Oracle Press™

OCM Java® EE 6 Enterprise Architect Exam Guide

(Exams 1Z0-807, 1Z0-865 & 1Z0-866)

Paul R. Allen and Joseph J. Bambara

New York Chicago San Francisco
Athens London Madrid Mexico City
Milan New Delhi Singapore Sydney Toronto

Cataloging-in-Publication Data is on file with the Library of Congress

McGraw-Hill Education books are available at special quantity discounts to use as premiums and sales promotions, or for use in corporate training programs. To contact a representative, please visit the Contact Us pages at www.mhprofessional.com.

OCM Java® EE 6 Enterprise Architect Exam Guide (Exams 1Z0-807, 1Z0-865 & 1Z0-866)

1234567890 DOC DOC 10987654

ISBN: Book p/n 978-0-07-182672-3 and CD p/n 978-0-07-182673-0
of set 978-0-07-182678-5

MHID: Book p/n 0-07-182672-6 and CD p/n 0-07-182673-4
of set 0-07-182678-5

Sponsoring Editor
Meghan Manfre

Editorial Supervisor
Jody McKenzie

Project Editor
Howie Severson, Fortuitous Publishing

Acquisitions Coordinator
Mary Demery

Technical Editor
Thomas Garben

Copy Editor
Bart Reed

Proofreader
Richard Camp

Indexer
Jack Lewis

Production Supervisor
Jean Bodeaux

Composition
Cenveo® Publishing Services

Illustration
Cenveo Publishing Services

Art Director, Cover
Jeff Weeks

I would like to dedicate this book to my children, Sophia and Terence.
I am so happy to be able to share time with you as you navigate
your own paths and build your own castles.

—Paul R. Allen

I would like to dedicate this book to my family (Roseanne, Vanessa, and Michael)
and friends (especially Hillary Brower and Rolando Marino) and to the hope
that we in America can properly educate our young and continue to lead
the world in technology and innovation.

—Joseph J. Bambara

ABOUT THE AUTHORS

Paul R. Allen is a principal of UCNY, Inc., an international consulting firm that helps Fortune 500 companies improve and streamline operations through the use of software technology. His e-mail address is pallen@ucny.com. He has been developing applications systems for over 20 years. His industry experience includes financial, brokerage, pharmaceutical, and manufacturing verticals. He has taught numerous courses in computing at the Columbia University of New York. He has co-authored several books, including *Sun Certified Enterprise Architect for Java EE Study Guide* (McGraw-Hill, 2007 and 2003), *J2EE Unleashed* (Sams, 2002), *SQL Server 7 Developer's Guide* (IDG, 2000), *Informix: Universal Data Option* (McGraw Hill, 1998), and *PowerBuilder: A Guide to Developing Client/Server Applications* (McGraw-Hill, 1995). He has taught numerous courses and given presentations on computing in several cities, including Berlin, Copenhagen, London, Los Angeles, Nashville, New York, Orlando, Oslo, Paris, Stockholm, Vienna, and Washington, D.C. over the past 15 years.

Joseph J. Bambara is a principal of UCNY, Inc., an international consulting firm that helps Fortune 500 companies improve operations through the use of database and object technology. His e-mail address is jbambara@ucny.com. He has been developing applications systems for over 30 years, including relational database development for the last 25 years and Java application server for web development for the past 15 years. He is a Certified Trainer and Developer. His industry experience includes financial, brokerage, manufacturing, medical, and entertainment. Mr. Bambara has a Bachelor's and Master's degree in Computer Science. He also holds a Juris Doctorate in Law and is admitted to the New York Bar. He has taught various computer courses for CCNY's School of Engineering. He has co-authored the following books: *PowerBuilder: A Guide to Developing Client/Server Applications* (McGraw-Hill, 1995), *Informix: Client /Server Application Development* (McGraw Hill, 1997), *Informix: Universal Server* (McGraw Hill, 1998), *Informix: Universal Data Option* (McGraw Hill, 1998), *SQL Server 7 Developer's Guide* (IDG, 2000), and *J2EE Unleashed* (Sams, 2002). He has presented numerous courses and presentations for WebLogic, WebSphere, and Sybase in several cities and countries, including Los Angeles, Vienna, Paris, Berlin, Orlando, Nashville, New York, Copenhagen, Oslo, and Stockholm over the past 15 years.

About the Technical Editor

Thomas Garben has developed applications for several different industries—from guided missile systems for the U.S. Navy to financial applications for many major banks and clearing houses on Wall Street to content distribution systems for major sports entertainment firms—and is currently working with Azul Systems supporting real-time business needs with their low-latency Java Virtual Machines. He has been developing applications since 1985 and has immersed himself in Java and J2EE technologies since their inception. He holds degrees in Physics, Math, and Computer Engineering and a Master's degree in Systems and Computer Engineering. He is the co-author of the book *J2EE Unleashed* (Sams, 2002).

CONTENTS

ACKNOWLEDGMENTS

We would like to acknowledge all the incredibly hard-working folks at McGraw-Hill, especially Meghan Manfre and Mary Demery. We would also like to thank Tom Garben and Kiran Narayana for their help in editing the technical material in this book and for being solid team players.

—Paul R. Allen and Joseph J. Bambara

A very special thank-you to my wife, Evelyn, for being a source of strength, support, and ideas both to me and to our children. Also, a very special thanks to my co-author, Joseph J. Bambara, especially for his encouragement, determination, and perseverance, which make it possible to succeed at all of our endeavors.

—Paul R. Allen
New York, New York

A very special thanks to my co-author Paul R. Allen, especially for his friendship and for being a great partner no matter what we try. Thanks to my family, who are always there when I need them.

—Joseph J. Bambara
Port Washington, New York

PREFACE

Because of the complexities involved in enterprise application development, it is becoming increasingly important for Information Technology architects to become certified as an Oracle Certified Master, Java EE Enterprise Architect (OCMJEA). Certification in Java technology will improve your career potential, provide credibility and respect, and increase job security. With certification, you prove that you are qualified to architect Java EE applications, which increases your opportunities for professional advancement.

The OCMJEA certification is the ultimate test in the Oracle Java certification series. The series is growing and presently includes, in addition to the Oracle Certified Master, Java EE 6 Enterprise Architect credential, the following certifications:

- Oracle Certified Professional, Java EE 5 Web Component Developer | Exam 1Z0-858 and Exam 1Z0-859 (upgrade exam)
- Oracle Certified Professional, Java EE 5 Business Component Developer | Exam 1Z0-860 and Exam 1Z0-861 (upgrade exam)
- Oracle Certified Professional, Java EE 5 Web Services Developer | Exam 1Z0-862 and Exam 1Z9-863 (upgrade exam)
- Oracle Certified Master, Java EE 5 Enterprise Architect | Exams 1Z0-864, 1Z0-865, 1Z0-866, and 1Z0-868 (upgrade exam)
- Oracle Certified Expert, Java Platform, EE 6 Enterprise JavaBeans Developer | Exam 1Z0-895
- Oracle Certified Expert, Java EE 6 JavaServer Faces Developer | Exam 1Z0-896
- Oracle Certified Expert, Java EE 6 Web Services Developer | Exam 1Z0-897
- Oracle Certified Expert, Java EE 6 Java Persistence API Developer | Exam 1Z0-898
- Oracle Certified Expert, Java EE 6 Web Component Developer | Exam 1Z0-899

The OCMJEA exam tests the concepts you've gained as a professional architect. These concepts are typically gained in a career that spans 10 or more years and includes experience with a diverse set of computing languages and technology beyond Java. The exam tests your ability to produce an enterprise architecture using Java EE. Chapter 1 provides a detailed overview of the exam and the objectives, along with test-taking tips. We cover all of the objectives in the book's chapters.

In This Book

OCM *Java EE 6 Enterprise Architect Exam Guide (Exams 1Z0-807, 1Z0-865 & 1Z0-866)* is organized in such a way as to serve as an in-depth review for the exams for everyone from experienced Java EE architects to professionals, developers, and even newcomers to Java EE and related technologies. Each chapter covers the specific stated objectives of the current exams. The emphasis is placed not only on the "why" and the "how to" of working with and supporting Java EE–based applications and related enterprise technologies but also on how best to prepare for the successful completion of the exams.

On the CD

For more information on the CD-ROM, please see Appendix C.

In Every Chapter

We've created a set of chapter components that call your attention to important items, reinforce important points, and provide helpful exam-taking hints. In Appendix A and B we cover the assignment and essay exams

- Every chapter of the exam begins with the **Certification Objectives**—what you need to know in order to pass the section on the exam dealing with the chapter topic. The Objective headings identify the objectives within the chapter, so you'll always know an objective when you see it!
- **Exam Watch** notes call attention to information about, and potential pitfalls in, the exams. These helpful hints are written by authors who have taken the exams and received their certification—who better to tell you what to worry about? They know what you're about to go through!

- **Exercises** are interspersed throughout the chapters. These exercises help you master skills that are likely to be an area of focus on the exams and give you practice for the OCMJEA essay exam. Don't just read through the exercises; they are hands-on practice that you should be comfortable completing. Learning by doing is an effective way to increase your competency with a product.

- **On the Job** notes describe the issues that come up most often in real-world settings. They provide a valuable perspective on certification- and product-related topics. They point out common mistakes and address questions that have arisen from on-the-job discussions and experience.
- **Scenario and Solutions** sections lay out potential problems and solutions in a quick-to-read format.

SCENARIO & SOLUTION	
James must be available to troubleshoot the computers in any office in the four buildings of the company that he works for...	Implement a roaming profile for James so that he can access his desktop no matter what computer he is using. This is especially handy. since his roaming profile can include the mapping to a network drive that holds his diagnostic tools.

- The **Certification Summary** is a succinct review of the chapter and a restatement of salient points regarding the exams.

- The **Two-Minute Drill** at the end of every chapter is a checklist of the main points of the chapter. It can be used for last-minute review.

- The **Self Test** offers questions similar to those found on the multiple-choice exam. The answers to these questions, as well as explanations of the answers, can be found at the end of each chapter. By taking the Self Test after completing each chapter, you'll reinforce what you've learned from that chapter while becoming familiar with the structure of the exam questions.

Some Pointers

Once you've finished reading this book, set aside some time to do a thorough review. You might want to return to the book several times and make use of all the methods it offers for reviewing the material.

1. *Re-read all the Two-Minute Drills*, or have someone quiz you. You also can use the drills as a way to do a quick cram before the exams. You might want to make some flash cards out of 3×5 index cards that have the Two-Minute Drill material on them.
2. *Re-read all the Exam Watch notes*. Remember that these notes are written by authors who have taken the exams and passed. They know what you should expect—and what you should be on the lookout for.
3. *Review all the S&S sections* for quick problem solving.
4. *Re-take the Self Tests*. Taking the tests right after you've read the chapter is a good idea, because the questions help reinforce what you've just learned. However, it's an even better idea to go back later and do all the questions in the book in one sitting. Pretend that you're taking the live multiple-choice exam. (When you go through the questions the first time, you should mark your answers on a separate piece of paper. That way, you can run through the questions as many times as you need to until you feel comfortable with the material.)
5. *Complete the Exercises*. Did you do the exercises when you read through each chapter? If not, do them! These exercises are designed to cover exam topics, and there's no better way to get to know this material than by practicing. If there is something you are not clear on, re-read that section in the chapter.

INTRODUCTION

Oracle's most advanced certification in Java technology is the Oracle Certified Master, Java EE Enterprise Architect (OCMJEA) credential. This book, *OCM Java EE 6 Enterprise Architect Exam Guide (Exams 1Z0-807, 1Z0-865 & 1Z0-866)*, provides all the information you may need to prepare for the OCMJEA exams. It has detailed chapters and a CD-ROM covering all the topics of the OCMJEA. To pass the exams, the candidate should be familiar with the fundamentals of Java applications programming, but no longer necessarily has to have in-depth skills in Java programming. Additionally, there are some specific technologies that the candidate should know well. These topical areas are as follows:

- Application Design Concepts and Principles
- Common Architectures
- Integration and Messaging
- Business Tier Technologies
- Web Tier Technologies
- Design Patterns
- Security

Appendix A and B present a sample assignment: an enterprise architecture case study (using UML) and sample essay answers for defending your assignment solution. These two appendices will help you prepare for the Java (EE) Enterprise Architect Certified Master Assignment and the Java (EE) Enterprise Architect Certified Master Essay Exam.

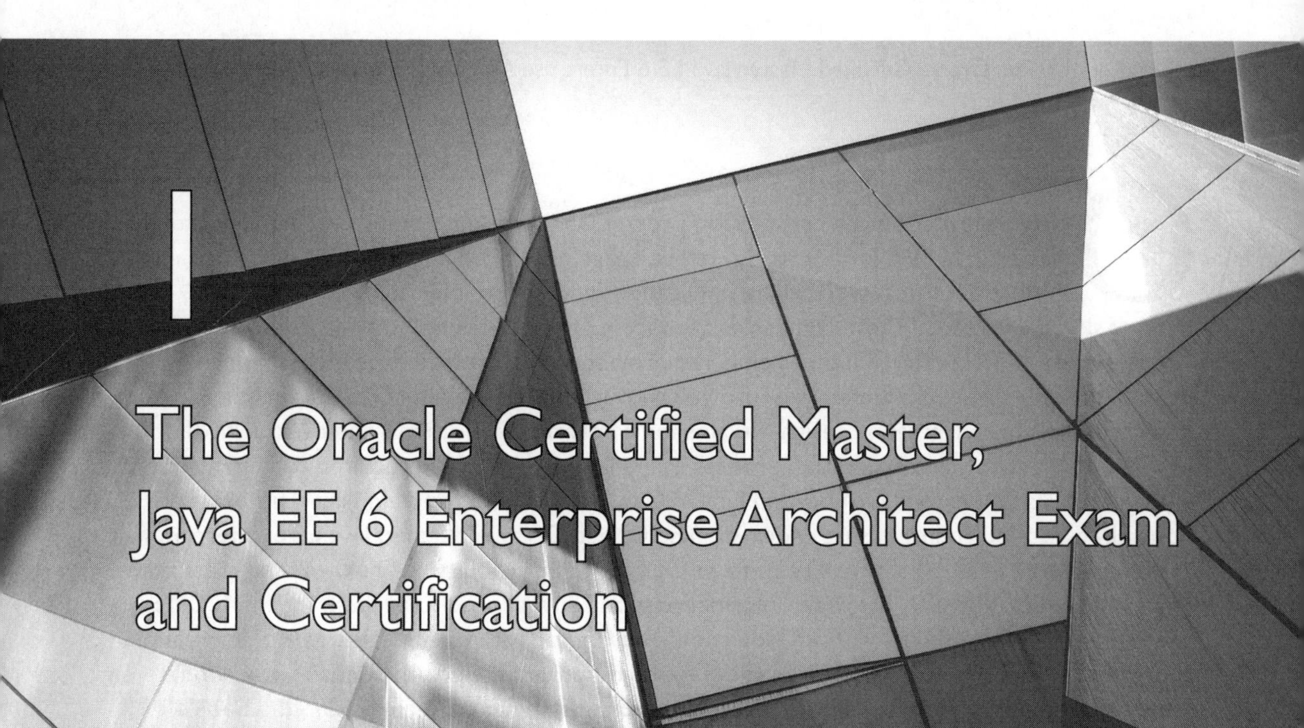

I

The Oracle Certified Master, Java EE 6 Enterprise Architect Exam and Certification

Oracle's most advanced certification program in Java technology is the Oracle Certified Master, Java EE 6 Enterprise Architect. Large enterprise organizations (for example, Wall Street firms) with critical applications and environments are constantly in need of skilled architects. These companies are looking for well-trained and highly experienced specialists to architect their systems, define requirements, and oversee execution. Playing key roles in the enterprise, the architect is involved throughout the system life cycle: analyzing and defining requirements, creating design artifacts for enterprise applications, and overseeing the process. As a part of the certification process, candidate architects are required to demonstrate a range of skills that extend well beyond fundamental or core Java programming. This book will hopefully assist you greatly in that endeavor. The Oracle Certified Master, Java EE 6 Enterprise Architect certification, which we'll refer to as OCMJEA throughout this book, will set you apart from your peers. This book provides information that you will need to prepare for the OCMJEA exam. To pass the certification exam, you should be familiar with the fundamentals of applications programming and should have some proficiency in Java programming. Additionally, you should know specific enterprise technologies. All of the topics listed next are covered in the book's chapters and on the CD-ROM accompanying the book:

- Basic principles of enterprise architectures
- Object-oriented design using UML
- Application design concepts and principles
- Common architectures
- Integration and messaging
- Business-tier technologies
- Web-tier technologies
- Design patterns
- Security
- Enterprise architecture case study (using UML)

Twenty-plus years into its life, Java is now the technology most commonly used behind the strategic scenes for an enterprise. After years in which Java development seemed to be reserved primarily for Internet applications, larger firms in the corporate world are using Java as the language of choice over C and C++ for most of their new development, including but not limited to mobile applications (for example, a majority of mobile handsets support Java), messaging, back-end night-cycle functions such as corporate "books and records" maintenance, database repair, warehousing, and data capture from external data feeds.

Java's appeal lies not only in its affinity for network and distributed computing but also in Java's other qualities, such as ease of programming and cross-platform capabilities (that is, the "write once, run anywhere" promise), garbage collection, as well as the global knowledge base: it is the most commonly used programming language ahead of C, its next closest contender, with all the others far behind.

Widespread Capabilities for Application Development

A large portion of the appeal of Java is the ease with which it allows the creation of web-based, self-service applications that enable customers to do their work and perform other tasks over the Internet through a browser using a laptop or mobile device. Most new applications are HTML5/JavaScript/JSON on the web server front end with Java-based Web Services on the application server back end that run on the company's web server. Figure 1-1 shows the JEE application server hierarchy.

Java isn't just for e-business. Some are developing Java applications for internal use, occasionally deploying Java clients to employee desktops.

Still, many issues stand in the way of Java Platform Enterprise Edition (JEE) adoption by corporate application development groups. These include concerns

FIGURE 1-1

The Java Platform Enterprise Edition (JEE) application server is the focal point.

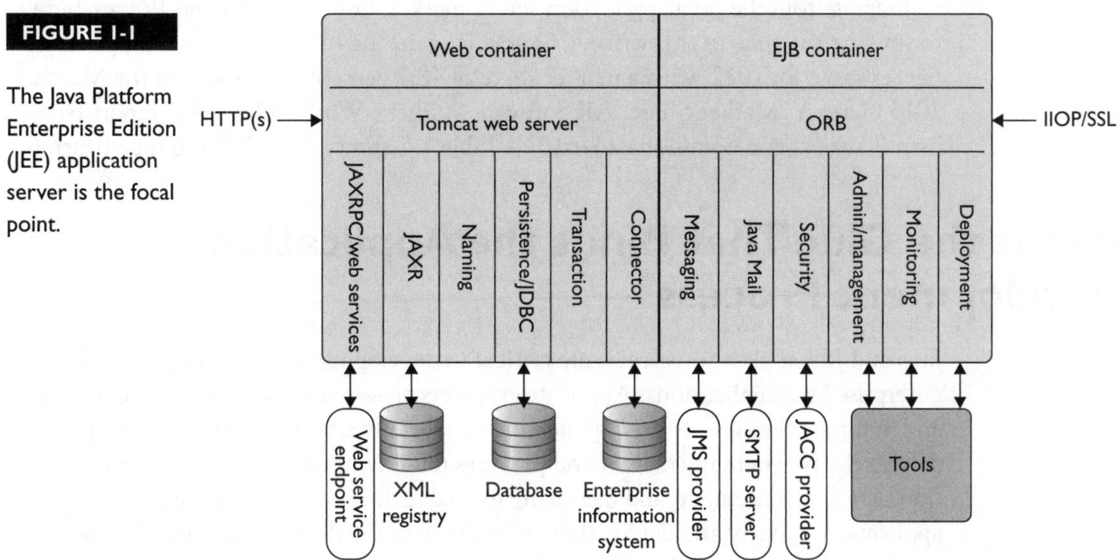

TABLE 1-1 JEE 6 API's and Current Release

Full Java EE 6.0 Implementation					
	Web Profile			**Enterprise Service**	
Servlet 3.0	JSP 2.2	EL 2.2	EJB 3.1	JMS 1.1	JavaMail 1.1
JSR-45 1.0	JSTL 1.2	JSRF 2.0	Connector 1.6	WebServices 1.3	JAX-RPC 1.1
Common Annotations 1.1	EJB 3.1 Lite	JTA 1.1	JAX-WS 2.2	JAX-RS 1.1	JAXB 2.2
JPA 2.0	Bean Validation 1.0	Managed Beans 1.0	JAXR 1.0	Java EE Management 1.1	Java EE Deployment 1.2
Interceptors 1.0	JSR 299 1.0	Dependency Injection 1.0	JACC 1.4	JASPIC 1.0	WebServicesMetadata 2.1

about the development environment, the need to locate or train Java developers, and the need to upgrade to the new generation of JEE application servers to take full advantage of the technology. This is where the JEE architect is most needed. The right architect can step into the enterprise to resolve these issues and make the dream of a JEE-based enterprise a reality.

An undercurrent of concern also exists about what Microsoft is doing with its .NET product line and what impact, if any, those actions will have on a development group's Java plans.

Judging from the Java application server market, however, Java and JEE are here to stay. At the time of this writing, Oracle is again the #1 vendor in the Application Server space for 2012, with a market share of 40.7 percent, according to the March 2013 Gartner "Market Share: All Software Markets, Worldwide, 2012" report (see http://java.sys-con.com/node/2616103). Table 1-1 shows the full JEE 6 specification.

Java Is the Glue That Binds the Application Development Process

Java and JEE application servers are critical to developing and deploying scalable enterprise Java applications. Application servers provide the infrastructure to execute and maintain business-critical applications, especially e-business applications. JEE defines the programming model and provides underlying services such as security, transaction management, and messaging to enable developers to build networked Java applications quickly and deploy them effectively in the distributed world. Figure 1-2 shows the multiple functions of the JEE application server.

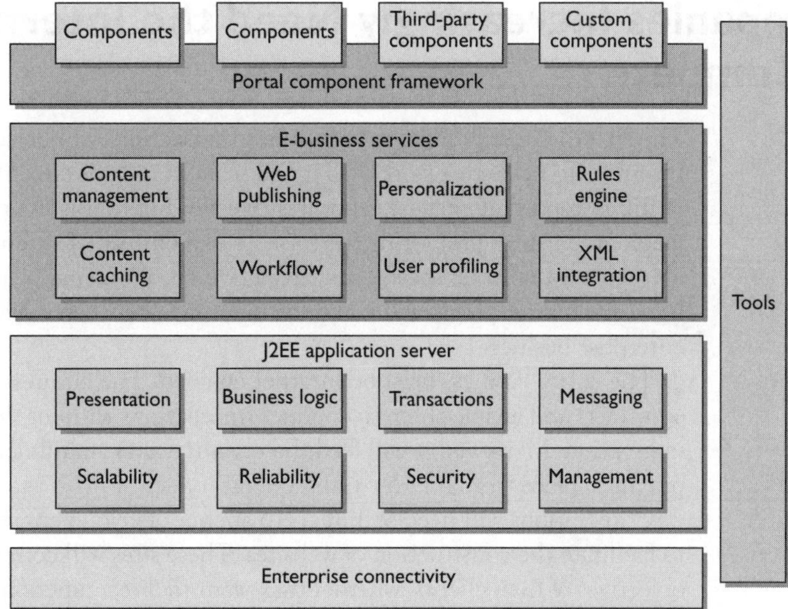

FIGURE 1-2 The Java Platform Enterprise Edition (JEE) application server is multifunctional.

A rush to deploy the latest JEE as well as servlet-based application servers (for example, Tomcat) in the business environment is fueling growth. A plethora of application server combinations are being offered on the market today and used in the enterprise environment, with more appearing weekly. However, only a few dominate the market. Three companies—Oracle, IBM, and VMware—claim most of the market, and several other vendors that specialize in market niches claim less than 10 percent each. The application server has emerged as the focal point of the evolving distributed, networked corporate development. The application server acts as middleware, making services necessary back-end connections, running business logic and messaging, and managing functions such as transaction management and security. The latest application servers are adding support for mobile computing and integrated Extensible Markup Language (XML) capabilities.

You can create distributed applications without an application server, but you'll end up having to build from scratch much of the functionality the application server provides—such as database connection pooling. For example, one of our UCNY, Inc. (www.ucny.com) clients uses Lotus Domino as its web server and does not use an application server. "We've already built a lot of the functionality we'd get in an application server," reasoned the application manager. Long story short, the company is now in the process of porting its applications to IBM's WebSphere JEE application server.

Companies Increasingly Need the Internet to Compete

Through the next decade, most business transactions will be conducted over the Internet. To make this work on a grand scale, standards are critical. The success of JEE is important because it ensures that the Internet is the most cost-effective medium to use for promoting the services of a business. Conducting business with a user-friendly, reliable, speedy, and attractive set of web pages supported by reliable back-end business logic will make the difference between success and failure in the enterprise business.

The entire business must be Internet enabled. The business site must engage the customers and enable them to conduct transactions without the necessity of human interaction. Moreover, it will feed the organization's "fulfillment" engine as well as provide a place to go for post-transaction services.

Corporations will need architects to anchor development standards such as JEE to facilitate the construction of websites. These sites will communicate the business objectives of their clients, whether they want to direct functionality to local, national, or international markets.

Development roles are now more important than ever. The architect must work together with other technical and graphic design personnel to ensure that the web pages not only meet the business's needs but that they also maintain a perfect balance between performance and professional graphics work. The design of each component must follow a standard such as JEE to ensure that the end product looks professional, loads faster, and effectively communicates the company's business objectives to the world.

Challenges of Application Development for the Enterprise

Timing has always been a critical factor for adopting new technologies, but the accelerated pace inherent in a virtual, information-driven business model has put even greater emphasis on response times. To leverage Internet economics, it is imperative that the architect not only project, build, and display enterprise systems, but that he or she do so repeatedly and in a timely manner, with frequent updates to both information and services. Just as the SQL standard facilitated data access, widespread acceptance and inherited experience with the JEE standard will make it easier for architects to construct enterprise systems. The architect's principal challenge is one of keeping up with the Internet's hyper-competitive pace while maintaining and leveraging the value of existing business systems.

In this economic environment, timeliness is critical in gaining and maintaining a competitive edge. A number of factors can enhance or impede an organization's ability to deliver custom enterprise applications quickly and to maximize their value over their lifetime.

Increasing Programmer Productivity

The ability to develop and deploy applications is a key to success in the information economy. Applications must go quickly from prototype to production, and they must continue evolving even after they have been deployed. Productivity, therefore, is vital to responsive application development. JEE provides application development teams with a set of standard application programming interfaces (APIs)—that is, the means to access the services required by multitier applications and standard ways to support a variety of clients. This can contribute to both responsiveness and flexibility.

In contrast to data access that is standardized and stabilized by SQL, a destabilizing factor in Internet and other distributed computing applications is the divergence of programming models. Historically (in web terms) and progressively, technologies such as Hypertext Markup Language (now HTML5) have provided a front-end mechanism for distributing dynamic content, whereas back-end systems such as transaction processors are based on SOAP/REST Web Services, which act as a façade to such legacy software as IBM Customer Information Control System (CICS), Tuxedo, IBM Message Queuing (MQ), Lotus Notes, and other data access systems. These technologies present a diversity of nonstandard programming models based on proprietary architectures.

With no single standard for application models, it is difficult for architecture, development, and production teams to communicate application requirements effectively and productively. As a result, the process of architecting applications is extremely complex. What's more, the skill sets required to integrate these technologies is not organized well for an effective division of labor.

Another complicating factor in application development time is the client type. Although many applications can be distributed to web browser clients through static or dynamically generated HTML5, others may need to support a specific type of client or several types of clients simultaneously (for example, mobile devices as well as desktop browsers). The programming model should support a variety of client configurations with minimal consequence to basic application architecture or the core business logic of the application.

JEE enables development to be role oriented. Components are architected by one group, developed and assembled by another, and deployed by still another, which is critical for enterprise-level code control and application governance.

JEE Architecture Must Respond to Consumer Demand

Imagine a multilocation retail business trying to increase its customer base by a factor of 10. How much time and effort would be expended on remodeling storefronts, building new warehouses, and so on, to keep up? Realistically, constant rework would impact the business's ability to serve its customers.

This holds for businesses in the e-commerce arena as well. The ability to architect applications that scale easily to accommodate growth is critical to achieving the company's goals. To scale effectively, systems require mechanisms to ensure efficient management of system resources and services such as database connections and transactions. They need access to features such as automatic load balancing without any effort on the part of the application developer. Applications should be able to run on any server appropriate to anticipate client volumes and to switch server configurations easily when the need arises. JEE-compliant application servers such as WebSphere, WebLogic, and JBOSS, for example, provide these features in the form of database pooling, server clustering, and failover functionality.

The Architect Must Be Able to Integrate JEE and Legacy Systems

In many enterprises, the data of value to organizations, also called "books and records," has been collected over the years by existing information systems. The investment resides in applications on those same systems. The business rules, the procedures, and legacy code all work, perform the business functionality properly, and cost a great deal of time and money to produce. Yes, its hard to believe, but there are RPG, Fortran, Cobol, and many other legacy platforms still in use at the big Wall Street financial firms. The challenge for developers of enterprise applications is how to reuse and capitalize on this value by betting on middleware, which can converse with the legacy systems.

Architects need to use the JEE standard to help application developers by providing standard ways to access middle-tier and back-end services such as database management systems and transaction monitors.

The JEE Standard Promotes Competition and Choices

Today's agile development environments advance programmer productivity by facilitating the assembly of software components. As JEE is maturing, integrated development environments (IDEs), such as Eclipse, are starting to increase the productivity of developers dramatically. With extensible development environments that allow developers to add open source or purchased components, or so-called "plug-ins," the competition to enhance the development environment is great. Architects must possess the ability to mix and match solutions to come up with the optimum configuration to accommodate the task at hand. As the vendor application server shakeout continues, freedom of choice in enterprise application development should soon extend from servers to tools to components.

As vendors adhere to and advance the JEE standard, choices among server products will give an organization the ability to select configurations tailored to its application requirements. Much like SQL, the JEE standard provides the organization the ability to move quickly and easily from one configuration to another (for example, SQL: Sybase DB converted to Oracle), as internal and external demand requires.

Access to the proper development tools for the job is another important choice. Development teams should be able to use new tools as needs arise, including tools from server vendors and third-party tool developers. What's more, each member of a development team should have access to the tools most appropriate to his or her skill set and contribution.

Finally, developers should be able to choose from a market of off-the-shelf application components to take advantage of external expertise and to enhance development productivity. JEE standardization over the coming years will advance systems development just as SQL advanced database development.

Design Goals of JEE Architecture

The web architecture required for JEE is somewhat analogous to the architecture required to run vendor-based SQL database servers. The same qualities of performance, reliability, and security must be present for web application servers to provide a host for an application. Speed is key, and the good architect must find a way to provide it. The competition will win out every time if it is able to provide faster response to the client. The user can click away to a competitor if a response is too slow on your site.

Mastering this requirement is a difficult task for the architect, because the user base can change rapidly. Not only should the architect be concerned with domestic customers and business hours, but he or she must consider the effects of globalization.

JEE application servers need to be efficient and scalable. These qualities will pare down the field to those few vendors who can provide the speed to handle a local customer base with thousands of simultaneous hits.

JEE Architects Should Strive for Service Availability

Users want the application to be available 24×7. This is the attraction of doing business on the web, as users don't have to worry about the doors being closed after hours. Moreover, the advancing global economy has made availability a "must" requirement. The sun is always shining somewhere on potential global system users. Additionally, users want to be able to speak to customer service representatives without having to wait until Monday. In addition to general availability, the reliability of the application server and the application software it runs is critical. Interruption of the business cycle—that is, downtime—is unacceptable. The business depends on the application being up and ready to serve.

JEE architects must provide reliable server configurations (clustering) as well as safe and clear failover procedures. JEE application server architects also must consider privacy issues. They must be able to maintain passwords and logins and to hide sensitive data. The data must be tamperproof, and architects must be able to allow for encrypted communication for sensitive portions of the business transactions.

JEE Architecture and Connectivity to Existing Data

Having been part of the development of mainframe systems that still maintain the "books and records" of large enterprises such as Merrill Lynch, Goldman Sachs, and most of the banks located in New York City, it is easy for this author to understand why some of these systems are still in operation 30 years later. They simply work, and replacing them has been expensive. The problem will meet a tipping point when the knowledge base of developers who know these technologies retires.

Specialized access to enterprise resource planning and mainframe systems such as IBM's CICS has been provided in JEE through the *connector* architecture. Because each of these systems is highly complex and specialized, each requires unique tools and support to ensure utmost simplicity to application developers. As JEE has evolved, enterprise beans are able to combine the use of connector access objects and service APIs with middle-tier business logic to accomplish their business functions, as demonstrated in Figure 1-3.

FIGURE 1-3

Java Platform Enterprise Edition (JEE) combines client tier, presentation, business processes, and enterprise connectivity.

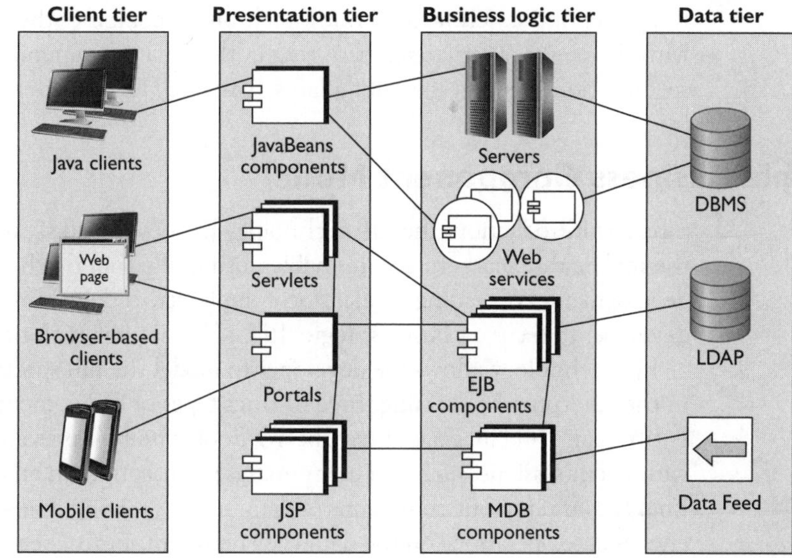

Expanded User Definition: Customers, Employees, and Partners

In the past, a desktop was the sole means of interfacing with an enterprise system, but those days are gone. Users today want to connect from virtually anywhere. The access begins during their commute and might continue through the workday and while traveling to remote business sites.

Flexible User Interaction

JEE provides choices for graphical user interfaces (GUIs) across an enterprise intranet or on the World Wide Web. Clients can use desktops, laptops, PDAs (personal digital assistants), cell phones, and other devices. Pure client-side user interfaces can use standard HTML and Java applets. Support for HTML facilitates prototypes and support for a broader range of clients. In addition, JEE supports automatic download of the Java plug-in to add applet support. JEE also supports standalone Java application clients.

For server-side deployment of dynamic content, JEE supports both the Java Servlets API and JavaServer Pages (JSP) technology. The Java Servlets API enables developers to easily implement server-side behaviors that take full advantage of the power of the rich Java API. JSP technology combines the ubiquity of HTML with the power of server-side scripting in the Java programming language. The JSP specification supports static templates, dynamic HTML generation, and custom tags.

Flexible Business Component Model

Since its introduction, the EJB technology has developed significant momentum in the middleware marketplace. It enables a simplified approach to multitier application development, concealing application complexity, and enabling the component developer to focus on business logic. JEE is the natural evolution of EJB technology.

EJB technology allows the developer to model the full spectrum of patterns useful in the enterprise by defining three distinct types of EJB components: session beans, entity beans, and message-driven beans. *Session beans* represent behaviors associated with client sessions, such as a user purchase transaction on an e-commerce site. *Entity beans* represent collections of data, such as rows in a relational database, and encapsulate operations on the data they represent. Entity beans are intended to be persistent, surviving as long as the data with which they are associated remains viable. The *message-driven bean* is the coupling of Java Message Service (JMS) with EJB to create an EJB type designed to handle asynchronous JMS messages.

JEE extends the power and portability of EJB components by defining a complete infrastructure that includes standard clients and service APIs for their use.

The New Architect Role: Comprehensive Skill Set Required

Many changes have occurred in software engineering. The most critical one is the scale of use. Scale obviously has been increasing since the first computers were used in the business world (for example, Wall Street circa 1970). In web and mobile applications, the scale of systems is an especially important issue because you never know exactly how many users will be accessing the services. The use of new wave web applications, especially those in the social media space, require that their design consider scaling and the distribution of software components across multiple servers. For example, because web applications are distributed by nature, the huge increases in load that are typical of Internet-deployed systems tend to make multiple parallel servers necessary, even further increasing distribution. Thus, distribution has created even more need for the architect.

Large-scale, Distributed Enterprise Systems and Integration Risk

As systems move from a single host to large-scale, distributed enterprise systems, the risks and difficulty of meeting project requirements increases. In a system that runs entirely on a single host, all pieces of the system communicate with each other reasonably quickly and at approximately the same speed. In distributed systems, making the right choices about where components are located and how they communicate becomes critical. The importance of these decisions has expanded the need for architects. The architect performs planning for the location of, and the communication among, software components. This role distinguishes the architect from the designer and other programmers. The goal of this planning is to ensure that the system includes a failover process if partial outages occur, performs load balancing, and is scalable when the demand for concurrent use exceeds the original design parameters.

Quality of Service

The architect is primarily concerned with quality of service: ensuring that the performance and reliability of the system provides all users the same service-level agreement (SLA). The architect works with use cases and provides crucial insight into the architectural development, especially with respect to quality of service (QoS).

Nonfunctional Requirements

Another focus of the architect is so-called "nonfunctional requirements." This focus has become necessary because distributed systems mandate an architectural design that ensures that the system is maintainable and performs sufficiently well even after all the functional requirements are met.

The focus on quality of service is a surprise to many experienced designers. They often find focusing on quality of service to be frustrating, and they want to work with more tangible design aspects. However, experience is proving that as long as a system has a good architecture, other problems are fixable. By contrast, the system lacking a good architecture might be functionally perfect, but still require a total rewrite to be usable or to revise the functionality.

Risk Evaluation and Control

A good architect controls risk to guarantee that the nonfunctional requirements are met by the system design. This means risk control is a project cost, and it must be treated as such.

To make qualified decisions about how much risk control is enough and how much is too much, you evaluate and compare the risks and mitigation strategies based on cost and probability of occurrence. You do not want to create high-cost solutions to mitigate low-probability risks. If designing such a solution was your goal, you could simply design systems that provide T1 connections and mainframes for every client that connects. This is not the best solution, and an architect should not take a position of *throw more hardware at it... that will fix all the problems*.

The best way to approach the problem is to perform a cost analysis of several options for controlling risk. Some options might be less costly, but leave some risk in place; others might be more costly, but control the risk completely. You can always look at the "do nothing" option: assume that the risk is realized and examine the cost impact. This "pay me now, or pay me later" approach to deciding what architectural solutions fit best is formalized in the return on investment (ROI).

For example, consider the use of a single server to provide availability compared to the implementation of the system on a server cluster. The cost of implementing a single-system environment is significantly less than that of the cluster: usually three to five times cheaper, possibly even more. This savings is due to the number of systems required to create a cluster (two to five or more, depending on the configuration and types of systems used) and the level of expertise required to install and maintain the configuration.

On the other hand, you must consider the cost of lost time and business in the single-system configuration. If the system goes down, how long would it take to replace it? How much money could be lost while the system is being replaced? And how often is the single system likely to fail? This analysis might indicate that, even though the cost of implementing and maintaining a cluster might appear to be more costly at first, the long-term cost of not using a cluster might justify its use.

Technology Responsibilities

The architect is involved with the significant use cases—that is to say, the use cases that need attention because they involve some degree of risk. Perhaps the single most important aspect of an architect's work is preparing for the unexpected.

The architect is responsible for guiding the development of the architectural prototype. This prototype might be a purely theoretical construction, realized only in documents and diagrams. Or, more commonly, it might involve an element of implemented code. The purpose of the prototype is to develop enough of the final system to determine that the key risks have been successfully addressed.

In developing the architectural prototype, the architect creates the following:

- **Checklist of assumptions and constraints** The architect documents all the assumptions made, so far as they have been recognized. Incorrect assumptions about potentially critical issues, such as user-base growth and transaction volumes, often require the system to be reworked. Documenting these assumptions ensures that you realize as quickly as possible that something is changing that might require such rework. The architect documents all the constraints about the platform upon which the software is constructed and deployed.
- **Plan for risk identification and mitigation** The architect provides a list of known risks, an assessment of the risks, and mitigation plans intended to address the risks.
- **Descriptive documentation of deployment environment** The architect specifies the deployment environment and shows how and where software and service components should *be located and how those components should communicate.*
- **UML diagrams** The architect uses these diagrams to verify that the architectural prototype supports all the functional requirements. This view of the architectural prototype ensures the domain model is complete enough to enable the architect to map elements of the domain model correctly and to complete the closure of the model.

Management Responsibilities

The architect also has some management responsibilities. The responsibilities generally include some degree of cost management, because other budget holders are not qualified to make decisions about the technologies and risk mitigation approaches. The architect should have soft skills for working effectively with stakeholders and team members.

Excellent interpersonal skills are required for tasks such as the following:

- Communicating to other stakeholders the validity of the decisions that have been made. It is likely that many of the stakeholders have preconceived ideas about what technologies should be used in what parts of the system. Many stakeholders tend, quite naturally, to overvalue certain parts of the system that relate to their needs, while simultaneously undervaluing other parts of the system.
- Mentoring other team members in the proper use of the technologies that have been chosen to implement a solution.
- Building media to describe how the task of selecting technologies was completed. To ensure the technologies are applied correctly, especially when they are new or cutting-edge technologies, the architect oversees the prototype development and uses it as a training tool for lead designers and developers.

Difference Between Architecture and Design

The role of the architect is sometimes hard to distinguish from that of designer. Indeed, the role of an architect is difficult to define. In part, this is because the role varies from company to company, and even from project to project. However, some important generalizations about the architect's role can be drawn from investigating the common elements of a number of projects.

Although business analysts, system architects, and system designers have distinct roles, the architect often performs many of their functions. This helps to explain the difficulty of defining the architect's role. In different companies or projects, the architect role might be quite different, depending on exactly which of these additional roles the architect fills.

The architect is not responsible for the project over its entire life cycle. Instead, the architect is primarily involved in the project at the point where its life cycle is moving from the Definition of Requirements phase into the Detailed Design phase. This occurs in the Inception and Elaboration phases. However, the architect must ensure that the final product conforms to the original vision of the architecture model. Some projects request that the architect attend project meetings or critical design reviews throughout the Construction phase.

Architectural Principles

Architecture principles are axioms or assumptions that suggest good practices when constructing an system architecture. These principles form the basis of many architectural patterns and form the decisions an architect makes to satisfy the quality of service requirements.

There are potentially hundreds of architectural principles. However, the next two modules will use the following principles:

- *Use a client component that depends on an interface to make the software more flexible*. This way, the supplier component can be changed or replaced without affecting the client component.
- *Separate volatile from stable components*. As a system changes, you want to reduce the changes to a small number of packages. This principle guides the grouping of components into volatile elements (such as the user interface) and more stable elements (such as the domain entities).
- *Use component and container frameworks*. A component is a software element that is managed by a container. For example, a servlet is managed by a web container. Typically, a software developer creates components. These components are built to fulfill interface or language specifications.

  A container is a software framework that manages components built to a certain specification. For example, a web container is a framework for managing HTTP requests and dispatching the requests to a servlet. A container is a system (or library) that you can build or acquire. For example, Tomcat is an implementation of a web container.

  A container framework is a powerful tool for the architect. These frameworks enable the architect to purchase software that provides infrastructure for the rest of the software system. This enables the designers and programmers to concentrate on the business logic components rather than the infrastructure.
- *Keep component interfaces simple and clear*. The more complex a component's interface, the harder it is for software developers to understand how to use the component. Component interfaces should also be highly cohesive.
- *Keep remote component interfaces coarse-grained*. Remote components require network traffic to communicate. You should keep the number of remote requests (which requires sending network messages) to a minimum. Therefore, keep remote interfaces simple and coarse-grained.

Registering for Oracle Certified Master, Java EE 6 Enterprise Architect Distinguishes the Java Professional

Because of the complexities involved, it is becoming increasingly important for IT architects to become an Oracle Certified Master, Java EE 6 Enterprise Architect. With certification, you prove that you are qualified to architect JEE applications. This will hopefully mean opportunities for professional advancement, such as salary increases, job role modifications, and promotions.

The OCMJEA (formerly the SCEA) exam is the ultimate test in the Oracle series. The series currently includes the following certifications:

- Oracle Certified Expert, Java EE 6 Enterprise JavaBeans Developer
- Oracle Certified Expert, Java EE 6 Java Persistence API Developer
- Oracle Certified Expert, Java EE 6 Web Services Developer
- Oracle Certified Expert, Java Platform, EE 6 Web Component Developer
- Oracle Certified Enterprise Architect (OCMJEA)

For the OCMJEA information, see http://education.oracle.com. The OCMJEE6EA exam tests the concepts you've gained as a professional architect. These concepts are typically gained in a career that spans 10 or more years. It includes diverse languages and technology beyond Java. The exam tests your ability to produce an enterprise architecture using JEE. The OCMJEA certification covers the topics discussed in the following sections.

Objectives of the Exam

The objectives tested are listed following each topic. All of these objectives are covered in the chapters that follow.

Application Design Concepts and Principles

- Identify the effects of an object-oriented approach to system design, including the effect of encapsulation, inheritance, and use of interfaces.
- Identify how the Separation of Concerns principle applies to the component model of a Java EE application, including client, the web and business component containers, and the integration and resource layers.

- Identify the correct interpretation of Separation of Concerns as it applies to the Java EE service layers, including component APIs, run-time containers, the operating system, and hardware resources.
- Identify nonfunctional and quality of service (QoS) requirements that influence application design, including trade-offs in performance, availability, and serviceability.

Common Architectures

- Identify the appropriate strategy for deploying client applications to desktop and mobile platforms, the principles for designing a user interface, and the benefits of applying client tier patterns.
- Identify best practices for exception handling, logging, and utilization of business tier patterns.
- Identify design patterns that address specific challenges in the web tier, including authentication, authorization, and scaling and clustering to meet demand.
- Identify Java EE technologies, including JMS, JCA, and Web Services, and design patterns that address specific challenges in enterprise integration.
- Identify the challenges with integrating enterprise resources, the Java EE technologies that address them (including JPA and JDBC), and the communication protocols that support tier-to-tier communication (including RMI, IIOP, and CORBA).

Integration and Messaging

- Identify the APIs available for a Java EE technology–based system for communicating with external resources, including JPA, JDBC, RMI, Web Services, JMS, and JCA. Outline the benefits and drawbacks of each approach.
- Describe the technologies used to integrate business components with Web Services, including XML over HTTP, JSON, SOAP, and REST.
- Identify and detail the technologies used to integrate business components with external resources, including JMS and JCA.
- Identify how a Service Oriented Architecture (SOA) facilitates system integration and best practices.

Business Tier Technologies

- Identify the correct EJB technology to apply for a given scenario, including entity classes, session beans, message-driven beans, timers, interceptors, and POJOs.
- Identify benefits and drawbacks of different persistence technologies such as BMP, CMP, and JPA, including ease of development, performance, scalability, extensibility, and security.
- Identify the benefits and drawbacks of implementing Web Services in the EJB component container.
- Select the appropriate use of JPA and JPQL in a given scenario.

Web Tier Technologies

- Identify the benefits and drawbacks of using URL rewriting and cookies to manage HTTP session state.
- Identify appropriate uses for JSP and Servlet technology as well as JavaServer Faces in a given Java EE application.
- Identify the benefits of using an EJB container with a web container instead of a web container alone.
- Identify the differences between client pull and server push architectures.
- Identify the benefits and drawbacks of using a browser to access asynchronous, lightweight processes on the server.

Design Patterns

- Demonstrate knowledge of Java EE design patterns, including Service Starter, Singleton, Bean Locator, Resource Binder, Dependency Injection, Payload Extractor, Context Holder, and Thread Tracker.
- Select an appropriate pattern for a given application challenge from the following: Facade, Strategy, Observer, Composite, and Abstract Factory.
- Identify a design pattern, using a description of its features, from the following: Facade, Strategy, Observer, Composite, and Abstract Factory.
- Identify the use of the law of leaky abstractions or a specific anti-pattern in a given scenario.

- Select the appropriate pattern for a given scenario from the following Web Services patterns: Web Service Cache, Web Service Broker, Asynchronous Interactions, and JMS Bridge.

Security

- Identify elements of the security model in the Java SE environment for remote clients, including Web Start, applets, and the role of the SecurityManager class.
- Select appropriate locations to implement Java EE security technologies or features in a UML component and deployment diagram.
- Classify the security threats to an enterprise application and select the measures an architect can propose to mitigate them.
- Identify techniques associated with declarative and programmatic security, including the use of annotations, deployment descriptors, and JAAS technology.
- Identify the security technologies that apply to an application's code, messaging, and transport layers.

Starting Point

To become an OCMJEA, start at http://education.oracle.com and follow your way to OCMJEE6EA. This presents you with the Oracle Certified Master, Java EE 6 Enterprise Architect Certification path. As the site suggests, we Java developers should all try to move our careers forward.

So let's start with what you need to do to attain this Oracle Certified Master, Java EE 6 Enterprise Architect Certification (see Figure 1-4). The OCMJEA exam consists of three parts: a multiple-choice exam, an architecture and UML design project, and an essay exam.

The exam is administered by Pearson VUE, a leading worldwide provider of comprehensive technology-based testing and assessment services (see www.pearsonvue.com). Applicants must complete one of the approved courses before taking the exam.

After you have successfully completed one of the designated courses and all three of the exam components, you will have earned the title of Oracle Certified Master, Java EE 6 Enterprise Architect. You can even have your certification listed on the Oracle website at http://education.oracle.com/education/otn/OCMEA.

FIGURE 1-4

OCMJEA exam steps

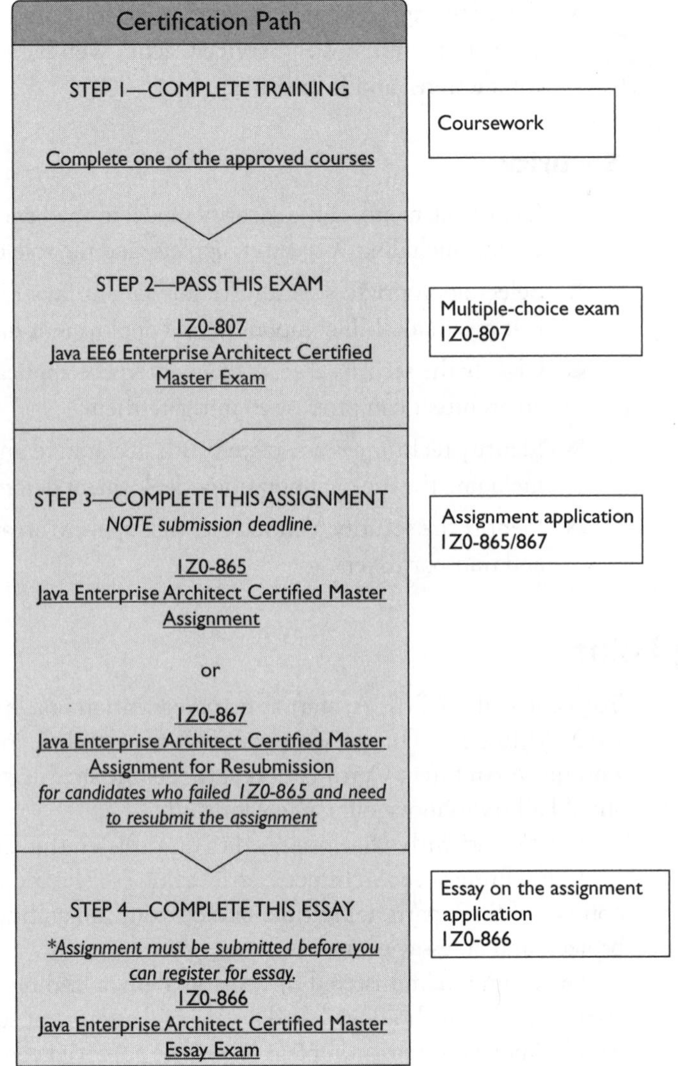

The exam components and summary details are as follows:

- Candidates must complete one of the instructor-led in-class, online, or recorded courses listed next—including Live Web Classes (LWC), Live Virtual Classes (LVC), and Training On-Demand courses—to obtain this certification. Self-Study CDs are excellent study and reference tools but do *not* meet the course requirement for certification.

    - Java EE 6: Develop Database Applications with JPA
    - Java EE 6: Develop Business Components with JMS & EJBs
    - Architect Enterprise Applications with Java EE
    - Building Database Driven Applications with JPA
    - Business Component Development with EJB Technology, Java EE 6
    - Creating Web Services Using Java Technology
    - Developing Applications for the Java EE 6 Platform
    - Developing Web Applications Using JSF Technologies
    - Developing Web Services Using Java Technology
    - Java Design Patterns
    - Java Programming Language, Java SE 6
    - Java SE 7 Fundamentals
    - Java SE 7 Programming
    - Object-Oriented Analysis and Design Using UML
    - Web Component Development with Servlets & JSPs, Java EE 6
- **OCMJEA Part 1** Exam 1Z0-807 is currently available at Pearson VUE (pearsonvue.com/oracle) for US$245. There is a course prerequisite. The exam includes 80 multiple-choice, short answer, and drag-and-drop questions. Candidates have 150 minutes to take the exam, and the pass score is 71 percent, up from the 68 percent in earlier versions. See Figure 1-5 for Part 1 test attributes and details.

  Particular coursework is available that is helpful. See Figure 1-6 for the Part 1 recommended coursework.
- **OCMJEA Part 2** Exam 1Z0-865 is the architecture and design project, which must be completed via Oracle certification database. You must complete exam 1Z0-807 before completing the project. There is a six-month time limit.

FIGURE 1-5 OCMJEA Exam 1Z0-807 details

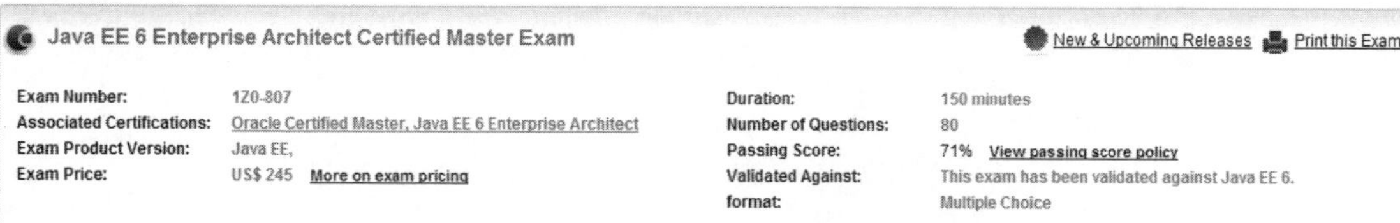

Java EE 6 Enterprise Architect Certified Master Exam

New & Upcoming Releases | Print this Exam

Exam Number:	1Z0-807	Duration:	150 minutes
Associated Certifications:	Oracle Certified Master, Java EE 6 Enterprise Architect	Number of Questions:	80
Exam Product Version:	Java EE,	Passing Score:	71% View passing score policy
Exam Price:	US$ 245 More on exam pricing	Validated Against:	This exam has been validated against Java EE 6.
		format:	Multiple Choice

FIGURE 1-6 OCMJEA Exam 1Z0-807 recommended course work

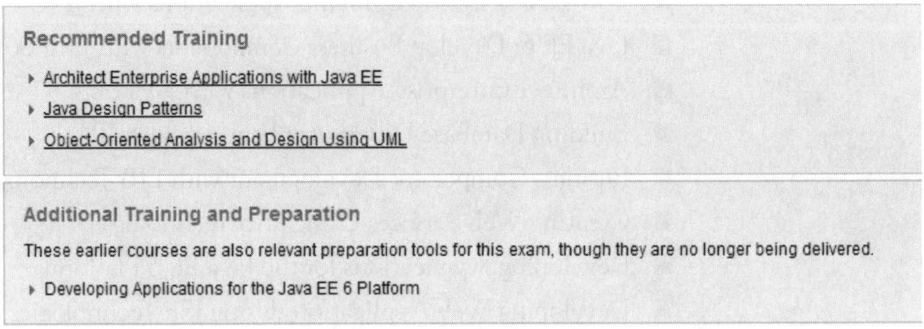

Recommended Training

- Architect Enterprise Applications with Java EE
- Java Design Patterns
- Object-Oriented Analysis and Design Using UML

Additional Training and Preparation

These earlier courses are also relevant preparation tools for this exam, though they are no longer being delivered.

- Developing Applications for the Java EE 6 Platform

The previous versions had no time limit. The passing score is 70 percent, subject to the evaluation of the essay exam and validation of the authenticity of the assignment. The current cost is US$245. See Figure 1-7 for Part 1 master assignment attributes.

For example, an assignment might be as follows:

"You are the architect for RemotePharma Corporation, a remote retail pharmacy company with significant operations in the U.S. RemotePharma operates its own pharmacy fulfillment operation to supply and provide discount subscribed drugs and non-subscription products to supplement treatment. RemotePharma has decided to build a web and mobile enrollment and fulfillment system to coop its competitors to effectively pool capacity."

FIGURE 1-7 OCMJEA Exam 1Z0-865 details

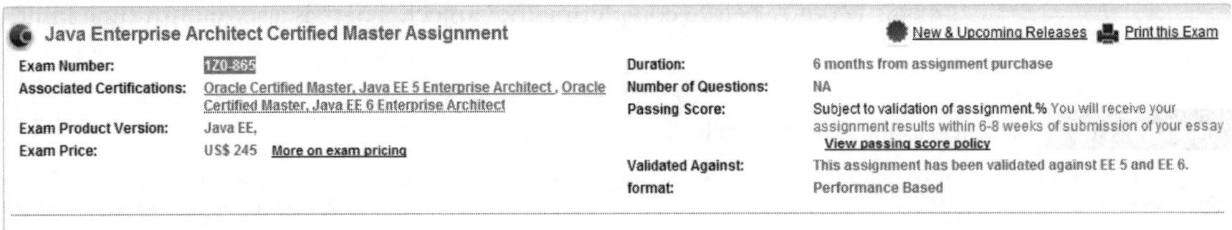

Java Enterprise Architect Certified Master Assignment New & Upcoming Releases Print this Exam

Exam Number:	1Z0-865	**Duration:**	6 months from assignment purchase
Associated Certifications:	Oracle Certified Master, Java EE 5 Enterprise Architect , Oracle Certified Master, Java EE 6 Enterprise Architect	**Number of Questions:**	NA
Exam Product Version:	Java EE,	**Passing Score:**	Subject to validation of assignment.% You will receive your assignment results within 6-8 weeks of submission of your essay View passing score policy
Exam Price:	US$ 245 More on exam pricing	**Validated Against:**	This assignment has been validated against EE 5 and EE 6.
		format:	Performance Based

FIGURE 1-8 OCMJEA Exam 1Z0-866 details

Java Enterprise Architect Certified Master Essay Exam New & Upcoming Releases Print this Exam

Exam Number:	1Z0-866	**Duration:**	120 minutes
Associated Certifications:	Oracle Certified Master, Java EE 5 Enterprise Architect, Oracle Certified Master, Java EE 6 Enterprise Architect	**Number of Questions:**	NA
Exam Product Version:	Java EE,	**Passing Score:**	Subject to validation of assignment % You will receive your assignment results within 6-8 weeks of submission of your essay. **View passing score policy**
Exam Price:	US$ 245 **More on exam pricing**	**Validated Against:**	This exam is validated against EE 5 and EE 6
		format:	Essay

You are given the following:

- A detailed textual description
- A domain model
- Use cases
- Directions on required deliverables

You will have to deliver the following for the system under discussion:

- Deliverable 1: Class diagram
- Deliverable 2: Component diagram
- Deliverable 3: Deployment diagram
- Deliverable 4: Use cases (as sequence or collaboration diagrams)
- Deliverable 5: Top three technical risks and mitigations for the same

- **OCMJEA Part 3** Exam 1Z0-866, an essay exam, can be completed at testing centers for a current cost of US$245. To take this exam, you must have passed Parts 1 and 2 and had your assignment validated. You have 120 minutes to complete the essay questions. See Figure 1-8 for the Part 1 master essay attributes.

General OCMJEA Test Preparation Tips

To prepare for Part 1, you must understand each of the exam objectives mentioned at the beginning of this chapter and within the chapters that follow. Those with comprehensive experience need only concentrate on their weaknesses. Others with less experience can take anywhere from weeks to months to learn what needs to be known.

- As a whole, Part 1 may require that you spend a few hours (for an experienced architect) to six months or more of dedicated preparation (for a beginner).
- Part 2 is project work, which requires a lot of focused and concentrated effort. On average, it may require 100 hours of study, typically spread over a period of a few months.

- Part 3 is an essay exam on your work in Part 2. Your success depends on your efforts during Part 2. If you did your homework, no special preparation is required at this stage.

Let's review some test-taking tips:

- *Prepare summary notes for Part 1*. Even though you may have read everything for the exam, having a few summary pages is a good idea. You can do a quick revision of all topics before the exam.
- *Cramming doesn't work*. If you have followed a study plan, the night before Part 1 you should do a quick review and get to sleep early. Remember that your brain and body need rest to function well.
- *Approach the exam as you would approach any large task*. It might be daunting, but you can do it! A positive attitude goes a long way toward success.
- *Those tricky problems can knock you off balance*. Don't get frustrated. Reread the question to make sure you understand it, and then try to solve it. If you're still clueless, mark it and move on. You can come back to it later. What if you have no idea about the answer? Review your options and take your best shot.
- *The process of elimination can help you choose the correct answer in a multiple-choice question*. Start by crossing off the answers that are obviously incorrect. Then spend your time focusing on the potentially correct choices before selecting your answer.
- *Prepare for scenario-based questions*. The test is geared toward testing your architectural skills. Hence, many lengthy scenarios are described, followed by questions that test your knowledge on what technology may be most appropriate in the given situation and why.
- *Read each scenario question twice*. Often the real issues will be embedded within a descriptive situation, and the real question will be hidden. Concentrate on the architecture issues and try to put the scenario to the back of your mind.
- *They say a picture is worth a thousand words, so when attempting to answer scenario questions, try to diagram what is being described*. If, for example, the question is describing a legacy system communicating with an application server, it helps to draw a diagram.
- *Use scrap paper*. Before you start the test, create a grid to represent the questions and your comfort level with the answer. Even when you mark off questions for review, having this in front of you will help you estimate the time required for revision.

- *This exam tests your architectural abilities, not necessarily your coding ability, so you should focus on the concepts, not on the code.* Although the test wants you to know what code performance is, it will not give you a code snippet and ask you to optimize it.
- *Although it's not in the requirements, a sound understanding of the JEE patterns is useful in Part 1 and essential in Parts 2 and 3.*
- *Try to build up a broad knowledge of other technologies, not just JEE.* Learn about messaging, mainframe technology, and perhaps some file and database terminology, because Oracle assumes you have overview of all the technologies.

Essay Test Preparation Tips

Here are a few suggestions for the essay portion of the exam.

Set Up a Documentation Template

While developing your solution, you should begin to document it. For example, you need to compile the following artifacts:

- Description of the company's story line
- Description of legacy systems used by the company
- Description of use cases
- Description of necessary infrastructure

Documentation requirements of the certification may be less than clear, and perhaps incomplete, and they may be in need of adjustments, which a good architect is trained to detect. You may make some amendments and enhancements to the design based on your interpretation. The objective is viability, as well as the ability to implement the solution. This is why you should document design decisions and describe your assumptions and how they affect your final solution. Also, be mindful to abstract the nonfunctional requirements and highlight the descriptions associated with each requirement. Here are some examples:

- How many will use the solution (a potential increase in usage requires scalability)
- The SLA and response time required by the end user
- The SLA and response time required for integrating external systems

Assumptions and Amendments Regarding the Requirement

Along the path of assumptions, you have two ways to go:

- If functionality already exists in the proposed solution, document this assumption.
- If functionality does not exist in the proposed solution, state the reasoning for adding functionality, components, and so on. Keep it basic, but be sure to cover the requirement and focus on diagrams depicting the solution.

Build Diagrams of the Solution

Here are a few tips for building diagrams:

- The diagrams need to be agnostic with respect to a particular technology or framework.
- Document all assumptions and design strategies and justify the decisions you are making.
- The diagrams must present a solution to the requirement based on the assumptions and strategy adopted.
- Keep the diagrams at a high level.
- Include deployment, class, sequence, and components diagrams.

Prepare for Potential Questions Related to the Project

To complete the certification, you will need to answer questions related to the project you developed. These questions might cover, for example, how you handled a system requirement and what the pros and cons of your choice are. Here are some potential questions you may encounter and should document prior to the exam:

- How does your design handle availability?
- How does your design handle reliability?
- How does your design handle scalability?
- How does your design handle performance?
- How does your design handle security?
- How does your design handle extensibility?
- How does your design handle maintainability?

- What design patterns are used on which layer and why?
- How does your design support session/state handling?
- How does your design handle persistence?
- How does your client tier communicate to the business tier?
- How does your design handle transactions?
- How does your design handle authentication and authorization?
- What technology did you use in the presentation and business tiers, and why?
- Why have you chosen to use a particular framework?

CERTIFICATION SUMMARY

The most important issue with regard to OCMJEA certification is how it promotes your career goals and helps you to earn a better job (and, hence, more money). With the current economy, it is somewhat difficult to compare the service rates, quantity, and quality of development opportunities. However, your opportunities will increase.

What you learn while preparing for the certification is what matters the most. The objectives for the architect certification are the best self-study curriculum for a Java architect and developer. They are practical and cover most of the issues, not only with respect to Java technologies, but also with respect to computing architecture and software development. The test preparation is a forced technique for mastering the material. It pumps up your confidence as well. It helps you to organize what you know and to find the voids. It also prepares you for interviews. Many recruiting companies are using their own tests to determine the programmer's qualification. Someone with an OCMJEA certification, generally speaking, is:

- Knowledgeable in Enterprise JavaBeans
- Knowledgeable in Uniform Modeling Language
- Knowledgeable in design patterns
- Knowledgeable in the architecture and protocols of distributed applications
- A potential project leader

The following chapters will put you in a position to take and pass all three parts of the OCMJEA and provide you with a quick review for any interview or Java architect skills test.

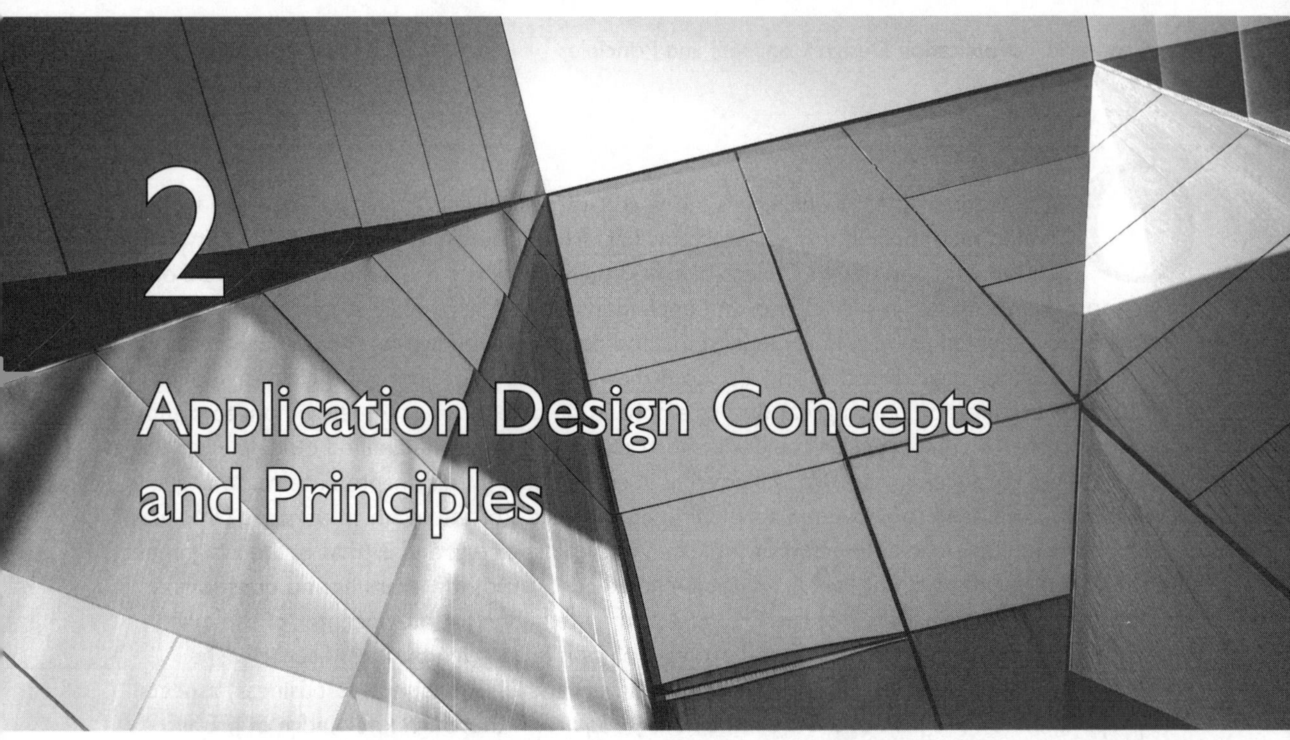

2 Application Design Concepts and Principles

CERTIFICATION OBJECTIVES

2.01	Identify Nonfunctional and Quality of Service Requirements That Influence Application Design	2.03	Identify the Correct Interpretation of Separation of Concerns as It Applies to the Java EE Service Layers
2.02	Identify How the Separation of Concerns Principle Applies to the Componengt Model of a Java EE Application	2.04	Identify the Effects of an Object-Oriented Approach to System Design
		✓	Two-Minute Drill
		Q&A	Self Test

One of the fundamental challenges facing software architects is change. The need to develop maintainable software systems has driven interest in approaches to software development and design. Object-oriented technology has proved over time to be one of the most mature paradigms for design and implementation of large-scale systems. Software architects are expected to be able to understand and communicate high-level design concepts to programmers under their direction and also to higher-ups who must approve their designs. Thus, the OCMJEA certification puts a great deal of emphasis on object-oriented design concepts and less on concrete APIs. In particular, the design abstraction known as the Unified Modeling Language (UML) receives strong emphasis. We will cover it in some detail in this chapter. The reasoning is as follows: you will need to know and apply UML during Part 2 of the exam. In the past, UML was tested on the multiple-choice portion of the exam as well as Parts 2 and 3 (that is, the assignment and the essay), but the current Part I (multiple-choice portion) of the exam has no questions on UML per se. That said, Part 2 of the OCMJEA is the literal and figurative center of the exam. Here, candidates must submit a JEE-based project solution for a given business scenario. The scenarios may contain both B2C (business-to-consumer) and B2B (business-to-business) aspects. The preparation for this part of the exam obviously requires a thorough knowledge of JEE and whatever is current in terms of assembled components. But most importantly your preparation for this exam part revolves around the UML. Your project will be evaluated on a number of objective criteria. Additionally, the project is evaluated based on UML compliance. The most important diagrams fall into three categories:

- **Class Diagrams** This category covers how well your class diagrams address the object model needed to satisfy the requirements.
- **Component Diagrams** This category covers how well your component diagrams convey the structure of the architecture in satisfying the requirements.
- **Sequence/Collaboration Diagrams** This category covers how well your sequence or collaboration diagrams satisfy the requirements of the assignment.

exam watch

This chapter covers UML with a view toward providing what you need to deliver a project for Part 2 of the exam.

With that said, UML is a system for drawing diagrams of object-oriented designs and using these diagrams throughout the design process. UML evolved out of a synthesis of several design methodologies to become an industry standard overseen by the Object Management Group (OMG; see www.omg.org/uml).

CERTIFICATION OBJECTIVE 2.01

Identify Nonfunctional and Quality of Service Requirements That Influence Application Design

Object-oriented concepts affect the whole development process, starting with gathering requirements, domain modeling, design, and implementation. Humans think in terms of nouns (objects) and verbs (behaviors of objects). Human languages and thought patterns are formed around objects in the world, such as people, places, and things (especially mobile devices, which are the most plentiful objects on the planet) as well as around the actions that manipulate the world of objects (for example, accessing your bank account from your iPhone). Object-oriented principles put our focus on objects and what actions these objects perform (their so-called "responsibilities"). Objects can also collaborate with other objects to perform an action. In object-oriented software development (OOSD), both problem and solution domains are modeled using object-oriented concepts. In OOSD, the development team is asked to create a software system that supports business processes. These processes are modeled with objects, responsibilities, and collaborations, because these notions fit our mental model of the business process.

Nonfunctional Requirements

Nonfunctional requirements (NFRs) define the qualitative characteristics of the system. The NFRs describe the Quality of Service of the system. These requirements include such characteristics as performance (measured in response time) and throughput (measured by how many simultaneous users can be accommodated). The NFRs describe relative capabilities of the system: that is, the speed, agility, elasticity, and so on, of the internal features of the system. NFRs describe the features of a system that support how an operation is performed. NFRs include how fast an operation is processed, how many operations can be performed simultaneously, how easy it is to add new features to the system, how easy the system is to manage, how easy the system is to use, and so on. Several factors contribute to the quality of service that a system delivers:

- **Transaction load** The system must support 2,000 simultaneous traders in the web application.
- **Transaction rate** The process for completing a stock/equity transaction must take no more than 150 milliseconds to finish.

- **Number of concurrent requests** The system must support 200 concurrent logons in the web application.
- **Request response time** The process for completing a stock/equity transaction must take the average user no more than 10 seconds to finish.
- **System availability** The system must be available 24 hours a day, 365 days a year (24×365). The applications can be shut down for scheduled maintenance once a week for two hours.

Quality of Service and Architecture

The nonfunctional Quality of Service features of an architecture include scalability, manageability, performance, availability, reliability, and security, which are defined in terms of context. Measures of system quality typically focus on performance characteristics of the system under study. Some research has examined resource utilization and investment utilization, hardware utilization efficiency, reliability, response time, ease of terminal use, content of the database, aggregation of details, human factors, and system accuracy.

Table 2-1 lists some well-known system quality measures.

TABLE 2-1 Capabilities and System Quality

System Quality	Definition
Availability	The degree to which a system is accessible. The term "24×7" describes total availability. This aspect of a system is often coupled with performance.
Reliability	The ability to ensure the integrity and consistency of an application and its transactions.
Manageability	The ability to administer and thereby manage the system resources to ensure the availability and performance of a system with respect to the other capabilities.
Flexibility	The ability to address architectural and hardware configuration changes without a great deal of impact to the underlying system.
Performance	The ability to carry out functionality in a timeframe that meets specified goals.
Capacity	The ability of a system to run multiple tasks per unit of time.
Scalability	The ability to support the required availability and performance as transactional load increases.
Extensibility	The ability to extend functionality.
Validity	The ability to predict and confirm results based on a specified input or user gesture.
Reusability	The ability to use a component in more than one context without changing its internals.
Security	The ability to ensure that information is not accessed and modified unless done so in accordance with the enterprise policy.

Availability

The availability of a system is often coupled with performance. *Availability* is the degree to which a system, subsystem, or equipment is operable and in a committable state at the start of a session, when the session is called for at an unknown (or random) time. The conditions determining operability must be specified. Expressed mathematically, availability is 1 minus the unavailability. Availability is the ratio of (a) the total time a functional unit is capable of being used during a given interval to (b) the length of the interval. An example of availability is 100/168, if the unit is capable of being used for 100 hours in a week. Typical availability objectives are specified in decimal fractions, such as 0.9998.

Reliability

Reliability is the ability of an item to perform a required function under stated conditions for a specified period of time. It is the probability that a functional unit will perform its required function for a specified interval under stated conditions.

The proper functioning of a company's computer systems is now critical to the operation of the company. An outage of an airline's computer systems, for example, can effectively shut down the airline. Many computer failures may be invisible to customers—a temporary hiccup during the catalog order process ("I can't check the availability of that item right now, but I'll take your order and call you back if there's a problem") or cashiers having to use hand calculators to ring up sales. However, on the Internet a company's computing infrastructure is on display in the store window—in fact, the company's infrastructure *is* the store window, so a computer problem at Amazon.com would be tantamount to every Barnes and Noble branch in the world locking its doors.

In the arena of Internet appliances and ubiquitous computing, the consumer cannot be placed in the position of troubleshooting the computer system. Reliability is critical because, eventually, people will expect their computers to work just as well as any other appliance in their home. After all, who has heard of a TV program that is "incompatible with the release level of your television"?

What does *reliability* mean from the standpoint of computer architecture? It is instructive to examine a system that is designed to have high fault tolerance and to allow repair without shutting down the system. For example, the IBM G5 series of S/390 mainframes has shown mean time to failure of 45 years, with 84 percent of all repairs performed while the system continues to run. To achieve this level of fault tolerance, the G5 includes duplicate instruction decode and execution pipeline stages. If an error is seen, the system retries the failing instruction. Repeated failures result in the last good state of the CPU being moved to another CPU, the failed

CPU being stopped, and a spare CPU being activated (if one is available). At the other end of the design spectrum, most PC systems do not have parity checking of their memory, even though many of these systems can now hold gigabytes of memory. Clearly, there is much room for computer architects to move high-end reliability and serviceability down into low-end servers, personal computers, and ubiquitous computing devices.

Manageability and Flexibility

Manageability refers to the set of services that ensures the continued integrity, or correctness, of the component application. It includes security, concurrency control, and server management. A metric example of manageability would be the number of staff hours per month required to perform normal upgrades. *Server management* refers to the set of system facilities used for starting and stopping the server, installing new components, managing security permissions, and performing other tasks. These services can be implemented through a "best of breed" third-party product approach, integrated in a middle-tier server product or implemented through operating system facilities.

Flexibility is the key to an available, reliable, and scalable application. Flexibility can be improved through location independence of application code. An example of flexibility would be a JEE system that uses internationalization code and property files to allow changes in the presentation language (for example, English to German). Regarding metrics, there is no standard way of measuring flexibility. The business measure is the cost of change in time and money, but this depends on what types of change can be anticipated.

As flexibility, reliability, and availability are increased, manageability can suffer. Flexibility is also essential for keeping pace with rapid change. It's enhanced when the middle-tier technology is a component-based solution that easily accommodates the integration of multiple technologies. Independence from hardware, operating system, and language creates the most adaptable and portable solutions. The connectivity mechanisms to multiple data sources also increase adaptability. Fortunately, this area is one in which several solutions are available, including the database connection standards (ODBC and JDBC), native database drivers, messaging, remote procedure calls (to database stored procedures), object request brokers, and database gateways.

Performance

Response time and response ratio are important to an application. The most important task resulting in good performance is to identify and control expensive calls.

The architect should state target performance criteria before implementing within a production environment. For example, the first visible response in any application browser view when the application is under maximum specified load must occur in less than 3 seconds, 95 percent of the time. Measurement is made at the enterprise's external firewall.

Today, when measuring performance, the architect must consider and attempt to quantify the cost of an operation (data or computational)—which can involve a myriad of servers across a sea of network connections—before finally returning a response view to the user requestor.

Today, performance is the ability to execute functions fast enough to meet goals. Response time (the time it takes to respond) and response ratio (the time it takes to perform the function) are important to an application. Both figures should be as low as possible, but a ratio of 1 is the target. For example, suppose a user requests functionality requiring a great deal of processing or database searching and it takes a minute to process. The user will not see a result for a minute—seemingly a long time to wait—but if the result can be viewed in 1 minute plus 20 seconds (a response ratio of 1.3333), that is still good performance. Alternatively, suppose that the processing takes only 1 second but the user does not see the result for 20 seconds (response ratio of 20), that is not good performance.

Capacity

Capacity is a measure of the extent or ability of the computer hardware, software, and connection infrastructure resources over some period of time. A typical capacity concern of many enterprises is whether resources will be in place to handle an increasing number of requests as the number of users or interactions increases. The aim of the capacity planner is to plan so well that new capacity is added just in time to meet the anticipated need but not so early that resources go unused for a long period. The successful capacity planner is one that makes the trade-offs between the present and the future that overall prove to be the most cost-efficient. No benchmark can predict the performance of every application. It is easy to find two applications and two computers with opposite rankings, depending on the application; therefore, any benchmark that produces a performance ranking must be wrong on at least one of the applications. However, memory references dominate most applications.

For example, there is considerable difference between a kernel-like information-retrieval product and one that performs the complex business rules of a heuristic trading system that does matrix multiplication. Most "kernels" are code excerpts. The work measure is typically something like the number of iterations in the loop structure, or an operation count (ignoring precision or differing weights for differing operations). The kernel accomplishes a petty but useful calculation and defines its work measure strictly in terms of the quality of the answer instead of what was done to get there. Although each iteration is simple, it still involves more than 100 instructions on a typical serial computer and includes decisions and variety that make it unlikely to be improved by a hardware engineer.

Scalability

Vertical scalability comes from adding capacity (memory and CPUs) to existing servers. Horizontal scalability comes from adding servers. In terms of scalability, a system can scale to accommodate more users and higher transaction volumes in several different ways:

- *Upgrade the hardware platform.* Solutions that offer platform independence enable rapid deployment and easier integration of new technology.
- *Improve the efficiency of communications.* In a distributed environment, the communications overhead is often a performance bottleneck. Session management will improve communication among clients and servers through session pooling.
- *Provide transparent access to multiple servers to increase throughput during peak loads.* Load balancing is especially necessary to support the unpredictable and uncontrollable demands of Internet applications. Some application server products offer load balancing.
- *Improve communication between the application component server and various data sources through connection pooling management.*

Scalability is more a system problem than a CPU architecture problem. The attributes that a system needs include the following:

- Graceful degradation all the way up to 100 percent system load
- The ability to add capacity incrementally (CPUs, memory, I/O, and/or disk storage) without disrupting system operation
- The ability to prioritize the workload so that unneeded work can be suspended at times of peak activity

Some websites, such as CNN.com, revert to lower overhead pages (smaller pages with less graphics) during traffic peaks. One possibility for the future would be to provide peak offload facilities for web merchants. If groups of sites used relatively similar architectures, a site with spare capacity could be kept ready for whoever needs it. If an unexpected peak occurred—or an expected peak that didn't justify buying more hardware—the contents of the site could be shadowed to the offload facility and traffic divided between the two sites.

Techniques such as logical partitioning can also be used to shift system resources. Logical partitioning is available in mainframe systems and allows one large CPU complex to contain multiple logical system images, which are kept completely separate by the hardware and operating system. Portions of the system resources can be assigned to the partitions, with the assignments enforced by the hardware. This allows resources to be shifted from development to production, or between different systems involved in production, by simply shifting the percentages assigned to the partitions. Capacity is affected by scalability—for example, one machine handles 500 transactions or five machines handle 100 transactions each.

Extensibility, Validity, and Reusability

Extensibility requires careful modeling of the business domain to add new features based on a model. Validity, or testability, is the ability to determine what the expected results should be. Multi-tier architecture provides for many connection points and hence many points of failure for intermediate testing and debugging. Reusability of software components can be achieved by employing the interfaces provided by frameworks. This is accomplished by defining generic components that can be reapplied to create new applications. Framework reusability leverages the domain knowledge and prior effort of experienced developers to avoid re-creating and revalidating common solutions to recurring application requirements and software design challenges. Reuse of framework components can yield substantial improvements in programmer productivity, as well as enhance other system qualities such as performance, reliability, and interoperability.

Security

Security is essential for ensuring access to component services and for ensuring that data is appropriately managed; these issues are particularly important in Internet applications. Integrated network, Internet, server, and application security is the most manageable solution. This approach can be described by Single Sign-On (SSO), which requires a rich infrastructure of network and system services. Firewalls and authentication mechanisms must also be supported for Internet security. With concurrency control, multiuser access can be managed without requiring explicit application code.

A goal of information security is to protect resources and assets from loss. Resources may include information, services, and equipment such as servers and networking components. Each resource has several assets that require protection:

- **Privacy** Preventing information disclosure to unauthorized persons
- **Integrity** Preventing corruption or modification of resources
- **Authenticity** Proof that a person has been correctly identified or that a message is received as transmitted
- **Availability** Assurance that information, services, and equipment are working and available for use

The classes of threats include accidental threats, intentional threats, passive threats (those that do not change the state of the system but may include loss of confidentiality but not of integrity or availability), and active threats (those that change the state of the system, including changes to data and to software).

A *security policy* is an enterprise's statement defining the rules that regulate how it will provide security, handle intrusions, and recover from damage caused by security breaches. Based on a risk analysis and cost considerations, such policies are most effective when users understand them and agree to abide by them.

Security services are provided by a system for implementing the security policy of an organization. A standard set of such services includes the following:

- **Identification and authentication** Unique identification and verification of users via certification servers and global authentication services (Single Sign-On services, also known as SSO)
- **Access control and authorization** Rights and permissions that control what resources users may access
- **Accountability and auditing** Services for logging activities on network systems and linking them to specific user accounts or sources of attacks
- **Data confidentiality** Services to prevent unauthorized data disclosure
- **Data integrity and recovery** Methods for protecting resources against corruption and unauthorized modification—for example, mechanisms using checksums and encryption technologies
- **Data exchange** Services that secure data transmissions over communication channels
- **Object reuse** Services that provide multiple users secure access to individual resources

- **Nonrepudiation of origin and delivery** Services to protect against attempts by the sender to falsely deny sending the data, or subsequent attempts by the recipient to falsely deny receiving the data
- **Reliability** Methods for ensuring that systems and resources are available and protected against failure

CERTIFICATION OBJECTIVE 2.02

Identify How the Separation of Concerns Principle Applies to the Component Model of a Java EE Application

In object-oriented programming, a complex system is decomposed into a hierarchy of collaborating objects—or as described and used in the exam, the principle of a "separation of concerns." This approach to structure tends to be more flexible and extensible because you are recomposing different collaborations between existing objects to solve new problems. This principle provides the designer with a handle on system complexity by shielding the complex details of one layer behind an abstraction (a method or object) on a higher level. This principle also affects modeling. You do not have to show all of the system complexity in one view; rather, you can create different views at different levels of abstraction.

Decomposition and the Separation of Concerns

A system can be split by intra- and inter-component relationships—that is, "separation of concerns." For example, a UI component deals with a user's actions, such as processing a click to a button or verifying that a data field has a legitimate value. A business logic component does not need to know how the data is entered when it processes some operation. This principle tells the architect to separate components into different functional or infrastructure purposes. This principle is important also because the exam constantly tests your ability to separate out or abstract the different components needed to provide a good solution. For example, on the exam, you may need to exhibit the ability to separate the user interface from business logic (Model). Even user interfaces can be separated into visual elements

(View) and user interaction logic (Controller). This separation of concerns leads to the Model-View-Controller (MVC) architecture pattern.

Moreover, the application of the Presentation Abstraction Control (PAC) pattern introduces a level of decoupling between tiers and further defines the separation of concerns that was initiated with the MVC pattern. The presentation components reside on the presentation tier, and the control and abstraction components reside on the business tier. This makes the model flexible and allows for rapid changes in presentation without impacting the business model that is managed by the control and abstraction components.

This principle of "separation of concerns" is tested on the Part I multiple-choice portion of the exam, as well as Parts 2 and 3.

The application of the "separation of concerns" principle enables one to study each component part of a system in relative isolation. So we see that the separation of concerns is an important principle in designing and building complex systems. Regarding separation of concerns, of special value is the ability to later modify/enhance one component part without having to know the details of the other component parts, and without having to make corresponding changes to those component parts. This is so because typically the interface does not change just the implementation. On the exam, you will be responsible for applying the separation of concerns to concepts such as tiers and layers.

Tiers

Tiers are the logical or physical components in the hierarchy of service. Not unlike the classic client/server model, in two- and three-tier hierarchies each component within a tier can be a client and/or a service provider. As a client, the tier may consume the services of the next tier. As a server, the tier may provide services to the client consumer tiers. For this exam, the tiers in the architecture are client, web/presentation, business, integration, and resource:

- **Client** A client tier is a component that manages display processing.
- **Web or presentation** Web tiers consist of services that manage user sessions and route requests to services.
- **Business** Business tier services execute the particular business logic and manage transactions.

- **Integration or middle** Integration tier services provide the access to external resources typically on behalf of the business tier.
- **Resource or database** The resource tier includes databases, flat data feeds, and, of course, the legacy systems such as IBM mainframes. The resource tier provides the access to data and legacy systems typically on behalf of the integration tier.

CERTIFICATION OBJECTIVE 2.03

Identify the Correct Interpretation of Separation of Concerns as It Applies to the Java EE Service Layers

In procedural programming, tasks are decomposed into a hierarchy of procedures. This decomposition seems natural until you try to extend the program. Alternatively, using object-oriented principles, a system is composed of a hierarchy of collaborating objects (for example, the "tiers" of an architecture).

For the exam, the tiers in the architecture are client, web/presentation, business, integration, and resource.

Breaking an architecture into tiers is one way in which we address the "separation of concerns." These principles can reduce development costs. Object-oriented (OO) principles provide a natural technique for modeling business entities and processes from the early stages of a project to address the separation of concerns. Developing software in an object-oriented language also increases productivity by enabling the programmers to write code that maps closely to the design models.

OO principles can reduce maintenance costs in the following ways:

- Maintainability and adaptability of software are important to keep software running for a long time. Sadly, a good percentage of the cost of software is devoted to the maintenance effort or changes to user requirements ("scope creep"). Object-oriented designs tend to be more flexible and adaptable than procedural designs, thus reducing maintenance costs.

- Object-oriented modeled business entities and processes that address the separation of concerns can be adapted to new functional requirements because the interface typically is not affected.
- Object-oriented designs that address the separation of concerns are easier to change in response to new business requirements. Object-oriented designs focus on identifying stable business objects that can be made to interact in new ways.

Layers

A *layer* can be thought of as an architecture pattern in which components use services in the layers below. Layering helps maintainability. The communication between two layers determines how well the application can be partitioned at that point for physical distribution across tiers. Strict layering schemes do not allow layers to access anything but the layers immediately below, whereas relaxed layering schemes allow a given layer to use any other layer below it. Layers are similar to tiers because they represent the interface-based relationships between system boundaries. Layers represent component relationships in the service implementation. For the exam, the following are the layers you will need to recognize and refer to when answering the exam questions:

- **Application** The application layer is the user and business functionality of a system (for example, the .war or .ear files).
- **Virtual platform (component APIs)** The virtual platform layer contains interfaces to the application infrastructure component APIs (for example, REST web services and servlets).
- **Application infrastructure (containers)** The application infrastructure layer contains products (for example, JBOSS and IBM's WebSphere) that provide for the operation and development of the application. The virtual platform components are housed in an application infrastructure container.
- **Enterprise services (OS and virtualization)** The enterprise services layer is the operating system (for example, Linux) and the software (for example, Oracle DBMS) that runs on top of the compute and storage layer. This layer provides the interfaces to operating system and storage functions needed by the application infrastructure layer.
- **Compute and storage** The compute and storage layer consists of the physical hardware used in the architecture.

CERTIFICATION OBJECTIVE 2.04

Identify the Effects of an Object-Oriented Approach to System Design

Object-oriented analysis and design (OOAD) is an engineering technique that models a system as a group of interacting objects. Each object represents an entity of interest in the system being modeled, and is characterized by its class, state, and behavior. Models can be created to illustrate the static structure, dynamic behavior, and run-time deployment of these collaborating objects. There are a number of different notations for representing these models, such as the Unified Modeling Language (UML), which we will cover in detail as needed, especially for Part 2 of the exam.

Fundamental Object-Oriented Concepts

Many other concepts and terminologies are essential an object-oriented approach to system design. Here is a quick review.

Objects

An object equals state plus behavior. Objects are run-time features of an object-oriented system. Here are some key points concerning objects:

- *Objects have identity*. Every object at run time has an identity that is unique and is independent of its attribute values. In the Java programming language, program variables refer to objects such that object references can be passed between objects and methods.
- *Objects are an instance of only one class*. A class defines a type of object. At run time, an object is defined by one class. However, that class might be an extension of other classes as a result of using inheritance.
- *Objects have attribute values that are unique to them*. Every object of the same class has the same set of attributes, but the values of these attributes are unique for every object. This means that you can change an attribute of one Account object without affecting any other Account object in memory.

Figure 2-1 illustrates an object example. The outer boxes represent aspects of a program's run-time environment. The Stack box (lower rectangle) represents the current execution frame (a stack frame) with program variables for that frame.

FIGURE 2-1

An example of an object at run time

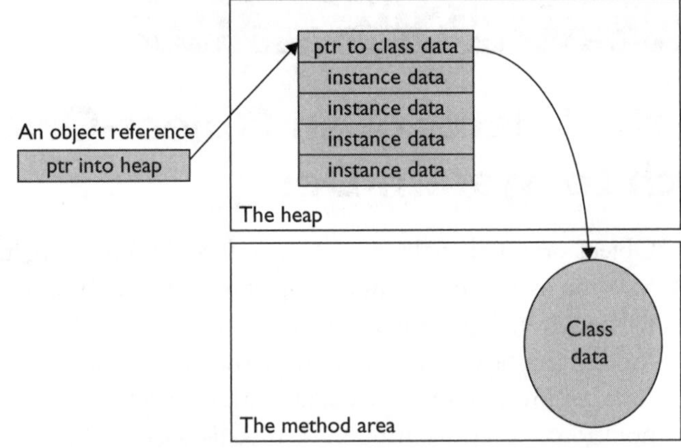

The Objects box (upper rectangle) represents the space in run-time memory that holds objects (this is usually called the "heap").

Classes

A class is the DNA from which objects are created. In object-oriented programming, a class is usually a language construct that forms the common structure and behavior from which objects are instantiated. Classes provide the following features:

- **The metadata for attributes** The class maintains the metadata of each attribute. This metadata includes the data type and the initial value.
- **The signature for methods** The operations of an object are called *methods*. Methods have two elements: a signature and implementation. The signature includes the name of the method, the list of parameters (parameter name and type), and the return type. The implementation of a method is the set of programming statements that specify how the operation is to be performed.
- **The constructors to initialize attributes at creation time** A constructor is a set of instructions that initializes an instance.

Abstraction

Abstraction is the summarization of a larger thing. Abstraction enables you to create a simplified and relevant view of an object within the context of the problem domain. Abstraction enables you to design features defined by the system requirements and to ignore irrelevant details.

Encapsulation

Encapsulation means "to enclose in" or "as if in a capsule." Encapsulation is a property of an object. An object is a capsule that holds the object's internal state within its boundaries. To create proper encapsulation you must make all attributes private and provide "getter" and "setter" methods to provide an abstract interface to the data held within the object capsule. To use an encapsulated class, you only need to know the purpose and signature of the public methods of the class. This tactic enables the programmer of the class to change the implementation of the class without changing the public interface.

Inheritance

Inheritance is "a mechanism whereby a class is defined in reference to others, adding all their features to its own," as Bertrand Meyer defines it in *Object-Oriented Software Construction*. The features of inheritance are as follows:

- Attributes and methods from the superclass are included in the subclass.
- Subclass methods can override superclass methods.
- A subclass can inherit from multiple super classes (called multiple inheritance) or a subclass can only inherit from a single superclass (single inheritance).

Inheritance should conform to Liskov's Substitution Principle (LSP). A brief simplified interpretation of LSP is that if you substitute a subclass (for example, Audi) for a superclass (for example, Car), then anyone who makes use of the superclass should discover that all the methods it expected to find in the superclass are still provided and accessible, with any overridden methods having the same semantic meaning.

Abstract Classes

An abstract class contains one or more abstract methods, and therefore can never be instantiated. The features of an abstract class include:

- Attributes are permitted. An abstract class may declare instance variables. These attributes are inherited by the subclasses of the abstract class.
- Methods are permitted, and some might be declared abstract. Methods may be declared in an abstract class. One or more of the methods might also be declared abstract, meaning that this class does not define an implementation of that method.

- Constructors are permitted, but no client may directly instantiate an abstract class. Constructors may be declared in an abstract class. These constructors can be used by the constructors of subclasses.
- Subclasses of abstract classes must provide implementations of all abstract methods; otherwise, the subclass must also be declared abstract. A subclass of an abstract class may implement any of the abstract methods in its abstract superclass. The subclass may also override any non-abstract methods in the abstract superclass. However, if the subclass does not provide implementations for all abstract methods, that subclass must also be declared abstract.

In the UML, a method or a class is denoted as abstract via the use of italics, or you can append the method name or class name with {abstract}. It is difficult to use italics in handwritten drawings, which tend to use the {abstract} notation. A concrete class is the opposite of an abstract class. A concrete class must have no abstract methods.

Interfaces

An interface is the contract between the application and its implementation.

The features of Java technology interfaces include:

- Attributes are not permitted (except constants). Interfaces by definition do not have attributes. However, interface may declare constants (with the modifiers public, static, and final).
- Methods are permitted, but they must be abstract. An interface is a set of abstract methods. An interface may not declare a method with an implementation.
- Constructors are not permitted.
- Interfaces are not classes, and no objects may be constructed from an interface. However, a class might implement an interface, and objects of that class may be said to be "instances" of the interface. However, it is more appropriate to say the instance supports the interface.
- Subinterfaces may be defined, forming an inheritance hierarchy of interfaces.

The Java programming language supports interfaces directly. Other languages, such as C++, can support the concept of interfaces by defining classes that are completely abstract (all methods are virtual and empty) with no attributes. Interfaces can be implemented by any class in any hierarchy; classes that implement an interface are not bound to a single class hierarchy.

Polymorphism

Polymorphism is a concept in type theory in which a name (such as a variable declaration) may denote objects of many different classes that are related by some common superclass (type).

Here are some aspects of polymorphism:

- A variable declared to reference type T can be assigned different types of objects at run time provided they are a subtype of the variable's type T.
- Method implementation is determined by the type of object, not the type of the declaration.

Analysis and Design of Object-Oriented Architecture

As mentioned, modeling is a visual process used for creating in a preserved form the design and structure of an application. Before, during, and after development, it is typical and prudent to outline an application, depicting dependencies and relationships among the components and subsystems. Like any good development tool, today's modeling tools facilitate this process by tracking changes made in the model to reflect the cascading effects of changes. Use of modeling tools gives developers a high-level and accurate view of the system.

Modeling can be used at any point in a project. Most modeling tools can reengineer and use code as input to create a visual model. The standard for modeling tools is the Unified Modeling Language (UML). This standard unifies the many proprietary and incompatible modeling languages to create one modeling specification. Use of modeling tools for development projects is increasing. With the increasing complexity of enterprise Java applications and components, modeling is a virtual necessity. It can reduce development time while ensuring that code is well formed.

Modeling is useful whether the objective is to understand and modify an existing computer-based business system or to create an entirely new one. An obstacle to engineering successfully is the inability to analyze and communicate the numerous interactive activities that make up a business process. Conversational languages, such as English, are ambiguous and therefore ineffective for communicating such objectives and activities. Formal languages are unintelligible to most functional (business) experts. What is needed instead is a technique that structures conversational language to eliminate ambiguity, thus facilitating effective communication and understanding.

In a process model, extraneous detail is eliminated, thus reducing the apparent complexity of the system under study. The remaining detail is structured to eliminate any ambiguity, while highlighting important information. Graphics (pictures, lines, arrows, and other graphic standards) are used to provide much of the structure, so most people consider process models to be pictorial representations. However, well-written definitions of the objects, as well as supporting text, are also critical to a successful model.

In engineering disciplines, the model is typically constructed before an actual working system is built. In most cases, modeling the target business process is a necessary first step in developing an application. The model becomes the roadmap that will establish the route to the final destination. Deciding the functionality of the target destination is essential. To be effective, it must be captured and depicted in detail.

In today's software development environment, we speak of objects as things that encapsulate attributes and operations. Before we proceed to the modeling standards being used today by software architects, let's begin with some basic definitions of object programming and its intending analysis, design, and life cycle.

Key Features of OOP: Objects and Classes

Object-oriented programming (OOP) is the methodology used for programming classes based on defined and cooperating objects. OOP is based on objects rather than procedural actions, and data rather than logic. In days past, a program had been viewed as a logical procedure that used input data to process and produce output data. Object-oriented programming focuses on the objects we want to manipulate rather than the logic required to manipulate them. Object examples range from human beings (described by name, address, and so forth) to inanimate objects whose properties can be described and managed, such as the controls on your computer desktop—buttons, scroll bars, and so on.

Step one in OOP is to identify the objects to be manipulated and their relationships to each other. That is the essence of modeling. Once you've identified an object, you generalize it as a class of objects and define the kind of data it contains and the logic that can manipulate it. The logic is known as "methods." A real instance of a class is called an object or an instance of a class. The object or class instance is executed on the computer. Its methods provide computer instructions, and the class object characteristics provide relevant data. You communicate with objects, and they communicate with each other with defined interfaces called "messages."

The concepts and rules used in OOP provide these important benefits:

- The concept of a data class makes it possible to define subclasses of data objects that share some or all of the main class characteristics. This is known as inheritance, and it is a property of OOP that facilitates thorough data analysis, reduces development time, and ensures more accurate coding.

- Because a class defines only the data it needs, when an instance of that class is run, the code will not be able to access other program data improperly. This characteristic of data hiding provides greater system security and avoids unintended data corruption.
- The definition of a class is reusable not only by the program for which it is initially created but also by other object-oriented programs. This facilitates distribution for use in other domains.
- The concept of data classes allows a programmer to create new data types that are not defined in the language itself.

Defining Object-Oriented Analysis and Design

In terms of computing software, analysis is the development activity consisting of the discovery, modeling, specification, and evaluation of requirements. Object-oriented analysis (OOA) is the discovery, analysis, and specification of requirements in terms of objects with identities that encapsulate properties and operations, message passing, classes, inheritance, polymorphism, and dynamic binding. Object-oriented design (OOD) is the design of an application in terms of objects, classes, clusters, frameworks, and their interactions.

In comparing the definition of traditional analysis with that of object-oriented analysis and design (OOAD), the only aspect that is new is thinking of the world or the problem in terms of objects and object classes. A class is any uniquely identified abstraction—that is, a model—of a set of logically related instances that share the same or similar characteristics. An object is any abstraction that models a single element, and the term "object," as mentioned, is synonymous with "instance." Classes have attributes and methods, as they are more commonly known.

Project Life Cycle Workflow

The project life cycle is a pivotal concept in terms of understanding what a project is; the life cycle is a mapping of the progress of the project from start to finish. Projects, by definition, have a start and finish, like any good game. At the simplest level, projects have two phases: planning and executing. Planning and executing are okay for a simple, short-term project. Larger, long-term endeavors require another layer to be added to the life cycle of the projects. This can be achieved by subdividing each phase—planning and executing—into two further phases, leading to a life cycle of analysis, design, development, and implementation. Table 2-2 summarizes the classic project life cycle phases and mentions activities to be planned

TABLE 2-2 Project Life Cycle Phases

Primary Phase/ Subphase	Activities
Analysis/ Requirements analysis	Take a concept statement and define detailed requirements and the externally visible characteristics of the system. Write a validation plan that maps to the requirements specification. Short form: Is it possible to resolve the requirements?
System-context analysis	Define the context of the system via use cases and scenarios. External messages, events, and actions are defined. The system is treated as a black box. Use case and scenario models are the deliverables. For real-time systems, characterize the sequence and synchronization details of the messages/responses. Short form: What would the big picture solution look like?
Model analysis	Identify the classes, objects, and associations that solve the problem, using class and object diagrams. Response behavior is modeled using state charts. Interaction among objects is shown with sequence or collaboration diagrams. Short form: a further refinement of the big-picture solution arrived at by decomposing subsystems into high-level classes.
Design/ Architectural design	Define the important architectural decisions. Physical architecture of the system is modeled using deployment diagrams, software component architecture is modeled using component diagrams, and concurrency models are captured using class diagrams identifying the active objects. Design patterns are used here as well. Note that one key element of design is that "hard" dependencies on specific hardware, software, and other infrastructure are fleshed out as we move closer to implementation. For example, an architect may decide to use BEA WebLogic as the J2EE server. A designer may find that, while trying to build some XML parsing components, a decision needs to be made about whether to use BEA-specific APIs or perhaps use JAXP APIs.
Mechanistic design	Define the collaborative behavior of classes and objects. This information is captured on class and object diagrams. Sequence and collaboration diagrams capture specific instances of collaborations, and state charts are enhanced to define the full behavior.
Detailed design	Define the detailed behavior and structure of individual classes using activity diagrams and notations.
Development	Develop class code, database definition, and message structures in the target language, DBMS, and messaging system.
Implementation/ Unit testing	Test the internal structure and behavior of each class.
Integration testing	Test the integration of various components. This takes place recursively at multiple levels of decomposition based on the scale of the system.
Validation testing	Test the delivered system against the requirements as defined in the validation test plan.
System delivered	Pass the delivered system and user guide and other operational documentation to the user and technical support staff.

and executed for each phase. UML deliverables mentioned in this table are discussed in the sections that follow.

For the sake of completeness, we should also mention the Unified Process—or RUP (Rational Unified Process), as it has been trademarked by Rational (www.rational.com). The RUP is an incremental process used by development managers to oversee a software project. Using the RUP, the project is broken down into phases and iterations. The iterations are oriented toward decreasing risk. Each phase should deliver a product, usually software that can be demonstrated and validated against the project's requirements and use cases. The development manager uses iteration plans to manage the project. An iteration plan provides a detailed description of the upcoming phase of work. It defines the roles involved as well as activities and artifacts to be delivered in that iteration. The RUP outlines a set of criteria by which productivity and progress can be measured during the iteration. As with all planning tools, it defines specific start and end dates for product delivery.

The RUP identifies four phases for projects. Each phase focuses the team on an aspect of the project and has associated milestones:

1. **Inception** The focus of this phase is the project scope versus resource capacity.
2. **Elaboration** The architecture as well as the requirements of the product being built must be defined by the end of this phase.
3. **Construction** The software must be developed or constructed in this phase.
4. **Transition** The software must be rolled out to users during this phase.

The RUP phases in some respects parallel the classic life cycle phases—analysis, design, development, and implementation. They are, however, targeted at managing risks in project development. They consider that today's development is iterative. They are a framework geared for project leaders as opposed to architects and developers. The RUP management discipline provides a process that software development managers use to produce an overall project plan. The plan must be focused on deliverables, and it must be measurable, flexible, and aligned to real progress. The plan also must define the responsibilities and dependencies of the development team.

Modeling and the Software Development Process

The software industry has experienced exponential growth. There has been a great deal of change in the technologies of programming: languages, operating systems, networking, communication protocols, component-based application programming interfaces (APIs), and application server software. The software development process has changed along with the technologies. When using object-oriented (OO) technologies for development, you should use OOSD processes because the object-oriented technologies influence the software development processes.

Software Methodology

Methodology is "a body of methods, rules, and postulates employed by a discipline," as defined by Merriam-Webster. In software development, a methodology refers to the highest-level of organization of the development process itself. OO methodologies incorporate object-oriented concepts throughout the OOSD process. Many modern object-oriented methodologies break down the development process into large-scale phases, such as Inception, Elaboration, Construction, and Transition. These phases are composed of workflows (disciplines), and these workflows are composed of specific activities. Activities involve workers and artifacts. A worker is a person who performs the activity. An artifact is a tangible piece of information that is produced by an activity. Artifacts such as diagrams, documents, and the software code itself are produced with tools. The Unified Modeling Language (UML) is one of our most powerful tools for modeling software.

To support the activities, the development team uses various tools to analyze, model, and construct the software solution. These tools include word processors, the Unified Modeling Language, UML modeling tools, advanced text editors, and integrated development environments.

An artifact produced in one activity might be an input into another activity. For example, a Use Case diagram is used during the design workflow to determine the software components needed to satisfy the functional requirements defined by the use cases.

Artifacts can be documents, diagrams, and even a functioning system. The goal of software development is to produce a functioning system (that is, an artifact) that satisfies the requirements of the business owner, users, and other client-side stakeholders.

Software Team Roles

A stakeholder is any person or group that has an interest in the project. The set of stakeholders includes users and managers on the client side and the complete project team on the development side. As previously mentioned, workers perform activities that generate artifacts that document, model, and implement the software solution. For example, the workers fall into categories such as the following:

- The **business owner** is the lead stakeholder on the client side of the project. This person is responsible for making final decisions about the behavior of the system.
- The **user** is any person who will be using the proposed system.
- The **business analyst** is the one who gathers requirements from the client-side stakeholders and analyzes the functional requirements by modeling the enduring business themes of the system. This role is responsible for the Business Domain diagrams, which include Use Case diagrams and Business Domain (Analysis) class diagrams.
- The **architect** defines the architecture of the system, leads the development of the architectural baseline during the Inception and Elaboration phases, analyses the NFRs, identifies project risk, and creates a risk mitigation plan.
- The **software designer** creates the Solution model of the system based on the Business Domain diagrams within the framework of the architecture.
- The **software programmer** implements the software solution. In many small development teams, the programmer and designer roles are filled by the same person.
- The **software tester** tests the implementation to verify that the system meets the requirements (both FRs and NFRs). This role might include the development team for unit and integration testing, as well as the client-side quality assurance (QA) personnel for acceptance testing.
- The **deployment specialist/system administrator** is the one who deploys the implementation onto the production platform. This role is typically performed by the development team during construction, but when the system goes to production this role should be filled by the client organization.

Requirements Gathering Workflow

The requirements of a system are divided into two fundamental categories: functional requirements (FRs) and nonfunctional requirements (NFRs). The FRs describe the behavior of the system relative to the perspective of the actors that use the system. High-level FRs are visualized as use cases. The NFRs describe the quality of service of the system. These requirements include such characteristics as performance (measured in response time), throughput (measured by how many simultaneous users can be accommodated), and so on. The purpose of the Requirements Gathering workflow is to determine the requirements of the system by meeting the business owner and users of the proposed system. The Requirements Gathering workflow activities are usually performed by the business analyst and architect job roles.

Requirements Analysis Workflow

There are two views of the Requirements model created in this workflow:

- The completed Use Case forms, containing full details of the actor's interaction with the system and what the system does in response
- The Domain model (a Class diagram of the key abstractions of the problem space)

These artifacts and the previously created artifacts together make up the problem space. The language used in these artifacts should be understandable to the client-side stakeholders because they use this language to discuss their business (also known as a "domain"). These terms are often the key abstractions of the problem space, and they are fashioned using a Domain model.

The purpose of Requirements Analysis workflow is to analyze, refine, and model the requirements of the system. The Requirements Analysis workflow activities are usually performed by the business analyst and architect job roles. The Requirements Analysis activities are as follows:

- Analyze the use case scenarios to discover more detail. Use scenarios to refine the Use Case forms. Add or refine the main flow and alternative flows to this form. Also, analyzing use case scenarios often identifies common patterns in use cases. These common patterns can be made explicit in the Use Case form. For example, a common pattern of many use cases might be the need to log on to the system.
- Refine the Use Case diagram from the analysis. For example, the logon behavior can be captured in a separate use case node and have other use cases refer to the logon use case.

Optionally, the analyst can create an Activity diagram that provides a visual view of the flow of events to augment and verify the textual Use Case forms.

A graphical view of the flow of events can be used to augment and verify the stakeholders' understanding of the problem. A UML Activity diagram can be used to model the activities of a use case at a fine level of granularity.

The Architecture Workflow

The Architecture workflow is complex. However, you will see how the Architecture model (developed in this workflow) affects the Design workflow. From the perspective of the designer, the Architecture model provides a template of the high-level system structure into which the designer plugs in designed components. The purpose of the Architecture workflow is to identify risk in the project and to mitigate the risk by modeling the high-level structure of the system. The Architecture workflow activities are performed by the architect. The architect creates a detailed Deployment diagram that shows the main components necessary to support the architecturally significant use cases. This diagram shows the low-level components and their dependencies with the high-level Deployment diagram.

The architect uses architectural patterns to transform the high-level architecture type into a robust hardware topology that supports the NFRs. The architect implements the architecturally significant use cases in an evolutionary prototype. When all architecturally significant use cases have been developed, the evolutionary prototype is called the *Architecture baseline*, which represents the version of the system solution that manages all risks. The Architecture baseline is the final product of the Elaboration phase and becomes the starting point of the Construction phase. The Architecture baseline is tested to verify that the selected systemic qualities have been satisfied. The Architecture baseline is refined by applying additional patterns to satisfy the systemic qualities.

The Design Workflow

The ultimate goal of the Design workflow is to develop a Solution model that the development team can use to construct the code for the proposed system. The purpose of the Design workflow is to create a Solution model of the system that satisfies the requirements. The Design model for the use cases is based on the classes discovered during analysis, which are the business objects. The Design model is then merged with the Architecture model. This combined model is called the Solution model in this book. The Solution model also includes the Domain model. The Solution model is also refined by a variety of Design patterns that are applicable to the design problem and context. The components in the Solution model can be implemented in code. The Design workflow activities are performed by the software designer job role.

EXERCISE 2-1

Design Activities

Question What are the design activities needed for developing a solution model that the development team can use to construct the code for the proposed system?
Answer The design activities are as follows:

- Create a Design model to enable the Domain objects to work with the computer system. By following the flows, you discover a collection of collaborating software components that satisfy the functional requirements of the use case. During this process, you discover missing methods and attributes in your Domain classes.
- Identify and model objects with nontrivial states using a State Machine diagram. State Machine diagrams are often used to check that every scenario that could occur has been considered.
- Apply design patterns to the Design model. This activity enables the designer to refine the Design model with applicable patterns to make the software more flexible and robust.
- Create the Solution model by merging the Design and Architecture models. Here, the designer inserts the components from the Design model into the Architectural model. This structure provides about 80 percent of the components that must be coded during the Implementation workflow.
- Refine the Domain model to satisfy the Solution model.

Implementation, Testing, and Deployment Workflows

The purpose of the Implementation workflow is to build the software components defined in the Solution model. The Implementation workflow is performed by the software programmer job role. The purpose of the Testing workflow is to test the implementation against the expectations defined in the requirements. The Testing workflow is performed by the software tester job role. The purpose of the Deployment workflow is to deploy the implementation into the production environment. The Deployment workflow is performed by the deployment specialist job role.

The Implementation activity is: Implement the software solution using the Solution model. This activity maps the class structure defined in the refined Domain model into a physical, Java technology class structure.

The Testing activities are numerous and varied. This book focuses on acceptance testing. This activity is: Test the software solution against the use case scenarios. In this activity, the tester generates the Functional test plan from the use case scenarios. The tests are performed to verify that the functional behavior of the system matches the use case requirements.

The Deployment activity is: Deploy the software solution using the architecture Deployment diagram. In this activity, the deployment specialist uses the Deployment diagram to set up the computer, network, and component structure of the production environment.

Unified Modeling Language

The Unified Modeling Language (UML) is a language used for specifying, constructing, visualizing, and documenting the components of a software system. The UML combines the concepts of Booch, the Object Modeling Technique (OMT), and object-oriented software engineering (OOSE). The result is a standard modeling language. The UML authors targeted the modeling of concurrent and distributed systems; therefore, UML contains the elements required to address these domains. UML concentrates on a common model that brings together the syntax and semantics using a common notation.

This nonexhaustive treatment of UML is arranged in parts. First, we describe the basic elements used in UML. Then we discuss UML relationships among elements. The follow-up is the resultant UML diagrams. Within each UML diagram type, the model elements that are found on that diagram are listed. It is important to note that most model elements are usable in more than one diagram. When we describe each element, relationship, and diagram in this chapter, we will use an example from a later chapter where we review an example of an OCMJEA Part 2 project.

on the job

UML is an evolving language. This chapter was written when OMG UML version 2.4 was the official version.

Using the UML, a model is composed of the following items:

- Elements (things and relationships)
- Diagrams (built from elements)
- Views (diagrams showing different perspectives of a model)

UML Diagrams

UML diagrams enable you to create visualizations of your mental models of a software system. These diagrams are used to construct many of the artifacts in the workflows described in this book.

Following is a brief description of each diagram:

- A **Use Case diagram** represents the set of high-level behaviors that the system must perform for a given actor.
- A **Class diagram** represents a collection of software classes and their interrelationships.
- An **Object diagram** represents a run-time snapshot of software objects and their interrelationships.
- A **Communication diagram** (formerly Collaboration diagram) represents a collection of objects that work together to support some system behavior.
- A **Sequence diagram** represents a time-oriented perspective of an object communication.
- An **Activity diagram** represents a flow of activities that might be performed by either a system or an actor.
- A **State Machine diagram** represents the set of states that an object might experience and the triggers that transition the object from one state to another.
- A **Component diagram** represents a collection of physical software components and their interrelationships.
- A **Deployment diagram** represents a collection of components and shows how these are distributed across one or more hardware nodes.
- A **Package diagram** represents a collection of other modeling elements and diagrams.
- An **Interaction Overview diagram** represents a form of Activity diagram where nodes can represent interaction diagram fragments. These fragments are usually sequence diagram fragments, but can also be Communication, Timing, or Interaction Overview diagram fragments.
- A **Timing diagram** represents changes in state (state lifeline view) or value (value lifeline view). It can also show time and duration constraints and interactions between timed events.

- A **Composite Structure diagram** represents the internal structure of a classifier, usually in the form of parts, and can include the interaction ports and interfaces (provided or required).
- A **Profile diagram** might define additional diagram types or extend existing diagrams with additional notations.

UML Tools

UML itself is a tool. You can create UML diagrams on paper, a whiteboard, or flip-chart–sized plastic sheets (which are statically charged, will adhere to most surfaces, and can be written on using whiteboard markers). For example, you can create models by drawing on napkins over lunch, you can have team meetings to collaborate on a Class diagram on a conference room whiteboard, and you can even paper the walls and windows of a room with numerous plastic sheets, draw on these sheets, and then move them to another room. This enables a great deal of flexibility in the creation of models and team collaboration. But when a model must be captured as a long-lived artifact, the diagram should be drawn in a tool that will enable printing and archiving.

UML tools can be divided into roughly two categories: drawing and modeling tools. Tools such as StarOffice, Illustrator, and Visio can draw UML diagrams, but using such tools puts the burden on the developer to verify that the diagram is drawn correctly.

UML modeling tools provide computer-aided drawing of UML diagrams. For example, UML modeling tools may prohibit you from placing an actor node in an Object diagram. This verification is accomplished by restricting the drawing operations of the UML tool by the syntactic constraints of the UML specification. This restriction may be relaxed because UML 2.2 does not strictly enforce the boundaries between diagrams. Therefore, it should be possible to include a state machine inside an internal structure.

Elements Used in UML

In UML, an element is an atomic constituent of a model. A model element is an element that represents an abstraction drawn from the system being modeled. Elements are used in UML diagrams, which will be covered in the following sections. UML defines the elements listed next.

Class

As mentioned, a class is any uniquely identified abstraction that models a single thing, and the term "object" is synonymous with "instance." Classes have attributes and methods. The class is represented in UML by a rectangle with three horizontal parts: name, attributes, and operations. The name part is required and contains the class name and other documentation-related information. For example, the name could be data_access_object <<javabean>>. The attributes part is optional and contains characteristics of the class. The operations part is also optional and contains method definitions. Here is an example of a method that returns a hashmap of name/value pairs describing the attributes of an order whose identifier is order_id:

```
method (argument(s)) return type: get_order ( order_id ) hashmap
```

Interface

An interface is a collection of operations that represent a class or that specify a set of methods that must be implemented by the derived class. An interface typically contains nothing but virtual methods and their signatures. Java supports interfaces directly. The interface is represented in UML by a rectangle with three horizontal parts: name, attributes, and operations. The name part, which is required, contains the class name and other documentation-related information. For example, the name could be data_access_object <<javabean>>. The attributes part (optional) contains characteristics of the class. The operations part (optional) contains method definitions. For example, in our case study we might have a method like this one:

```
method (argument(s)) return type: get_order ( order_id ) hashmap
```

Package

A package is used to organize groups of like elements. The package is the only group type element, and its function is to represent a collection of functionally similar classes. Packages can nest. Outer packages are sometimes called "domains." Some outer packages are depicted by an "upside-down tuning fork" symbol, denoting them as subsystems. The package name is part of the class name—for example, given the class accessdata in the ucny.trading.com package, the fully qualified class name is ucny.trading.com.accessdata.

Collaboration

Collaboration defines the interaction of one or more roles along with their contents, associations, relationships, and classes. To use collaboration, the roles must be bound to a class that supports the operations required of the role. A use of collaboration is shown as a dashed ellipse containing the name of the collaboration. A dashed line is drawn from the collaboration symbol to each of the objects, depending on whether it appears within an object diagram that participates in the collaboration. Each line is labeled by the role of the participant.

Use Case

A use case is a description that represents a complete unit of functionality provided by something as large as a system or as small as a class. The result of this functionality is manifested by a sequence of messages exchanged among the system (or class) and one or more outside actors combined with actions performed by another system (or class).

There are two types of use cases: essential and real. Essential use cases are expressed in an ideal form that remains free of technology and implementation detail. The design decisions are abstracted, especially those related to the user interface. A real use case describes the process in terms of its real design and implementation. Essential use cases are important early in the project. Their purpose is to illustrate and document the business process. Real use cases become important after implementation because they document how the user interface supports the business processes documented in the essential use case. In either type, a use case is represented as a solid line ellipse containing the name of the use case. A stereotype keyword may be placed above the name, and a list of properties is included below the name.

Component

The component represents a modular and deployable system part. It encapsulates an implementation and exposes a set of interfaces. The interfaces represent services provided by elements that reside on the component. A component is typically deployed on a node. A component is shown as a rectangle with two smaller rectangles extending from its left side. A component type has a type name: component-type. A component instance has a name and a type. The name of the component and its type may be shown as an underlined string, either within the component symbol or above or below it, with the syntax component-name ':' component-type. Either or both elements are optional.

Node

The node is a physical element object that represents a processing resource, generally having memory and processing capability (for example, a JEE application server). Obviously, nodes include computers and other devices, but they can also be human resources or any processing resources. Nodes may be represented as types and instances. Run-time computational instances—both objects and component instances—may reside on node instances. A node is typically depicted as a cube. A node type has a type name: node-type. A node instance has a name and a type name. The node may have an underlined name within the cube or below it. The name string has the syntax name ':' node-type. The name is the name of the individual node, and the node-type says what kind of a node it is.

State

The state is a condition that can occur during the life of an object. It can also be an interaction that satisfies some condition, performs some action, or waits for some event. A composite state has a graphical decomposition. An object remains in a particular state for an interval of time. A state may be used to model the status of in-flight activity. Such an activity can be depicted as a state machine. A state is graphically shown as a rectangle with rounded corners. Optionally, it may have an attached name tab. The name tab is a rectangle and contains the name of that state.

Relationships Used in UML

The object is the center of an object-oriented (OO) system. The object-oriented model defines the system structure by describing objects (such as classes) and the relationships that exist among them. Class diagrams, as you will see, comprise classes, objects, and their relationships. The classes appear as rectangles that contain the class name. This rectangle is divided into sections, with the class name appearing in the first section, class attributes in the second section, class operations in the third, class exceptions in the fourth, and so on. The object names are underlined and have a colon as a suffix. As in any system, objects are connected by relationships. UML defines and includes the types of relationships detailed in Table 2-3.

Diagrams Used in UML

The following sections introduce the graphical diagrams defined within UML. These descriptions are expanded upon later in the chapter.

TABLE 2-3 UML Relationships

Relationship	Description	Notation
Generalization (aka Inheritance)	A specialized version of another class.	Solid line with a closed arrowhead pointing to the more general class
Association	Uses the services of another class.	Solid line connecting the associated classes, with an optional open arrowhead showing the direction of navigation
Aggregation	A class "owns" another class.	A form of association with an unfilled diamond at the "owner" end of the association
Composition	A class is composed of another class; refers to an aggregation within which the component parts and the larger encompassing whole share a lifetime.	A form of aggregation, shown either with a filled diamond at the "composite" end or with the composite graphically containing the "component"
Refinement	A refined version of another class; refinement within a given model can be shown as a dependency with the stereotype <<refines>> or one of its more specific forms, such as <<implements>>.	Dashed line with a closed hollow arrowhead pointing to the more refined class
Dependency	A class dependent on another class.	Dashed line with an open arrowhead pointing to the dependency

Use Case Diagram

The Use Case diagram shows actors, a set of use cases enclosed by a system boundary, communication or participation associations among the actors and the use cases, and generalizations among the use cases (see Figure 2-2).

Class Diagram

The Class diagram shows modeling elements. It may also contain types, packages, relationships, and even instances such as objects and links. A class is the descriptor for a set of objects that have a similar structure, behavior, and relationships. UML provides notation for declaring, specifying, and using classes. Some modeling elements that are similar to classes (such as types, signals, or utilities) are notated as stereotypes of classes. Classes are declared in Class diagrams and used in most of the other diagrams. See Figure 2-3, which depicts the Java EJB SessionBean class

FIGURE 2-2

Use Case diagram

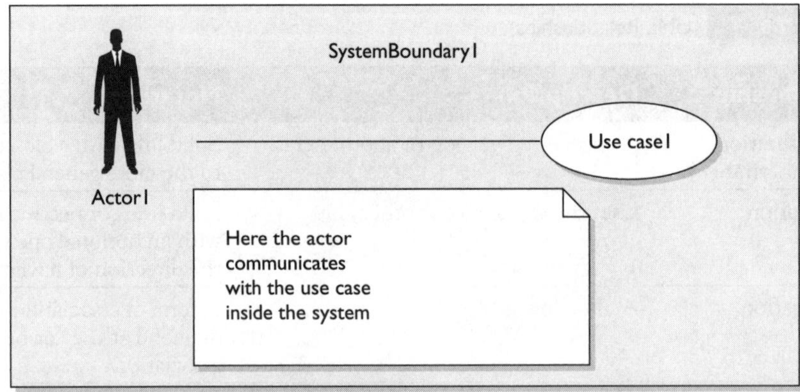

AccessDataBean as well as its attributes and methods. Here, the class includes methods and attributes sufficient to make and access securities trade orders. For you to do well on the OCMJEA exam, your class diagrams must be well thought out and provide the required functionality to carry out the business requirement.

Package Diagram

The Package diagram is a mechanism used for dividing and grouping model elements such as classes. In UML, a folder represents a package. The package provides a namespace so that two elements with the same name can exist by being placed in two separate packages. Packages can also be nested within other packages. Dependencies between two packages indicate dependencies between any two classes in the packages (see Figure 2-4).

State Diagram

The State diagram is a two-part diagram showing states and transitions. It shows states connected by physical containment and tiling. The entire state diagram is attached through the model to a class or a method—that is, an operation implementation (see Figure 2-5).

Activity Diagram

An Activity diagram is a special case of a State diagram in which all or most of the states are action states and in which all or most of the transitions are triggered by completion of the actions in the source states. The entire activity diagram is

FIGURE 2-3

Class diagram

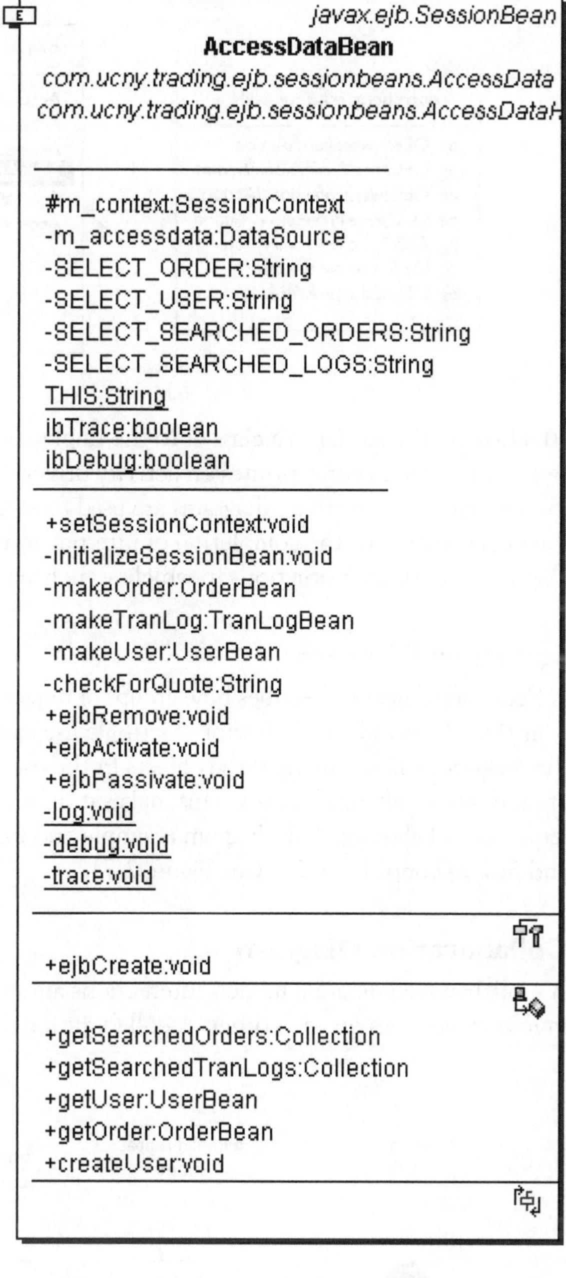
javax.ejb.SessionBean
AccessDataBean
com.ucny.trading.ejb.sessionbeans.AccessData
com.ucny.trading.ejb.sessionbeans.AccessDataH
#m_context:SessionContext
-m_accessdata:DataSource
-SELECT_ORDER:String
-SELECT_USER:String
-SELECT_SEARCHED_ORDERS:String
-SELECT_SEARCHED_LOGS:String
THIS:String
ibTrace:boolean
ibDebug:boolean
+setSessionContext:void
-initializeSessionBean:void
-makeOrder:OrderBean
-makeTranLog:TranLogBean
-makeUser:UserBean
-checkForQuote:String
+ejbRemove:void
+ejbActivate:void
+ejbPassivate:void
-log:void
-debug:void
-trace:void
+ejbCreate:void
+getSearchedOrders:Collection
+getSearchedTranLogs:Collection
+getUser:UserBean
+getOrder:OrderBean
+createUser:void

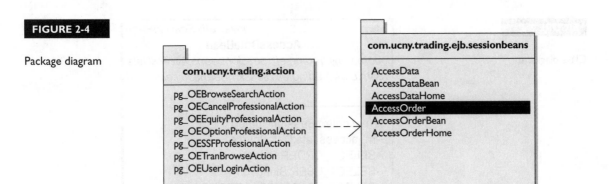

FIGURE 2-4

Package diagram

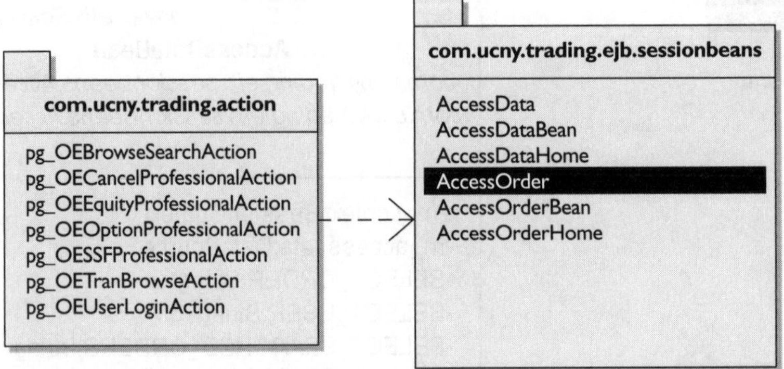

attached via the model to a class or to the implementation of an operation or a use case. This diagram concentrates on activity driven by internal processing as opposed to external forces. Activity diagrams are used for situations in which all or most of the events represent the completion of internal actions. Alternatively, ordinary state diagrams are used for situations in which asynchronous events occur (see Figure 2-6).

Sequence Diagram

A Sequence diagram describes how groups of objects collaborate in some behavior over time. It records the behavior of a single use case. It displays objects and the messages passed among these objects in the use case. A design can have lots of methods in different classes. This makes it difficult to determine the overall sequence of behavior. This diagram is simple and logical, so as to make the sequence and flow of control obvious (see Figure 2-7).

Collaboration Diagram

A Collaboration diagram models interactions among objects; objects interact by invoking messages on each other. A collaboration diagram groups together the

FIGURE 2-5

State diagram

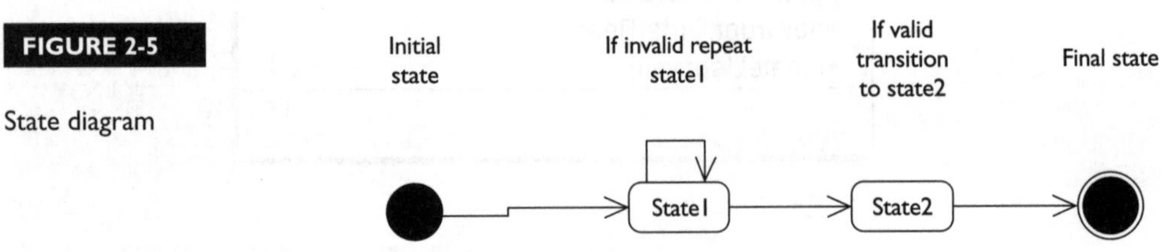

FIGURE 2-6

Activity diagram

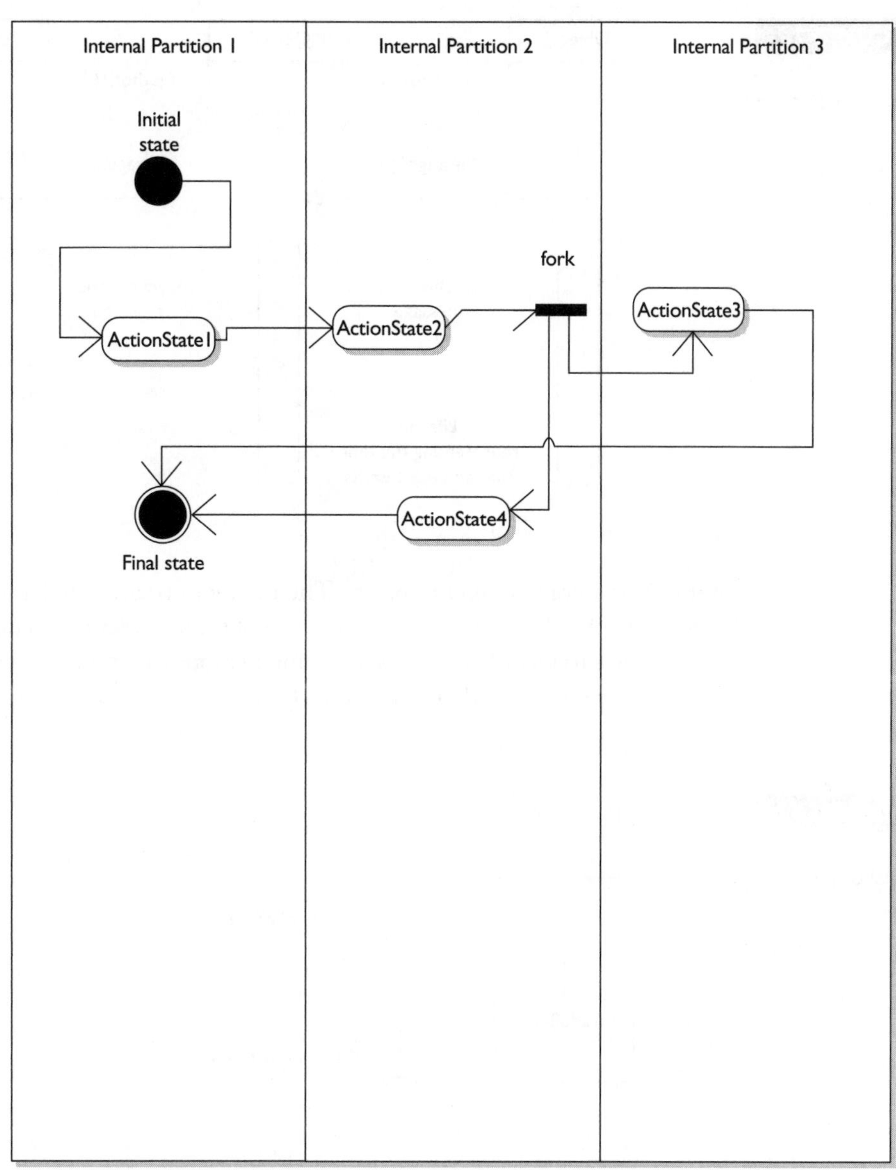

FIGURE 2-7

Sequence diagram

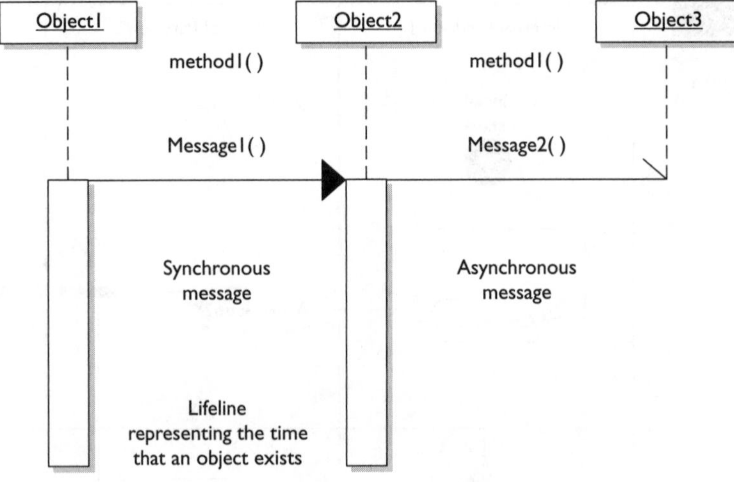

interactions among different objects. The interactions are listed as numbered interactions that help to trace the sequence of the interactions. The Collaboration diagram helps to identify all the possible interactions that each object has with other objects. See Figure 2-8, where the interactions required to make a trade are illustrated.

FIGURE 2-8

Collaboration diagram

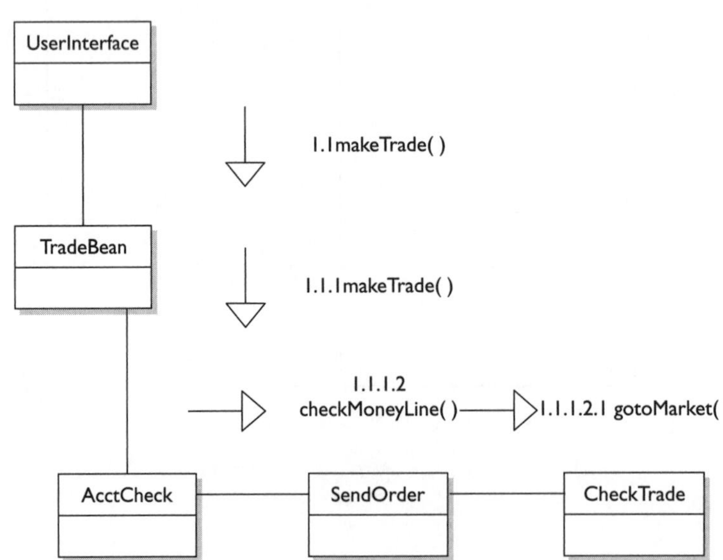

Communication Diagram

UML 2.4 includes the Communication diagram. Communication diagrams represent a combination of information taken from Class, Sequence, and Use Case diagrams describing both the static and dynamic parts of a system. Communication and Sequence diagrams describe similar information and can typically be transformed into one another easily. However, Communication diagrams use the free-form arrangement of objects and links, as used in object diagrams. In order to maintain the ordering of messages in such a free-form diagram, messages are labeled with a chronological number and placed near the link the message is sent over. Reading a Communication diagram involves starting at message 1.0 and following the messages from object to object.

Component Diagram

The Component diagram represents the high-level parts that make up the modeled application. This diagram is a high-level depiction of the components and their relationships. A component diagram depicts the components' refined post-development or construction phase. See Figure 2-9, which depicts a trading application, the JEE application server it executes on, and the session beans used in the application.

Deployment Diagram

A Deployment diagram puts it all together and captures the configuration of the run-time elements of the application. This diagram is obviously most useful when an application is complete and ready to be deployed. See Figure 2-10, which depicts the nodes in our trading application—that is, a JEE server, the database server it accesses, and the user workstation used to access the JEE application. Each of these nodes hosts components whose interaction is also illustrated.

FIGURE 2-9

Component diagram

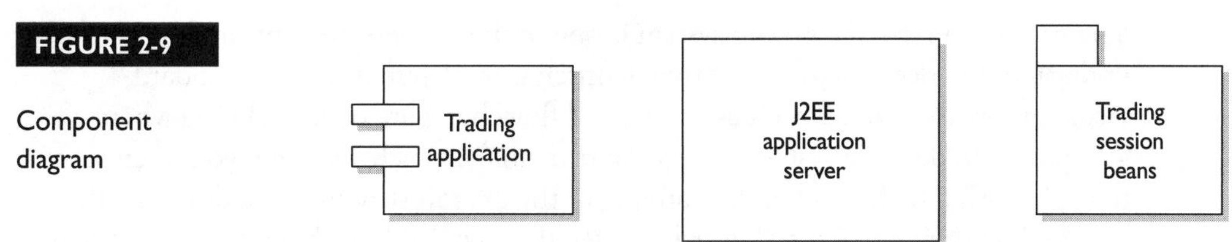

FIGURE 2-10

Deployment diagram

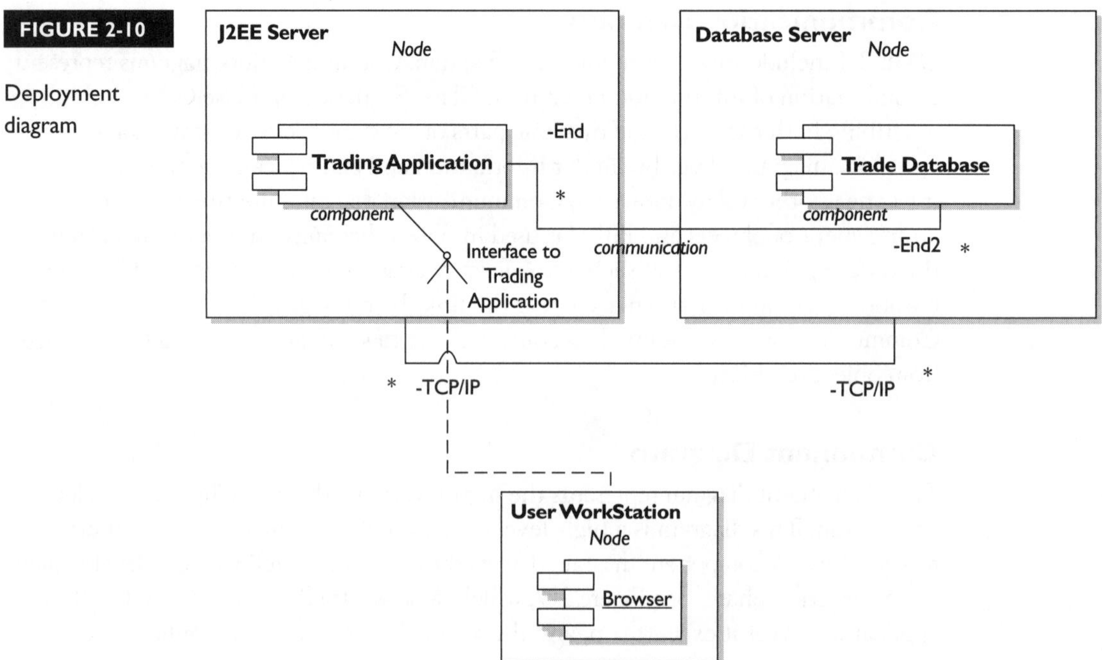

Stereotypes

A stereotype is a new class of modeling element that is introduced during modeling time. Certain restrictions are in place: stereotypes must be based on certain existing classes in the Meta model, and they may extend those classes only in certain predefined ways. They provide an extensibility mechanism for UML.

Practical Use of UML Diagrams

The scope of a typical software system is one of the barriers preventing the thorough understanding necessary for effective maintenance of systems. Even standard visualization approaches such as graphs and flowcharts are overwhelming when attempting to depict a system. As you start to analyze such a system, you often want to begin with a high-level understanding of the overall structure and design of the system. You then delve into lower-level details once you have bounded the problem at hand. And at other times, the scope of the problem requires that you continue to work from the higher-level view.

UML provides a number of abstraction mechanisms to help you study the high-level architecture of your software. Within the Unified Modeling Language notation, diagrams are the primary representation of a system. UML will help you understand the objects, interactions, and relationships of your system software and hardware.

Use Case Diagram

The use case lends itself to a problem-centric approach to analysis and design, providing an understanding and a model of your system from a high-level business perspective—that is, how a system or business works or how you wish it to work. The Use Case diagram represents the functionality of a system as displayed to external interactions as actors of the system. A use case view represents the interface or interfaces that a system makes visible to the outside world, the external entities that interact with it, and their interrelationships.

Each use case step is either automated or manual. The objective of each step is to make a business decision or carry out an action. We typically assign responsibility for each business decision and action either to the system (in the case of an automated action) or to the actor (in the manual case). This responsibility impacts the system delivered because the automated steps manifest themselves as system operations to make these decisions or execute these actions.

The diagram represents the processes within the system, which are visible to the outside world—that is, the actors of the system being modeled and the relationships among them.

Use cases are the functions or services of the system—those that are visible to its actors. They constitute a complete unit of functionality provided by a system as manifested by sequences of messages exchanged among the system and one or more actors, together with actions performed by the system.

Actors are representative of the role of an object outside of a system that interacts directly with it as part of a complete work unit. An actor element characterizes the role played by an outside object, where one physical object may play multiple positions. For example, one entity may actually play different positions and assume different identities.

You can think of a use case as a model that describes the processes of a business—order processing, for example—and its interactions with external parties such as clients and vendors. It is helpful in identifying the fundamental components of a system, namely the following:

- The business processes of the system
- External entities of the system
- The relationships among them

A Use Case diagram enables you to identify—by modeling—the high-level functional requirements (FRs) that are required to satisfy each user's goals. A Use Case diagram provides a visual representation of the high-level FRs. The Use Case diagram is often easier to model with the client-side stakeholders than the alternative textual representation.

on the job

The client-side stakeholders need a big-picture view of the system. A Use Case diagram provides a high-level view of the entire system. All nontrivial systems will have too many use cases to view at the same time. The use of UML packages allows you to see a high-level view of the packages, each containing either use cases or subpackages. The packages are simply views of related use cases that can be categorized in different ways—for example, Sales, Marketing, and Shipping. This view can be the basis of a common language between the client-side stakeholders and the development team.

The use cases form the basis from which the detailed FRs are developed. Use cases are the central focus of system development. A Use Case diagram is the high-level guide for the development team. The lower-level functionality of the system can be identified by exploring the internal behavior of each use case, which will be covered in the following section.

Use cases can be prioritized and developed in order of priority. Use cases can be assigned priorities based on business need, complexity, and dependency on other use cases. In an incremental development process, the priority affects the iteration in which the use case will be developed.

Use cases often have minimal dependencies, which enables a degree of independent development. Because use cases often have minimal dependencies, they can be developed in parallel or by more specialist teams.

Identifying the Elements of a Use Case Diagram

A Use Case diagram shows the relationships between actors and the goals they wish to achieve.

A Use Case diagram provides a visual representation of the system, the use cases that the system provides, and the actors (job roles) that use the system to perform specific functions.

Actors are simply roles. Any physical person, system, or device can assume multiple roles. Therefore, the job title Receptionist can assume the Receptionist role and also the Booking Agent role. If this was not the case, then the Duty Manager actor would need associations to most of the use cases in the hotel, as would the Hotel Manager and other actors.

Actors

An Actor models a type of role played by an entity that interacts with the subject (for example, by exchanging signals and data), but which is external to the subject (that is, in the sense that an instance of an actor is not a part of the instance of its corresponding subject). Actors may represent roles played by human users, external hardware, or other subjects. Note that an actor does not necessarily represent a specific physical entity but merely a particular facet (that is, "role") of some entity that is relevant to the specification of its associated use cases. Thus, a single physical instance may play the role of several different actors and, conversely, a given actor may be played by multiple different instances (UML Superstructure Specification, v2.2). The subject is the system under consideration to which the use cases apply.

Use Case diagrams are closely connected to scenarios. A scenario is an example of what happens when someone interacts with the system. For example, Figure 2-11 shows a scenario for a security trade: a trader accesses an Internet-based system and chooses the type of security for which he or she wants to place a trade order to buy or sell.

Figure 2-11 shows a trade use case for the online trading site. The actor is a trader. The connection between actor and use case is a communication association. Actors are represented by stick figures. Use cases are represented by ovals. A common issue regarding drawing use cases is having two "actions" tied to each other, essentially showing a "flowchart." In Figure 2-11, the case study trading system menu is invoked for the "Order entry and browse" functionality and subsequent calls to the Stratus CTPS and Oracle database. Lines that link actors to use cases represent communications.

A use case diagram is a collection of actors, use cases, and their communications. A single use case can have multiple actors. A system boundary rectangle separates the system from the external actors. A use case generalization shows that one use case is a special kind of another use case. Use Case diagrams are important to use when you are:

- **Determining new requirements**
- **Communicating with clients** Their simplicity makes Use Case diagrams a good way to communicate the system to users.
- **Validating the system** The different scenarios for a use case make a good set of test cases.

FIGURE 2-11 Annotated use case diagram

Class Diagram

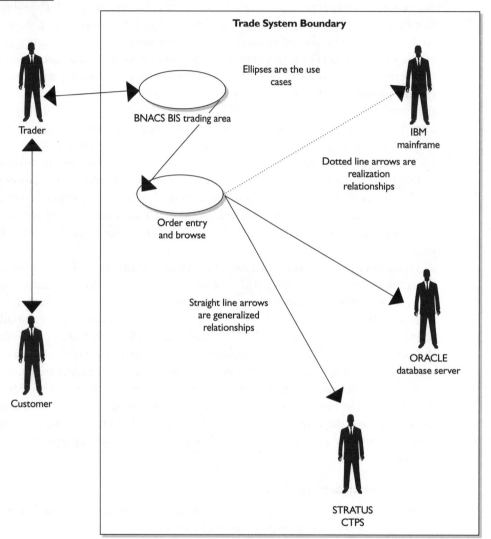

A Class diagram provides an overview of a system by showing its classes and the relationships among them. Class diagrams are static; they display what interacts but not what happens when they do interact. The Class diagram in the UML is probably the most recognized. It is used to visually represent classes, the members of the classes, and the relationships between classes (usually called "associations"). Class nodes represent classes of objects within the model. Class nodes can take many visual forms in UML; however, a class node is represented by a rectangle with the name of the class in a bold, monospaced font. A class node can represent the following:

- Conceptual entities, such as key abstractions during the Analysis workflow. Class nodes in the Domain model represent key abstractions. These are conceptual entities that do not correspond to software components.
- Real software components.

During the Design workflow, class nodes usually represent a physical software component. The component is usually a class, but can also be other components. For example, a class node might represent an EJB technology entity bean.

A stereotype can help identify the type of the class node. A stereotype in UML can take one of two forms. The textual form uses a word or phrase surrounded by guillemet characters (for example, «Entity»). A stereotype can also take an iconic form; for example, an Entity can also be symbolized by a circle with a line under it.

A class node may be split into three or more compartments:

- The Name compartment records the name of the class. This compartment is always the top of the node. The stereotype of the class must also be placed in the Name compartment.
- The Attributes compartment records attributes of the class. This compartment is placed below the Name compartment.
- The Operations compartment records operations of the class. This compartment is placed below the Attributes compartment. Methods can be conceptual or actual method signatures.

Associations represent relationships between classes. Associations are manifested at run time in which two objects are associated with each other, usually with an object reference. It is important to understand that Class diagrams represent static information about the relationships between classes. A Class diagram does not represent the dynamic relationships of objects at run time.

Relationships and roles are indicated by the direction arrow, which indicates which direction to read the association. Role names indicate what role that a particular class is taking in the association.

Multiplicity determines how many objects might participate in the relationship.

Navigation arrows on the association determine what direction an association can be traversed at run time. This additional information is most important during design, but it can also be useful in analysis. An association without navigation arrows means that you can navigate from one object to the other, and the other way around as well. This is very flexible, but in some situations it might not be meaningful to the problem domain.

Association classes indicate that information is included in the association between two classes. For example, a person works for many employers. If you need to record details about each term of employment, this information belongs to the association between the person and the employer. You can show this using an association class.

The Class diagram shown in Figure 2-12 models an EJB session bean used to order equities from a securities market. The central method is makeOrder, which creates and returns an OrderBean. Associated with it is the makeUser, which creates and returns a UserBean. UML class notation is a rectangle divided into three parts: class name, attributes, and operations. Names of abstract classes, such as com.ucny.trading.ejb.sessionbeans.AccessData, are in italics. Relationships among classes are the connecting links.

A Class diagram can have three kinds of relationships:

- Association is a relationship between instances of the two classes. An association exists between two classes if an instance of one class must know about the other to perform its work. In a diagram, an association is a link connecting two classes.
- Aggregation is an association in which one class belongs to a collection. An aggregation shows a diamond end pointing to the part containing the whole.
- Generalization is an inheritance link indicating one class is a superclass of another. A generalization shows a triangle pointing to the superclass.

An association has two ends. An end may include a role name to clarify the nature of the association. For example, an OrderDetail is a line item of each Order.

A navigability arrow on an association shows which direction the association can be traversed or queried. An OrderDetail can be queried about its Item, but not the other way around. The arrow also lets you know who "owns" the association's implementation; in this case, OrderDetail has an Item. Associations with no navigability arrows are bidirectional.

FIGURE 2-12

Annotated Class diagram

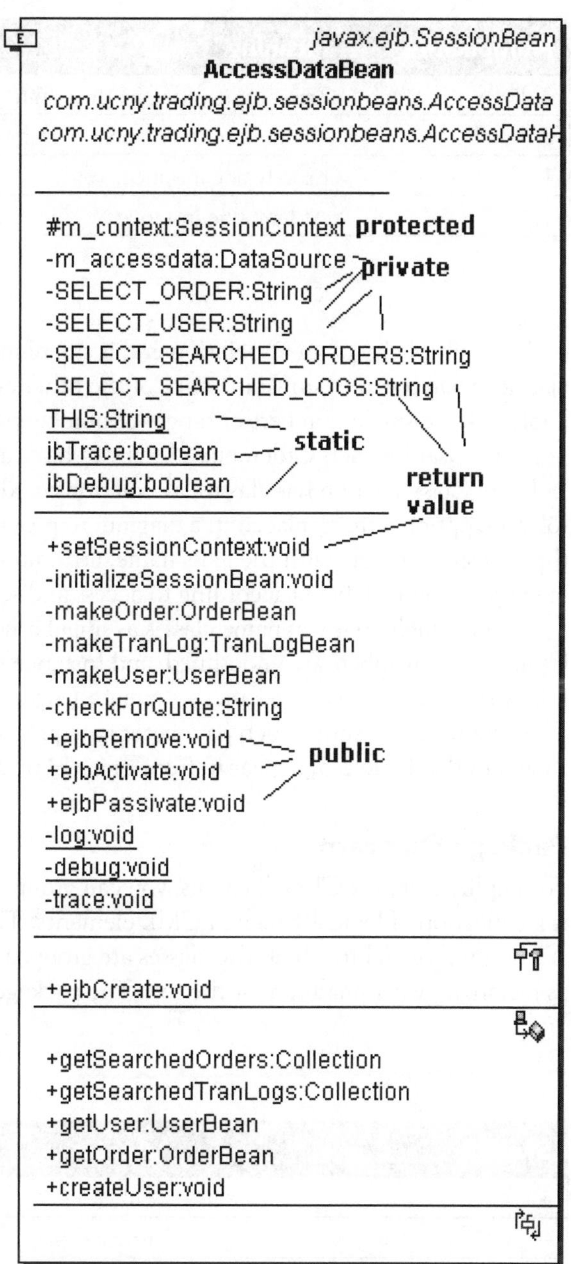

TABLE 2-4

Multiplicities

Multiplicities	Meaning
0..1	Zero or one instance; the notation n..m indicates n to m instances.
0..* or *	No limit on the number of instances (including none).
1	Exactly one instance.
1..*	At least one instance.

The multiplicity of an association end is the number of possible instances of the class associated with a single instance of the other end. Multiplicities, shown in Table 2-4, are single numbers or ranges of numbers. In our example, there can be only one User for each Order, but a User can have any number of Orders.

Every Class diagram has classes, associations, and multiplicities. Navigability and roles are optional items placed in a diagram to provide clarity. The class notation is a three-piece rectangle with the class name, attributes, and operations. Attributes and operations can be labeled according to access and scope.

It is preferable that you name classes as singular nouns, such as User instead of Users. Static members are underlined, and Instance members are not. The operations follow this form: <access specifier> <name> (<parameter list>) : <return type>. The parameter list shows each parameter type preceded by a colon. Access specifiers, shown in the Table 2-5, appear in front of each member.

Package Diagram

To simplify complex Class diagrams, you can group classes into packages. A package is a collection of logically related UML elements. The diagram shown in Figure 2-13 is a business model in which the classes are grouped into packages. Packages appear as rectangles with small tabs at the top. The package name is on the tab or inside the

TABLE 2-5

Access Specifiers

Symbol	Access
+	Public
–	Private
#	Protected

FIGURE 2-13 Annotated Package diagram

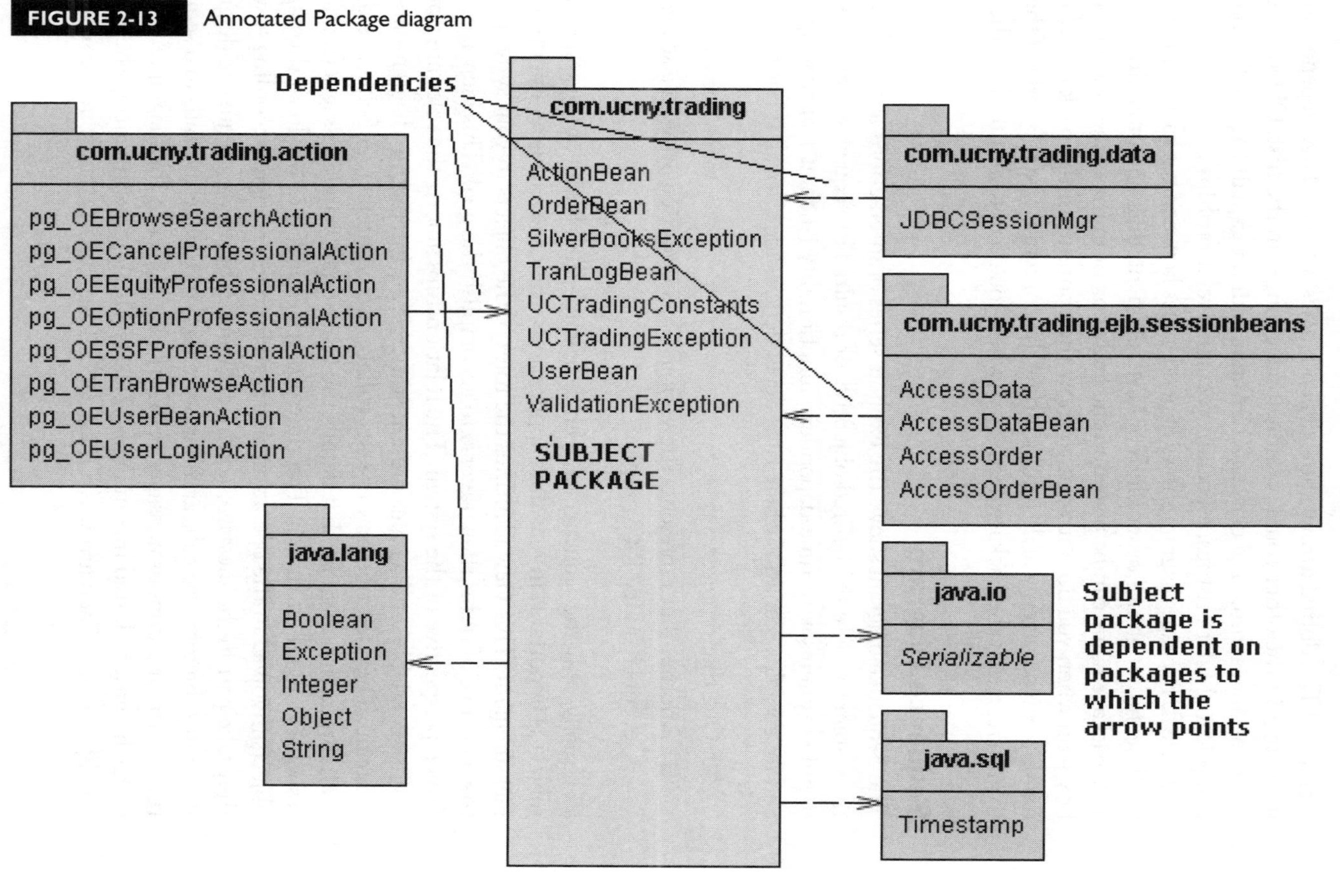

rectangle. The dotted arrows show dependencies. One package depends on another if changes in the other could possibly force changes in the first. Object diagrams show instances instead of classes. They are useful for explaining small pieces with complicated relationships, especially recursive relationships.

A UML Package diagram shows dependencies between packages. A package is a UML icon that groups other kinds of UML element, diagram, or additional packages. The package name can be placed in the body box or in the name box. Use the body box icon when you do not want to show the contents of the package. Use the name box icon when you do want to show the contents. Use this form of the package icon to represent the package abstractly (when you do not want to show the contents).

Sequence Diagram

The Sequence diagram shows the explicit series of interactions as they flow through the system to cause the desired objective or result. The sequence view is especially useful in systems with time-dependent functionality (such as real-time applications) and for complex scenarios where time dependencies are critical. It has two dimensions:

- One that represents time
- Another that represents the various objects participating in a sequence of events required for a purpose

Usually, only the sequence of events to which the objects of the system are subject is important; in real-time applications, the time axis is an important measurement. This view identifies the roles of the objects in your system through the sequence of states they traverse to accomplish the goal. This view is an event-driven perspective of the system. The relationships among the roles are not shown.

Class and Object diagrams present static views. Interaction diagrams are dynamic. They describe how objects collaborate or interact. A Sequence diagram is an interaction diagram that details the functionality and messages (requests and responses) and their timing. The time progresses as you move down the page. The objects involved in the operation are listed from left to right according to when they take part in the message sequence. Figure 2-14 shows a sequence diagram that illustrates the software calls and hardware used to service the calls in a sequence of time, with synchronous messages between each object in the diagram.

Each vertical dotted line in Figure 2-14 is a lifeline, representing the time that an object exists. Each arrow is a message call. An arrow goes from the sender to the

FIGURE 2-14

Annotated Sequence diagram

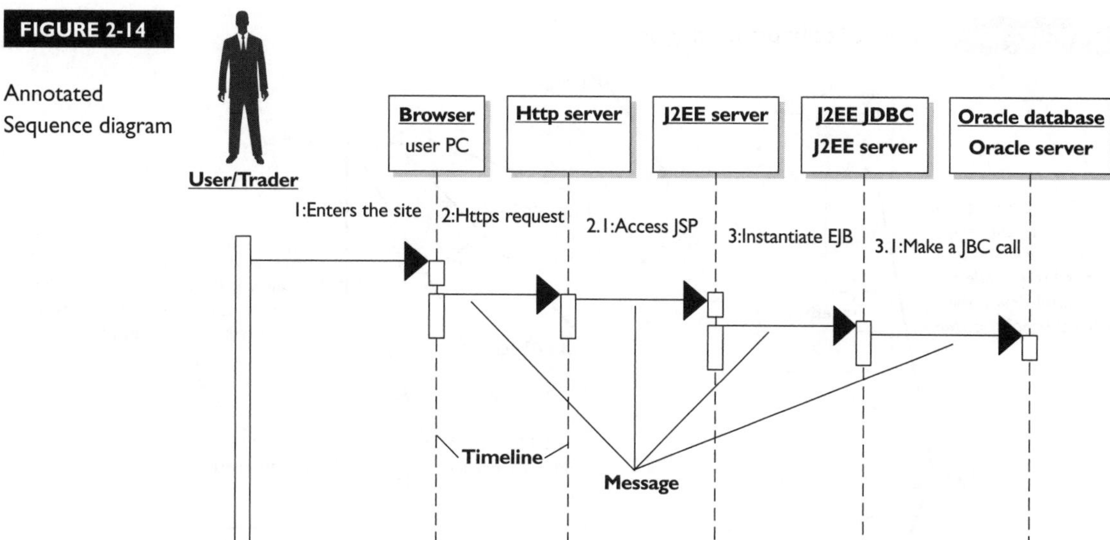

top of the activation bar of the message on the receiver's lifeline. The activation bar represents the duration of the execution of the message. The Sequence diagram can have a clarifying note (text inside a dog-eared rectangle). Notes can be put into any kind of UML diagram.

Collaboration Diagram

Collaboration diagrams are also interaction diagrams. They convey the same information as sequence diagrams, but they focus on object roles instead of the times that messages are sent. In a Sequence diagram, object roles are the vertices and messages are the connecting links. The object-role rectangles are labeled with either class or object names (or both). Class names are preceded by colons (:). Each message in a Collaboration diagram has a sequence number. The top-level message is number 1. Messages at the same level (sent during the same call) have the same decimal prefix but suffixes of 1, 2, 3, and so on, according to when they occur.

The Collaboration diagram is similar to the Sequence diagram in terms of the information displayed, but it's different in its depiction. A Collaboration diagram shows the relationships among objects. It is intended to assist in the understanding

FIGURE 2-15 Annotated collaboration diagram

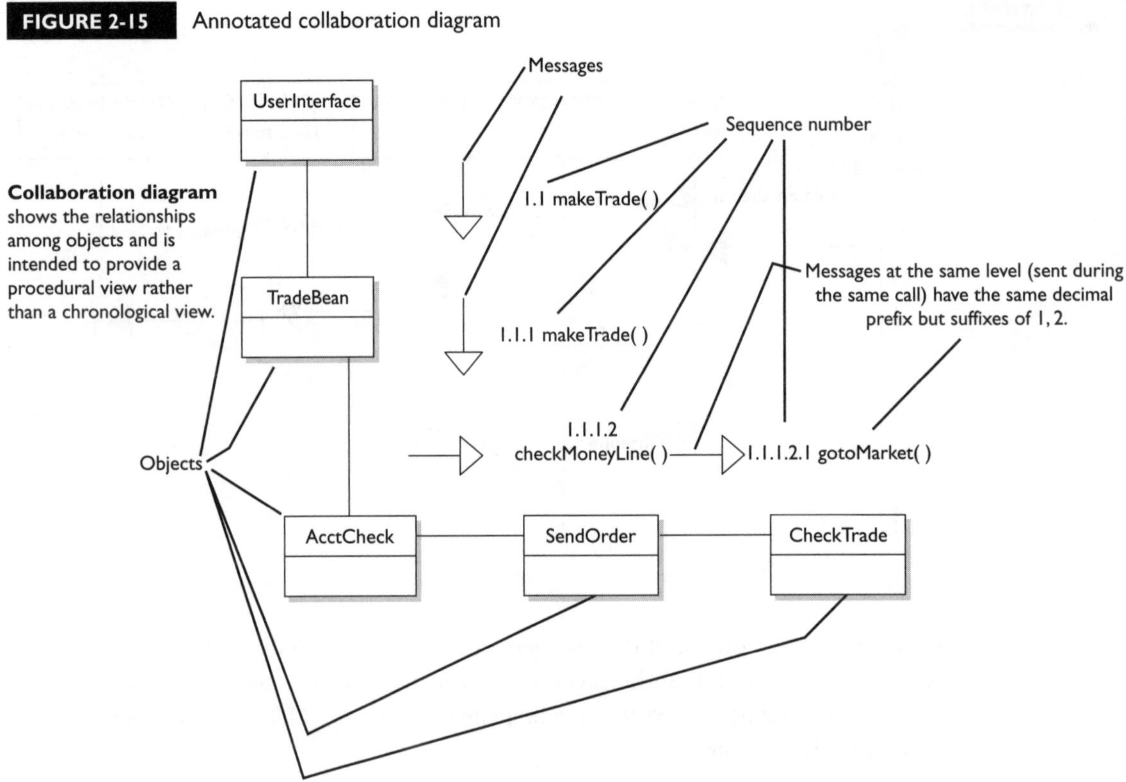

the effects on a given object. It provides a procedural perspective rather than a chronological view. A Collaboration diagram shows interactions organized around the objects in a particular interaction, especially their links to one another. A Collaboration diagram shows the relationships among the object roles.

The Collaboration diagram in Figure 2-15 shows you a model of the behavior of the objects in the trading system and the messages involved in accomplishing a purpose—in this case, making a trade (checking the trader account for sufficient funds and sending the order to the marketplace), projected from the larger trading system of which this collaboration is just a part. It is a representation of a set of participants and relationships that are meaningful for a given set of functionality.

The description of behavior itself involves two characteristics:

- The structural description of its participants
- The behavioral description of its execution

These two characteristics are combined, but they can be separated, because at times it is useful to describe the structure and behavior separately.

Collaboration diagrams can be enhanced by the inclusion of the dynamic behavior of the message sequences exchanged among objects to accomplish a specific purpose. This is called an interaction, and it helps in understanding the dynamics of the system and its participating objects.

State Diagram

Objects have state or status. The state of an object depends on the current activity or condition. A state diagram illustrates the states of the object and the input and transitions that cause changes in the state. The State diagram shows the sequences of states that an object passes through during its lifetime. They correspond to prompts for input, coupled with the responses and actions.

A state machine is a diagram of states and transitions that describe the response of an object of a given class to the receipt of external stimuli, and it is generally attached to a class or a method. A State diagram represents a state machine: a state being a condition during the life of an object or an interaction during which it satisfies some condition, performs some action, or waits for some event. A state may correspond to ongoing activity. Such activity is expressed as a nested state machine. For example, you may re-prompt the user to enter missing form items that are required to process a transaction, such as user login. Alternatively, ongoing activity may be represented by a pair of actions—one that starts the activity on entry to the state and one that terminates the activity on exit from the state.

The sample State diagram shown in Figure 2-16 models the login part of an online trading system. Logging in consists of entering a valid user ID and password, and then submitting the information for validation against a security database of valid users and their passwords. Logging in can be factored into four non-overlapping states: checking whether the user ID is logged in, getting the user ID and password, validating the same, and rejecting/accepting the user. From each state comes a complete set of transitions that determine the subsequent state.

FIGURE 2-16

Annotated State diagram

User login for trading system
Is user already logged in?
If yes, then final state.
If no, then prompt for userID and password.
State1: User login page entered.
State2: Prompt for userID and password.
Has user entered userID and password?
If yes, then check same against the security database.
If no, then reprompt and stay in State2.
State3: Check userID and password against security database.
Do user and password match the security database?
If yes, then build user session and go to the final state.
If no, then reprompt and stay in State3 for three tries.
If no and more than three tries, report attempt to Audit and remove user and go to the final state.
State4: Audit user and remove user from system.

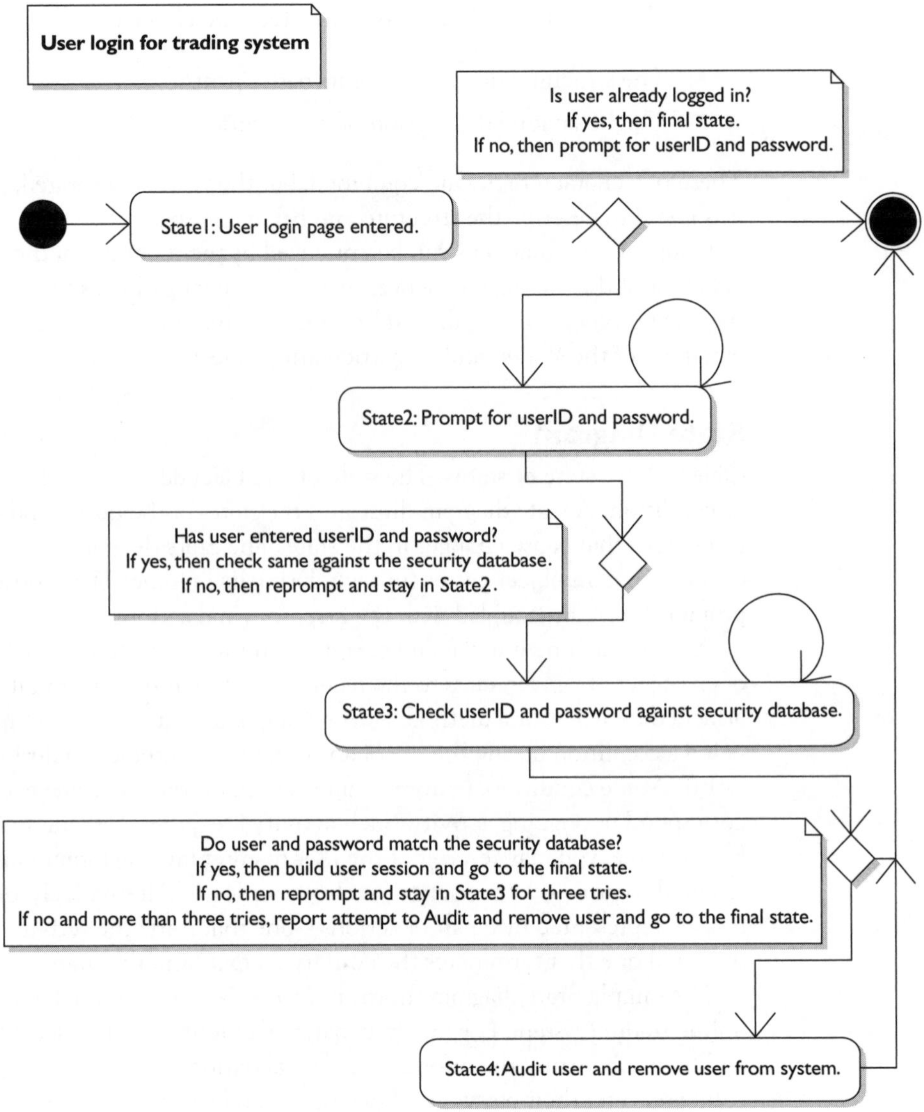

Activity Diagram

An Activity diagram is essentially a fancy flowchart. Activity diagrams and State diagrams are related. An Activity diagram—in a similar manner to the relationship between an Object and Class diagram—is a special case of a State diagram in which all the states are action states and all the transitions are triggered by completion of the actions in the source states. The entire Activity diagram is attached to a class or a use case. The purpose of this diagram is to focus on the functionality that flows from internal processing. Activity diagrams are used in situations for which the events represent the completion of internally generated actions—that is, procedure flow. State diagrams, on the other hand, are used in situations for which asynchronous events predominate. Figure 2-17 shows the process for making a trade.

Component Diagram

Component diagrams are physical versions of Class diagrams. A Component diagram shows the relationships and dependencies between software components, including Java source code components, Java class components, and Java deployable components—JAR (Java Archive) files. Within the Deployment diagram, a software component may be represented as a component type.

With respect to Java and JEE, some components exist at compile time (such as makeTrade.java), some exist at archive time (makeTrade.class), and some exist at run time (Trade.ear); some exist at more than one time. Therefore, you can say that a compile-only component is one that is meaningful only at compile time; the run-time component in this case would be an executable program. You can think of this diagram as a kind of compile, JAR, and deploy description.

Deployment Diagram

Deployment diagrams show the physical configurations of software and hardware. The Deployment diagram complements the Component diagram. It shows the configuration of run-time processing elements such as servers and other hardware and the software components, processes, and objects they comprise. Software component instances represent run-time manifestations of classes. Components that do not exist as run-time entities (such as makeTrade.java) do not appear on these diagrams; they are shown on Component diagrams. A Deployment diagram is a graphical representation of nodes connected by communication links or associations.

FIGURE 2-17 Annotated activity diagram

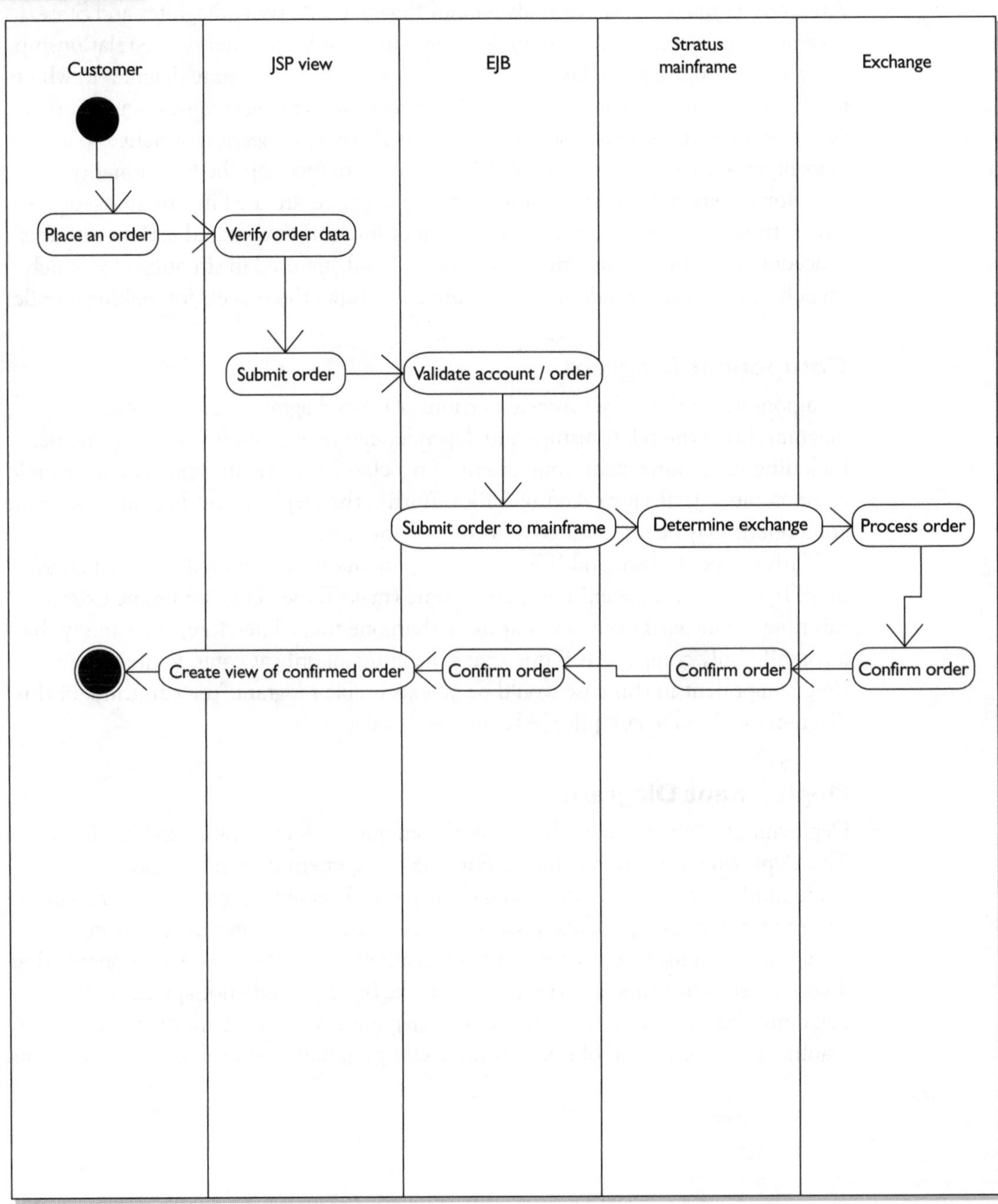

Nodes may contain component instances, which indicate that the component resides and runs on the node. Components may contain objects, which indicate that the object is part of the component. The Deployment diagram can be used to show which components run on which nodes. The migration of components from node to node or of objects from component to component may also be represented. The Deployment diagram shown in Figure 2-18 depicts the relationships among software and hardware components involved in security trading transactions.

A Deployment diagram contains the following elements:

- Hardware nodes can represent any type of physical hardware. A hardware node is usually a computer, but it can also be any physical device that communicates with a computer network. Such devices include printers, scanners, personal digital assistants (PDAs), cell phones, network routers, firewalls, and so on.
- Links between hardware nodes indicate connectivity and can include the communication protocol used between the nodes. A Deployment diagram represents a graph of links that show the topology of a real computer network. These links are shown as solid lines with no arrows. There is usually a stereotype label on the link that specifies the communication protocol used between the nodes.

Software components are placed within hardware nodes to show the distribution of the software across the network.

A Deployment diagram can show how to deploy software components onto the hardware nodes of the system solution. These software components are usually large-scale components, such as complete executable applications and class libraries.

Here's how to create a detailed Deployment diagram:

- Design the components for the architecturally significant use cases. This step requires the architect to design the boundary, service, and entity components that support each architecturally significant use cases.
- Place Design components into the Architecture model. The Design components are then placed within an infrastructure that supports the high-level architecture. Therefore, if there is a Presentation tier, the servlet and JSP page components are required.
- Draw the detailed Deployment diagram from the merger of the Design and Infrastructure components.

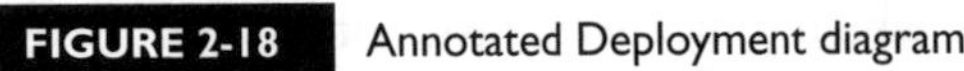

FIGURE 2-18 Annotated Deployment diagram

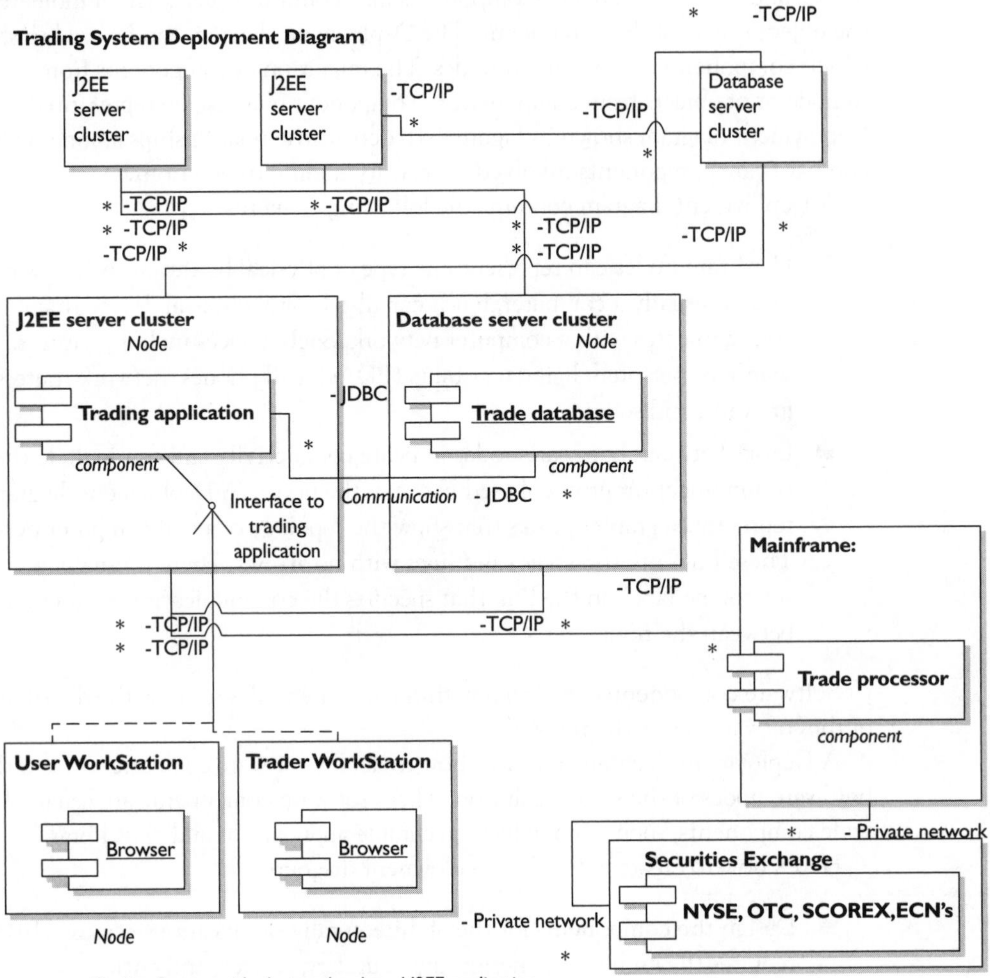

CERTIFICATION SUMMARY

The UML is a language used for specifying, constructing, visualizing, and documenting the components of a software system. The primary design goals of the UML areas follow:

- Provide users with a visual modeling language to develop and exchange comprehensive models.
- Provide mechanisms for extensibility and specialization that extend the core concepts.
- Create a standard specification that is independent of particular computing languages.
- Provide a formal base for a modeling language.
- Support high-level development concepts such as components, collaborations, frameworks, and patterns.
- Integrate best practices.

The principle of "separation of concerns" can be applied such that a complex system is decomposed into a hierarchy of collaborating objects. This principle provides the designer with a handle on system complexity by shielding the complex details of one layer/tier behind an abstraction (a method or object) on an adjacent layer/tier.

TWO-MINUTE DRILL

Identify Nonfunctional and Quality of Service Requirements That Influence Application Design

- The nonfunctional/QoS requirements are as follows:
  - **Availability** The degree to which a system is accessible. The term "24×7" describes total availability. This aspect of a system is often coupled with performance.
  - **Reliability** The ability to ensure the integrity and consistency of an application and its transactions.
  - **Manageability** The ability to administer and thereby manage the system resources to ensure the availability and performance of a system with respect to the other capabilities.
  - **Flexibility** The ability to address architectural and hardware configuration changes without a great deal of impact to the underlying system.
  - **Performance** The ability to carry out functionality in a timeframe that meets specified goals.
  - **Capacity** The ability of a system to run multiple tasks per unit of time.
  - **Scalability** The ability to support the required availability and performance as the transactional load increases.
  - **Extensibility** The ability to extend functionality.
  - **Validity** The ability to predict and confirm results based on a specified input or user gesture.
  - **Reusability** The ability to use a component in more than one context without changing its internals.
  - **Security** The ability to ensure that information is not accessed and modified unless done so in accordance with the enterprise policy.

Identify How the Separation of Concerns Principle Applies to the Component Model of a Java EE Application

- Separation of concerns is a principle for separating a system into distinct tiers/layers/components, such that each tier/layer/component addresses a separate concern.
- A concern is a set of information that affects the tier/layer/component.

- A concern can be as general as the details of the hardware the code is being optimized for, or as specific as the name of a class to instantiate. For example, layered designs in information systems are another embodiment of separation of concerns (for example, presentation layer, business logic layer, data access layer, and database layer). The value of separation of concerns is in simplifying the development and maintenance of the tier/layer/component.
- When concerns are well separated, individual tiers/layers/components can be developed and updated independently. Of special value is the ability to later improve or modify one tier/layer/component without having to know the details of another tier/layer/component, and without having to make corresponding changes to the tier/layer/component.

Identify the Correct Interpretation of Separation of Concerns as It Applies to the Java EE Service Layers

- Separation of concerns means a system can be split by intra- and inter-component relationships. For example, a UI component deals with a user's actions, such as processing a click to a button or verifying that a data field has a legitimate value. A business logic component does not need to know how the data is entered when it processes some operation.
- The separation of concerns principle tells the architect to separate components into different functional or infrastructure layers:
  - **Application** The application layer is the user and business functionality of a system (for example, the .war or .ear files).
  - **Virtual platform (component APIs)** The virtual platform layer contains interfaces to the application infrastructure component APIs (for example, REST web services and servlets).
  - **Application infrastructure (containers)** The application infrastructure layer contains products (for example, JBOSS and IBM's WebSphere) that provide for the operation and development of the application. The virtual platform components are housed in an application infrastructure container.
  - **Enterprise services (OS and virtualization)** The enterprise services layer includes the operating system (for example, Linux) and software (for example, Oracle DBMS) that runs on top of the compute and storage layer. This layer provides the interfaces to the operating system and storage functions needed by the application infrastructure layer.
  - **Compute and storage** The compute and storage layer consists of the physical hardware used in the architecture.

Identify the Effects of an Object-Oriented Approach to System Design

- UML provides an object-oriented approach to system design and defines the following elements:
  - **Class** Any uniquely identified abstraction that models a single thing, where the term "object" is synonymous with "instance." Classes have attributes and methods.
  - **Interface** A collection of operations that represents a class or specifies a set of methods that must be implemented by the derived class. An interface typically contains nothing but virtual methods and their signatures.
  - **Package** Used to organize groups of like kind elements. The package is the only group type element, and its function is to represent a collection of functionally similar classes.
  - **Collaboration** Defines the interaction of one or more roles along with their contents, associations, relationships, and classes.
  - **Use Case** A description that represents a complete unit of functionality provided by something as large as a system or as small as a class.
  - **Component** Represents a modular and deployable system part. It encapsulates an implementation and exposes a set of interfaces.
  - **Node** A physical element object that represents a processing resource, generally having memory and processing capability, such as a server.
  - **State** A condition that can occur during the life of an object. It can also be an interaction that satisfies some condition, performs some action, or waits for some event.
- UML defines the following relationships:
  - **Generalization** A specialized version of another class.
  - **Association** Uses the services of another class.
  - **Aggregation** A class "owns" another class.
  - **Composition** A class is composed of another class. Composition refers to an aggregation within which the component parts and the larger encompassing whole share a lifetime.
  - **Refinement** A refined version of another class.
  - **Dependency** A class dependent on another class.

- UML defines the following diagrams:
  - **Use Case diagram** Used to identify the primary elements and processes that form the system. The primary elements are termed "actors," and the processes are called "use cases." The Use Case diagram shows which actors interact with each use case.
  - **Class diagram** Used to define a detailed design of the system. Each class in the class diagram may be capable of providing certain functionalities. The functionalities provided by the class are called methods of the class.
  - **Package diagram** Groups objects or classes.
  - **State diagram** Represents the different states that objects in the system undergo during their life cycle. Objects in the system change states in response to events.
  - **Activity diagram** Captures the process flow of the system. An Activity diagram also consists of activities, actions, transitions, and initial and final states.
  - **Sequence diagram** Represents the interaction between different objects in the system. The important aspect of a sequence diagram is that it is time ordered. Objects in the sequence diagram interact by passing messages.
  - **Collaboration diagram** Groups together the interactions between different objects. The interactions are listed as numbered interactions that help to trace the sequence of the interactions. The Collaboration diagram helps to identify all the possible interactions that each object has with other objects.
  - **Component diagram** Represents the high-level parts that make up the system. This diagram depicts what components form part of the system and how they are interrelated. It depicts the components culled after the system has undergone the development or construction phase.
  - **Deployment diagram** Captures the configuration of the run-time elements of the application. This diagram is useful when a system is complete and ready for deployment.
- UML can be used to view a system from various perspectives:
  - **Design view** Structural view of the system; Class diagrams and Package diagrams form this view of the system.
  - **Process view** Dynamic behavior of a system; State diagrams, Activity diagrams, Sequence diagrams, and Collaboration diagrams form this view.

- **Component view** Software and hardware modules of the system modeled using the component diagram.
- **Deployment view** The Deployment diagram of UML is used to combine Component diagrams to depict the implementation and deployment of a system.
- **Use Case view** You can view a system from this perspective as a set of activities or transactions via the Use Case diagrams.

SELF TEST

The following questions will help you measure your understanding of the material presented in this chapter. Read all the choices carefully because there may be more than one correct answer. Choose all correct answers for each question.

Identify Nonfunctional and Quality of Service Requirements That Influence Application Design

1. Which of the following is true about the requirements of a banking system?
   - A. The need for security is a classic example of a functional service level requirement, and a checking account rule is an example of a nonfunctional requirement.
   - B. Security and the mandatory checking account both illustrate functional service-level requirements.
   - C. Neither security nor the mandatory checking account is an example of any kind of requirement, theoretically speaking.
   - D. Security is an architectural nonfunctional requirement, and the mandatory checking account is a functional design requirement.
   - E. They are both examples of business use cases.
2. Which of the following are nonfunctional requirements?
   - A. Scalability, availability, extensibility, manageability, and security
   - B. Performance, reliability, elaboration, transition, documentation, and security
   - C. Specification, elaboration, construction, transition, use cases, and security
   - D. Performance, availability, scalability, and security
   - E. Reliability, availability, scalability, manageability, and security
3. Which of the following is the most important item that should be considered when designing an application?
   - A. Scalability
   - B. Maintainability
   - C. Reliability
   - D. Meeting the needs of the customer
   - E. Performance
   - F. Ensuring the application is produced on time and within budget
4. You have been contracted by a company to help them improve the performance of their e-commerce application. You have suggested that the hardware on which the application is

currently deployed (two web servers and a database server) be migrated to three web servers, an application server, and a database server (all on different machines). You assure them that all the required software rewrites will be worth it in the long run. What are the characteristics of your suggested architecture?

A. Fat clients.

B. Thin clients.

C. Good separation of business logic.

D. Good scalability.

E. Poor separation of business logic.

F. Poor scalability.

G. There is no difference in the separation of business logic.

Identify How the Separation of Concerns Principle Applies to the Component Model of a Java EE Application

5. The MVC pattern is an example of the separation of concerns because:

A. It is defined in reference to others, adding all their features to its own.

B. It is defined in reference to others, adding selected features to its own.

C. The Model elements (the business Entities and Services) are kept separate from the GUI Views and Controller mechanisms.

D. It conforms to Liskov's Substitution Principle, adding all features from multiple superclasses.

6. The DAO pattern provides for a separation of concerns because:

A. It separates the business logic components from the data integration components.

B. It provides the integration components that the system software uses to communicate with the data store.

C. It separates the implementation of the CRUD operations from the application tier.

D. It applies Liskov's Substitution Principle, adding all features from multiple superclasses.

Identify the Correct Interpretation of Separation of Concerns as It Applies to the Java EE Service Layers

7. Layers represent component-to-container relationships. This suggests the separation of the software system into five major layers and is an example of the separation of concerns.

A. True

B. False

Identify the Effects of an Object-Oriented Approach to System Design

8. Inheritance is a mechanism whereby a class:

A. Is defined in reference to others, adding all their features to its own

B. Is defined in reference to others, adding selected features to its own

C. Is defined in deference to others, adding new features as its own

D. Conforms to Liskov's Substitution Principle, adding all features from multiple superclasses

9. When we utilize inheritance:

A. Attributes and methods from the superclass are included in the subclass.

B. Subclass methods cannot override superclass methods.

C. Subclass methods can only include superclass methods.

D. Subclasses can extend the superclass with new features.

10. Which of the following conditions must be true for the inheritance relationship to be plausible?

A. A subclass object *is a kind of* the superclass object.

B. If you substitute a subclass for a superclass, the code should find that all the methods it expected to find in the superclass are still provided and accessible.

C. A subclass can inherit from multiple superclasses.

D. A subclass can inherit from one and only one superclass.

11. The Java programming language supports all forms of inheritance.

A. True

B. False

12. What must one do to create proper encapsulation?

A. Make all attributes private.

B. Provide an abstract interface to the data held within the object capsule.

C. Make all attributes static.

D. Hide implementation details behind a set of non-private methods.

Additional questions to test your knowledge of UML for parts 2 and 3 of the exam

13. Which of the following items is not one of the phases of the Unified Process?

A. Inception

B. Design

C. Construction

D. Transition

14. Which of the following statements are true about a use case?

A. It is a complete end-to-end business process that satisfies the needs of a user.

B. It is a description that represents a complete unit of functionality provided by something as large as a system or as small as a class.

C. It defines the interaction of one or more roles along with their contents, associations, relationships, and classes.

D. It is a collection of operations that represents a class or specifies a set of methods that must be implemented by the derived class.

15. Which of the following statements is not true when speaking of a class?

A. A class is a nonunique structure.

B. An instance is one computer executable copy of a class, also referred to as an "object."

C. Multiple instances of a particular class can exist in a computer's main memory at any given time.

D. A class is a structure that defines the attribute data and the methods or functions that operate on that data.

16. Which of the following statements are not true about use cases?

A. There are three types of use cases: essential, real, and virtual.

B. A virtual use case describes the user's virtual view of the problem and is technology independent.

C. A real use case describes the process in terms of its real design and implementation.

D. Essential use cases are of importance early in the project. Their purpose is to illustrate and document the business process.

17. Which of the following statements is not true about a Sequence diagram?

A. It has two dimensions.

B. One sequence diagram dimension represents time.

C. One sequence diagram dimension represents the different objects participating in a sequence of events required for a purpose.

D. Sequence diagrams are static model views.

18. Which item is not an example of something that a State diagram could effectively model?

A. Life could be modeled as birth, puberty, adulthood, and death.

B. A computer system infrastructure.

C. A banking transaction.

D. A soccer match could be modeled as start, halftime, injury time, end.

19. Which of the following statements is not true about a Collaboration diagram?

A. A Collaboration diagram models interactions among objects, and objects interact by invoking messages on each other.

B. A Collaboration diagram groups together the interactions among different objects.

C. The interactions in a Collaboration diagram are listed as alphabetically collated letters that help to trace the sequence of the interactions.

D. The Collaboration diagram helps to identify all the possible interactions that each object has with other objects.

20. Which of the following statements is not true about a component?

A. A component represents a modular and deployable system part. It encapsulates an implementation and exposes a set of interfaces.

B. The component interfaces represent services provided by elements that reside on the component.

C. A node may be deployed on a component.

D. A component is shown as a rectangle with two smaller rectangles extending from its left side. A component type has a type name of component-type.

21. Which item is not part of a class in a UML class diagram?

A. Name

B. Attributes

C. Method

D. Comments

22. Which item is not one of the three kinds of relationships a Class diagram can have?

A. Association

B. Aggregation

C. Generalization

D. Specialization

23. In a Class diagram, what does a line with an arrow from one class to another denote?

A. Attribute visibility

B. Class visibility

C. Method visibility

D. Global visibility

24. Which of the following is not a type of visibility between objects?

A. Local

B. Method

C. Attribute

D. Global

25. Which statement is not true about state machine and state diagrams?

A. A state machine is basically a diagram of states and transitions that describes the response of an object of a given class to the receipt of external stimuli, and it is generally attached to a class or a method.

B. The state diagram shows the sequences of states that an object passes through during its lifetime.

C. A state diagram represents a state machine—a state being a condition during the life of an object or an interaction during which it satisfies some condition, performs some action, or waits for some event.

D. State diagrams are used in situations for which all or most of the events represent the completion of internally generated actions (that is, procedural flow of control).

26. Which of the following UML diagrams may be best suited for a business analyst?

A. Deployment

B. Class

C. Use Case

D. Activity

E. Collaboration

F. Sequence

27. In a UML Class diagram, the Private, Protected, and Public attributes are shown by which one of the following sets of symbols?

A. -, +, #

B. +, -, hash

C. #, -, +

D. -, #, +

E. +, #, -

F. #, +, -

SELF TEST ANSWERS

Identify Nonfunctional and Quality of Service Requirements That Influence Application Design

1. ☑ **D.** Successful software architecture deals with addressing the nonfunctional service-level requirements of a system. The design process takes all functional business requirements into account. Security is considered a nonfunctional requirement, and specific business rules, such as the one described for the checking account, are considered functional requirements. **D** is the only choice that accurately describes this.
☒ **A, B, C,** and **E** are incorrect. **A** is incorrect because the functional and nonfunctional requirements are switched. **B** is incorrect because only one of them is a functional requirement. **C** is incorrect because, as just described, one of these is a functional requirement and the other is a nonfunctional requirement. Finally, **E** is incorrect because business analysis may start with use cases.

2. ☑ **D.** The nonfunctional service-level requirements discussed are performance (the system needs to respond within five seconds), availability (the system needs to have a 99.9 percent uptime), scalability (an additional 200,000 subscribers will be added), and security (HTTPS is to be used). Hence, **D** is correct.
☒ **A, B, C,** and **E** are incorrect. There is no mention of extensibility (the ability to easily add or extend functionality) and manageability (the ability to monitor the health of the system). Hence, **A** is incorrect. Specification, elaboration, construction, transition, documentation, and use cases are not nonfunctional service-level requirements. Hence, **B** and **C** are incorrect. Although scalability and reliability may be related (will the system perform as reliably when more users operate on it?), there is no mention of reliability in the question. Hence, **E** is incorrect.

3. ☑ **D.** The most important consideration when designing an application is that it meets the needs of the customer.
☒ **A, B, C, E,** and **F** are incorrect. Ensuring the application is produced on time and within budget is something that should be done, but it is not the number-one concern. The application does not have to be the best possible solution under the circumstances. As long as it meets the customer's needs, it is considered adequate. All of the other considerations are secondary to meeting the customer's needs.

4. ☑ **B, C,** and **D** are correct. The system you have suggested they migrate to is a three-tier system. The characteristics of a three-tier system are thin clients, good separation of business logic, and good scalability. This is due to the fact that each tier is separate from the others (for example, it would be possible to change the data store without affecting the business logic).

☒ **A, E, F,** and **G** are incorrect. **A** is incorrect because the suggested system has thin clients, with the business logic residing on the application server, in the middle tier. Because there is a good separation of business logic, **E** and **G** are incorrect. **F** is incorrect because the three-tier nature of the system makes it very scalable.

Identify How the Separation of Concerns Principle Applies to the Component Model of a Java EE Application

5. ☑ **C.** MVC is another GUI architectural pattern. This pattern is an example of the separation of concerns principle in which the Model elements (the business Entities and Services) are kept separate from the GUI Views and Controller mechanisms. The MVC pattern uses a notification mechanism similar to that used in Swing. A View component can register with the Model to listen to events when the Model changes.
☒ **A, B,** and **D** are incorrect. They are not relevant, because they describe features not associated with the MVC pattern.

6. ☑ **A** and **C**. The DAO pattern provides the integration components that the system software uses to communicate with the data store. This pattern has the following characteristics: It separates the implementation of the CRUD operations from the application tier. It applies the principle of "separation of concerns" to separate the business logic components from the data integration components.
☒ **B** and **D** are incorrect. **B,** although descriptive, but does not apply separation of concerns, and **D** is not relevant to separation of concerns.

Identify the Correct Interpretation of Separation of Concerns as It Applies to the Java EE Service Layers

7. ☑ **A.** The statement is true because separation of concerns and layering components are crucial, for example, to the design of the Internet. In the Internet Protocol suite, great efforts have been made to separate concerns into well-defined layers. This allows protocol designers to focus on the concerns in one layer and to ignore the other layers. The Application layer protocol SMTP, for example, is concerned about all the details of conducting an e-mail session over a reliable transport service (usually TCP), but is not in the least concerned about how the transport service makes that service reliable. Similarly, TCP is not concerned about the routing of data packets, which is handled at the Internet layer.
☒ **B** is incorrect. This answer is incorrect because the statement is true.

Identify the Effects of an Object-Oriented Approach to System Design

8. ☑ **A.** Inheritance is a mechanism whereby a class is defined in reference to others, adding all their features to its own.
☒ B, C and D are incorrect. They are false statements.

9. ☑ A and **D.** Attributes and methods from the superclass are included in the subclass. Subclasses inherit all of the features of the superclass; plus, these classes can extend the superclass with new features specific to that type of employee. Subclass methods can override superclass methods. A subclass object *is a* superclass object (or *is a kind of* the superclass object). Using the *is a* or *is a kind of* test helps you avoid using the inheritance relationship when it is either inappropriate now or in the future (if changes are made). Inheritance should conform to Liskov's Substitution Principle (LSP). This principle was introduced by Barbara Liskov in 1987. A simplified interpretation is that if you substitute a subclass for a superclass, the code should find that all the methods it expected to find in the superclass are still provided and accessible, with any overridden methods having the same semantic meaning. A subclass can inherit from multiple superclasses (called multiple inheritance) *or* a subclass can *only* inherit from a single superclass (single inheritance). Some OO languages support multiple inheritance, which enables a subclass to inherit members from multiple superclasses. C++ supports this feature.
☒ B and C are incorrect. They are both are false.

10. ☑ **A, B,** and C. These are correct because a subclass object *is a kind of* the superclass object, and all attributes and methods from the superclass are included in the subclass.
☒ D is incorrect. A subclass can inherit from multiple superclasses.

11. ☑ **A.** This statement is true.
☒ B is incorrect. This statement is false because the Java programming language only supports single inheritance.

12. ☑ **A, B,** and **D.** In OO languages, the term "encapsulation" means information hiding, which can be defined as hiding implementation details behind a set of non-private methods. In order to create proper encapsulation, you must make all attributes private as well as provide accessor and mutator methods to give an abstract interface to the data held within the object capsule.
☒ C is incorrect. Making all attributes static is not part of encapsulation.

Additional questions to test your knowledge of UML

13. ☑ **B.** Design is not a phase in the Unified Process.
☒ **A, C,** and D are incorrect. The phases of the Unified Process include Inception, whose focus is the scope of the project; Elaboration, in which the architecture and the requirements of the product being built must be defined by the end of this phase; Construction, during which the software must be developed or constructed; and Transition, during which the software must be rolled out to users.

14. ☑ **A** and **B.** These statements are correct because a use case is a complete end-to-end business process that satisfies the needs of a user. It is also a description that represents a complete unit of functionality provided by something as large as a system or as small as a class.
☒ **C** and **D** are incorrect. A collaboration defines the interaction of one or more roles along with their contents, associations, relationships, and classes. A Class diagram is a collection of operations that represents a class or specifies a set of methods that must be implemented by the derived class.

15. ☑ **A.** A class is unique.
☒ **B, C,** and **D** are incorrect. These are all true statements. A class is a unique structure that defines the attribute data and the methods or functions that operate on that data. An instance is one computer executable copy of a class, also referred to as an object. Multiple instances of a particular class can exist in a computer's main memory at any given time.

16. ☑ **A** and **B.** These are correct because they are false statements. There are only two types of use cases: essential and real.
☒ **C** and **D** are incorrect. These are true statements. Essential use cases are expressed in an ideal form that remains free of technology and implementation detail. The design decisions are abstracted, especially those related to the user interface. A real use case describes the process in terms of its real design and implementation. Essential use cases are of importance early in the project. Their purpose is to illustrate and document the business process. Real use cases become important after implementation because they document how the user interface supports the business process documented in the essential use case.

17. ☑ **D.** This answer is correct because it is a false statement. Class and Object diagrams are static model views; Sequence diagrams are dynamic.
☒ **A, B,** and **C** are incorrect. They are true statements. The Sequence diagram shows the explicit sequence of interactions as they flow through the system to affect a desired operation or result. It has two dimensions; one dimension represents time, and the other dimension represents the different objects participating in a sequence of events required for a purpose. Class and Object diagrams are static model views.

18. ☑ **B.** A computer system infrastructure does not have dynamic states; it is more or less static, and the modeler would use a deployment diagram to depict the infrastructure.
☒ **A, C,** and **D** are incorrect. Life could be modeled, and a banking transaction and a soccer match could also be modeled.

19. ☑ **C.** This answer is correct because it is a false statement. The interactions in a Collaboration diagram are listed as numbered interactions that help to trace the sequence of the interactions.

☒ **A, B,** and **D** are incorrect. They are all true statements. A Collaboration diagram models interactions among objects, and objects interact by invoking messages on each other. A Collaboration diagram groups together the interactions among different objects. The interactions in a Collaboration diagram are listed as numbered interactions that help to trace the sequence of the interactions.

20. ☑ **C.** This answer is correct because it is a false statement. A component may be deployed on a node.
☒ **A, B,** and **D** are incorrect. They are all true statements. A component represents a modular and deployable system part. It encapsulates an implementation and exposes a set of interfaces. The interfaces represent services provided by elements that reside on the component. A component is shown as a rectangle with two smaller rectangles extending from its left side.

21. ☑ **D.** A comment is not part of a UML class diagram.
☒ **A, B,** and **C** are incorrect. UML class notation is a rectangle divided into three parts: class name, attributes, and operations.

22. ☑ **D.** Specialization is not a relationship type.
☒ **A, B,** and **C** are incorrect. Association is a relationship between instances of the two classes. An association exists between two classes if an instance of one class must know about the other to perform its work. In a diagram, an association is a link connecting two classes. Aggregation is an association in which one class belongs to a collection. An aggregation has a diamond end pointing to the part containing the whole. Generalization is an inheritance link indicating one class is a superclass of the other. A generalization has a triangle pointing to the superclass.

23. ☑ **A.** A line with an arrow from one class to another denotes attribute visibility.
☒ **B, C,** and **D** are incorrect. It does not denote class visibility, method visibility, or global visibility.

24. ☑ **B.** Method is not a type of visibility between objects
☒ **A, C,** and **D** are incorrect. These are all visibility types.

25. ☑ **D.** This answer is correct because it is a false statement. Activity diagrams are used in situations for which all or most of the events represent the completion of internally generated actions (that is, procedural flow of control). State diagrams, on the other hand, are used in situations for which asynchronous events predominate.
☒ **A, B,** and **C** are incorrect. They are all true statements. The State diagram shows the sequences of states through which an object passes during its lifetime. They correspond to prompts for input, coupled with the responses and actions. A state machine is basically a diagram of states and transitions that describe the response of an object of a given class to the receipt of external stimuli, and it is generally attached to a class or a method. A State diagram represents a state machine—a state being a condition during the life of an object or an interaction during which it satisfies some condition, performs some action, or waits for some event.

26. ☑ **C.** Use Case diagrams show a set of use cases and actors and their relationships. Use Case diagrams show the static view of a system. These diagrams are especially important in organizing and modeling the behaviors of a system. Use Case diagrams are frequently used by business analysts to capture the business requirements of a system.
☒ **A, B, D, E,** and **F** are incorrect. Deployment diagrams show the configuration of run-time processing nodes and the components that live within these nodes. Deployment diagrams address the static view of the architecture. Architects frequently use Deployment diagrams. A Class diagram shows a set of classes, interfaces, and collaborations and their relationships. Class diagrams address the static design view of a system. Software designers frequently use Class diagrams. Activity diagrams are a special kind of state chart diagram that shows the flow from activity to activity within the system. This type of diagram is important in modeling the function of a system and emphasizing the flow of control among objects. Designers and developers frequently use Activity diagrams. A Collaboration diagram is an interaction diagram that emphasizes the structural organization of objects that send and receive messages. Designers and developers frequently use interaction diagrams. A *sequence diagram* depicts the ordering and interaction of processes which operate with one another.

27. ☑ **D.** In UML notation, access modifiers are shown by the –, #, and + symbols to represent private, protected, and public, respectively.
☒ **A, B, C, E,** and **F** are incorrect. These do not offer the right combination.

3

Common Architectures

CERTIFICATION OBJECTIVES

3.01	Identify the Appropriate Strategy for Deploying Client Applications to Desktop and Mobile Platforms, the Principles for Designing a User Interface and the Benefits of Applying Client Tier Patterns
3.02	Identify Best Practices for Exception Handling, Logging, and Business Tier Patterns
3.03	Identify Design Patterns That Address Specific Challenges in the Web Tier, Including Authentication, Authorization, and Scaling and Clustering to Meet Demand
3.04	Identify Java EE Technologies, Including JMS, JCA, and Web Services, and Design Patterns That Address Specific Challenges in Enterprise Integration
3.05	Identify the Challenges in Integrating Enterprise Resources, the Java EE Technologies That Address Them (Including JPA and JDBC), and the Communication Protocols That Support Tier-to-Tier Communication (Including RMI, IIOP, and CORBA)
✓	Two-Minute Drill
Q&A	Self Test

This chapter covers common architectures, which for the exam creators encompasses deploying client applications, exception handling, and nonfunctional requirements, including web tier security, performance, and JEE technologies that handle messaging, data stores, persistence, and so on, all of which facilitate enterprise integration.

exam watch

This chapter covers enterprise integration from the vantage point of common architectures—that is, technologies that are commonly used to handle end-to-end integration of applications in the enterprise space. The exam coverage extends from client browser to back-end data persistence, expecting the candidate to understand integration from end to end.

CERTIFICATION OBJECTIVE 3.01

Identify the Appropriate Strategy for Deploying Client Applications to Desktop and Mobile Platforms, the Principles for Designing a User Interface and the Benefits of Applying Client Tier Patterns

One of the fundamental challenges facing software architects is change. The need to develop maintainable software systems has driven interest in approaches to software development and design. Simply put, the main objective of a user interface is to provide the best possible user experience for interacting with the application. That said, the user experience depends on the capabilities of the platform technology the end user is using to access the application interface. Additionally, the client tier is unlike the other tiers of the enterprise architecture. The other tiers tend to focus on aspects of a software architecture that support the implementation of a business process. The client tier is subject to the type of the technology hosting the user interface (for example, laptop, tablet, phablet, or phone).

With respect to the design of user interface, it is important to consider how a user is going to use the application, and what the functional requirements are, as they also have an impact on the design and selection of devices and technologies for such an interface. Usability Engineering (UE) extends the subjective notion of design principles, with a pragmatic approach. See Table 3-1 for a list of design principles. UE focuses on an iterative metric-gathering process to determine the level of user acceptance of a given interface. UE encourages regular interface prototyping, beginning at the early stages of the development cycle. Such prototypes are often mock-ups with no back-end functionality. They measure user acceptance. Presenting prototypes to end users for feedback is called usability testing. It is less formal than a full quality assurance (QA) or system test process. It is not uncommon for usability testing of prototypes early in the development cycle to effect and clarify the application requirements. End users cannot fully quantify and qualify the behavior and features of the application until they begin usability testing. Per the emerging agile development process, all the key players of the development process, including architects, designers, business analysts, and project managers, should attend the initial usability tests. There is value in catching significant functional changes early in the development process.

Table 3-1 lists a synopsis of client tier design principles.

Client Tier Design Principles

Before beginning full-scale development, it is important to review existing Human Computer Interaction (HCI) pattern catalogs. It is also prudent to consider creating a set of user interface design guidelines that establish the style and method of presentation and interaction components for the enterprise. Additionally, look at http://developer.yahoo.com/ypatterns for sets of client tier patterns. Another important aspect to consider when designing the software architecture of the client tier is the end-user hardware resources. What the user is likely to use (for example desktop, tablet, and so on) for input and output of information from your application tends to drive many factors relating to information architecture and interface development. We must also consider how resource intensive the client application is expected to be. The answers might immediately rule out the possibility of using devices such as mobile phones as platforms for hosting client interfaces. HCI studies are quite extensive with regard to the mechanisms that humans use to interact with computer systems. In general, the smaller the device, the more limited the possibilities for complex user interactions. Larger devices, with extensive resources available, might have the ability to accommodate advanced user input mechanisms. The most commonly used technology for the display of enterprise application user interfaces is the desktop web browser. Inherently, all popular browsers support recent versions of the Hypertext Markup Language (HTML) specification and some sort

TABLE 3-1 Client Tier Design Principles

Principle	Description
Visibility	Clarity of the visual goal. Visibility in the context of UI design means making it clear what a UI element is used for. To achieve visibility, think about the goal that will be achieved by using that element. For example, are there any icons that could be used to draw the user's attention (that is, is there a "standard" symbol for the goal)?
Feedback	Feedback is related to the concept of visibility. In the context of UI design, it means making it clear what action has been achieved through the use of the UI element. All UI elements should provide adequate feedback in response to the user's actions. That is to say, let the user know that their request has been acknowledged.
Affordance	Element usage that is obvious to user. Affordance in the context of UI design means making it clear how a UI element should be used. To afford means "to give a clue." The clue is of how to interact. The element's appearance should make it obvious how a user should interact with it. UI controls should be designed so that it is obvious how they should be used.
Simplicity	Simplicity in the context of UI design means keeping things as simple as possible. To achieve simplicity, employ UI controls, icons, and words that are comfortable for the user. Use the user's own language. Break complex tasks into simpler subtasks.
Structure	Structure in this context means that a UI will be more usable if it is structured in a way that is meaningful and useful to user. For example, if the dialog involves printing, then things that the user will think of as related should be clearly and closely related and appear together in the UI, such as network printer choice, page range, and so on, and should be clearly and closely associated. Features that are unrelated, either in terms of a user's activities or in their mind, should be separated or distinguished in the UI.
Consistency	Consistency in visual patterns, navigation, appearance, positioning, and behavior within the UI makes a system easy to learn and remember. Bottom line: the presentation of the UI should be consistent. If two UI elements are to serve the same or similar purpose, they should be made as consistent as possible. For example, buttons for OK and Cancel on most interfaces have the same appearance, perhaps even the same size, because they serve similar purposes in ending a user interaction.
Tolerance	Tolerance refers to the ability of a UI to prevent errors, if possible, or to make them easy to recover from if not. The UI design should reduce the number of user errors and facilitate recovery from them. For an interface to be tolerant of errors, you should think of the ways in which the user can make errors. Is there a message that would help a user make the correct choice? If so, include examples of good choices in the UI message. For example, offer the format of a date that is to be entered.

of scripting language for dynamically manipulating the visual components within a page displayed on a web browser. However, supporting multiple user browsers simultaneously tends to be problematic with respect to the scripting languages.

Rich Internet Application Frameworks

Rich Internet Application (RIA) frameworks facilitate development for multiple browsers by providing browser-specific JavaScript source code generation and browser-specific JavaScript libraries with ECMA Script interfaces. There are also RIAs designed to run inside browser plug-ins such as Flash. HTML5 supports developers to create interactive websites and applications. HTML5 is seen as a trending alternative to Adobe Flash. HTML5 includes tags and support for drawing, video, and sound as well as geolocation, client-side databases, offline application caches, thread-like operations, and smarter forms. Adobe Flash (formerly Macromedia Flash) is a multimedia platform that adds animation, video, and interactivity to web pages. With the increasing presence of Apple's iOS platform for iPhone and iPad, some have seen this a signaling the end of Flash's dominance. Recent tests have also shown Flash performance on Android, a strong competitor with the iOS platform, to be significantly slower. The bottom line is that HTML5 in concert with an RIA framework will be the UI development front-runner.

Java on the Client Tier

Java applets offer the ability to run client applications within a confined Java Virtual Machine (JVM) Security Manager, often referred to as a sandbox. Applets run inside web browsers and usually have Rich Client Interfaces (RCIs), because they make use of Java GUI toolkits. Those who desire the RCI capabilities of Java applets tend to implement RIAs with JavaScript technology instead. As we all know, "smartphone" is the name given to the class of mobile phones that offer more advanced computing ability and connectivity than a contemporary basic "feature phone." Although both smartphones and feature phones can be thought of as handheld computers, feature phones run applications based on platforms such as Java ME and BREW. Smartphones enable the user to install and run more advanced applications based on a specific, different platform. Also, smartphones run complete operating systems, thus providing a rich development environment for application developers. Operating systems that can be found on smartphones include Symbian OS (including S60 series), iOS for Apple mobile devices, Palm WebOS, and BlackBerry OS, as well as Linux, Windows Mobile, and Android for Samsung phones. The current popular choice is between the iPhone and Android. The iPhone is a "closed" platform, based on Apple's iOS operating system, which is derived from

Mac OS X, with the hardware and software controlled by Apple. Android is an open architecture, but is experiencing OS fragmentation due to different models and carriers. This puts a lot of strain on application developers to support different versions of the software, and it can impede forward progress on application features. Android applications do not have to go through the application process like the iPhone, so there are more applications available. However, without an approval process, the quality, usefulness, and tastefulness of Android apps can be questionable. Also, Android devices do not sync to the desktop as easily or cleanly as the Apple devices. The mobile device space is evolving with the iPad and other tablet devices. These tablets and phablets (iPhone/iPad), initially marketed as a platform for audio and visual media such as books, periodicals, movies, music, and games, as well as web content, are expanding to include business functionality for the enterprise.

Application Client Installation Utilities

When it comes to the client tier, the emergence and comprehensive functionality imbedded in HTML5/CSS has made the interface of choice the browser, so it may just be a question of which browser or which release. For example, the WebSQL or SQLlite Web SQL Database browser-based API can store data in offline client databases that can be queried using a variant of SQL, and it requires the user to use the Google Chrome/Safari/Opera browser. That said, for native applications, we can use installation utilities such as InstallShield and others. Application developers typically use an installation utility, such as the commercial InstallShield, to simplify software installation and subsequent application execution. Although desktop GUI toolkit-based applications might seem attractive on the surface for their Rich Client Interface and broad flexibility, they suffer from issues relating to installation and maintenance. For example, getting users to properly install and execute Java applications can be problematic. Users might have to download and install a Java Runtime Environment (JRE). They might also need to download and save an application JAR file in a directory as well as modify the system path to include the bin directory containing the `java` command and open a command shell and execute `java -jar sampleapp.jar` to start the application.

The trend is demonstrably toward mobile applications. Emerging, iOS-, and Android-based applications present a challenge. Each environment should have methodology to facilitate acquiring, distributing, securing, and tracking mobile applications. Mobile Device Management (MDM) solutions are needed to manage internal, public, and purchased applications across employee-owned (BYOD), enterprise-supplied, and shared devices from a central administrative console.

CERTIFICATION OBJECTIVE 3.02

Identify Best Practices for Exception Handling, Logging, and Business Tier Patterns

In this objective we cover exception handling in standalone Java as well EJB-based applications. We start with a review of exception-handling basics, including the use of logging utilities, then move to a description of how EJB technology defines and manages different types of exceptions. Exception handling is a programming language construct designed to handle the occurrence of some condition/exception that changes the normal flow of execution. Exception handling seems simple enough, but IT shops should implement enterprise-wide handlers to integrate the logs and thereby facilitate the correction of issues that detrimentally affect the business.

Exceptions in General

To chart all of the failures possible, it is important to understand where potential exceptions/failure can occur within the process or service. Two types of exceptions can occur:

- **Process exception** This occurs when there is a failure with components used by a process or service. Process exceptions are environmental errors (for example, memory issues, connectivity failure, and so on). These are also called nonrecoverable exceptions.
- **Business exception** This occurs as a result of a business rules decision being internally triggered. A business exception is happens when a process is unable to proceed due to one of the following:
  - A validation issue
  - Some condition that puts a hold on a transaction (for example, the stock market has closed)

Business exceptions allow you to create cleaner processes and to define exceptional situations of the process as true exceptions. These are checked exceptions that indicate that certain business conditions have not been met. These are recoverable exceptions that allow the EJB layer to handle them using an alternative processing path.

Process Exception Classes

Process exceptions are further classified in different ways from an EJB perspective. The EJB specification classifies exceptions into broad categories:

- **JVM exceptions** This type of exception is thrown by the JVM, perhaps because of an OutOfMemoryError. These are fatal situations.
- **System exceptions** Most often system exceptions are thrown as subclasses of the Runtime Exception by the JVM. A NullPointer Exception or an ArrayOutOfBoundsException is due to a coding issue that only appears at run time.

Exception Handling Overview

The exception handling solution approach should give the user a facility to handle these two types of exceptions independently. Trivial process and business exceptions should not cause the process to abort. A proper exception-handling approach should make a provision for handling such nonfatal exceptions and allows the process to continue or retry once these exceptions are addressed. All run-time exceptions are handled either in the individual activity or in the process level, depending on the type of the exception. A proper exception handler gives the calling service an opportunity to address the exception, such as:

- Pertinent logging information
- Passing information to the user
- Taking an alternate execution path based on the exception

Best practice dictates that exception handling should include retry logic or route the task to an administrator for resolution. Business exceptions are also raised and explicitly routed to the support team. For reference, each transaction/process should be assigned a unique identifier. If there is an exception at a particular point, the exception is caught and an error message and identifier are passed on to the issue logger. Based on the severity of the exception, the issue logger can take action:

- Log the message or send an e-mail to support and return the control back to the activity where the exception has occurred.
- Pass on the details so that the support user can take action and then kick start the instance from the portal. The identifier is a reference to all of the processing that has taken place before the exception has occurred. The error message has detailed exception information.

Common Exception-Handling Strategies

There should be a strategy for exception handling, and developers will likely write code to handle exceptions differently. This results in confusion for the production support team because a single exception may be described and handled differently in different areas of the system. Lack of strategy also results in logging at multiple places throughout the system. Logging should be centralized or broken out into multiple manageable units. Ideally, exception logging should occur in as few places as possible without compromising the content.

When such an exception occurs, the end user normally expects the following:

- A description and error code indicating what has occurred
- A unique error number that they can use upon accessing a readily available customer support system
- Timely resolution of the problem, and the assurance that their request has been processed

EXERCISE 3-1

Issue Resolution

Question: How can a support group after receiving notification of a problem be able to quickly find all of the logs for the problem before the user calls for resolution?
Answer: If properly deigned, all logs of the problem are tagged with a unique ID to cross-reference the production logs for quick identification of the problem.

EJB Exception Handling for the Web Tier

In a web tier design, it is often easier and more efficient to place your exception-logging mechanism on the client side. For this to work, the web tier must be the only client for the EJB tier. In addition, the web tier must be based on one of the following patterns or frameworks:

- **Patterns** Business Delegate, FrontController, or Intercepting Filters
- **Frameworks** Struts or any similar MVC framework that contains hierarchies

Why should exception logging take place on the client side? Well, first, the control hasn't passed outside of the application server yet. The so-called client tier, which is composed of JSP pages, servlets, or their helper classes, runs on the JEE app server itself. Second, the classes in a well-designed web tier have a hierarchy (for example, in the Business Delegate classes, Intercepting Filter classes, HTTP request handler classes, JSP base class, or in the Struts Action classes) or single point of invocation in the form of a FrontController servlet. The base classes of these hierarchies or the central point in Controller classes can contain the exception-logging code. In the case of session EJB-based logging, each of the methods in the EJB component must have logging code. As the business logic grows, so will the number of session EJB methods, and so will the amount of logging code. A web tier system will require less logging code. You should consider this alternative if you have co-located web and EJB tiers and you don't have a requirement to support any other type of client. Regardless, the logging mechanism doesn't change; you can use the same techniques as described in previous sections.

Logging for All Applications

At the time of this writing, the most common Java-based logging solution is based on the Apache Log4j API and uses a file-based logging approach.

An Approach to Logging

An approach to logging that has been successful in a number of enterprises includes the following requirements/factors:

- Defining a logging object template that contains date, time, name of component, error message, and other pertinent information.
- Developing a generic logging service that can be invoked from every application.
- Ensuring that all applications call the generic logging service when they encounter an exception.
- The logging needs to take into consideration requirements if they are already standardized or structured at the enterprise level.
- Considering the amount of data required in the log (time, event, and user information) or additional information such as payload, custom messages, and so on.
- The level of logging can vary from process to process based on the urgency and needs of the process.
- The logging data storage can be file based or database based, subject to requirements.

- There can be an additional need for logging intimation, which can be in the form of an e-mail to the support group to study the log if or when it is needed.
- If a certain threshold is reached, consider backing up the logging files.

Best Practices for Logging

Logging is done using the following activities:

- **Invoke the log** A business process activity (generally the exception handler activity) invokes a log API. If an event or service call needs to be logged, create a logging task at the beginning and end of each service where logging is required.
- **Populate the wrapper object** The logger object is populated with relevant payload information. The object can generate process instance–specific data, such as process name, current activity, current logged-in user, and the current instance ID.
- **Call the customized logging service** This information is passed along with the log message to the generic logger service, which needs to be mapped. This service can also add features to send notification or intimation to the users of the log.
- **Call the generic logging service to log the information to the file** There should be a built-in service that is specifically used for logging. Based on the requirement, even this service can be customized.

CERTIFICATION OBJECTIVE 3.03

Identify Design Patterns That Address Specific Challenges in the Web Tier, Including Authentication, Authorization, and Scaling and Clustering to Meet Demand

Nowadays, well thought-out application design strategies implement best practices using design patterns. Design patterns that address authentication/authorization ("Auth/Auth") have emerged as an addition to the original Gang-of-Four patterns.

As in all patterns, Auth/Auth patterns use a standard template that includes a common or recurring problem and a solution for solving the problem.

Security Patterns by Tier

Security and Authentication/Authorization (Auth/Auth) patterns can be utilized in the delivery of end-to-end security solutions for a JEE-based application architecture (see Figure 3-1). They handle all aspects of user authentication and the roles and responsibilities they have to access components at each logical tiers. The tables in the following sections contain a non-exhaustive catalog of patterns for each logical tier. The description discusses how each provides solutions that, when integrated together, sum up an end-to-end security solution for an enterprise application.

FIGURE 3-1 Security: Authentication/Authorization patterns by tier

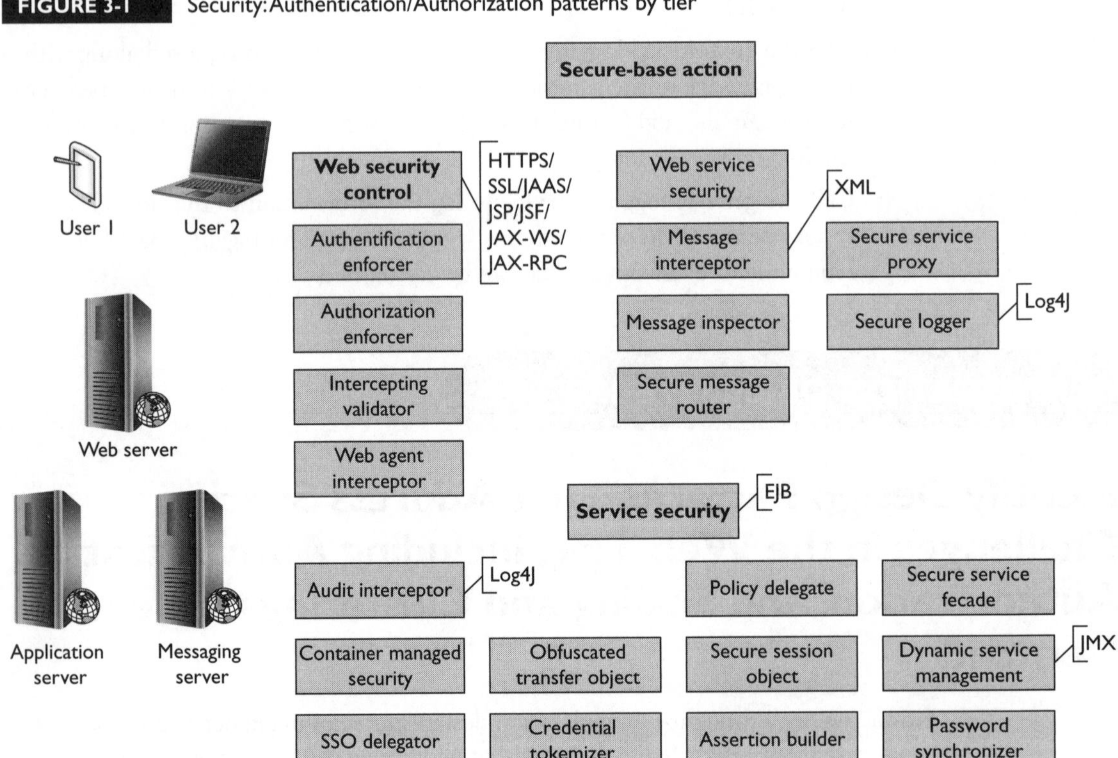

Web Tier Security Patterns

The following table details the web tier security patterns.

Pattern Name	Description
Authentication Enforcer	This pattern describes how a JEE-based application client should authenticate with a JEE application and how the application manages and delegates authentication processes. The solution is to create a single point of access to receive the interactions of a subject and apply a protocol to verify the identity of the subject. The application will then create a proof of identity if the subject is successfully authenticated.
Authorization Enforcer	This pattern describes how a JEE-based application client should authorize with a JEE application and how the application manages and delegates authorization. Indicate, in a suitable representation, who is authorized to access what and in what way. Specify policies to define all the needed access to resources.
Intercepting Validator	This pattern describes how a JEE-based application provides secure mechanisms for validating parameters. Unchecked parameters may lead to unintended command execution (for example, SQL injection attacks). The validation of application parameters includes all input data and their attributes, such as data type, format, length, and reasonableness. Apply filters declaratively based on URL, allowing different requests to be mapped to different filter chains. Restrict filter tasks to pre-processing of requests and providing validation (that is, a yes or no decision). Server-side validation is key, because client-side validation is potentially insecure. Renegotiate trust between users for long transactions. Record the volatility of the data.
Secure Logger	The pattern provides centralized control of logging functionality to be used throughout the application request and response. As suggested by the name, this pattern describes how to log the application events/exceptions in a secure/reliable way to facilitate auditing. It supports HTTP servlets, EJBs, SOAP/REST messages, and other designated events. The Secure Logger must log messages/events in a secure manner so that they cannot be altered or deleted.
Secure Pipe	A Secure Pipe pattern is used to guarantee that the data is not tampered with in transit to the Secure Store. That is to say, that the pattern implemented secures the connection between the client and the server. It adds value by requiring mutual authentication and establishing confidentiality or nonrepudiation between a specific client and server. This is important in the ever-expanding world of B2B integration using web services.
Secure Service Proxy	This pattern implemented secures and controls access to JEE components that provide web services endpoints/facade. It acts as a proxy/common interface to the underlying service provider components, thereby restricting direct access to the actual web services provider components.
Intercepting Web Agent	This pattern, when implemented, provides authentication, authorization, encryption, and auditing capabilities for controlling access from outside the application. The intercepting web agent installed on the server authenticates and determines authorization of incoming requests by intercepting them and enforcing access control policy at the web server level. Bottom line: isolate the application logic from security logic.

Business Tier Security Patterns

The following table details the business tier security patterns.

Pattern Name	Description
Audit Interceptor	An Audit Interceptor can be used to collect events that are stored by the secure logger, which provides instrumentation of the logging aspects. Audit Interceptor pattern enables the administration and manages the logging and audit in the back end, allowing for creation of audit events based on the information in the request/response pair using declarative mechanisms defined externally to the application. The declarative approach is crucial to maintainability of the application.
Container Managed Security	This pattern describes when and how to use standard security features provided by an application container to declare security-related information for users by defining application-level roles. It then performs a mapping of users and their application-level logical roles in the deployment environment (for example, EJBs in a deployment descriptor).
Dynamic Service Management	This pattern provides dynamically adjustable instrumentation of components for monitoring and active management and fine-grained instrumentation of business objects to prevent improper user action. This is done on an as-needed basis.
Obfuscated Transfer Object	This pattern describes ways of protecting business data represented in transfer objects and passed within/between tiers by obfuscating the data in the object that needs to be protected. The producers and consumers of data agree upon the sensitive data elements that need to be protected. This pattern must protect the data from any intermediary components. It potentially encrypts critical data using an agreed-upon key between the source and the target component.
Policy Delegate	This pattern administers security management policies governing how EJB tier objects are accessed and routed. Use a mediator to coordinate requests between clients and security services. Use the delegate to locate and mediate back-end security services. Perform pertinent message translation to accommodate disparate message formats and protocols.
Secure Service Facade	This pattern provides a session façade to centralize interactions between business components under a secure session. It provides dynamic and declarative security to back-end business objects in the service façade. It denies foreign entities attempting direct unauthorized service invocations. It integrates a fine-grained, security-unaware service implementation into a unified, security-enabled interface to clients. It uses a gateway where client requests are securely validated and routed to the appropriate fine-grained service implementation. It maintains and mediates the security and workflow context between client requests and fine-grained services that fulfill portions of client requests.
Secure Session Object	This pattern defines ways to secure session information in EJBs facilitating distributed access and seamless propagation of security context.

Services Tier Security Patterns

The following table details the services tier security patterns.

Pattern Name	Description
Message Inspector	This pattern checks for and verifies the quality of XML message-level security mechanisms, such as XML Signature and XML Encryption, in conjunction with a security token. The Message Inspector pattern also helps in verifying and validating applied security mechanisms in a SOAP message when processed by multiple intermediaries (actors). It supports a variety of signature formats and encryption technologies used by these intermediaries
Message Interceptor	This pattern provides a single entry point and allows centralization of security enforcement for incoming and outgoing messages. The security tasks include creating, modifying, and administering security policies for sending and receiving SOAP messages. It helps to apply transport-level and message-level security mechanisms required for securely communicating with a web services endpoint.
Secure Message Router	This pattern facilitates secure XML communication with multiple partner endpoints that adopt message-level security and identity-federation mechanisms. It acts as a security intermediary component that applies message-level security mechanisms to deliver messages to multiple recipients, where the intended recipient would be able to access only the required portion of the message and remaining message fragments are made confidential.

Identity Management and Service Provisioning

The following table details the identity management and service provisioning patterns.

Pattern Name	Description
Assertion Builder	This pattern defines how an identity assertion (for example, authentication assertion or authorization assertion) can be built.
Credential Tokenizer	This pattern describes how a principal's security token can be encapsulated, embedded in a SOAP message, routed, and processed.
Single Sign-On (SSO) Delegator	This pattern describes how to construct a delegator agent for handling a legacy system for Single Sign-On (SSO).
Password Synchronizer	This pattern describes how to securely synchronize principals across multiple applications using service provisioning.

Scaling and Clustering Patterns

High-use web applications such as Amazon, eBay, and online banking and billing require high availability (HA), whereas those large-scale systems such as Google ask for more scalability. JEE clustering provides high available and scalable services with fault tolerance.

Scalability

In some large-scale systems, it is hard to predict the number and behavior of end users. Scalability refers to a system's ability to support fast-increasing numbers of users. The intuitive way to scale up the number of concurrent sessions handled by a server is to add resources (memory, CPUs, or hard disks) to it. Clustering is an alternative way to resolve the scalability issue. It allows a group of servers to share the heavy tasks and operate as a single server logically.

Scalability refers to growing computing resources to support an application. There are two ways to scale: vertically and horizontally. Vertical scaling is where you grow a single server by adding RAM, CPU, and I/O resources and speed. Horizontal scaling is where you would add additional servers, load balancers, and so on.

High Availability

The single-server solution (add memory and CPU) to scalability is not a robust one because of its single point of failure. Those mission-critical applications (such as banking and billing) cannot tolerate service outage even for one single minute. It is required that those services are accessible with reasonable/predictable response times at any time. Clustering is a solution to achieve this kind of high availability by providing redundant servers in the cluster in case one server fails to provide service.

Load Balancing

Load balancing is one of the key technologies behind clustering, which is a way to obtain high availability and better performance by dispatching incoming requests to different servers. A load balancer can be anything from a simple servlet to expensive hardware with an SSL accelerator embedded in it. In addition to dispatching requests, a load balancer should perform some other important tasks, such as "session stickiness" to have a user session live entirely on one server and "health check" (or "heartbeat") to prevent dispatching requests to a failing server.

Fault Tolerance

Highly available data is not necessarily strictly correct data. In a JEE cluster, when a server instance fails, the service is still available, because new requests can be handled by other redundant server instances in the cluster. It is important to note that the requests that are "in flight" on the failed server may not get the correct data; whereas a "fault-tolerant" service always guarantees strictly correct behavior despite a certain number of faults.

Failover

Failover is another key technology behind clustering to achieve fault tolerance. By choosing another node in the cluster, the process will continue when the original node fails. Failing over to another node can be coded explicitly or performed automatically by the underlying platform, which transparently reroutes communication to another server.

JEE Clustering

JEE clustering technology includes load balancing and failover. Clustering in the web tier is the most important and fundamental function in JEE clustering. Web clustering technique includes web load balancing and HTTPSession failover.

Web Load Balancing

The JEE vendors achieve web load balancing in many ways. Basically, a load balancer intervenes between browsers and web servers. A load balancer could be a hardware product such as F5 load balancer, or it also could just be another web server with load-balancing plug-ins. The load balancer normally has the following features:

- **Implements load-balancing algorithms** When client requests come, the load balancer will decide how to dispatch the requests to the back-end server instances. Popular algorithms include round-robin, random, and weight based. The load balancer tries to achieve equal workload to every server instance, but none of these algorithms can really get ideal equality because they are all only based on the number of requests dispatched to a certain server instance. Some sophisticated load balancer implements special algorithm that will detect every server's workload before dispatching the requests to the servers.

- **Health check** When some server instance fails, the load balancer should detect this failure and never dispatch requests to it any more. The load balancer also needs to monitor when the failed server comes back and resume dispatching requests to it.
- **Session stickiness** Nearly every web application has some session state, which might be as simple as remembering whether you are logged in or the contents of your shopping cart. Because the HTTP protocol is itself stateless, session state needs to be stored somewhere and associated with your browsing session in a way that can be easily retrieved the next time you request a page from the same web application. When load balancing, it is the best choice to dispatch the request to the same server instance as the last time for a certain browser session. Otherwise, the application may not work properly. Because the session state is stored in the memory of certain web server instances, the feature of "session stickiness" is important for load balancing. However, if one of the server instances fails due to some reason such as powering off, all the session state in this server will get lost. The load balancer should detect this failure and won't dispatch any requests to it anymore. However, those requests whose session state was stored in the failed server will lose all the session information, which will cause errors.

HTTPSession Failover

Almost all popular JEE vendors implement HTTPSession failover in their cluster products to ensure that all client requests can be processed properly without losing any session state in case of the failure of some server instances. To realize the preceding functionality, the following issues should be addressed in HTTPSession failover implementations:

- **Global HTTPSession ID** An HTTPSession ID is used to identify an in-memory session object in a certain server instance uniquely. In JEE, HTTPSession ID depends on JVM instances. Every JVM instance can hold multiple web applications, and each of these applications can hold many HTTPSessions for different users. HTTPSession ID is the key to accessing the related session object in the current JVM instance. In session failover implementations, it is required that different JVM instances should not produce two identical HTTPSession IDs, because when failover happens, sessions in one JVM may be backed up and restored in another. Therefore, a global HTTPSession ID mechanism should be established.

- **How to back up session states** How to back up the session states is a key factor in making one JEE server special and stand out from the others. HTTPSession state backup has performance costs, including CPU cycles, network bandwidth, and I/O cost of writing to the disk or database. The frequency of backup operations and the granularity of backup objects will impact the performance of the cluster heavily.

Database Persistence Approach

JEE cluster products also let you choose to back up your session state to a relational database through the JPA/JDBC interface. The approach is simply to let server instances serialize the session contents and write to a database at the proper time. When failover happens, another available server instance takes the responsibility for the failed server, and it restores all session states from the database. Serialization of objects is the key point, which make the in-memory session data persistent and transportable.

Because database transactions are expensive, the main drawback of this approach is limited scalability when storing large or numerous objects in sessions. Most application servers that utilize database session persistence advocate minimal use of HTTPSessions to store objects, but this limits your web application's architecture and design, especially if you are using HTTPSession to store cached user data. The database approach has advantages:

- It's simple to implement. Because requests processing is separate from session backup processing, a cluster is more manageable and robust.
- A session can fail over to any other host because the database is shared.
- Session data can survive the failure of the entire cluster.

Memory Replication Approach

Memory-based session persistence stores session information in the memory of one or more backup servers instead of a database. This is a high-performance approach. Compared to the database approach, direct network communication between the original server and backup servers is really lightweight. Also note that in this approach, the "restore" phase in database persistence approach is not needed, because, after session backup, all session data is already in the backup servers' memory for the coming requests.

CERTIFICATION OBJECTIVE 3.04

Identify Java EE Technologies, Including JMS, JCA, and Web Services, and Design Patterns That Address Specific Challenges in Enterprise Integration

In Java EE, technologies including JMS, JCA, and Web Services provide a bridge or thoroughfare to connect disparate environments and pass data between them. We examine the when and how to use them in an enterprise architecture.

Java EE Technologies: JMS and Design Patterns In Enterprise Integration

In JEE, the Java Messaging Service (JMS) offers a generic way to access and integrate enterprise applications by exchanging messages. A message is a unit of serializable data exchanged between two or more distributed components running in the same machine or different machine. By using a message-oriented middleware (MOM) infrastructure, an application can create, send, and receive messages. This lets you combine separate business components into a reliable yet flexible system. There are two modes of communication, depending on the level of coupling between the sender and receiver:

- Synchronous
- Asynchronous

In synchronous mode, a distributed component sends a message via the MOM message queue to another component and waits for the reply to proceed further. The synchronous communication is "tightly coupled"—that is, both the sender and receiver know each other and rely on each other. The sender is responsible for retries in case of failures. This mode is typically used for transaction processing, where the sender needs the reliable response in real time (for example, stock purchase). When multiple messages are sent, they reach the destination in the same order in which they are sent. In asynchronous mode, the distributed component sends messages via the MOM message queue to the listening component and continues its processing without waiting for the response. This communication mechanism is "loosely coupled," where sender and receiver need not have specific knowledge about each other. Messages arrive at the destination but not necessarily in same order in which they are sent. MOM is responsible for retry in case of failure in the communication. The asynchronous communication is desirable if the sender wants to broadcast messages to multiple receivers efficiently to handle high-volume processing.

There are two types of messaging models, depending on whether you require one-to-one message delivery or a one-to-many broadcast delivery. With "point-to-point" messaging, the sender puts the messages into a destination queue. The receiver consumes the messages from the queue. A queue is designated to only one receiver. More than one sender can send the messages to a queue, but only one consumer receives those messages from the queue. The messages in the queue are processed on a first-in-first-out (FIFO) basis. The messages stay in the queue until they are consumed by the consumer or until their expiry time. A sender can also send the message directly to the consumer instead of placing it in the queue. A consumer can acknowledge the successful processing of the message.

EXERCISE 3-2

Publish/Subscribe Messaging

Question: If a "publish-subscribe" messaging application publishes the messages to a topic and some subscribers are not active, are the messages delivered to them?
Answer: There is a special type of subscription known as a "durable subscription," in which the messages will not be lost if the subscriber is not active. Rather, the messages are delivered once the subscriber becomes active.

Java EE Technologies: JCA and Design Patterns in Enterprise Integration

It is quite common for the enterprise to take legacy applications and apply web-enabling facades to these existing applications. Alternatively, they may be added to supply chains using business-to-business (B2B) software. These scenarios are best implemented as design patterns related to enterprise application integration (EAI) or integrating internal systems. The basic pattern is the adapter pattern. The logical definition of an application integration adapter is a software component that enables the adapted application to participate and function in one or more integration patterns without significant changes to the application. The primary integration patterns used must handle common requirements such as the following:

- Data synchronization
- Online services
- Process automation

This definition can be extended to include other integration patterns as they evolve. These three patterns are generic and cover most of the e-business technologies, including mobile computing, e-commerce, web services, business process automation, supply chain automation, data integrity, and business intelligence. The physical definition of the adapter depends on the technical environment and the specific adapter architecture. In the context of JEE, an adapter is known as a resource adapter, and must comply with the JCA specification.

Java EE Connector Architecture

Java EE Connector Architecture (JCA) is a Java-based technology solution for connecting application servers and enterprise information systems (EIS) as part of enterprise application integration (EAI) solutions. JCA is a generic architecture for connection to legacy systems. JCA was developed under the Java Community Process as JSR 16 (JCA 1.0), JSR 112 (JCA 1.5), and JSR 322 (JCA 1.6). Java EE version 6 requires application servers to support JCA version 1.6.

Contracts

The Java EE Connector Architecture defines a standard for connecting a compliant application server to an EIS. It defines a standard set of system-level contracts between the Java EE application server and a resource adapter. The system contracts of the Java EE Connector Architecture are described by the specification as follows:

- **Connection management** Connection management enables an application server to pool connections to the underlying EIS and enables application components to connect. This leads to a scalable application environment that can support a large number of clients.
- **Transaction management** Transaction management enables an application server to use a transaction manager to manage transactions across multiple resource managers. This contract also supports transactions that are managed internal to an EIS resource manager without the necessity of involving an external transaction manager.

- **Security management** Security management reduces security threats to the EIS and protects valuable information resources managed by the EIS.
- **Life cycle management** Life cycle management enables an application server to manage the life cycle of a resource adapter from initiation through upgrades to obsolescence. This contract provides a mechanism for the application server to bootstrap a resource adapter instance during its deployment or application server startup, and to notify the resource adapter instance during its un-deployment/removal or during an orderly shutdown.
- **Work management** Work management enables a resource adapter to do work (monitor network endpoints, invoke application components, and so on) by submitting work instances to an application server for execution. The application server dispatches threads to execute submitted work instances. This allows a resource adapter to avoid creating or managing threads directly, and allows an application server to efficiently pool threads and have more control over its run-time environment. The resource adapter can control the transaction context with which work instances are executed.
- **Transaction inflow management** Transaction inflow management enables a resource adapter to propagate an imported transaction to an application server. This contract also allows a resource adapter to transmit transaction completion and crash recovery calls initiated by an EIS, and ensures that the Atomicity, Consistency, Isolation, and Durability (ACID) properties of the imported transaction are preserved.
- **Message inflow management** Message inflow management enables a resource adapter to asynchronously deliver messages to message endpoints residing in the application server, independent of the specific messaging style, messaging semantics, and messaging infrastructure used to deliver messages. This contract also serves as the standard message provider pluggability contract that allows a wide range of message providers—Java Message Service (JMS), Java API for XML Messaging (JAXM), and so on—to be plugged into any Java EE–compatible application server with a resource adapter.

EIS Integration

JCA adapters can be built to integrate with various enterprise information systems, such SAP AG, Oracle Applications, and so on. SAP provides an interface for Java called SAP Java Connector.

Java EE Technologies: Web Services and Design Patterns in Enterprise Integration

Web services are client and server applications that communicate via HTTP. Web services provide a standard means of interoperating between software applications running on a variety of platforms and frameworks. Web services are characterized by their interoperability and extensibility. Web services can be combined in a loosely coupled way to achieve complex operations. Web services make it relatively easy to reuse and share common logic with such diverse clients as mobile, desktop, and web applications. The broad reach of web services is possible because they rely on open standards that are ubiquitous, interoperable across different computing platforms, and independent of the underlying execution technologies. All web services, at the very least, use HTTP and leverage data-interchange standards, such as XML and JSON, and common media types. Beyond that, web services use HTTP in two distinct ways. Some use it as an application protocol to define standard service behaviors. Others simply use HTTP as a transport mechanism to convey data. Regardless, web services facilitate rapid application integration because, when compared to their predecessors, they tend to be much easier to learn and implement. Due to their inherent interoperability and simplicity, web services facilitate the creation of complex business processes through service composition. This is a practice in which compound services can be created by assembling simpler services into workflows.

Before making everything a service, an architect might consider alternatives. In some cases, it may be better to create "service libraries" (for example, JARs or .NET assemblies) that can be imported, called, and executed from within the client's process. Even if the client and service have been created for different platforms (for example, Java and .NET), there are techniques that enable disparate clients and services to collaborate from within the same process. That said, these options are complex and their use may prolong the tight coupling to the service's technologies. Web services are ideal, however, for fast-tracking B2B and B2C transactions. Here are some examples:

- The client and service belong to different application domains and the "service functions" cannot be easily imported into the client.
- The client is a complex business process that incorporates functions from multiple application domains. The logical services are owned and managed by different organizations and change at different rates.

- The divide between the client and server is natural. The client may, for example, be a mobile or desktop application that uses common business functions. Developers would be wise to consider alternatives to web services even when cross-machine calls seem justified.
- MOM (for example, MSMQ, WebSphere MQ, Apache ActiveMQ, and so on) can be used to integrate applications. These technologies, however, are best reserved for use within a secured environment, far behind the corporate firewall. Furthermore, they require the adoption of an asynchronous communications style that forces all parties to tackle several new design challenges. MOM solutions often use proprietary technologies that are platform specific.

Services and Loose Coupling

Web services often forward requests to MOM. A certain amount of overhead should be expected with HTTP due to the time it takes for clients and servers to establish connections. This added time may not be acceptable in certain high-performance/high-load scenarios. Most web service frameworks can be configured to stream data. This helps to minimize memory utilization on both the sender's and receiver's end because data doesn't have to be buffered. Response times are also minimized because the receiver can consume the data as it arrives rather than having to wait for the entire dataset to be transferred. However, this option is best used for the transfer of large documents or messages rather than for real-time delivery of large multimedia files such as video and audio.

RESTful Web Services

Representational State Transfer (REST) is an architectural style that specifies constraints, such as the uniform interface, that if applied to a web service induce desirable properties, such as performance, scalability, and modifiability that enable services to work best on the Web. In the REST architectural style, data and functionality are considered resources and are accessed using Uniform Resource Identifiers (URIs), typically links on the Web. The resources are acted upon by using a set of simple, well-defined operations. The REST architectural style constrains architecture to a client/server architecture and is designed to use a stateless communication protocol, typically HTTP. In the REST architecture style, clients and servers exchange representations of resources by using a standardized interface and protocol.

The following principles encourage RESTful applications to be simple, lightweight, and fast:

- **Resource identification through URI** A RESTful web service exposes a set of resources that identify the targets of the interaction with its clients. Resources are identified by URIs, which provide a global addressing space for resource and service discovery.
- **Uniform interface** Resources are manipulated using a fixed set of four Create, Read, Update, Delete (CRUD) operations: PUT, GET, POST, and DELETE. PUT creates a new resource, which can be then deleted via DELETE. GET retrieves the current state of a resource in some representation. POST transfers a new state onto a resource.
- **Self-descriptive messages** Resources are decoupled from their representation so that their content can be accessed in a variety of formats, such as HTML, XML, plain text, PDF, JPEG, JSON, and others. Metadata about the resource is available and used, for example, to control caching, detect transmission errors, negotiate the appropriate representation format, and perform authentication or access control.
- **Stateful interactions through hyperlinks** Every interaction with a resource is stateless; that is, request messages are self-contained. Stateful interactions are based on the concept of explicit state transfer. Several techniques exist to exchange state, such as URI rewriting, cookies, and hidden form fields. State can be embedded in response messages to point to valid future states of the interaction.

Developing RESTful Web Services with JAX-RS

JAX-RS is a Java programming language API designed to develop applications that use the REST architecture. The JAX-RS API uses Java programming language annotations for the development of RESTful web services. Developers decorate Java programming language class files with JAX-RS annotations to define resources and the actions that can be performed on those resources. JAX-RS annotations are run-time annotations; therefore, run-time reflection will generate the helper classes and artifacts for the resource. A Java EE application archive containing JAX-RS resource classes will have the resources configured, the helper classes and artifacts generated, and the resource exposed to clients by deploying the archive to a Java EE server. A design methodology for REST might include the following steps:

- Identify resources to be exposed as services (for example, yearly risk report, book catalog, purchase order, open bugs, polls, and votes).
- Model relationships (for example, containment, reference, and state transitions) between resources with hyperlinks that can be followed to get more details (or perform state transitions).
- Define URIs to address the resources.
- Understand what it means to do a GET, POST, PUT, DELETE for each resource (and whether it is allowed or not).
- Design and document resource representations.
- Implement and deploy on web server.

CERTIFICATION OBJECTIVE 3.05

Identify the Challenges in Integrating Enterprise Resources, the Java EE Technologies That Address Them (Including JPA and JDBC), and the Communication Protocols That Support Tier-to-Tier Communication (Including RMI, IIOP, and CORBA)

The integration of enterprise resources is any viable approach to providing interoperability between the multiple disparate systems that make up a typical enterprise infrastructure. Enterprise architectures for most established business entities typically consist of many systems and applications, which provide services the enterprise relies upon to conduct their day-to-day business. The typical enterprise uses separate systems (for example, Oracle and DB2, Java and .Net, and so on), either developed in-house or licensed from a third-party vendor, to manage their various subject area systems and business logic. This results from the fact that a business (for example, a Wall Street brokerage) consists of multiple smaller businesses with similar but distinct functionalities, where the management in each area chooses what they believe is the best technology for their changing business needs.

Integration of Enterprise Resources

To benefit from these distributed systems, an enterprise must implement technologies that handle the downside of this architecture:

- **Interoperability** The various components of the infrastructure may use different operating systems, data formats, and languages, thus preventing connection via a standard interface.
- **Data integration** In order for a distributed system to be functional, a standard method of handling the flow of data between applications and systems to enforce consistency across the database is crucial.
- **Robustness, stability, and scalability** Because they are the glue that holds together a modular infrastructure, integration solutions must be highly robust, stable, and scalable.

Prior to the development of Enterprise Integration–type approaches, the problems of integration were largely handled using point-to-point integration. In the old point-to-point integration model, a connection component was implemented for each application pair so that they could communicate. This connector handles all data transformation, integration, and any other messaging-related services that must take place between only the specific pair of components it is designed to integrate. When and where only a few systems must be integrated, this model can work, providing a simple "tightly coupled" integration solution tailor-made to the needs of the infrastructure. However, as additional components are added to an infrastructure, the number of point-to-point connections required to create a comprehensive integration architecture begins to increase exponentially. A three-component infrastructure requires only three point-to-point connections to be considered fully integrated. By comparison, the addition of just two more components increases this number to 10 connectors. This is already approaching an unmanageable level of complexity, and once an infrastructure includes eight or nine component systems, and the number of connections jumps into the thirties, point-to-point integration is no longer a viable option. This obviously is unsustainable as each of these connectors must be separately developed and maintained across system version changes, making it unsuitable for complex enterprise environments.

In today's enterprise, valuable data and vital business logic code are locked away in different applications, platforms, and databases. The challenge is flexibility and the ability to respond rapidly to change. As enterprises expand, they need to build new systems, integrate different and disbursed applications, and to update applications to take advantage of emerging technologies and opportunities. Java introduces many standards, including Java RMI, JDBC, JPA, JMS, JNDI, and Java IDL for CORBA. These standards are all applicable integrating enterprise resources in that they provide a Java-enabled infrastructure. They are database oriented (JDBC and JPA), interprocess capable (Java RMI), message oriented (JMS to ESB), and distributed object technology (Java RMI and Java IDL).

JDBC

Java Database Connectivity (JDBC) is an application programming interface (API) that allows the programmer to connect and interact with databases. It provides methods to query and update data in the database through update statements such as SQL's CREATE, UPDATE, DELETE, and INSERT and query statements such as SELECT. Additionally, JDBC can run stored procedures. The JDBC API uses Java standard classes and interfaces to connect to databases. In order to use JDBC to connect Java applications to a specific database server, a JDBC driver that supports the JDBC API for that database server is required. To establish a connection between the Java application and the database, JDBC needs to load a driver and create a connection to the target database using the URL and credentials.

JPA

The Java Persistence Architecture (JPA) API is a Java specification for accessing, persisting, and managing data between Java objects/classes and a relational database. JPA was defined as part of the EJB 3.0 specification as a replacement for the EJB 2 CMP Entity Beans specification. JPA is the standard industry approach for Object Relational Mapping (ORM). JPA itself is a specification. JPA is a set of interfaces and requires an implementation. There are open-source and commercial JPA implementations to choose from, and any Java EE 6 application server will provide support for its use. Obviously, JPA requires a target database to persist data. JPA allows Plain Old Java Objects to be persisted without requiring the classes to implement any interfaces or methods as the complex EJB 2 CMP specification required. JPA allows an object's Object Relational Mappings to be defined through standard annotations or XML defining how the Java class maps to a relational database table. JPA also defines a run-time EntityManager API for processing queries and transactions on the objects against the database. JPA defines an object-level query language, JPQL, to allow querying of the objects from the database.

CORBA

The Common Object Request Broker Architecture (CORBA) enables separate pieces of software written in different languages and running on different computers to work with each other like a single application or set of services. CORBA provides a mechanism in software for normalizing the method-call semantics between application objects residing either in the same address space (application) or in remote address spaces. CORBA uses an interface definition language (IDL) to specify the interfaces that objects present to the outer world. CORBA then specifies a mapping from IDL to a specific implementation language such as C++ or Java. Standard mappings exist for Java and many other languages linking C and Python. There are also nonstandard mappings for Perl implemented by object request brokers (ORBs) written for those languages. The CORBA specification dictates that there shall be an ORB through which an application would interact with other objects.

RMI

RMI denotes the Java Remote Method Invocation interface over the Internet Inter-Orb Protocol (IIOP), which delivers Common Object Request Broker Architecture (CORBA) distributed computing capabilities to the Java platform. It was initially based on two specifications: the Java Language Mapping to OMG IDL, and CORBA/IIOP 2.3.1.

With features inherited from CORBA, software components that work together can be written in multiple computer languages and run on multiple computers. In other words, it supports multiple platforms and can make remote procedure calls to execute subroutines on another computer as defined by RMI.

IIOP

IOP (Internet Inter-ORB Protocol) is a protocol that makes it possible for distributed programs written in different programming languages to communicate over the Internet. IIOP is part of an industry standard CORBA. Using IIOP, one can write programs to communicate with their company's programs wherever they are located and without anything other than program service(s) and a name. CORBA and IIOP assume the client/server model of computing, in which a client program always makes requests and a server program waits to receive requests from clients. For a client to make a request of a program somewhere in a network, it must have an address for the program. This address is known as the Interoperable Object Reference (IOR). Using IIOP, part of the address is based on the server's port number and IP address.

The Evolution of Enterprise Integration

To avoid the complexity and fallibility of integrating complex infrastructures using a point-to-point approach, Enterprise Integration solutions use various models of middleware to centralize and standardize integration practices across an entire infrastructure. Rather than each application requiring a separate connector to connect to every other connector, components in an Enterprise Integration–based infrastructure use standardized methods to connect to a common system that is responsible for providing integration, message brokering, and reliability functionalities to the entire network. Enterprise Integration systems bundle together adapters for connectivity, data transformation engines to convert data to an appropriate format for use by the consumer, modular integration engines to handle many different complex routing scenarios simultaneously, and other components to present a unified integration solution. Enterprise Integration creates "loosely coupled" connections to eliminate the tightly coupled connections of point-to-point integration. An application can send a message without any knowledge of the consumer's location, data requirements, or use for the message. This allows for flexible architecture, where new components can be added and removed as needed, simply by changing the configuration of the Enterprise Integration provider, and simplified modular development, where a single service can be reused by multiple applications. Many modern Enterprise Integration approaches also take advantage of the opportunity presented by adding a central integration mechanism to further consolidate messaging tasks. In addition to data integration, a modern Enterprise Integration may also include functionalities such as network administration, security, and scalability.

Enterprise Service Bus

The broker model of Enterprise Integration was successfully implemented by some companies, but the vast majority of integration projects using this model ultimately failed. The lack of clear standards for Enterprise Integration architecture and the fact that most early solutions were proprietary meant that early Enterprise Integration products were expensive, heavyweight, and sometimes did not work as intended unless a system was fairly homogenous. The effects of these problems were amplified by the fact that the broker model made the Enterprise Integration system a single point of failure for the network. A malfunctioning component meant total failure for the entire network. To move away from the problems caused by a brokered hub-and-spoke Enterprise Integration approach, a new Enterprise Integration model emerged—the bus. Although it still used a central routing component to pass messages from system to system, the bus architecture sought to lessen the burden of functionality placed on a single component by distributing some of the integration tasks to other parts of the network. These components could then be grouped in various configurations via configuration files to handle any integration scenario in the most efficient way possible, and could be hosted anywhere within the infrastructure or duplicated for scalability across large geographic regions. As bus-based Enterprise Integration evolved, a number of other necessary functionalities were identified, such as security transaction processing, error handling, and more. Rather than requiring hard-coding these features into the central integration logic, as would have been required by a broker architecture, the bus architecture allowed these functions to be enclosed in separate components. The ultimate result is a lightweight, tailor-made integration solutions with guaranteed reliability that are fully abstracted from the application layer, follow a consistent pattern, and can be designed and configured with minimal additional code with no modification to the systems that need to be integrated. This mature version of the bus-based Enterprise Integration model eventually came to be known as the Enterprise Service Bus (ESB).

ESB Features

Most ESBs include all or most of the following core features (or "services"):

- **Location transparency** A way of centrally configuring endpoints for messages, so that a consumer application does not require information about a message producer in order to receive messages.
- **Transformation** The ability of the ESB to convert messages into a format that is usable by the consumer application.
- **Protocol conversion** Similar to the transformation requirement, the ESB must be able to accept messages sent in all major protocols, and convert them to the format required by the end consumer.
- **Routing** The ability to determine the appropriate end consumer or consumers based on both preconfigured rules and dynamically created requests.
- **Enhancement** The ability to retrieve missing data in an incoming message, based on the existing message data, and append it to the message before delivery to its final destination.
- **Monitoring/administration** The goal of ESB is to make integration a simple task. As such, an ESB must provide an easy method of monitoring the performance of the system, the flow of messages through the ESB architecture, and a simple means of managing the system in order to deliver its proposed value to an infrastructure.

- **Security** ESB security involves two main components—making sure the ESB itself handles messages in a fully secure manner, and negotiating between the security assurance systems used by each of the systems that will be integrated.

ESB Architectural Benefits

Here's a look at the advantages offered by an ESB approach to application integration:

- **Lightweight** Because an ESB is made up of many interoperating services, rather than a single hub that contains every possible service, ESBs can be as heavy or light as an organization needs them to be, making them the most efficient integration solution available.
- **Easy to expand** If an organization knows that they will need to connect additional applications or systems to their architecture in the future, an ESB allows them to integrate their systems right away, instead of worrying about whether or not a new system will work with their existing infrastructure. When the new application is ready, all the organization needs to do to get it working with the rest of their infrastructure is hook it up to the bus.
- **Scalable and distributable** Unlike broker architectures, ESB functionality can easily be dispersed across a geographically distributed network as needed. Additionally, because individual components are used to offer each feature, it is much simpler and cost-effective to ensure high availability and scalability for critical parts of the architecture when using an ESB solution.
- **SOA friendly** ESBs are built with Service-Oriented Architecture in mind. This means that an organization seeking to migrate toward an SOA can do so incrementally, continuing to use their existing systems while plugging in reusable services as they implement them.
- **Incremental adoption** At first glance, the number of features offered by the best ESBs can seem intimidating. However, it's best to think of the ESB as an integration "platform," of which you only need to use the components that meet your current integration needs. The large number of modular components offers unrivaled flexibility that allows incremental adoption of an integration architecture as the resources become available, while guaranteeing that unexpected needs in the future will not prevent ROI.

Enterprise Integration Architectural Decisions

All integration solutions have strengths and weaknesses, which are often dependent on the environment in which they are deployed. For this reason, making informed decisions about your Enterprise Integration strategy is vital to the success of your integration initiative.

In order for your Enterprise Integration and SOA efforts to be successful, you don't just need the "best" technology around—you need hard facts about the product's intended use scenario, performance under load, maturity, and a deep understanding of the present and future integration challenges your organization must overcome.

Before you make a decision about Enterprise Integration, it's important to have a good idea of how you would answer questions like these:

- How many applications do I need to integrate?
- Will I need to add additional applications in the future?
- How many communication protocols will I need to use?
- Do my integration needs include routing, forking, or aggregation?
- How important is scalability to my organization?
- Does my integration situation require asynchronous messaging, publish/consume messaging models, or other complex multi-application messaging scenarios?

The benefits of an ESB include:

- Firm-wide integration on a common system
- Improves internal communications
- Reduces or eliminates manual processes
- Enables higher availability of systems
- Integrated workflow, industry best practices, and reduced dependence on paper
- Reduces or eliminates the need for backup or shadow systems
- Platform for reengineering business practices and continued process improvements
- Develops and maintains consistent data definitions
- Increases data integrity, validity, and reliability
- Assures system-wide security and protection of confidential information
- Creates a more seamless integration between technologies

ESB products swept onto the scene as the latest generation of enterprise application integration technology and a replacement for older message-oriented middleware. ESBs have become the foundation for Service-Oriented Architecture (SOA) deployments.

CERTIFICATION SUMMARY

In this chapter we reviewed the following:

- Strategies for deploying client applications to desktop and mobile platforms
- The principles for designing a user interface and the benefits of applying client tier patterns
- The best practices for exception handling, logging, and business tier patterns
- The design patterns that address the web tier authentication, authorization, scaling, and clustering
- Java EE JMS, JCA, and Web Services as well as design patterns; these are techniques that address enterprise integration
- JPA and JDBC and the tier-to-tier communication protocols.

These "common architectures" are the glue that binds Enterprise Applications.

TWO-MINUTE DRILL

Identify the Appropriate Strategy for Deploying Client Applications to Desktop and Mobile Platforms, the Principles for Designing a User Interface and the Benefits of Applying Client Tier Patterns

- ❑ Create a set of user interface design guidelines that establishes the style and method of presentation and interaction components for the enterprise.
- ❑ Within the UI guidelines include the design principles:
  - ❑ **Visibility** Clarity of the visual goal.
  - ❑ **Feedback** Make it clear what action has been achieved.
  - ❑ **Affordance** Make it clear how a UI element should be used.
  - ❑ **Simplicity** Employ UI controls, icons, and words that are comfortable for the user.
  - ❑ **Structure** The UI will be more usable if it is structured in way that is meaningful and useful to user.
  - ❑ **Consistency** Consistent visual patterns, navigation, appearance, positioning, and behavior within the UI make a system easy to learn and remember.
  - ❑ **Tolerance** Design the UI to prevent errors if possible, or to make them easy to recover from if not.
- ❑ Rich Internet Application (RIA) frameworks facilitate development for multiple browsers by providing browser-specific JavaScript source code generation and browser-specific JavaScript libraries with ECMA Script interfaces.
- ❑ Within the client tier, the emergence and comprehensive functionality imbedded in HTML5/CSS makes the browser the interface of choice.
- ❑ For iOS- and Android-based applications, each environment should have the methodology to facilitate acquiring, distributing, securing, and tracking mobile applications. Mobile Device Management (MDM) solutions are needed to manage internal, public, and purchased applications across employee-owned (BYOD), enterprise-supplied, and shared devices from a central administrative console.

Identify Best Practices for Exception Handling, Logging, and Business Tier Patterns

- Exception handling is a programming language construct designed to handle the occurrence of some condition/exception that changes the normal flow of execution.
- Two types of exceptions can occur:
  - **Process exception** This occurs when there is a problem with one of the components used by a process or service. Process exceptions are often caused due to temporary errors such as connectivity failures, timeouts, and basic code failures.
  - **Business exception** This is an exception that occurs due to the outcome of a decision in the process. The actual process internally triggers this type of fault. A business exception is designed as part of a business process and is raised by the business process if the process cannot proceed due to:
    - Data validation failure
    - Insufficient privileges
    - Known business conditions for which the process should be put on hold
- An exception-handling solution approach should give the user a facility to handle these two types of exception independently:
  - If an exception is a system-level error, handle the error at the process level so that the exception can be caught in the process level.
  - If a process-level exception occurs, route it to the support group. The support group can view the error and act accordingly.
- An approach to logging that has been successful in a number of enterprises includes the following requirements/factors:
  - Define a logging object template that contains date, time, name of component, error message, and other pertinent information.
  - Develop a generic logging service that can be invoked from every application.
  - Ensure that all applications call the generic logging service when they encounter an exception.

- The logging needs to take into consideration requirements if they are already standardized or structured at the enterprise level.
- Consider the amount of data required in the log (time, event, and user information) or additional information such as payload, custom messages, and so on.
- The level of logging can vary from process to process based on the urgency and needs of the process.
- The logging data storage can be file based or database based, subject to requirements.
- There can be an additional need for logging intimation, which can be in the form of an e-mail to the support group to study the log if or when it is needed.
- If a certain threshold is reached, consider backing up the logging files.

Identify Design Patterns That Address Specific Challenges in the Web Tier, Including Authentication, Authorization, and Scaling and Clustering to Meet Demand

- Web tier Auth/Auth patterns:
  - Authentication Enforcer
  - Authorization Enforcer
  - Intercepting Validator
  - Secure Logger
  - Secure Pipe
  - Secure Service Proxy
  - Intercepting Web Agent
- Scaling and clustering patterns:
  - High Availability
  - Load balancing
  - Fault Tolerance
  - Failover

Identify Java EE Technologies, Including JMS, JCA, and Web Services, and Design Patterns That Address Specific Challenges in Enterprise Integration

- Java Messaging Service (JMS) offers a generic way to access and integrate enterprise applications by exchanging messages. There are two modes of communication, depending on the level of coupling between the sender and receiver:
  - Synchronous
  - Asynchronous
- In JMS, there are two types of messaging models, depending on whether you require one-to-one message delivery or a one-to-many broadcast delivery.
- Java EE Connector Architecture (JCA) is a Java-based technology solution for connecting application servers and enterprise information systems (EIS) as part of enterprise application integration (EAI) solutions. JCA is a generic architecture for connection to legacy systems.
- Web services are client and server applications that communicate via HTTP. Web services provide a standard means of interoperating between software applications running on a variety of platforms and frameworks.
- All web services, at the very least, use HTTP and leverage data-interchange standards, such as XML and JSON, and common media types. Beyond that, web services use HTTP in two distinct ways. Some use it as an application protocol to define standard service behaviors. Others simply use HTTP as a transport mechanism to convey data.

Identify the Challenges in Integrating Enterprise Resources, the Java EE Technologies That Address Them (Including JPA and JDBC), and the Communication Protocols That Support Tier-to-Tier Communication (Including RMI, IIOP, and CORBA)

- The integration of enterprise resources is any viable approach to providing interoperability between the multiple disparate systems that make up a typical enterprise infrastructure.

- Java Database Connectivity (JDBC) is an application programming interface (API) that allows the programmer to connect and interact with databases. It provides methods to query and update data in the database through update statements such as SQL's CREATE, UPDATE, DELETE, and INSERT and query statements such as SELECT.
- The Java Persistence Architecture API (JPA) is a Java specification for accessing, persisting, and managing data between Java objects/classes and a relational database. JPA was defined as part of the EJB 3.0 specification as a replacement for the EJB 2 CMP Entity Beans specification. JPA is the standard industry approach for Object Relational Mapping (ORM).
- The Common Object Request Broker Architecture (CORBA) enables separate pieces of software written in different languages and running on different computers to work with each other like a single application or set of services. CORBA provides a mechanism in software for normalizing the method-call semantics between application objects residing either in the same address space (application) or in remote address spaces. CORBA uses an interface definition language (IDL) to specify the interfaces that objects present to the outer world. CORBA then specifies a mapping from IDL to a specific implementation language such as C++ or Java.
- RMI denotes the Java Remote Method Invocation (RMI) interface over the Internet Inter-Orb Protocol (IIOP), which delivers CORBA-distributed computing capabilities to the Java platform.
- IOP (Internet Inter-ORB Protocol) is a protocol that makes it possible for distributed programs written in different programming languages to communicate over the Internet. IIOP is part of an industry-standard CORBA.

SELF TEST

The following questions will help you measure your understanding of the material presented in this chapter. Read all the choices carefully because there may be more than one correct answer. Choose all correct answers for each question.

Identify the Appropriate Strategy for Deploying Client Applications to Desktop and Mobile Platforms, the Principles for Designing a User Interface and the Benefits of Applying Client Tier Patterns

1. In contrast to the other tiers of an Enterprise Architecture, the client tier is most successful when:

A. End users have a positive experience with the user interface.

B. All of the web browser types are supported.

C. Response time is less than a second for every screen.

D. A Model-View-Controller pattern is used.

2. Which of the following roles are key for the development of the client tier?

A. User interface designer

B. Network engineer

C. Graphic artist

D. Database architect

3. With respect to the UI design principles, "affordance" means:

A. Making it clear what action has been achieved

B. Designing the UI to prevent errors, if possible, or to make them easy to recover from if not

C. Making it clear how a UI element should be used

D. Clarity of the visual goal

4. With respect to the UI design principles, "feedback" means:

A. Making it clear what action has been achieved

B. Designing the UI to prevent errors, if possible, or to make them easy to recover from, if not

C. Making it clear how a UI element should be used

D. Clarity of the visual goal

5. Rich Internet Application (RIA) frameworks facilitate development for multiple browsers by:
   A. Providing browser-specific JavaScript source code generation and browser-specific JavaScript libraries with ECMA Script interfaces
   B. Offering the ability to run client applications within a confined Java Virtual Machine (JVM) Security Manager

Identify Best Practices for Exception Handling, Logging, and Business Tier Patterns

6. A business exception is one that occurs due to the outcome of a decision in the process and not a code or component failure. The actual process internally triggers this type of fault.
   A. True
   B. False
7. A process exception is often caused due to temporary errors such as connectivity failures, timeouts, or basic code failures.
   A. True
   B. False
8. From an EJB perspective, a process exception can be:
   A. OutOfMemoryError
   B. NullPointerException
   C. Database row not found
   D. ArrayOutOfBoundsException
9. When an exception occurs in a well-designed production application, the end user should be provided with which of the following?
   A. A clear message indicating that an error has occurred
   B. An error confirmation/tag number that they can use upon accessing a readily available customer support system
   C. A phone call from a member of the support team
   D. Quick resolution of the problem, and the assurance that their request has been processed, or will be processed within a set timeframe

Identify Design Patterns That Address Specific Challenges in the Web Tier, Including Authentication, Authorization, and Scaling and Clustering to Meet Demand

10. The Intercepting Validator describes how a JEE-based application provides secure mechanisms for validating parameters.

A. True

B. False

11. A Secure Pipe pattern is used to guarantee authentication, authorization, encryption, and auditing capabilities outside the application.

A. True

B. False

12. The Authorization Enforcer pattern secures and controls access to JEE components that provide web service endpoints/façade.

A. True

B. False

13. Adaptability refers to a system's ability to support fast-increasing numbers of users.

A. True

B. False

14. To scale up the number of concurrent sessions handled by a server:

A. Add memory and disk

B. Allow a group of servers to share the heavy tasks and operate as a single server logically

C. Add CPU

D. Switch the machine's OS to Windows

15. Fault tolerance means dispatching incoming requests to different servers.

A. True

B. False

16. With respect to round-robin, random, and weight based, which statements are true?

A. These are different types of database optimizers.

B. These are different types of clustering algorithms.

C. These are different types of load-balancing algorithms.

D. These are different types of health check algorithms.

Identify Java EE Technologies, Including JMS, JCA, and Web Services, and Design Patterns That Address Specific Challenges in Enterprise Integration

17. Java Messaging Service (JMS) messaging modes include which of the following?

A. Synchronous

B. Push

C. Store and forward

D. Asynchronous

E. Pull

18. JCA is a generic architecture for connecting to legacy systems.

A. True

B. False

Identify the Challenges in Integrating Enterprise Resources, the Java EE Technologies That Address Them (Including JPA and JDBC), and the Communication Protocols That Support Tier-to-Tier Communication (Including RMI, IIOP, and CORBA)

19. Java Database Connectivity (JDBC) is an application programming interface (API) that allows the programmer to connect and interact with databases using statements, including which of the following?

A. INSERT

B. DELETE

C. UPSERT

D. SELECT

20. Java Database Connectivity (JDBC) is a Java specification for accessing, persisting, and managing data between Java objects/classes and a relational database.

A. True

B. False

SELF TEST ANSWERS

Identify the Appropriate Strategy for Deploying Client Applications to Desktop and Mobile Platforms, the Principles for Designing a User Interface and the Benefits of Applying Client-Tier Patterns

1. ☑ **A** and **C.** The client tier user interface and response time are most important
☒ **B** and **D** are incorrect. The client tier does not necessarily dictate the use of a browser, and the MVC pattern does not dictate how successful the client tier will be.

2. ☑ **A** and **C.** The client tier relies on the user interface designer and to some degree the graphic artist. These roles are key to the development of the client tier.
☒ **B** and **D** are incorrect. The network engineer and database architect do not dictate how successful the client tier will be.

3. ☑ **C.** Affordance means making it clear how a UI element should be used.
☒ **A, B,** and **D** are incorrect. Feedback means making it clear what action has been achieved. Tolerance means designing the UI to prevent errors if possible, or to make them easy to recover from. Visibility is clarity of the visual goal.

4. ☑ **A.** Feedback means making it clear to the user what action has been achieved.
☒ **B, C,** and **D** are incorrect. Affordance is making it clear how a UI element should be used. Tolerance means you design the UI to prevent errors if possible, or to make them easy to recover from. Visibility is clarity of the visual goal.

5. ☑ **A.** Rich Internet Application (RIA) frameworks facilitate development for multiple browsers by providing browser-specific JavaScript source code generation and browser-specific JavaScript libraries with ECMA Script interfaces.
☒ **B** is incorrect. Java applets offer the ability to run client applications within a confined Java Virtual Machine (JVM) Security Manager, often referred to as a sandbox.

Identify Best Practices for Exception Handling, Logging, and Business Tier Patterns

6. ☑ **A.** True, a business exception is one that occurs due to the outcome of a decision in the process. The actual process internally triggers this type of fault. A business exception is designed as part of a business process and is raised by the business process if the process cannot proceed.
☒ **B** is incorrect. This statement is false.

7. ☑ **A.** True, a process exception occurs when there is a problem with one of the components used by a process or service. Process exceptions are often caused due to temporary errors such as connectivity failures, timeouts, and basic code failures.
   ☒ B is incorrect. This statement is false.

8. ☑ **A, B,** and **D.** An OutOfMemoryError is a common JVM process exception. Likewise, a NullPointerException or an ArrayOutOfBoundsException will be thrown due to a code fault, and these are also process exceptions.
   ☒ C is incorrect. A "Database row not found" is a system exception and it should be thrown as an unchecked exception.

9. ☑ **A, B,** and **D.** A clear message, a confirmation, and a quick resolution of the problem, as well as the assurance that the user's request has been processed, or will be processed within a set time frame, are all practical ways of handling exceptions.
   ☒ C is incorrect. This option is impractical because it would be expensive and not as efficient as the other choices.

Identify Design Patterns That Address Specific Challenges in the Web Tier, Including Authentication, Authorization, and Scaling and Clustering to Meet Demand

10. ☑ **A.** True, the Intercepting Validator pattern describes how a JEE-based application provides secure mechanisms for validating parameters. Unchecked parameters may lead to unintended command execution (for example, SQL injection attacks). The validation of application parameters includes all input data and their attributes, such as data type, format, length, and reasonableness.
    ☒ B is incorrect. This statement is false.

11. ☑ **B.** False, a Secure Pipe pattern is used to guarantee that the data is not tampered with in transit to the Secure Store. The Intercepting Web Agent pattern provides authentication, authorization, encryption, and auditing capabilities outside the application.
    ☒ A is incorrect. The Intercepting Web Agent pattern provides authentication, authorization, encryption, and auditing capabilities outside the application.

12. ☑ **B.** False, the Authorization Enforcer pattern describes how a JEE-based application client should authorize with a JEE application and how the application manages and delegates authorization.
    ☒ A is incorrect. The Secure Service Proxy pattern secures and controls access to JEE components to provide web service endpoints/façade.

13. ☑ **B.** False, scalability refers to a system's ability to support fast-increasing numbers of users.
☒ **A** is incorrect. Adaptability relates to change in system usage, not number of users.

14. ☑ **A, B,** and **C.** The intuitive way to scale up the number of concurrent sessions handled by a server is to add resources (memory, CPU or hard disk) to it. Clustering is another way to resolve the scalability issue. It allows a group of servers to share the heavy tasks and to operate as a single server logically.
☒ **D** is incorrect. Although the OS is important, it does not provide any help with scaling.

15. ☑ **B.** False, fault tolerance means that a service always guarantees strictly correct behavior despite a certain number of faults.
☒ **A** is incorrect. Load balancing is one of the key technologies behind clustering, which is a way to obtain high availability and better performance by dispatching incoming requests to different servers.

16. ☑ **C.** When client requests come in, the load balancer will decide how to dispatch the requests to the back-end server instances. Popular algorithms include round-robin, random, and weight based. The load balancer tries to achieve equal workload to every server instance, but none of these algorithms can really get ideal equality because they are only based on the number of requests dispatched to a certain server instance.
☒ **A, B,** and **D** are incorrect. These statements are not true with respect to round-robin, random, and weight based.

Identify Java EE Technologies, Including JMS, JCA and Web Services, and Design Patterns That Address Specific Challenges in Enterprise Integration

17. ☑ **A** and **D.** There are two modes of communication, depending on the level of coupling between the sender and receiver: synchronous and asynchronous.
☒ **B, C,** and **E** are incorrect. Push, pull, and store and forward do not relate to JMS messaging modes.

18. ☑ **A.** Java EE Connector Architecture (JCA) is a Java-based technology solution for connecting application servers and Enterprise Information Systems (EIS) as part of Enterprise Application Integration (EAI) solutions. JCA is a generic architecture for connection to legacy systems. JCA was developed under the Java Community Process as JSR 16 (JCA 1.0), JSR 112 (JCA 1.5), and JSR 322 (JCA 1.6).
☒ **B** is incorrect.

Identify the Challenges in Integrating Enterprise Resources, the Java EE Technologies That Address Them (Including JPA and JDBC), and The Communication Protocols That Support Tier-to-Tier Communication (Including RMI, IIOP, and CORBA)

19. ☑ **A, B,** and **D.** JDBC provides methods to query and update data in the database through SQL statements such as UPDATE, DELETE, and INSERT and query statements such as SELECT.

☒ C is incorrect. UPSERT (that is, UPDATE and INSERT) is not a JDBC statement.

20. ☑ **B.** The Java Persistence Architecture API (JPA) is a Java specification for accessing, persisting, and managing data between Java objects/classes and a relational database.

☒ A is incorrect. Java Database Connectivity (JDBC) is an application programming interface (API) that allows the programmer to connect and interact with databases. JDBC provides methods to query and update data in the database through SQL statements such as UPDATE, DELETE, and INSERT and query statements such as SELECT.

4

Integration and Messaging

CERTIFICATION OBJECTIVES

4.01 Identify the APIs Available for a Java EE Technology-Based System to Communicate with External Resources, Including JPA, JDBC, RMI, Web Services, JMS, and JCA. Outline the Benefits and Drawbacks of Each Approach.

4.02 Identify and Detail the Technologies Used to Integrate Business Components with External Resources, Including JMS and JCA.

4.03 Describe the Technologies Used to Integrate Business Components with Web Services, Including XML over HTTP, JSON, SOAP, and REST.

4.04 Identify How a Service-Oriented Architecture (SOA) Facilitates System Integration and Best Practices.

✓ Two-Minute Drill

Q&A Self Test

This chapter covers a feature required by practically all Java EE applications: the ability to integrate and exchange data with another system or application. Java EE provides several components and APIs to integrate both synchronously and asynchronously:

- Java Message Service (JMS) API and message-driven beans (MDB)
- Java EE Connector Architecture (JCA)
- Java API for XML-based Web Services (JAX-WS) and Java API for Restful Web Services (JAX-RS)
- Java Database Connectivity (JDBC) API and Java Persistence API (JPA)

We first cover the technologies available in Java EE to communicate with external resources. We then take a look at the technologies for integrating business components with Web Services and external resources. Finally, we finish up with covering Service-Oriented Architecture in general and the best practices surrounding it.

CERTIFICATION OBJECTIVE 4.01

Identify the APIs Available for a Java EE Technology–Based System to Communicate with External Resources. Outline the Benefits and Drawbacks of Each Approach.

Several integration technologies (application programming interfaces, or APIs) are available for Java EE technology–based systems to communicate with external resources:

- Java Message Service (JMS)
- Java EE Connector Architecture (JCA)
- Java API For XML-based Web Services (JAX-WS)
- Java API for Restful Web Services (JAX-RS)

- Java Database Connectivity (JDBC)
- Java Persistence API (JPA)
- Common Object Request Broker Architecture (CORBA)
- Remote Method Invocation (Java/RMI)

Now let's cover these technologies at the level of detail necessary to pass the exam (for complete detail, you should review the material on Oracle's website).

Java Message Service (JMS)

JMS provides a standard Java interface to message-oriented middleware (MOM) products, allowing a developer to loosely couple applications together. The JMS API provides a convenient and easy way to create, send, receive, and read messages using Java.

Benefits	Drawbacks
Easier integration of incompatible systems.	Not recommended for non-Java integration (for example, legacy EIS).
Synchronous messaging: ■ Supports message acknowledgement (guaranteed delivery). ■ Support for transactions (via JTA).	Requires support for message-based integration.
Asynchronous messaging: ■ As transaction volumes increase, asynchronous messaging is better able to handle spikes by queuing requests until they can be processed instead of needing to service the requests instantaneously. ■ Asynchronous messaging is less affected by failures at the hardware, software, and network levels. ■ When processing capacities are exceeded, information is not lost; instead, it is delayed.	

Java EE Connector Architecture (JCA)

JCA provides a standardized access mechanism to and from enterprise information systems (EIS) from the Java EE platform. Although not as widespread as JDBC in terms of usage, JCA is a generic architecture for connecting to legacy systems.

JCA wraps legacy applications that provide value to a business by exposing their functionality as a well-formed API for consumption by Java EE applications.

Benefits	Drawbacks
Exposes resource in generic/high-level way.	Requires resource vendor's connector implementation. Tight coupling between EIS and application.

Java API for XML-based Web Services (JAX-WS)

JAX-WS is a technology for building Web Services and clients that communicate using XML. For this, a Web Service operation invocation is represented by an XML-based protocol (for example, Simple Object Access Protocol, or SOAP). SOAP defines the envelope structure, encoding rules, and conventions for representing Web Service invocations and responses.

Benefits	Drawbacks
Addresses enterprise QoS requirements for security (WS-Security) and reliability.	XML only. (Some workarounds are available, but these are nonstandard.)
Interoperates with other WS-*-conforming clients and servers.	Overhead of SOAP envelope/wrapper (bigger payload to transport).
Support for HTTP/HTTPS and SMTP transport layers.	No direct support in Java EE for asynchronous communication.

Metro Web Services Stack (Metro)

Metro Web Service stack, from the Glassfish community, is a reference implementation of JAX-WS and includes several extensible and easy-to-use features such as Web Services Interoperability Technologies (WSIT), Java Architecture for XML Binding (JAXB), and JAX-WS Commons.

Java API for RESTful Web Services (JAX-RS)

JAX-RS provides support for Web Services that conform to the Representational State Transfer (REST) architectural pattern. JAX-RS makes extensive use of annotations to simplify the development and deployment of Web Service clients and endpoints.

Benefits	Drawbacks
No configuration required for JEE version 6 (and above) containers. Prior versions need entry in web.xml deployment descriptor.	Only support for HTTP/HTTPS transport layer (this is usually not such a big deal though).
Uses annotations (over configuration files).	No automatic support for WS-Security.
HTTP methods (POST, GET, PUT, DEL) can simply represent CRUD (Create, Read, Update, and Delete) within application.	No direct support in Java EE for asynchronous communication.
Supports JSON for messages.	

Java Database Connectivity (JDBC)

JDBC is a low-level technology Java API that provides methods for querying and updating data in a database. JDBC is a very mature technology and is in widespread use within Java EE applications.

Benefits	Drawbacks
Mature technology for SQL data sources that is in widespread use.	A driver for specific database vendor is required.
Some performance-sensitive tasks may only be solved more efficiently with JDBC (compared to JPA).	Code needed to map table and column data to and from objects.
	Logic is often mixed in with SQL.
	No notion of objects or hierarchies. You to translate a result set into Java objects.

Java Persistence API (JPA)

JPA is a standard for Object Relational Mapping (ORM), a technology that deals with the way relational data (that is, rows and columns in database tables) is mapped to Java objects.

The latest version of JPA was developed by the EJB 3.0 software expert group on JSR 220 and utilizes a Plain Old Java Object (POJO) persistence model for ORM. JPA draws on concepts and ideas from major persistence frameworks such as Hibernate, TopLink, and Java Data Objects (JDO), in addition to the container-managed persistence (CMP) approach in earlier versions of the EJB specification. JPA can be utilized outside of EJB (for example, within a web application).

Benefits	Drawbacks
Uses annotations to specify details of database metadata (for example, table names and column names).	Some tasks cannot be solved efficiently using JPA (use JDBC for these).
Possible to utilize outside of EJB.	Performance may be affected due to additional layers between your application and the database.

exam watch

Java EE Connector Architecture (JCA) is the preferred choice as an integration method between Java and legacy Enterprise Information Systems (EIS).

Common Object Request Broker Architecture (CORBA)

CORBA is a language-independent, distributed object model specified by the Object Management Group (OMG). This architecture was created to support the development of object-oriented applications across heterogeneous computing environments that might contain different hardware platforms and operating systems.

CORBA relies on IIOP for communications between objects. The center of the CORBA architecture lies in the Object Request Broker (ORB). The ORB is a distributed programming service that enables CORBA objects to locate and communicate with one another. CORBA objects have interfaces that expose sets of methods to clients. To request access to an object's method, a CORBA client acquires an object reference to a CORBA server object. Then, the client makes method calls on the object reference as if the CORBA object were local to the client. The ORB finds the CORBA object and prepares it to receive requests, to communicate requests to it, and then to communicate replies back to the client. A CORBA object interacts with ORBs either through an ORB interface or through an Object Adapter.

Benefits	Drawbacks
Essentially the opposite of RMI. Heterogeneous objects are supported.	Objects are not passed by value; only the argument data is passed.
IIOP wire protocol guarantees interoperability between vendor products.	The server/client has to reconstitute the objects with the data.
Bundled with well-documented services such as COSNaming (name reference) and CORBASec (security) to extend the capabilities of the ORB.	Only commonly accepted data types can be passed as arguments, unless the CORBA 2.3 and later Objects By Value specification is used.

Remote Method Invocation (Java/RMI)

Java/RMI is a Java technology in which the methods of remote Java objects can be invoked from other Java virtual machines. RMI is the Java version of Remote Procedure Call (RPC), with the added ability to pass one or more objects along with the request.

Java/RMI relies on a protocol called the Java Remote Method Protocol (JRMP). Java relies heavily on Java Object Serialization, which allows objects to be marshaled (or transmitted) as a stream. Because Java Object Serialization is specific to Java, both the Java/RMI server object and the client object have to be written in Java. Each Java/RMI server object is defined by an interface that can be used to access the server object outside of the current JVM and on another machine's JVM. The interface exposes a set of methods that are indicative of the services offered by the server object.

For a client to locate a server object for the first time, RMI depends on a naming mechanism called an RMIRegistry that runs on the server machine and holds information about available server objects. A Java/RMI client acquires an object reference to a Java/RMI server object by performing a lookup for a server object reference and invokes methods on the server object as if the Java/RMI server object resided in the client's address space. Java/RMI server objects are named using URLs, and for a client to acquire a server object reference, it should specify the URL of the server object, as you would specify the URL to an HTML page. Because Java/RMI relies on Java, it also can be used on diverse operating system platforms—from IBM mainframes to Unix boxes to Windows machines to handheld devices—as long as a JVM implementation exists for that platform.

Benefits	Drawbacks
Object oriented. RMI can pass full objects as arguments and return values.	Must use Java on local and remote objects.
Objects are passed by value. The client or server can reconstitute the objects easily.	Arguments must implement the Serializable interface or extend the java.rmi.Remote object.
The data type can be any Java object (see the implement/extend restriction in the Drawbacks column).	

CERTIFICATION OBJECTIVE 4.02

Identify and Detail the Technologies Used to Integrate Business Components with External Resources, Including JMS and JCA.

In this section we look at the JMS, MDB, and JCA technologies. Before we look specifically at those technologies, we will review the basics around messaging technology.

Messaging Basics

The main subject areas in the messaging arena with which you need to be familiar are messages, message-oriented middleware, JMS, message types, and communication modes. We'll take a look at each of these subject areas before looking at the scenarios that are appropriate for messaging.

Messages

A *message* is a unit of data that is sent from one process to another process running on either the same or a different machine. The data in the message can range from simple text to a more complex data structure (such as a Java HashMap, which can be used to store name/value pairs). The only restriction is that the object must be *serializable* so that it can be easily transformed into a sequence of bytes, transmitted across a network, and then re-created into a copy of the original object.

Message-Oriented Middleware

Message-oriented middleware, also known as MOM, is a collection of server-based services used to support the sending and receiving of messages. This middleware is the infrastructure that provides dependable mechanisms that enable applications to create, send, and receive messages within an enterprise environment. The advantage of message-based applications is that they are event driven. They exchange messages in a wide variety of formats and deliver messages quickly and reliably.

Communication Modes

Frequently an application will use *synchronous* method calls for communication. In this type of communication, the requester is blocked from processing any further commands until the response (or a timeout) is received. Synchronous communication is conducted between two active participants. The receiver has to acknowledge receipt of the message before the sender can proceed. From the sender's perspective, this is known as a *blocking* call. As the volume of traffic increases, more bandwidth is required, and the need for additional hardware becomes critical. These implementations are more easily directly affected by hardware, software, and network failures. When capacities are exceeded, the opportunity to process the information is typically lost.

An example of synchronous communication is credit card authorization. When your card is swiped through a card reader and the details of the purchase are entered, the machine dials the authorization computer and waits for a response (approval or denial of the purchase).

In *asynchronous* communication, the parties are peers and can send and receive messages at will. Asynchronous communication does not require real-time acknowledgment of a message; the requester can continue with other processing once it sends the message. From the sender's perspective, this is known as a *nonblocking call.*

An example of asynchronous communication is e-mail. Even if your computer is switched off or your e-mail client is not running, other people can still send e-mail messages to you. When you start your e-mail client, you will be able to view the e-mail messages that have accumulated in your inbox.

Message Models

JMS supports two basic message models: publish/subscribe (pub/sub), in which messages are published on a one (or more)-to-many basis, and point-to-point (PTP), in which messages are sent on a one-to-one basis.

Java Message Service

Message-oriented middleware products allow a developer to couple applications loosely together. However, these products are proprietary and quite often complex and expensive. The JMS API provides a standard Java interface to these messaging middleware products, thus freeing developers from having to write low-level infrastructure code (or "plumbing") and allowing solutions to be built quickly and easily. In short, the JMS API provides a convenient and easy way to create, send, receive, and read an enterprise messaging system's messages using Java.

JMS applications can use databases to provide the storage to support the message persistence that is necessary for guaranteeing delivery and order of messages. The Enterprise JavaBeans (EJB) 2.0 specification, released in 2001, gave us the message-driven bean (MDB). Since then, the MDB has been able to receive and process messages asynchronously within the EJB container. These message-driven beans can be instantiated multiple times to provide concurrent processing (and therefore faster throughput) of a message queue.

JMS provides an interface from Java applications to messaging products. JMS enables clients (or peers) to exchange data in the form of messages. As mentioned earlier, the major advantages of using messaging for this exchange are:

- Easier integration of incompatible systems
- Asynchronous communications
- One-to-many communications
- Guaranteed messaging (message acknowledgement)
- Transactional messaging

Message-Driven Bean (MDB)

The message-driven bean (MDB) is a stateless component that is invoked by the EJB container when a JMS message arrives for the destination (topic or queue) for which the bean has registered. An MDB is a message consumer, and like other JMS message consumers it can receive messages from a destination because it implements the javax.jms.MessageListener interface. After receiving messages, it is then able to perform business logic based on the message contents.

MDBs receive JMS messages from clients in the same manner as any other JMS servicing object. A client that writes to a destination has no knowledge of the fact that an MDB is acting as the message consumer. MDBs were created to have an EJB that can be asynchronously invoked to process messages, while receiving all of the same EJB container services provided to session and entity beans.

When a message is sent to a message consumer, the EJB container ensures that the MDB registered to process the destination exists. If the MDB needs to be instantiated, the container will do this. The onMessage() method of the bean is called, and the message is passed in as an argument. MDBs and stateless session EJBs are similar in the sense that they do not maintain state across invocations. MDBs differ from stateless session beans and entity beans in that they have no home or remote interface. Internal or external clients cannot directly access methods of an MDB. Clients can only indirectly interact with an MDB by sending a message to the destination.

The EJB *deployer* is the person responsible for assigning MDBs to a destination at deployment time. The EJB container provides the service of creating and removing MDB instances as necessary or as specified at deployment time.

EJB Container and Message-Driven Beans

The EJB container allows for the concurrent consumption of messages and provides support for distributed transactions. This means that database updates, message processing, and connections to Enterprise Information Systems using the Java EE Connector Architecture (JCA) can all participate in the same transaction context.

The EJB container or application server provides many services for MDBs, so the bean developer can concentrate on implementing business logic. Here are some of the services provided by the EJB container:

- Handles all communication for JMS messages
- Checks the pool of available bean instances to see which MDB is to be used
- Enables the propagation of a security context by associating the role specified in the deployment descriptor to the appropriate execution thread
- Creates a transactional context, if one is specified in the deployment descriptor
- Passes the message as an argument to the onMessage() method of the appropriate MDB instance
- Reallocates MDB resources to a pool of available instances

The EJB container also provides the following services based on the entries in the deployment descriptor file.

MDB Life Cycle Management The life cycle of an MDB corresponds to the lifespan of the EJB container in which it is deployed. Because MDBs are stateless, bean instances are usually pooled by the EJB container and retrieved by the container when a message is written to the destination for which it is a message consumer.

The container creates a bean instance by invoking the newInstance() method of the bean instance class object. After the instance is created, the container creates an instance of javax.ejb.MessageDrivenContext and passes it to the bean instance via the setMessageDrivenContext() method. The ejbCreate() method is also called on the bean instance before it is placed in the pool and is then made available to process messages.

Exception Handling MDBs may not throw application exceptions while processing messages. This means that the only exceptions that may be thrown by an MDB are run-time exceptions indicating a system-level error. The container will handle these exceptions by removing the bean instance and rolling back any transaction started by the bean instance or by the container.

Threading and Concurrency An MDB instance is assumed to execute in a single thread of control. The EJB container will guarantee this behavior. In addition, the EJB container may provide a mode of operation that allows multiple messages to be handled concurrently by separate bean instances. This deployment option utilizes expert-level classes that are defined in the JMS specification. The JMS provider is not required to provide implementations for these classes, so the EJB container may not be able to take advantage of them with every JMS implementation. Using these classes involves a trade-off between performance and serialization of messages delivered to the server.

Message Acknowledgment The container always manages message acknowledgment for MDBs. It is prohibited for the bean to use any message acknowledgment methods—for example, acknowledge() or rollback(). The message acknowledgment can be set to either AUTO_ACKNOWLEDGE, allowing the message to be delivered once, or DUPS_OK_ACKNOWLEDGE, allowing the delivery of duplicate messages after a failure. Note that if a bean has the Required transaction attribute, it will process the onMessage() method inside a transaction.

Because the MDB has no client, no security principal is propagated to the EJB container on receipt of a message. The EJB framework provides facilities for a bean method to execute in a role specified in the deployment descriptor. As a result, the MDB can be configured to execute within a security context that can then be propagated to other EJBs that are called during the processing of a message.

Java EE Connector Architecture (JCA)

As mentioned earlier in this chapter, JCA connections provide access to EIS resources with the use of a nonproprietary API. JCA resource adapters use specific interfaces that are provided by the EIS resource vendor. The EIS resources are commonly (but not limited to) non-Java technology executing on mainframe hardware running transactional or legacy systems. Figure 4-1 shows the JCA contracts between application server, the resource adapter, and EIS.

FIGURE 4-1

Java EE Connector Architecture (JCA)

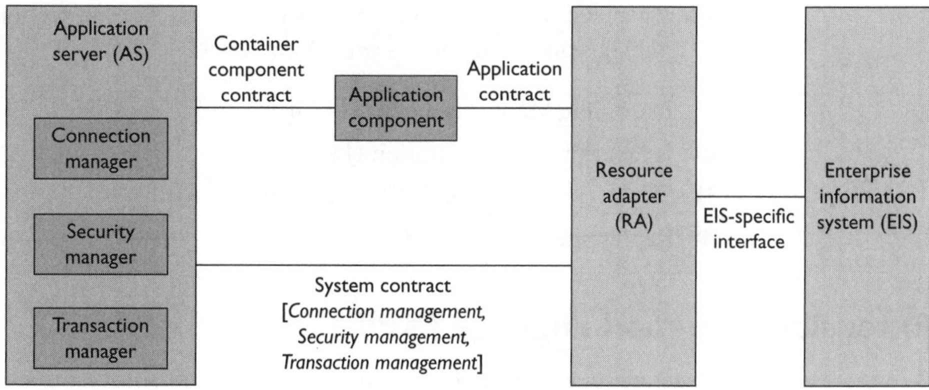

The Java EE application server manages connections, transactions, and the security of the JCA resource adapter via the system contract. The application component's contract with the JCA resource is via the provided common client interface (CCI), which provides a standard interface that is consistent with accessing other resources, such as JDBC and JMS.

CERTIFICATION OBJECTIVE 4.03

Describe the Technologies Used to Integrate Business Components with Web Services, Including XML over HTTP, JSON, SOAP, and REST.

In this section we look at the technologies that can be used to integrate business components with Web Services. This includes message transports and the message formats of XML and JSON, and the SOAP and REST approaches.

What Are Web Services?

Web Services provide a standard means of interoperating, via Hypertext Transfer Protocol (HTTP), between software applications. Web Services can be combined in a loosely coupled way to achieve complex operations. Several technologies are used to integrate business components with Web Services:

- Extensible Markup Language (XML)
- JavaScript Object Notation (JSON)
- SOAP (formally Simple Object Access Protocol)
- Representational State Transfer (REST)

Extensible Markup Language (XML)

XML defines a set of rules for encoding documents in a format that is readable by both human and machine. The properties of XML make it suitable for representing data, concepts, and contexts in an open, platform-, vendor-, and language-neutral manner. It uses *tags* (identifiers that signal the start and end of a related block of data) to create a hierarchy of related data components called *elements*. In turn, this hierarchy of elements provides encapsulation and context. As a result, there is a greater opportunity to reuse this data outside of the application and data sources from which it was derived. Here is an example of an XML document:

```
<?xml version="1.0"?>
<contact>
    <firstName>Terence</firstName>
    <lastName>Allen</lastName>
    <age>25</age>
    <address>
        <street>594 Broadway</street>
        <city>New York</city>
        <state>NY</state>
         <zip>10012</zip>
    </address>
    <phoneNumbers>
         <phoneNumber>
            <type>home</type>
            <phone>347 123 3972</phone>
         </phoneNumber>
         <phoneNumber>
            <type>cell</type>
            <phone>646 123 4567</phone>
         </phoneNumber>
    </phoneNumbers>
</contact>
```

JavaScript Object Notation (JSON)

JSON is based on a subset of the JavaScript Programming Language, Standard ECMA-262, Third Edition, December 1999. It is a lightweight data-interchange format that uses text, which humans can read and write and machines can parse and generate, to transmit data objects consisting of attribute/value pairs. It is now primarily used to transmit data between a server and web application, including those executing within a web browser or iOS/Android mobile application. It has gained significant ground as an alternative to XML because it is much less verbose and therefore has a lower payload overhead (messages are smaller). Here is an example of a JSON string:

```
{
    "firstName": "John",
    "lastName": "Doe",
    "age": 25,
    "address": {
        "street": "594 Broad Street",
        "city": "New York",
        "state": "NY",
        "zip": 10012
},
    "phoneNumbers": [
    {
        "type": "home",
        "phone": "347 123 3972"
    },
    {
        "type": "cell",
        "phone": "646 123 4567"
    }
  ]
}
```

SOAP

SOAP (Simple Object Access Protocol) is a protocol specification for exchanging structured information via services over a network. It uses the XML language to define the message architecture and message formats. SOAP relies on protocols for negotiation and transmission; however, this is almost always Hypertext Transfer Protocol (HTTP/HTTPS), although the specification allows for other transport protocols (such as SMTP, TCP, and JMS).

SOAP messages have the following elements (or parts):

- **Envelope** This defines what is in the message and how to process it (encoding rules and data representation conventions).
- **Header** Contains application-specific information about the message.
- **Body** Contains the actual SOAP message intended for the recipient.
- **Fault** Contains error messages describing faults encountered calling the service (if present, it will appear as a child element of the Body element).

When compared to a plain XML message (which is an alternative service approach), this additional information allows SOAP-based messaging to more easily use standards to address the issues of security, reliability, and transactions. However, with the additional complexity comes the overhead of increased message size (bigger bandwidth footprint) and message parsing (bigger CPU and memory footprint).

Web Service Description Language (WSDL)

WSDL (formerly, Web Service Definition Language) is an XML format language for describing Web Service functionality. WSDL is a machine-readable definition of how the Web Service can be called, the parameters that it needs, and the structures it can respond with.

XML Schema Definition (XSD)

An XSD is an XML format language that defines a set of rules that an XML document must conform to in order to be considered complete, valid, and correct.

Representational State Transfer (REST)

REST is an architectural style (not a standard) for designing networked applications. It was created as part of Roy Fielding's doctoral dissertation in 2000. REST, based on HTTP 1.1, is a lightweight alternative to the more complicated approaches, such as CORBA and Web Services (SOAP, WSDL, XSDs, and so on), for connecting between machines. It uses the HTTP methods to perform the four essential data access functions—that is, reading data using GET, updating data using PUT, creating data with POST, and removing data with DEL.

Web Application Description Language (WADL)

WADL is a machine-readable XML description of HTTP-based web applications, which are usually REST Web Services. WADL is the REST equivalent of SOAP's WSDL, in that it can also be used to describe REST Web Services. Although WADL has been around since 2009, it is not considered a standard and it is not as widely supported as WSDL is for SOAP-based Web Services.

CERTIFICATION OBJECTIVE 4.04

Identify How a Service-Oriented Architecture (SOA) Facilitates System Integration and Best Practices

Service-Oriented Architecture (SOA) is a strategy, or system integration process, for developing and integrating systems through interoperable standards-based services. Some benefits for an SOA strategy are:

- The ability to reuse functionality across multiple business segments and applications.
- Easier integration across systems because it is a standards-based approach.
- The use of standardized components and interfaces means that an agile approach to development can be utilized, which in turn allows the development process to quickly and more easily adapt to the changes of business needs.

There are no specific technologies stipulated by SOA; however, standards have emerged in the Web Service arena that provide flexibility and reusability and have been embraced by the SOA movement. The Web Service standards are shown in the Figure 4-2.

Architecture and Design for SOA

As mentioned earlier, businesses will redefine their processes and change course to meet the challenges of their industry domain. The SOA design approach will always keep the focus aligned with these changing business requirements and therefore the

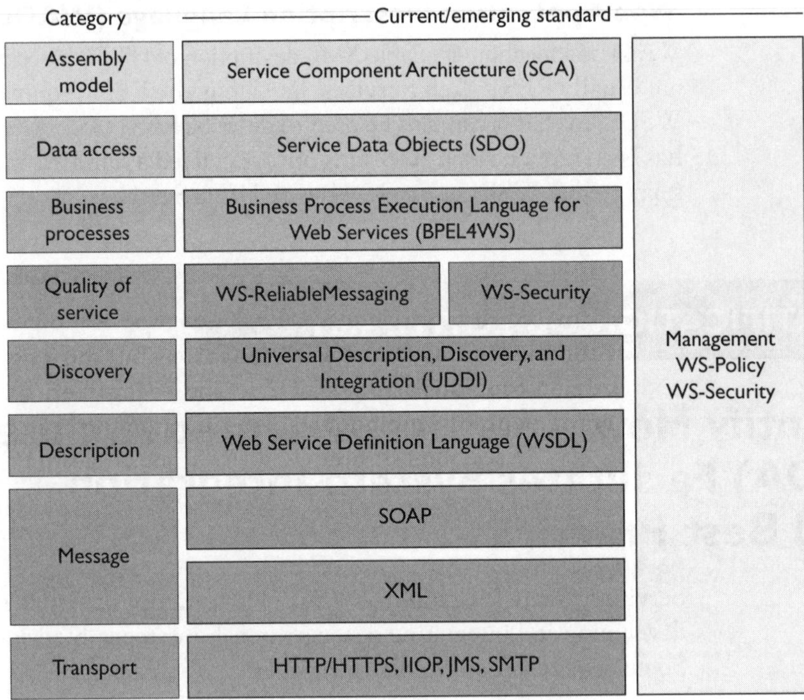

Category
Current/emerging standard
Assembly model
Service Component Architecture (SCA)
Data access
Service Data Objects (SDO)
Business processes
Business Process Execution Language for Web Services (BPEL4WS)
Quality of service
WS-ReliableMessaging
WS-Security
Discovery
Universal Description, Discovery, and Integration (UDDI)
Description
Web Service Definition Language (WSDL)
Message
SOAP
XML
Transport
HTTP/HTTPS, IIOP, JMS, SMTP
Management
WS-Policy
WS-Security

FIGURE 4-2

Service-Oriented Architecture (SOA) standards

development teams within these organizations will need to be agile in order to adapt to the business needs. The design for a service should be not only how it can be used the first time, but also how it can be reused. It is possible to have services that are not reusable; nonetheless, the key definitions for a service will be:

- Message formats, in XML Schema Documents (XSD), that define the data required by a service to perform its function.
- Interface definitions, in Web Services Definition Language (WSDL), that describe the operations and associated input and output messages for a service.
- The service implementation technology. Here are some possible choices:
  - Java Web Services (JAX-WS)
  - Business Process Execution Language (BPEL)
  - Service Component Architecture (SCA)
  - Service Data Objects (SDO)

Business Process Execution Language (BPEL)

BPEL is a language (based on XML, XSD, SOAP, and WSDL) for specifying actions within business processes. It is industry standard for business process orchestration and execution, in that you can design an end-to-end process flow for integrating one or more Web Services. BPEL provides a means to define how to perform the following actions:

- Asynchronously exchange XML messages with remote services.
- Manipulate XML data structures.
- Manage events and exceptions.
- Design parallel flows of process execution. (This includes being able to undo specific portions of flow if an exception occurs.)

Service Component Architecture (SCA) and Service Data Objects (SDO)

OASIS (Organization for the Advancement of Structured Information Standards) is a nonprofit consortium that drives the development, convergence, and adoption of open standards for the global information society. SCA and SDO are new standards, developed by OASIS as part of their Open Composite Services Architecture (Open CSA).

SCA is a set of specifications that describe a model for building an SOA application. SCA is based on the idea that business function is delivered as a series of services assembled together to create a solution that addresses a specific business need. In short, SCA is designed to simplify the representation of business logic.

SDO is a specification designed to simplify and unify the way in which applications handle data. Using SDO, developers can uniformly access/manipulate data from heterogeneous data sources, including relational databases, XML data sources, Web Services, and Enterprise Information Systems (EIS). In short, SDO is designed to simplify the representation of data access.

These new standards are designed to be used together in an application that is then known as a "composite application."

Enterprise Service Bus (ESB)

ESB is a software architecture model used to build and then deploy enterprise SOA-based applications. Its primary use is in Enterprise Application Integration (EAI) of heterogeneous application landscapes, and it promotes agility and flexibility

FIGURE 4-3

Service integration (without ESB)

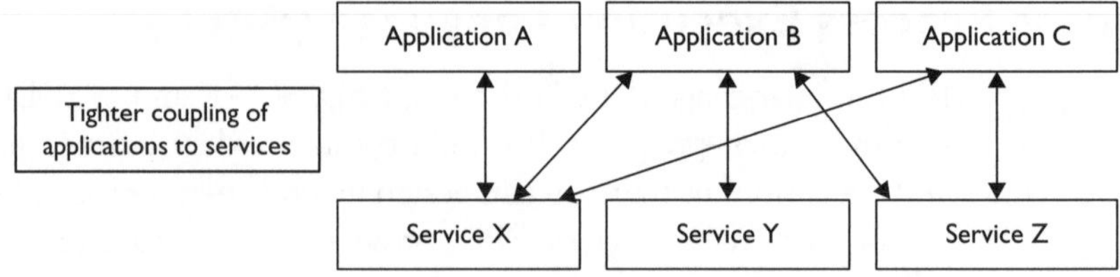

with regard to communication and interaction between SOA-based applications. It defines and provides an approach to resolving issues associated with an SOA-based application—typically functional orchestration (process flow), data synchronization (transport and transform), and monitoring. An ESB has the following characteristics:

- **Platform neutral** Support for Java, .NET, mainframes, and relational databases.
- **Support for SOA standards** This includes UDDI, WSDL, SOAP, WS-ReliableMessaging, and WS-Security.
- **Transformation** XML-to-XML mapping.
- **Content-based routing** Message inspection and intelligent routing to destinations.
- **Transportation** Asynchronous (store-and-forward) message delivery.

For SOA-based systems, applications (and new services) are developed by a composition of services that are in place within the enterprise (see Figure 4-3).

To more loosely couple what would be a more rigid point-to-point communication path among services, an Enterprise Service Bus (ESB) can be utilized (see Figure 4-4). This will also present the opportunity to provide the aforementioned characteristics (such as content-based routing) to an application.

FIGURE 4-4

Service integration (via ESB)

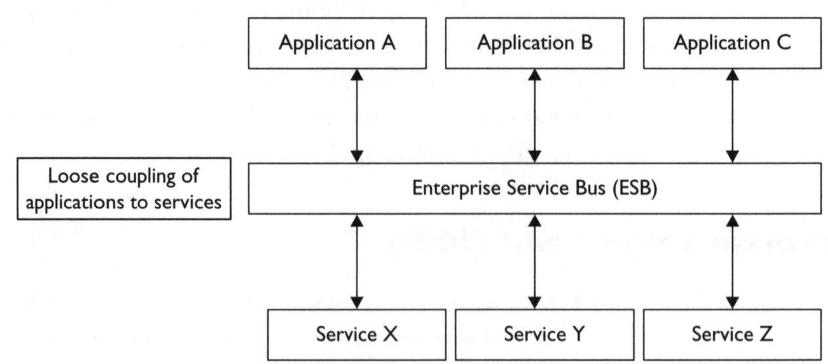

Best Practices for SOA

SOA is a more contemporary approach to designing information systems. It proposes a component assembly approach to bring together existing systems and/or services in order to deliver business value. It will take an organization some time to adopt and implement this approach. The infrastructure will evolve over time and organizations that wish to create systems based on SOA implementations will need to take into consideration design, implementation, and governance of this approach. These considerations include the following:

- **Define** Ensure service interfaces have no dependencies and typically allow the independent invocation of a complete set of steps to achieve a goal.
- **Associate** Map service interfaces to artifacts, example, XML Schema documents (XSD) and Web Service Definition Language (WSDL).
- **Catalog** Categorize and tag service interfaces into service portfolios and templates so that they are more likely to be reused later.
- **Quality of Service (QoS)** SOA solutions, for the most part, bring together application components with services, and therefore you should apply appropriate technologies at the various levels of the solution. For example, for distributed transactions you can use EJB to manage the transactional aspects.

SOA Governance

Governance is mostly about ensuring that a process is conducted in a proper manner in terms of providing guidance and making the most effective and equitable use of resources to achieve and maintain alignment with the overall objectives.

Governance is also about structure and controls. As such, when it applies to SOA, governance means putting in place a framework for managing the service assets so that they are compliant with the prevailing policies and standards. Governance focuses on *what* is covered by policies, *who* makes decisions, and *how* governance is carried out in terms of processes.

The benefits that governance brings to an SOA architecture are:

- **Agility** Increased speed in the ability to make (and change) decisions.
- **Alignment** Keeping aligned with business objectives.
- **Cost reduction** Standardization and reuse of SOA will drive down IT expenditures.

- **Risk reduction** Enforced policies, faster decision making, and control of dependencies reduce risks.
- **Value** Investment in services yield value (initially and especially upon reuse).

Comparing Integration Technologies

During Part 1 of the exam you will be given questions that describe scenarios for which you must supply the correct integration technology answer. Here is a quick study summary that will help you select the most appropriate integration technique for the exam (note that these answers are not necessarily what you may encounter in your workplace):

SCENARIO & SOLUTION

Given Scenarios	Appropriate Integration Method
Java-to-Java integration using a synchronous approach	Web Services (JAX-WS or JAX-RS) or Java Message Service (JMS).
Java-to-Java integration using a asynchronous approach	Java Message Service (JMS).
Java-to-non-Java (non-EIS) integration when one or more WS-*-standards–based features (security, reliability, and transactions) are required	Web Services using SOAP (JAX-WS).
Java-to-non-Java (non-EIS) integration when lightweight annotation-based features are required	Web Services using REST (JAX-RS).
Java-to-non-Java (EIS) integration	Java EE Connector Architecture (JCA) is the preferred way to interface to an Enterprise Information System (EIS).

CERTIFICATION SUMMARY

By studying this chapter, you now have an understanding of the messaging and integration technologies available for Java EE.

TWO-MINUTE DRILL

Identify the APIs Available for a Java EE Technology-Based System to Communicate with External Resources. Outline the Benefits and Drawbacks of Each Approach.

The following table shows the benefits and drawbacks for the Java EE integration APIs that you will be tested on during the exam.

API	Benefit	Drawback
Java Message Service (JMS)	Easier integration of incompatible systems. Provides support for acknowledgement, guaranteed delivery, and transactions (JTA) for synchronous messaging. Asynchronous messaging is better able to handle spikes in message volumes.	Not recommended for legacy EIS integration. Requires support for message-based integration.
Java EE Connector Architecture (JCA)	Exposes EIS resources in a generic/high-level way.	Requires resource vendor's connector implementation. Tight coupling between EIS and application.
Java API For XML-based Web Services (JAX-WS)	Uses standards to addresses QoS requirements for security and reliability. Interoperates with other WS-*-conforming clients and servers.	XML only. Overhead of SOAP envelope/wrapper (bigger payload to transport). No direct support in Java EE for asynchronous communication.
Java API for Restful Web Services (JAX-RS)	Zero (or near-zero) configuration. Uses annotations (over configuration files). HTTP methods (POST, GET, PUT, DEL) can simply represent CRUD (Create, Read, Update and Delete) within the application. Supports JSON for message.	HTTP/HTTPS only. No automatic support for WS-Security. No direct support in Java EE for asynchronous communication.
Java Database Connectivity (JDBC)	Mature technology in widespread use. Some performance-sensitive tasks may only be solved more efficiently with JDBC (compared to JPA).	Driver for specific database vendor is required. Code needed to map table and column data to and from objects. Logic is often mixed in with SQL. No notion of objects or hierarchies. You need to translate a result set into Java objects.

API	Benefit	Drawback
Java Persistence API (JPA)	Annotations specify details of database metadata (for example, table names and column names). Available outside of EJB.	Some tasks cannot be solved efficiently using JPA (use JDBC for instead). Performance may be affected due to additional layers between the application and the database.
Common Object Request Broker Architecture (CORBA)	Heterogeneous objects are supported. IIOP wire protocol guarantees interoperability between vendor products. Bundled with services that extend the capabilities of the ORB—for example, COSNaming (name reference) and CORBASec (security).	Objects are not passed by value; only the argument data is passed. The server/client has to reconstitute the objects with the data. Only commonly accepted data types can be passed as arguments unless CORBA 2.3 (and above) Objects By Value is used.
Remote Method Invocation (Java/RMI)	Object oriented. RMI can pass full objects as arguments and return values. Objects are passed by value. The client or server can reconstitute the objects easily. The data type can be any Java object. Any Java objects can be passed as arguments. Arguments must implement the Serializable interface or java.rmi.Remote object.	Must use Java on local and remote objects.

Identify and Detail the Technologies Used to Integrate Business Components with External Sources

- ❑ Java Message Service (JMS) provides a standard Java interface to message-oriented middleware (MOM). The JMS API provides a convenient and easy way to create, send, receive, and read an enterprise messaging system's messages using Java.
- ❑ Message-driven bean (MDB) is an enterprise bean that allows Java EE applications to process messages asynchronously. An MDB typically acts as a JMS message listener.
- ❑ Java Connector Architecture (JCA) is a Java technology that is used to create resource adapters that support access to Enterprise Information Systems (EIS).

Describe the Technologies Used to Integrate Business Components with Web Services

- ❑ Extensible Markup Language (XML) defines a set of rules for encoding and exchanging data in a format that is readable by both human and machine.
- ❑ JavaScript Object Notation (JSON) is a lightweight data-interchange format that uses text, which humans can read and write and machines can parse and generate, to transmit data objects consisting of attribute/value pairs.
- ❑ Simple Object Access Protocol (SOAP) is a protocol specification for exchanging structured information via services over a network.
- ❑ Web Service Description Language (WSDL—formerly, Web Service Definition Language) is an XML format language for describing Web Service functionality. WSDL is a machine-readable definition of how the Web Service can be called, the parameters it needs, and the structures it can respond with.
- ❑ XML Schema Definition (XSD) is an XML format language that defines a set of rules an XML document must conform to in order to be considered complete, valid, and correct.
- ❑ Representational State Transfer (REST) is an architectural style (not a standard) for designing networked applications. Based on HTTP 1.1, REST is a lightweight alternative to more complicated approaches such as CORBA and Web Services for connecting between machines.

Identify How a Service-Oriented Architecture (SOA) Facilitates System Integration and Best Practices

- ❑ SOA is a strategy for developing and integrating systems via standards-based services. Benefits include the following:
  - ❑ The ability to reuse functionality across multiple business segments and applications.
  - ❑ Easier integration across systems because it is a standards-based approach.
  - ❑ Suited to agile approach—more quickly and easily adapt to the business changes and needs.

- SOA standards include the following:
  - Extensible Markup Language (XML)
  - XML Schema Document (XSD)
  - Web Service Description Language (WSDL)
  - Java API For XML-based Web Services (JAX-WS)
  - Business Process Execution Language (BPEL)
  - Service Component Architecture (SCA)
  - Service Data Objects (SDO)
  - Enterprise Service Bus (ESB)
- The SOA governance approach ensures that a process is conducted in a proper manner, in terms of providing guidance and making the most effective and equitable use of resources to achieve and maintain alignment with the overall objectives. Governance focuses on *what* is covered by policies, *who* makes decisions, and *how* governance is carried out in terms of processes.
- The following are the SOA governance benefits:
  - **Agility** Increased speed in the ability to make (and change) decisions.
  - **Alignment** Keeping aligned with business objectives.
  - **Cost reduction** Standardization and reuse of SOA will drive down IT expenditures.
  - **Risk reduction** Enforced policies, faster decision making, and control of dependencies reduce risks.
  - **Value** Investment in services yield value (initially and especially upon reuse).

Comparing Integration Technologies

- This section does not fall into an individual integration and messaging objective, but spans several of the objectives for this chapter.
- For integration of Java-to-Java:
  - When synchronous communication is required use Web Services (JAX-WS or JAX-RS) or Java Message Service (JMS).
  - When asynchronous communication is required use Java Message Service (JMS).

- For integration of Java-to-non-Java (Non-EIS):
  - Use Web Services using SOAP (JAX-WS) for WS-* standards-based features of security, reliability, and transactions.
  - Use Web Services using REST (JAX-RS) for lightweight annotation-based communication.
- For integration of Java-to-EIS:
  - Java EE Connector Architecture (JCA) is the preferred way to interface with an Enterprise Information System (EIS).

SELF TEST

The following questions will help you measure your understanding of the material presented in this chapter. Read all the choices carefully because there may be more than one correct answer. Choose all correct answers for each question.

Identify the APIs Available for a Java EE Technology-Based System to Communicate with External Resources, Including JPA, JDBC, RMI, Web Services, JMS, and JCA. Outline the Benefits and Drawbacks of Each Approach.

1. What technology supports asynchronous and synchronous communication out of the box?
   A. JAX-WS
   B. JAX-RS
   C. JCA
   D. JMS
2. Which of the following exposes Enterprise Information System (EIS) resources in a generic way?
   A. JMS
   B. JCA
   C. JAX-WS
   D. JAX-RS
3. Which Web Service technology supports the industry standards for security, reliability, and transactions?
   A. JAX-SRT
   B. JAX-RS
   C. JAX-WS
   D. JAXB
4. Which technology uses annotations to map database tables and columns to Java objects?
   A. JPA
   B. JDBC
   C. JDO
   D. JCA

Identify and Detail the Technologies Used to Integrate Business Components with External Resources, Including JMS and JCA

5. Which API provides a convenient and easy way to create, send, receive, and read an enterprise messaging system's messages?

A. JDBC
B. JMS
C. JAX-WS
D. JPA

6. Which of the following allows Java EE applications to process messages asynchronously?

A. JDBC
B. MDB
C. JPA
D. JCA

7. Which integration technology supports the WS-*-type standards?

A. JAX-WS
B. REST
C. EJB
D. JAX-RS

8. Which technology is used to create resource adapters that support access to Enterprise Information Systems (EIS)?

A. JMS
B. JDBC
C. JCA
D. JPA

Describe the Technologies Used to Integrate Business Components with Web Services, Including XML over HTTP, JSON, SOAP, and REST

9. Which of the following is *not* used in Web Service communication?

A. XML
B. RMI
C. SOAP
D. JSON

10. Which of the following uses industry standards for Web Service communication?
    A. REST
    B. JAX-RS
    C. JCA
    D. JAX-WS

Identify How a Service-Oriented Architecture (SOA) Facilitates System Integration and Best Practices

11. Which of the following is a valid industry standard for SOA integration?
    A. JCA
    B. JAX-WS
    C. REST
    D. JAX-RS
12. Which of the following are valid considerations for SOA architecture and design?
    A. Define the service interface.
    B. Associate the service interface to XSD and WSDL.
    C. Catalog, categorize, and tag service interfaces.
    D. Provide Quality of Service (QoS) at the appropriate level.
    E. All of the above.
13. Which of the following is the most relevant characteristic of Service-Oriented Architecture (SOA)?
    A. Performance of Enterprise JavaBeans (EJB)
    B. Loosely coupled components
    C. Web Services
    D. Load-balanced resources

Additional Questions on Comparing Integration Technologies

14. You have been hired by a company to select the best technology for integrating its Java EE–based sales and marketing application with its Java EE accounting system using an asynchronous approach. What technology will you select?
    A. JCA
    B. JAX-WS
    C. JAX-RS
    D. JMS

15. You have been hired by a company to select the best technology for integrating its Java EE–based sales and marketing application with its legacy EIS accounting system. What technology will you select?

A. JCA

B. JAX-WS

C. JAX-RS

D. JMS

16. You are designing a solution to loosely couple multiple Java applications. Which of the following integration technologies is the best choice?

A. RMI

B. EJB

C. JCA

D. JDBC

E. None of the above

17. KNAB is a bank that has an existing Enterprise Information System (EIS) that is to be integrated with a new web-based banking application. It is your job to recommend how this will be achieved. Which if the following would you recommend?

A. EJB

B. JPA

C. JCA

D. JAX-WS

18. SeeEmmEss Corp is a futures exchange that receives millions of electronic bids and offers on commodity items (such as oil, gas, and cotton) during the day via a Java web application. The member bids and offers are queued and processed without immediate acknowledgment by a Java application server that hosts the marketplace. Successful bids and offers are notified when paired according to the marketplace rules (lot size, time, and so on). What integration technology would you recommend between the server that hosts the web application and the server that hosts the marketplace?

A. JCA

B. EJB using JPA

C. Java Web Services (JAX-WS or JAX-RS)

D. JMS queue with MDB

SELF TEST ANSWERS

Identify the APIs Available for a Java EE Technology-Based System to Communicate with External Resources, Including JPA, JDBC, RMI, Web Services, JMS, and JCA. Outline the Benefits and Drawbacks of Each Approach.

1. ☑ **D.** JMS supports asynchronous and synchronous communication.
☒ **A, B,** and **C** are incorrect. JAX-WS, JAX-RS, and JCA support synchronous communication and do not automatically support asynchronous communication.

2. ☑ **B.** JCA exposes EIS resources in a generic way.
☒ **A, C,** and **D** are incorrect. JMS, JAX-WS, and JAX-RS do not support communication with an Enterprise Information System (EIS).

3. ☑ **C.** JAX-WS is a Web Service technology that supports industry standards for security, reliability, and transactions.
☒ **A, B,** and **D** are incorrect. JAX-SRT is fictitious. JAX-RS and JAXB do not automatically support standards for security, reliability, and transactions.

4. ☑ **A.** JPA uses annotations to map database tables and columns to Java objects.
☒ **B, C,** and **D** are incorrect. JDBC, JDO, and JCA do not use annotations for ORM.

Identify and Detail the Technologies Used to Integrate Business Components with External Resources

5. ☑ **B.** Java Message Service (JMS) provides a convenient and easy way to create, send, receive, and read an enterprise messaging system's messages.
☒ **A, C,** and **D** are incorrect. JDBC, JAX-WS, and JPA are not messaging APIs.

6. ☑ **B.** Message-driven beans (MDB) allow Java EE applications to process messages asynchronously.
☒ **A, C,** and **D** are incorrect. JDBC, JPA, and JCA are not messaging related.

7. ☑ **A.** JAX-WS supports the WS-*-type standards.
☒ **B, C,** and **D** are incorrect. REST, EJB, and JAX-RS do not support the WS-* standards.

8. ☑ **C.** Java EE Connector Architecture (JCA) is used to create resource adapters that support access to Enterprise Information Systems (EIS).
☒ **A, B,** and **D** are incorrect. JMS, JDBC, and JPA are not resource adapter related.

Describe the Technologies Used to Integrate Business Components with Web Services

9. ☑ **B.** RMI is not used in Web Service communication.
☒ **A, C,** and **D** are incorrect. XML, SOAP, and JSON are used in Web Services (not necessarily all at the same time, though).

10. ☑ **D.** JAX-WS uses industry standards for Web Service communication.
☒ **A, B,** and **C** are incorrect. REST and JAX-RS do not use industry standards for Web Service communication. JCA is not Web Service related at all.

Identify How a Service-Oriented Architecture (SOA) Facilitates System Integration and Best Practices

11. ☑ **B.** JAX-WS is an industry standard for SOA integration.
☒ **A, C,** and **D** are incorrect. JCA is not Web Service related. JAX-RS and REST are not SOA integration industry standards (at least not yet).

12. ☑ **E.** All are valid considerations for SOA architecture and design.
☒ **A, B, C,** and **D** are incorrect. Each is incorrect on an individual basis because all are valid collectively.

13. ☑ **B.** From the given list, loosely coupled components is the most relevant characteristic of Service-Oriented Architecture (SOA).
☒ **A, C,** and **D** are incorrect. EJB performance, Web Services, and load-balanced resources, although valid characteristics, will not be improved or degraded with the adoption of SOA into an application architecture.

Comparing Integration Technology

14. ☑ **D.** JMS is the only technology listed with support for asynchronous Java-to-Java application integration.
☒ **A, B,** and **C** are incorrect. JCA, JAX-WS, and JAX-RS do not automatically support asynchronous communication.

15. ☑ **A.** JCA is the preferred choice for integration technology with EIS.
☒ **B, C,** and **D** are incorrect. JAX-WS, JAX-RS, and JMS are not the preferred integration choices with a legacy EIS.

16. ☑ **E.** None of the choices are valid for loosely coupling Java applications.
☒ **A, B, C,** and **D** are incorrect. RMI, EJB, JCA, and JDBC do not support loose coupling between Java applications.

17. ☑ **C.** JCA is the preferred choice for integration technology for EIS.
☒ **A, B,** and **D** are incorrect. EJB, JPA, and JAX-WS are not the preferred integration choices with a legacy EIS.

18. ☑ **D.** JMS with MDB supports the Java-to-Java integration, with the added ability that the marketplace does not need to immediately acknowledge the success or failure of the incoming bid or offer. Given JMS's ability to handle spikes in workload and the asynchronous pairing and notification of bids with offers, it is the ideal choice.
☒ **A, B,** and **C** are incorrect. JCA, EJB using JPA, and Java Web Services (JAX-WS or JAX-RS) do not meet the asynchronous and Java-to-Java requirements.

5

Business Tier Technologies

CERTIFICATION OBJECTIVES

5.01	Identify the Correct EJB Technology to Apply for a Given Scenario, Including Entity Classes, Session Beans, Message-Driven Beans, Timers, Interceptors, and POJOs
5.02	Identify Benefits and Drawbacks of Different Persistence Technologies such as BMP, CMP, and JPA, Including Ease of Development, Performance, Scalability, Extensibility, and Security
5.03	Identify the Benefits and Drawbacks of Implementing Web Services in the EJB Component Container
5.04	Select the Appropriate Use of JPA and JPQL in a Given Scenario
✓	Two-Minute Drill
Q&A	Self Test

The business tier contains the code that solves the needs of a business area, such as insurance, banking, retail, or finance. In a Java EE environment, business functionality is typically placed within enterprise beans running in the business tier (in some cases enterprise beans run in the web tier). An enterprise bean receives data from a client program, performs any necessary processing, and then sends data to a storage tier, such as a database or an enterprise information system tier. An enterprise bean can also receive data from a client program, retrieve data from a storage tier, perform any necessary processing, and then send it back to the client program. Figure 5-1 depicts the client, business, and persistence tiers of a Java EE application.

FIGURE 5-1

Java EE overview

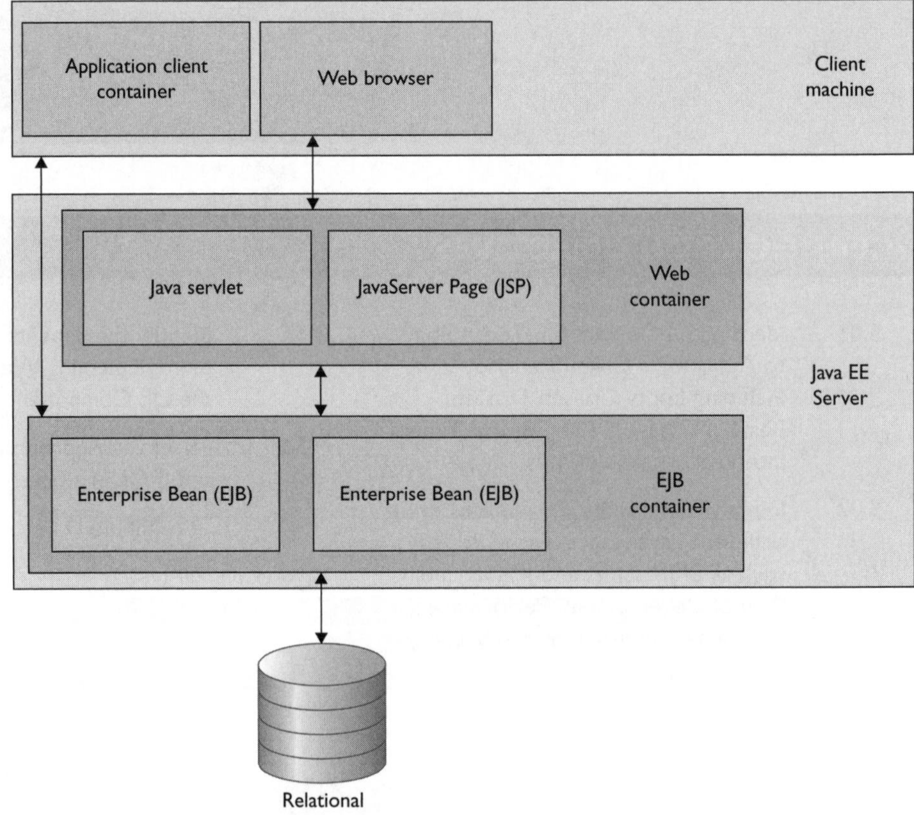

Background on New Features in Java EE 6

The exam focuses less, if at all, on prior releases of Java EE and essentially concentrates on the new features of Java EE 6. In general, the design goals for this Java EE 6 are:

- Provide the foundation for the various components that make up the Java EE platform.
- Focus and improve development productivity, as follows:
  - Add many new annotations.
  - Reduce, or eliminate, the need for XML configuration.
  - Move away from complex classes that implement interfaces and increase the ability to use Plain Old Java Objects (POJOs).

Java EE 6 continues the direction set by the Java EE 5 release, which can be summarized as follows:

- Utilize features supported by Java SE 5 (annotations, generics, type safe enums), making Java EE more declarative.
- Decouple EJBs from infrastructure.
- Add persistence for POJOs.
- Make code placed in business methods not required to declare checked exceptions.
- Make more of the deployment descriptors optional.

Java EE 6 also embraced many values that existed in complementary and competing frameworks. This brings forth a much cleaner and lighter framework with features, such as the following:

- **Contexts and dependency injection (CDI)** Looser coupling, scoping for components.
- **Dependency injection** Easier lookups. Declare external resources in code.
- **Convention over configuration** Also known as "configuration by exception." Simplifies decisions for the developer.
- **Simplified packaging**

Table 5-1 provides the details for the new features of enterprise beans (EJB) 3.1.

TABLE 5-1 New Features for Enterprise Beans (EJB)

EJB Feature	Description
No-interface view	In prior releases, the developer needed to create a Plain Old Java Interface (POJI) as the contract that defines the business methods exposed to the client and implemented on the bean class. Now enterprise beans that do not have a local business interface expose a no-interface view (same behavior as a local view) that automatically exposes public methods of the bean class to a caller.
Singleton	Takes the state (and functionality) contained in a single instance and share it between multiple components.
Asynchronous invocation	Support for asynchronous calls to session bean methods.
Simplified packaging	Now you can place EJB classes directly in the .war file along with web tier components.
Schedule-based timers	You can now schedule execution of events marked as timed events in all enterprise beans (all except the stateful session).
EJB Lite	A typical application only needs a subset of the features provided by EJB: ■ Stateless, stateful, and singleton session beans ■ Local (or no) EJB interfaces ■ Interceptors ■ Container- and bean-managed transactions ■ Declarative and programmatic security ■ Embeddable API (see next)
Embeddable	Provides an embeddable API and container to allow Java SE unit testing of EJB components. It can also be easily used for offline batch processing, messaging, scheduling, and so on.
Annotations	New annotations expose EJB as a REST service. Annotations are also provided to develop beans as Singleton, StartUp & Timer, and Schedule expressions.
Portable global JNDI names	JNDI names for session beans have become portable via the java:global namespace. Here is their syntax: `java:global[/<app-name>]/<module-name>/<bean-name>`

CERTIFICATION OBJECTIVE 5.01

Identify the Correct EJB Technology to Apply for a Given Scenario, Including Entity Classes, Session Beans, Message-Driven Beans, Timers, Interceptors, and POJOs

This section covers the enterprise bean (EJB) technology in Java EE. This includes describing the enterprise bean (EJB) technology that is appropriate for given scenarios.

Enterprise Bean Overview

A enterprise bean (or EJB) is a server-side component that contains business logic for an application. Enterprise beans contain fields (variables) and methods (functions) to implement business logic or functionality. Enterprise beans simplify the development of large, distributed applications, as follows:

- The enterprise bean (EJB) container provides system-level services to enterprise beans, such as security and transaction management, leaving the bean developer to focus on implementing the code to solve the business requirements.
- An enterprise bean (EJB) contains an application's business logic, leaving the developer of a client application to focus on the presentation of the client. When the client application contains less code, there are fewer opportunities for defects, and a smaller client code footprint can be an important consideration for smaller devices.
- Provided that it uses the standard APIs, an enterprise bean (EJB) is a portable component and will run on any compliant Java EE container.

With the simplification and streamlining aspects of the EJB 3.1 release, enterprise beans can be placed in a web application archive (.war) file alongside web tier components. In other words, enterprise beans do not have to be contained in a separate ejb-jar file. The ejb-jar.xml file is optionally required and can be packaged as part of the .war file (/WEB-INF/ folder).

Exam Scenarios to Utilize Enterprise Beans

For the exam, the use of enterprise beans is the most appropriate implementation for the following scenarios:

- **Scalability** To accommodate growing numbers of users, Java EE servers can be clustered (multiple machines), and enterprise beans of a deployed application will run on multiple members of the cluster.
- **Transactions** Transactions ensure data integrity; the performance of an operation that changes data from a known state to another known state. Enterprise beans support transactions, the mechanisms that manage the concurrent access of shared objects.
- **Fine-grained security** Enterprise beans support declarative and programmatic, fine-grained security.
- **Reuse** Involves using business logic (functionality) from multiple types of clients (Web Start, Applet, web browser). With minimal code, a client can easily locate and utilize enterprise beans.

Exam Watch: Since the release of Java EE 5, the use of EJB entity beans has been discouraged and essentially replaced by entity classes using the Java Persistence API (JPA).

As mentioned earlier, the enterprise bean solely implements business logic, and all low-level system services are taken care of by the EJB container. Enterprise bean technology comes in three high-level types: entity class, session bean, and message-driven bean. We cover each of these types in detail as well as the scheduling timer service and the Aspect Oriented Programming (AOP) interceptor features.

Entity Class

An entity class is a lightweight persistence domain object. For the most part, an instance of an entity class will represent a row in a table or view in a relational database. The state of an entity is represented either through fields or properties. These fields or properties use Object Relational Mapping (ORM) annotations to map an entity and its relationships to the relational data in the persistence data store. All entity classes must abide by the following:

- They must be annotated with `@Entity`.
- They must have a public or protected, no-argument constructor.
- The class must not be declared final.
- The methods or persistent instance variables must not be declared final.
- (Optional) They must implement the Serializable interface if they are parameters (such as via a stateless session beans remote interface).

Plain Old Java Object (POJO)

The release of EJB 3 vastly simplified the way a developer builds classes to represent entities in a persistence layer (for example, database tables). A Plain Old Java Object, or POJO, is all that is needed (along with the new EJB3 annotations and transaction management) to be used in an Enterprise application.

Entity Bean

Entity beans are a legacy from the EJB spec prior to EJB 3. Since Java EE 5 was released, the use of entity beans has been discouraged and essentially replaced by entity classes using the Java Persistence API (JPA). Like EJB 3 entity classes, entity beans are used in pre-Java EE 5 platform implementations in the following areas:

- To represent persistent data in an object with a clearly defined identity
- To provide secure, concurrent access to multiple clients
- To provide robust, long-lived persistent data management
- To provide access through query language (EJB-QL) for container-managed persistence (CMP) and SQL for bean-managed persistence (BMP)
- To provide simplified transaction handling

As mentioned previously, an entity bean can implement either bean-managed persistence (BMP) or container-managed persistence (CMP). In the case of BMP, the implementer of an entity bean stores and retrieves the information managed by the bean through direct database calls. One disadvantage to this approach is that it makes it more difficult to adapt BMP entity beans to alternative data sources. In the case of CMP, the container provider may implement access to the database using standard APIs. The container provider can offer tools to map instance variables of an entity bean to calls to an underlying database. This approach makes it easier to use CMP entity beans with different databases.

Look at the coverage for the exam objective that covers CMP and BMP later in this chapter for more information on EJB entity beans.

Session Bean

A session bean is an enterprise bean that contains business logic that implements a process or specific functionality (and/or workflow). A session bean would be the right type of enterprise bean to be used in the following scenarios:

- When only one client has access to the bean instance at any given time
- If the enterprise bean's state does not need to be persisted
- If the enterprise bean is implementing a web service

Session beans come in three subtypes: stateless, stateful, and singleton. Let's look at each of these subtypes.

Stateless Session Bean (SLSB)

A stateless session bean does not maintain a conversational state with the client. When a client invokes the methods of a stateless bean, the bean's instance variables may contain a state specific to that client, but only for the duration of the invocation. When the method is finished, the client-specific state should not be retained. Clients may, however, change the state of instance variables in pooled stateless beans, and this state is held over to the next invocation of the pooled stateless bean. Except during method invocation, all instances of a stateless bean are equivalent, allowing the container to assign an instance to any client. That is, the state of a stateless session bean should apply across all clients. Because stateless session beans can support multiple clients, they can offer better scalability for applications that require large numbers of clients. Typically, an application requires fewer stateless session beans than stateful session beans to support the same number of clients.

A stateless session bean can implement a web service, but other types of enterprise beans cannot.

Use a stateless session bean in the following scenarios:

- ***The bean's state has no data for a specific client.***
- ***The bean performs a task for any client during a single method invocation.***
- ***To implement a web service endpoint.***

Stateful Session Bean (SFSB)

In a stateful session bean, the instance variables represent the state of a specific client/bean session, and this state is available for the duration of the client/bean session. The session and its state ends when the client removes the bean or when the client terminates.

Use a stateful session bean for any of the following situations:

- ***The bean's state represents the interaction between the bean and a specific client.***
- ***The bean needs to hold information about the client access method invocations.***
- ***The bean mediates between the client and the other components of the application, presenting a simplified view to the client.***

Singleton Session Bean (SSB)

A singleton session bean follows the namesake design pattern and is instantiated once per application (per Java Virtual Machine) and then exists until the application is stopped. The purpose of the singleton session bean is to maintain session state and to provide functionality that can be accessed concurrently by clients (until the application is stopped, or the server crashes or is shut down).

Applications that use a singleton session bean may specify that the singleton should be instantiated upon application startup, which allows the singleton to perform initialization tasks for the application. The singleton may perform cleanup tasks on application shutdown as well, because the singleton will operate throughout the life cycle of the application.

Use a singleton session bean in the following situations:

- ***The state or functionality needs to be shared (accessed by multiple threads concurrently) across an application.***
- ***The application needs to perform tasks at startup and/or during shutdown.***
- ***The bean implements a web service endpoint.***

There are two choices for controlling concurrency for a singleton session bean:

- **Container-managed concurrency (CMC)** The Java EE container controls access to a singleton session bean instance based on method-level locking metadata. Annotate a singleton bean with `@ConcurrencyManagement(ConcurrencyManagementType.CONTAINER)`.
- **Bean-managed concurrency (BMC)** The Java EE container permits full concurrent access to a singleton session bean instance and defers state synchronization to code within the singleton session bean instance. Annotate a singleton bean with `@ConcurrencyManagement(ConcurrencyManagementType.BEAN)`.

Message-Driven Bean (MDB)

A message-driven bean (MDB) is an enterprise bean that allows a Java EE application to process messages in an asynchronous way, as opposed to session beans, which allow you to send JMS messages and to receive them synchronously. MDBs typically process JMS messages by acting as a JMS message consumer, but they can consume messages from other providers—for example, Java Connector Architecture (JCA). Messages can be inserted into a JMS Topic or JMS Queue from many sources, including other Java EE components, but a message can also be inserted from non-Java EE components. All instances of an MDB are equivalent and the Java EE container can pool these instances, in a manner similar to stateless session bean, to allow streams of messages to be processed simultaneously. MDBs have the following characteristics:

- They are stateless, but they can access and update shared data in a database.
- They execute upon receipt of a message from a client.
- They are invoked asynchronously.

- They execute for short periods.
- They can be made part of a transaction (redelivered upon rollback).

When a message arrives, the container calls the message-driven beans `onMessage` method to process the message. The `onMessage` method normally casts the message to one of the five JMS message types and handles it in accordance with the application's business logic.

Use a message-driven bean in the following situations:

- ***For long-running tasks to be processed asynchronously***
- ***When resources are not always available***
- ***If you want to parallelize processing***
- ***To receive and process messages from third-party applications***

Timer Service

The timer service of the enterprise bean container enables you to schedule timed notifications for all types of enterprise beans (except for stateful session beans). You can schedule a timed notification to occur according to a calendar schedule, at a specific time, after a duration of time, or at timed intervals. There are two types of timers:

- **Programmatic** Set by explicitly calling one of the timer-creation methods of the TimerService interface. When a programmatic timer expires, the container calls the method that is annotated with `@Timeout` in the bean's implementation class. This method has the business logic for such timed events.
- **Automatic** Created upon the successful deployment of an enterprise bean that contains a method annotated with the `java.ejb.Schedule` or `java.ejb.Schedules` annotation.

Interceptors (AOP)

Interceptors are the implementation of aspect-oriented programming (AOP) features in Java EE. AOP is a programming approach that increases modularity by separation of cross-cutting concerns. In Java EE, interceptors allow developers to invoke interceptor methods on an associated target class, in conjunction with method invocations or when life cycle events (bean creation/destruction) occur.

Common uses of interceptors are typical cross-cutting concerns such as logging, auditing, and profiling, but they can also be used to extend functionality to existing classes for which you do not have source code (for example, a third-party product).

An interceptor can be defined within a target class as an interceptor method, or in an associated class called an interceptor class. Interceptor classes contain methods that are invoked in conjunction with the methods or life cycle events of the target class. Interceptor classes and methods are defined using metadata annotations, or in the deployment descriptor of the application containing the interceptors and target classes.

on the Job

Use an interceptor to extend functionality. The interceptor is invoked when business methods on the target class are invoked. Any object managed by Java EE can have an interceptor associated with it.

The following scenario and solutions table shows the appropriate EJB technology for a list of scenarios.

SCENARIO & SOLUTION

Given Scenario	Appropriate EJB Technology
To represent data being retrieved from, and saved to, a persistence layer (for example, relational database)	Entity classes. (You will have to consider entity beans if you are extending the functionality of an existing EJB 2.x implementation.)
If you do not have to store state data for a specific client To perform business functionality for any client during a single method invocation To implement a web service endpoint	Stateless session bean (SLSB).
To represent state (or information) for a specific client To present a simplified view of a mediation between client and several server-side components of an application	Stateful session bean (SFSB).
If state (or functionality) needs to be shared across an application (internally) or via a web service end point (externally) To perform tasks at application startup and/or during shutdown	Singleton session bean (SSB).
To integrate with a third-party application where messages are received via JMS For long-running tasks to be processed asynchronously When resources are not always available If you want to parallelize processing	Message-driven bean (MDB).

CERTIFICATION OBJECTIVE 5.02

Identify Benefits and Drawbacks of Different Persistence Technologies such as BMP, CMP, and JPA, Including Ease of Development, Performance, Scalability, Extensibility, and Security

Several persistence technologies are available in Java EE that you must be familiar with in order to pass the exam.

Gauging Benefits and Drawbacks

Before we cover the persistence technologies, let's take a quick look at the nonfunctional requirements and qualities that are typically used to gauge the benefits and drawbacks of these persistence technologies.

Ease of Development

Ease of development typically refers to qualities that make developers more productive and able to implement more functionality in a shorter periods of time with simple or straightforward approaches. For Java EE specifically, we can look at examples of this with features such as annotations, which can be used to define and wire functionality along with the code instead of separately in configuration files. Another example is JPA, where persistence details are left up to the JPA implementation to deal with leaving the developer free from having to explicitly write SQL code, thus reducing development time.

The older EJB (2.x and prior) specification releases required significantly more overhead and implementation work by the developer. There was a big push in the EJB 3.0 specification, and continuing with EJB 3.1, to vastly simplify the process of developing EJBs of all types and thus improve developer productivity.

Performance

In terms of persistence and performance, there is typically a tradeoff in having the details of the persistence being delegated to a container or specific persistence implementation or having a developer implement the persistence details in code.

Examples of persistence delegation are JPA-based EJB 3.x entity classes and EJB 2.x CMP entity beans. In general, there is the potential for a run-time performance penalty to be paid for the productivity gains realized during development and ongoing maintenance. A contrasting example is where the developer takes more time and effort to implement SQL calls via JDBC, potentially producing the fastest possible performance in all or at least most test cases.

on the job

It is possible for delegated persistence approaches to be tuned to the point where they can be comparable to or even outperform developer-coded persistence. Persistence container services can be configured to incorporate caching and pre-fetching approaches, thus reducing the number of expensive I/O or network calls. In short, mileage can vary—there is no one clear winner just yet.

Scalability

In terms of the persistence approach to scalability, the EJB container has the ability to manage a pool of enterprise beans. The underlying Java EE servers have configuration properties for sizing and managing these bean pools. These properties can be set by taking into account the number, frequency, and duration of client requests. Here are some general rules of thumb:

- Stateless session beans are the most scalable because the container can reuse the bean instance after each method invocation.
- Stateful session beans are less scalable because the container must map one bean instance for every concurrent client until the client session is completed.

Extensibility

As additional functionality is added to an existing application, when it comes to a particular persistence approach, there are no clear advantages (or disadvantages) to either delegated persistence or explicitly coded persistence. In the case of a relational database table having additional columns, regardless of persistence approach, the additional effort is needed to meet the new requirements. The ease of extensibility has no clear winner.

Security

Again, no clear benefits or drawbacks among differing persistence strategies because security has always been one of the core feature of enterprise beans and the EJB container.

So now we have briefly covered the nonfunctional requirements and qualities that are typically used to gauge the benefits and drawbacks of these persistence technologies. We will now cover each of the persistence approaches in more detail before showing a comparison of the benefits and drawbacks of each.

Bean-Managed Persistence (BMP)

When using bean-managed persistence (BMP) entity beans, developers are required to implement code to save the state of the bean to the underlying persistence layer. This does provide the developer with exact control of the way the persistence takes place and often results in the improved performance over CMP implementations, but it comes with the overhead of an increasing amount of potentially more complicated code (increase in complexity not always the case, though). BMP is best suited for specific scenarios where CMP cannot deliver the performance or the underlying persistence layer is not supported by CMP.

The benefits of using bean-managed persistence include the following:

- **Standards based** The standard EJB and JDBC APIs can be used for data access calls.
- **Data type access** The ability to access nonstandard data types and legacy applications is supported.
- **Maximum flexibility** Data validation logic of any complexity is supported.
- **Database specific features** The application is able to take advantage of nonstandard SQL features of different SQL servers.

The drawbacks to using bean-managed persistence include the following:

- **Database specific** Because entity bean code is database specific, if access to multiple databases is required, the enterprise bean provider will have to account for this in its data access methods.
- **Knowledge of SQL** The enterprise bean provider must have knowledge of SQL.
- **Development time** These beans on average take a much longer time to develop.

Container-Managed Persistence (CMP)

When using container-managed persistence (CMP), entity beans leave the persistence of their state to the EJB container. This simplifies the amount of code that needs to be implemented, thus increasing the productivity of the developer. However, the SQL that is generated and submitted to the database server may not be optimal. Knowledge of SQL and the underlying database schema is still essential for the developer, if only to debug and troubleshoot the SQL the CMP implementation is issuing.

The benefits of using container-managed persistence include the following:

- **Database independence** The container, not the enterprise bean provider, maintains database access code to most popular databases.
- **Container-specific features** Features such as full text search are available for use by the enterprise bean provider.
- **Portability** Portability to other EJB containers is straightforward but does not guarantee the same performance.

The drawbacks to container-managed persistence include the following:

- **Algorithms** Only container-supported algorithms persistence can be used.
- **Access** The developer has no access to the view and cannot modify the actual code.
- **Efficiency** Sometimes the generated SQL is not the most efficient with respect to performance.

Java Data Objects (JDO)

The Java Data Objects (JDO) API is a standard interface-based Java model abstraction of persistence, developed under the auspices of the Java Community Process. A developer can use JDO to store Java domain model instances into the persistent store.

The benefits of using JDO are:

- **Ease of use** The developer focuses on the domain object model; the persistence details are taken care of by the JDO implementation.
- **Portability** JDO applications run on several JDO implementations without change. Also, JDO supports a large number of relationship and data types, and it has no proxy objects.

- **Database independence** JDO applications are independent of the underlying data store. The transactional data stores are not limited to relational databases; there is also support for NoSQL data sources, object databases, XML, flat files, and other persistence tiers. It is also possible to more easily switch from a SQL to a NoSQL data source, and vice versa.
- **High performance** The persistence details are taken care of by the JDO implementation, so there is an opportunity to obtain optimal performance through optimized data access patterns.
- **Integration with EJB** JDO applications can still take advantage of the major EJB features using the same domain object models—features such as transaction coordination, security, and remote message processing.

The main drawback of using JDO is that it is not as frequently updated.

Java Database Connectivity (JDBC)

The Java Database Connectivity (JDBC) API lets you invoke SQL commands from Java programming language methods. You use the JDBC API within multiple Java EE components (enterprise beans, servlets, and JSP) to access the database directly without using entity beans or entity classes. The JDBC API has two parts: an application-level interface used by the application components to access a database, and a service provider interface to attach a JDBC driver to the Java EE platform.

The benefits of using JDBC include the following:

- It is easy to test.
- It is platform independent.
- It offers the potential to maximize query performance.

The drawbacks of using JDBC include the following:

- The developer needs to code and handle all checked exceptions.
- There is no support for relationships, inheritance, and associations.
- Implementation is up to the developer.
- The developer needs to know SQL and relational model.

Java Persistence API (JPA)

The Java Persistence API (JPA) was introduced by the Java EE 5 specification and has been steadily enhanced. Its purpose is to simplify and standardize the approach to mapping Java objects to relational database tables, more commonly known as Object Relational Mapping (ORM). JPA also simplifies the programming model for entity persistence and adds capabilities that were not in EJB 2.1. JPA establishes standards for mapping entities to relational tables and creating the ORM configuration metadata. The EntityManager API exposes operations that INSERT, SELECT, UPDATE, and DELETE entities, where entities are persistence objects that model persistent data stored in a relational database. However, there are some cases where JPA is not recommended or possible, and we will cover those scenarios next.

The benefits of using JPA include the following:

- It can be used outside of the container and therefore is also easier to test.
- It can be used with pluggable, third-party persistence providers (Hibernate, TopLink, OpenJPA).
- It offers cleaner, easier, standardized Object Relational Mapping. In particular:
  - It eliminates the need for lookup code (annotations drive this).
  - It reduces or eliminates deployment descriptor entries (it use annotations instead).
  - It requires fewer classes and interfaces.
- Java Persistence Query Language (JPQL), an enhanced EJB QL, can be used to search through and retrieve data.

The drawbacks of using JPA include the following:

- There is the potential for suboptimal performance. The generated SQL statements may not perform as needed because of the data store design and implementation.
- If the existing implementation is not using JPA and you need to extend functionality in a minor way, a rewrite of the entire tier to use JPA is typically not permitted or justified (large cost and increased risk).
- If the underlying persistence layer is not supported sufficiently by the JPA implementation. This situation occurs mostly when the persistence layer is not one of the major relational databases.

TABLE 5-2 Benefits and Drawbacks of Java EE Persistence Technology

Persistence Type	Benefit	Drawback
Container Managed Persistence (CMP)—EJB2	Ease of development. Scalable. Secure.	Prior EJB specification, becoming obsolete. Possible performance hit. Less extensible.
Bean Managed Persistence (BMP)—EJB2	Scalable. Secure.	Prior EJB specification, becoming obsolete.
Java Persistence API (JPA)	Ease of development. Performance (potential). Scalable. Secure.	May not fit the underlying schema.
Java Data Objects (JDO)	Ease of development. Scalable. Secure.	Less frequently updated (latest update is April 2010).
Java Database Connectivity (JDBC)	Performance (fine-grained control over implementation).	Less extensible. Less secure (subject to SQL injection).

Comparing Persistence Types

Table 5-2 shows the benefits and drawbacks of each of the persistence types found for Java EE.

CERTIFICATION OBJECTIVE 5.03

Identify the Benefits and Drawbacks of Implementing Web Services in the EJB Component Container

For this objective we examine the advantages and disadvantages to implementing web services within the EJB container. We look at exposing enterprise beans as web services as well as calling web services from enterprise beans.

Web Services

Before looking at how enterprise beans (EJBs) can be exposed as web service end points and how they can call web services to consume data, we will first quickly review the web services available in the Java EE platform.

Java API for XML Web Services (JAX-WS)

JAX-WS is a technology for building web services and clients that communicate using XML. It defines the core specification for the web services standard in Java EE. It provides a way for the developer to expose singleton and stateless session beans (as well as other POJOs) as web services.

Java API for RESTful Web Services (JAX-RS)

JAX-RS provides support for web services that conform to the Representational State Transfer (REST) architectural pattern. It also provides a way for the developer to expose singleton and stateless session beans (as well as other POJOs) as web services.

Enterprise Beans and Web Services

In the new releases of the Java EE platform, it has become fairly straightforward for an enterprise bean (EJB) to become either a provider or a consumer of web services. Adding the `@WebService` annotation to an enterprise bean (stateless and singleton session beans only) will expose all the public methods of the EJB as a web service when deployed. The Java EE platform publishes the public methods as web service operations, mapping the arguments for each operation into an XML schema. Likewise, an enterprise bean (EJB) can access web services using either of the Java Web Service APIs (JAX-WS and JAX-RS) listed earlier in this section.

The benefits of using enterprise beans (EJB) and web services include the following:

- Increased developer productivity to meet changing business requirements and needs.
  - A provider is quickly able to expose business functionality as web services.
  - A consumer is quickly able to build or modify an enterprise bean (EJB) so it can consume web services.

The drawbacks of using enterprise beans (EJB) and web services include the following:

- As a provider:
  - Directly exposing business functionality instead of the preferred architectural approach of a well-defined and more centralized integration tier may be viewed as disorganized and somewhat messy.
  - There is a security concern with data and functionality being directly available to external applications/clients. This points to weakness in the direct approach in place of the centralized integration tier mentioned earlier.
- As a consumer:
  - If web service calls are added to an existing enterprise bean, then appropriate steps need to be taken to validate data being sent to the service and the data being received so that invalid data does not leak into the application or its persistence layer.

CERTIFICATION OBJECTIVE 5.04

Select the Appropriate Use of JPA and JPQL in a Given Scenario

For this objective we examine the scenarios for which JPA and JPQL are appropriate. Before covering the scenarios, we first quickly review the Java Persistence API and Java Persistence Query Language (JPQL) available in the Java EE platform. Figure 5-2 depicts an overview of the Java Persistence API for a Java EE application.

Java Persistence API (JPA)

As mentioned earlier in this chapter, the Java Persistence API (JPA) greatly simplifies Java persistence and provides an Object Relational Mapping (ORM) approach that enables developers to define how to map Java objects (entities) to relational database tables in a standard, portable, and declarative (within code) way. These are known as JPA entities and are discussed next.

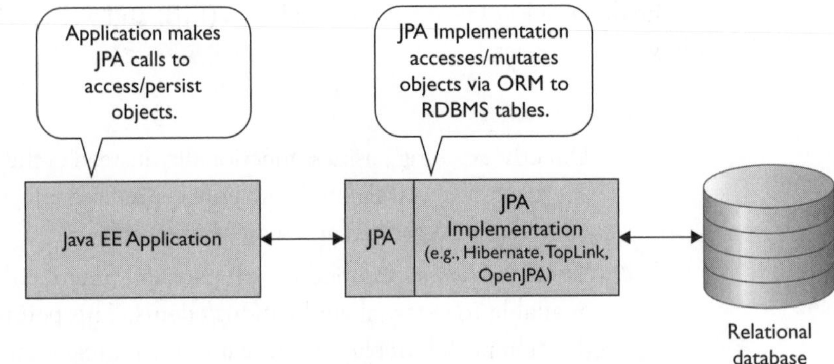

FIGURE 5-2

Java Persistence API (JPA) overview

JPA Entities

A JPA entity is a Plain Old Java Object (POJO) that manages persistent data. There is no requirement to implement an interface (it is able to, though), and as such it is a lightweight object. A developer places annotations within the code to map the fields within an entity to columns in a database table.

Java Persistence Query Language (JPQL)

The Java Persistence Query Language allows a developer to define queries for entities and their persistent state. JPQL uses a SQL-like syntax to select objects based on entity abstract schema types and relationships that exist among them. In other words, JPQL can be considered as an object-oriented version of SQL.

The advantages of JPQL are:

- JPQL queries look similar to SQL queries, which can be familiar, easy to use, and simple to understand.
- For simple static queries, string-based JPQL queries (for example, as named queries) may be preferred.

Named Query

A JPA named query is a statically predefined unchangeable query string. Its primary goal is to create more efficient queries by forcing developers to use query parameters in place of embedding literals in a string. Named queries, defined by the `@NamedQuery` and `@NamedQueries` annotations, are also placed separately from the Java code that uses them, and the separation is considered an improvement to the organization of the code.

SCENARIO & SOLUTION	
Given Scenario	**Appropriate Use of JPA and JPQL?**
The data model is simple, in terms of size and relationships, and the development team would like to start using an ORM approach to development.	Yes, JPA using JPQL and/or the JPA Criteria API is an appropriate fit for this scenario.
The development team is making minor updates to an existing EJB 2.x application.	No, existing EJB 2.x applications should keep to using CMP and/or BMP entity beans.
You are architecting a new Java EE application that persists data represented within Java objects to a relational database.	Yes, this is an appropriate scenario for using JPA and JPQL.

JPA Criteria API

A new feature introduced in JPA 2.0 is the JPA Criteria API, which allows a developer to dynamically build object-based queries instead of defining queries using Java Persistence Query Language (JPQL). Whereas JPQL queries are defined as strings (like SQL), JPA criteria queries are defined by instantiation of Java objects that represent query elements. Neither approach to queries has a power or efficiency advantage, so the choice comes down to the personal preference of the developer. The advantages of JPA Criteria API are:

- The Criteria API is a type-safe API, so type-checking errors will be detected during compilation instead of at run time.
- Mixing SQL strings throughout an application's logic can surface issues. For example, some developers are not comfortable with SQL, or those that are may not create good SQL anyway. Use of the Criteria API will alleviate these issues.
- For dynamic queries that are built at run time, the Criteria API may be preferred instead of building queries using many string concatenation operations.

Table 5-3 shows the appropriate use of JPA and JPQL for given scenarios.

CERTIFICATION SUMMARY

By studying this chapter, you will have an understanding of the business tier technologies that will be tested on the exam.

TWO-MINUTE DRILL

Identify the Correct EJB Technology to Apply for a Given Scenario, Including Entity Classes, Session Beans, Message-Driven Beans, Timers, Interceptors, and POJOs

- ❑ Use an entity class (EJB 3.x) to represent data being retrieved from, and saved to, a persistence layer (for example, relational database). Note: You will have to consider an entity bean if you are extending functionality of an existing EJB 2.x implementation.
- ❑ Use a stateless session bean (SLSB) for the following scenarios:
  - ❑ You do not have to store state data for a specific client.
  - ❑ To perform business functionality for any client during a single method invocation.
  - ❑ To implement a web service end point.
- ❑ Use a stateful session bean (SFSB) for the following scenarios:
  - ❑ To represent state (or information) for a specific client.
  - ❑ To present a simplified view of a mediation between the client and several server-side components of an application.
- ❑ Use a singleton session bean (SSB) for the following scenarios:
  - ❑ If state (or functionality) needs to be shared across an application (internally) or via a web service end point (externally).
  - ❑ To perform tasks at application startup and/or during shutdown.
- ❑ Use a message-driven bean (MDB) for the following scenarios:
  - ❑ To integrate with a third-party application where messages are received via JMS.
  - ❑ For long-running tasks to be processed asynchronously.
  - ❑ When resources are not always available.
  - ❑ If you want to parallelize processing.

Identify Benefits and Drawbacks of Different Persistence Technologies such as BMP, CMP, and JPA, Including Ease of Development, Performance, Scalability, Extensibility, and Security

- ❑ The benefits to bean-managed persistence (BMP) are:
  - ❑ **Standards based** Standard EJB and JDBC APIs for data access calls.
  - ❑ **Data type access** Support for nonstandard data types and legacy applications.
  - ❑ **Maximum flexibility** Support for complex data validation logic. For exact control over the SQL being sent to the database or to implement code to match a specific legacy database schema. For example, if your persistent store is not a database system or is a legacy database system that is not supported by the EJB container's CMP implementation.
  - ❑ **Database-specific features** Can take advantage of nonstandard SQL features.
  - ❑ **Performance** If the query needs of the application exceed the capabilities of CMP or if the application needs fine-grained coding of SQL to perform effectively. However, it is recommended that data access objects (DAOs) be used. DAOs better enable the bean to be adapted to a different database schema or to evolve into a CMP entity bean later on.
  - ❑ **Backward Compatibility** Better fit if you are extending an existing EJB 2.x BMP implementation.
- ❑ The drawbacks to bean-managed persistence (BMP) are:
  - ❑ **Database specific** Entity bean code is database specific and less portable.
  - ❑ Deeper knowledge of SQL is required.
  - ❑ **Development time** Takes longer time to develop.
- ❑ The benefits to container-managed persistence (CMP) are:
  - ❑ **Database independence** Container handles persistence details.
  - ❑ **Container-specific features** Additional container features are available.
  - ❑ **Portability** Very portable to other EJB containers.
  - ❑ Better fit if you are extending an existing EJB 2.x CMP implementation.

- The drawbacks to container-managed persistence (CMP) are:
  - **Algorithms** Only container-supported algorithms are available.
  - **Access** No access to the view, and generated code cannot be modified.
  - **Efficiency** Generated SQL may not perform as well as required.
- The benefits to Java Data Objects (JDO) are:
  - **Ease of use** Like JPA, the developer focuses on building the model and leaves persistence details to the JDO implementation.
  - **Portability** JDO applications run on several JDO implementations without change.
  - **Database independence** JDO applications are independent of the underlying data store. Support for SQL and NoSQL as well as other data store types.
  - **High performance** JDO implementations have optimized data access patterns.
  - **Integration with EJB** JDO applications can also have EJB features: transaction coordination, security, and remote message processing.
- The drawbacks to Java Data Objects (JDO) are:
  - **Older code** Not as frequently updated.
- The benefits of using Java Database Connectivity (JDBC) are:
  - **Testing** Easy to test components that use JDBC.
  - **Database Agnostic** Platform independent.
  - **Performance** Potential to maximize query performance.
- The drawbacks of using Java Database Connectivity (JDBC) are:
  - **Exceptions** Need to code and handle all checked exceptions.
  - **Relationships** No support for relationships, inheritance, and associations.
  - **More Coding** Implementation is up to the developer.
  - **SQL Knowledge** Developer needs to know SQL and relational model.
- The benefits of using Java Persistence API (JPA) are:
  - **Testing** Usable outside of the container and therefore also easier to test.
  - **Plugins** Usable with pluggable, third-party persistence providers (Hibernate, TopLink, OpenJPA).

- ❑ **Standard** Cleaner, easier, standardized object-relational mapping:
    - ❑ Eliminates the need for lookup code (annotations drive this).
    - ❑ Reduces or eliminates deployment descriptor entries (use annotations instead).
    - ❑ Requires fewer classes and interfaces.
- ❑ **Java Persistence Query Language (JPQL)** An enhanced EJB QL to search through and retrieve data.
- ❑ **Criteria API** Dynamically built object-based queries.

❑ The drawbacks of using Java Persistence API (JPA) are:

- ❑ **Potentially suboptimal performance** The generated SQL statements may not perform as needed because of the data store design and implementation.
- ❑ **If existing implementation is not using JPA and you need to extend functionality in a minor way** In these types of cases, a rewrite of the entire tier to use JPA is typically not permitted or justified (due to large cost and increased risk).
- ❑ **If the underlying persistence layer is not supported sufficiently by the JPA implementation** This situation occurs mostly when the persistence layer is not one of the major relational databases.

Identify the Benefits and Drawbacks of Implementing Web Services in the EJB Component Container

The benefit of using enterprise beans (EJB) and web services is:

- ❑ Increased developer productivity to meet changing business requirements and needs. It's easy to expose EJB as a web service provider and to create or modify an EJB to consume web service(s).

The drawbacks of using enterprise beans (EJB) and web services include the following:

- ❑ Direct exposure as a web service provider is a security concern as well as being counter to the preferred architectural approach of a well-defined and more centralized integration tier.
- ❑ As web service calls are added to an enterprise bean (EJB), the developer must ensure the data being sent and received is valid to prevent invalidate data leaking into the application or its persistence layer.

Select the Appropriate Use of JPA and JPQL in a Given Scenario

- ❑ If you are architecting an new Java EE application that persists data represented within Java objects to a relational database, this is an appropriate scenario for using JPA and JPQL.
- ❑ If you are making minor updates to an existing EJB 2.x application, it is probably not a good scenario for using JPA and JPQL technology. It makes more sense to keep to using EJB 2.x CMP and/or BMP entity beans.

SELF TEST

The following questions will help you measure your understanding of the material presented in this chapter. Read all the choices carefully because there may be more than one correct answer. Choose all correct answers for each question.

Identify the Correct EJB Technology to Apply for a Given Scenario, Including Entity Classes, Session Beans, Message-Driven Beans, Timers, Interceptors, and POJOs

1. Serengeti Trading Company is starting to develop a new system that enables its participants, who reside anywhere around the world, to buy and sell items in an open auction fashion. Serengeti has a primary goal to ensure that all participants are treated absolutely equally in all respects; this includes dedicating resources to each participant so that they do not impact each other. Serengeti has sufficient funding to procure whatever is needed on the technology budget to achieve its goal. Which one of the following solutions do you recommend?

A. Stateless session beans (SLSB)

B. Stateful session beans (SFSB)

C. Message-driven beans (MDB)

D. BMP entity beans

2. An application needs to read messages from a JMS queue, call a web service using data provided within the message, and persist data from the web service response in a database table. Which type of EJB will you use?

A. Stateful session bean (SFSB)

B. Stateless session bean (SLSB)

C. Message-driven bean (MDB)

D. Entity class

3. If you are to follow the best practice for Java EE architecture, where would you place business rules and functionality?

A. Java servlets

B. Enterprise beans (EJB)

C. JAX-RS Web Services

D. JAX-WS Web Services

4. Which of the following would you recommend for business logic for a highly available, complex transactional system?
   A. Use session beans with JPA
   B. Use JPA
   C. Use a web-centric architecture
   D. Use stateful session beans

5. Which of the following EJB types should be avoided where possible if you are architecting an application for use by a very high number of users?
   A. Entity bean
   B. Message-driven bean (MDB)
   C. Stateful session bean (SFSB)
   D. Stateless session bean (SLSB)

Identify Benefits and Drawbacks of Different Persistence Technologies such as BMP, CMP, and JPA, Including Ease of Development, Performance, Scalability, Extensibility, and Security

6. ABC Corp is a small B2C reverse-auctioneering online business. You have been asked to recommend a persistence strategy for their new platform, which is a green field (that is, no existing code or database schemas) project. Top priorities are ease of development and integration with EJB 3. What do you recommend?
   A. JDBC
   B. CMP entity beans
   C. BMP entity beans
   D. JPA

7. Which of the following is not a benefit of JPA persistence technology?
   A. Callable outside of the EJB container
   B. Eliminates JNDI lookups
   C. Utilizes POJOs
   D. Works with NoSQL data sources

8. Which of the following is not a benefit of CMP persistence technology?
   A. Container generates SQL.
   B. Can be switched to JPA later on.
   C. Deeper knowledge of SQL is required.
   D. Takes less time to develop.

Identify the Benefits and Drawbacks of Implementing Web Services in the EJB Component Container

9. You have been brought into a company to recommend an approach to exposing some existing EJB-based business functionality to their external customers for a short period of time that is fast approaching. What do you recommend if security is not a consideration?

A. Expose an existing EJB as web service.

B. Create a JAX-WS web service that calls EJB.

C. Create a Java servlet that calls EJB.

D. Create a JSP that calls EJB.

10. Which of the following is a drawback to calling web services from an EJB component?

A. Increased productivity.

B. Increased security.

C. It is counter to the preferred architectural approach.

D. It increases validity of data.

Select the Appropriate Use of JPA and JPQL in a Given Scenario

11. An existing application uses EJB 2.0 CMP entity beans heavily. The application has no major issues in production, and little future development is planned. You have been asked to recommend a methodology to adopt when making minor modifications to the application. What do you recommend?

A. JPA entity classes

B. BMP entity beans

C. CMP entity beans

D. Use DAO accessing JDBC directly

12. You are architecting an new Java EE application that persists data represented within Java objects to a relational database. Which of the following do you recommend?

A. JPA entity classes

B. BMP entity beans

C. CMP entity beans

D. Use DAO accessing JDBC directly

SELF TEST ANSWERS

Identify the Correct EJB Technology to Apply for a Given Scenario, Including Entity Classes, Session Beans, Message-Driven Beans, Timers, Interceptors, and POJOs

1. ☑ **B.** Stateful session beans allow a Java EE application to access and retain resources for a user for the lifetime of their session.
   ☒ **A, C,** and **D** are incorrect. These do not solve the core goal of dedicating resources for a user.

2. ☑ **C.** Message-driven bean reads from a JMS queue and initiates the work.
   ☒ **A, B,** and **D** are incorrect. These other options do not asynchronously read from a JMS queue, but can be invoked by a message-driven bean (MDB) to execute the work needed.

3. ☑ **B.** Enterprise beans (EJB) are architecturally the "best practice" location for business rules and functionality.
   ☒ **A, C,** and **D** are incorrect. Servlets and web services are architecturally not the best practice locations for business rules and functionality.

4. ☑ **A.** Session beans with JPA have the transactional support needed.
   ☒ **B, C,** and **D** are incorrect. A web-centric approach does not fundamentally imply transactional support. JPA does not provide transactional support by itself. There is no mention for the need for stateful architecture, so stateful session beans are not needed.

5. ☑ **C.** The EJB container needs a stateful session bean instance for each concurrent user, so this type of resource-intensive bean should be avoided unless requirements make it absolutely necessary.
   ☒ **A, B,** and **D** are incorrect. These bean types can be used in high-concurrent-user scenarios.

Identify Benefits and Drawbacks of Different Persistence Technologies such as BMP, CMP, and JPA, Including Ease of Development, Performance, Scalability, Extensibility, and Security

6. ☑ **D.** JPA offers the best integration with EJB 3 and has been designed with ease of development in mind.
   ☒ **A, B,** and **C** are incorrect. These choices are certainly viable, but JPA still offers the best integration with EJB 3.

7. ☑ **D.** JPA does not work with NoSQL implementations.
☒ **A, B,** and **C** are incorrect. They are all benefits of JPA, not drawbacks.

8. ☑ **C.** Deeper knowledge of SQL is not required (it may be useful, though).
☒ **A, B,** and **D** are incorrect. They are all benefits of CMP, not drawbacks.

Identify the Benefits and Drawbacks of Implementing Web Services in the EJB Component Container

9. ☑ **A.** Exposing an existing EJB as a web service can be done quickly, and with security not being a consideration, this is the best choice.
☒ **B, C,** and **D** are incorrect. Although **B** is not a wrong approach, the time pressure to deliver combined with security not being a consideration makes this a less-than-suitable approach. **C** and **D** do not expose a web service interface.

10. ☑ **C.** Calling a web service from an EJB component is considered running counter to the preferred architectural approach of using an integration tier.
☒ **A, B,** and **D** are incorrect. These are not drawbacks.

Select the Appropriate Use of JPA and JPQL in a Given Scenario

11. ☑ **C.** Continuing to use EJB 2.0 CMP entity beans is the pragmatic approach.
☒ **A, B,** and **D** are incorrect. These choices introduce significant new code that would need to be fully regression tested. For a very stable application that does not require very much new development, venturing into considerably more development is unwise.

12. ☑ **A.** Using JPA entity classes is the recommended approach for persisting Java objects in a relational database.
☒ **B, C,** and **D** are incorrect. These choices, although not wrong, are not the best fit for the given scenario.

6

Web Tier Technologies

CERTIFICATION OBJECTIVES

6.01	Identify the Benefits and Drawbacks of Using URL Rewriting and Cookies to Manage HTTP Session State
6.02	Identify Appropriate Uses for JSP and Servlet Technology, and JavaServer Faces in a Given Java EE Application
6.03	Identify the Benefits of Using an EJB Container with a Web Container Instead of a Web Container Alone
6.04	Identify the Differences Between Client Pull and Server Push Architectures
6.05	Identify the Benefits and Drawbacks of Using a Browser to Access Asynchronous, Lightweight Processes on the Server
✓	Two-Minute Drill
Q&A	Self Test

The focus of this chapter is the architecture of the web tier. This architecture at this level has become more comprehensive with the growth of mobile and web applications in all facets of life. We focus on the certification objectives as a view into this web tier architecture. Therefore, we mention specific web tier components when they pertain to the particular certification objectives. That said, a web application is one that uses a web and/or application server to carry out the requirement. Web applications can be user presentation or services oriented. A user presentation–oriented web application generates interactive web pages containing various types of markup language (HTML, XHTML, XML) and dynamic content in response to requests. A service-oriented web application implements the endpoint of a web service. Presentation-oriented applications are often clients of service-oriented web applications.

Web Tier Development Roles

The web tier is the face of an enterprise application and requires specific developers to build applications used in the web.

- **Web designer** Interface designer for web browser–based applications
- **Web developer** Implements all aspects of the web tier
- **Information architect** Creates the vision for site navigation and templating

Web Designer

A web designer fulfills the role of the interface designer for browser-based client applications. If the source code for the view components is sufficiently decoupled from the framework that manages the web tier, then the role of the web designer is purely a client tier concern. Otherwise, the web designing and developing might need to be handled by individuals fluent in the concerns of both the client and web tiers.

Web Developer

The web developer implements all aspects of the web tier. This person must also work closely with the web interface designer to ensure that domain entities and content are properly integrated into the XHTML presentation components. They might also develop the client proxies and business delegates to the business tier components. Although it might be considered more of a client tier concern, because of their expertise from a programming perspective, the web developer often provides assistance with the JavaScript-technology aspects of the web-client tier. That way, the web interface designer can focus on design-oriented issues.

on the job

The typical web developer not only implements all aspects of the web tier, they typically handle a good deal of the business tier functionality as well. The architect oversees internal and client web site construction, application development, and system integration.

CERTIFICATION OBJECTIVE 6.01

Identify the Benefits and Drawbacks of Using URL Rewriting and Cookies to Manage HTTP Session State

Techniques to handle application state using web tier components are not a new phenomenon. As a general rule, you do not persist client session state, but in some applications (such as shopping carts) it may be a requirement. For example, a JSF/JSP technology, such as a servlet, helper bean, or custom-tag, can be adequate and appropriate. Additionally, one might utilize a JPA database/data store entity to separate the persistence logic from the other aspects of the application. Client session state exists for the duration of the client's connection and is abandoned when the connection is closed. Consequently, the selection of components for managing client conversation information typically does not need to support data persistence. Also, the client's presentation content does not always require client state. Instead, you might be using only portions of the client state data or taking different views on that data. Consequently, although they are capable of managing client state, presentation-oriented components, such as JSP technology components and custom tags, are not useful for this application.

exam watch

The client tier can store state with cookies or URL rewriting. URL rewriting can store only enough state to tie a browser to a particular client session, whereas cookies can hold at least 4,096 bytes each, as per RFC 2109. State stored in cookies must pass from the client to the presentation tier before it can be used. This places a limit on the number of concurrent clients because of the network bandwidth used.

You can hold state on the presentation tier with the HTTPSession object, which is a collection that can hold any nonprimitive type. The web container ties the HTTPSession object to the client either with the use of cookies or URL rewriting, so no programming effort is required to do this function.

Many applications require a web-based workflow implemented as a series of requests/response pairs to and from a client. For example, the shopping cart application saves the state of a user's cart selections across requests. Web-based applications are responsible for maintaining such state, called a "session," because HTTP is stateless. To support applications that need to maintain state, Java servlet technology provides an API for managing sessions and allows several mechanisms for implementing sessions.

HttpSession Object

Sessions are represented by an HttpSession object. You access a session by calling the getSession method of a request object. This method returns the current session associated with this request, or, if the request does not have a session, it creates one. You can associate object-valued attributes with a session by name/value pairs. Such attributes are accessible by any web component that belongs to the same web context and is handling a request that is part of the same session. The shopping cart application stores a customer's cart as a session attribute. This allows the shopping cart to be saved between requests and also allows cooperating servlets to access the cart. See the following example, where ShoppingCartServlet retrieves the values in the cart:

```
public class ShoppingCartServlet extends HttpServlet {
     public void doGet (HttpServletRequest request,
        HttpServletResponse response)
        throws ServletException, IOException {
        // Get the user's session and shopping cart
        HttpSession session = request.getSession();
        ShoppingCart cart =
            (ShoppingCart)session.
               getAttribute("cart");
         ...  // access the getters and setters (e.g., cart.
getTotalPrice)
```

Notification and Session Objects

Your application can notify web context and session listener objects of servlet life cycle events. You can notify objects of certain events related to their association with a session, such as the following:

- **When the object is added to or removed from a session** To receive this notification, your object must implement the javax.servlet.http .HttpSessionBindingListener interface.
- **When the session to which the object is attached will be passivated or activated** A session will be passivated or activated when it is moved between virtual machines or saved to and restored from persistent storage. To receive this notification, your object must implement the javax.servlet .http.HttpSessionActivationListener interface.

In terms of HttpSession session management, there is no way for an HTTP client to signal that it no longer needs a session; each session has an associated timeout so that its resources can be reclaimed. The timeout period can be accessed by using a session's [get | set]MaxInactiveInterval methods. To ensure that an active session is not timed out, you should periodically access the session by using service methods because this resets the session's time-to-live counter. When a particular client interaction is finished, you use the session's invalidate method to invalidate a session on the server side and remove any session data:

```
public class ShoppingCartServlet extends HttpServlet {
     public void doPost(HttpServletRequest request,
                  HttpServletResponse response)
                   throws ServletException, IOException {
        // Get the user's session
        HttpSession session = request.getSession();
        // transaction complete -- invalidate the session
        session.invalidate();
        ...
```

Session State Tracking: Should We Use Cookies or URL Rewrite?

A web container can associate a session with a user, passing an identifier between the client and the server. The identifier can be maintained on the client machine as a cookie, or the web component can include the identifier in every URL that is returned to the client. If your application uses session objects, you must ensure that session tracking is enabled by having the application rewrite URLs whenever the client turns off cookies. You do this by calling the response's encodeURL(URL) method on all URLs returned by a servlet. This method includes the session ID in the URL only if cookies are disabled; otherwise, it returns the URL unchanged. The doGet method of ShowCartServlet encodes the three URLs at the bottom of the shopping cart display page, as follows:

```
ShoppingCartServlet

out.println("<a href=\"" +    response.encodeURL(request.getContextPath() +
        "/shopcatalog") + "\">" + messages.getString("ContinueShopping") +
        "<a href=\"" +    response.encodeURL(request.getContextPath() +
        "/shopcashier") +    "\">" + messages.getString("Checkout") +
        "<a href=\"" +   response.encodeURL(request.getContextPath() +
        "/shoppingcart?Clear=clear") +        "\">" + messages.getString("ClearCart");
```

If cookies are turned off, the session is encoded in the URL as follows: http://localhost:8000/onlinestore1/shopcashier;jsessionid=c0o7fszeb1

If cookies are turned on, the URL is http://localhost:8000/onlinestore1/shopcashier.

URL Rewriting

So how do you develop your servlets in order to perform session tracking using URL rewriting? By default, session tracking on the J2EE Engine is performed using cookies. However, in cases where the client browser does not accept cookies, you must use URL rewriting. Note that URL rewriting is always used when the first request from the client arrives. This guarantees that the client receives the session information even if it does not accept cookies. To perform URL rewriting, use the encodeURL() method of the HttpServletResponse object. You can perform a check whether a session has been retrieved from a cookie using the isRequestedSessionFromCookie() method of the HttpServletRequest object.

exam watch

The JEE Engine's Web Container provides an extension to the standard encodeURL(String url), encodeUrl(String s), encodeRedirectUrl(String location), and encodeRedirectURL(String location) methods. That is, if the forceEncoding:string is present at the very beginning of the request URL, it will encode the session information to the URL even if the request contained a session cookie.

You can perform session tracking in your application using URL rewriting only. You configure this behavior using the additional web deployment descriptor of your application and adding the <url-session-tracking/> tag to it. This case is applicable for Wireless Application Protocol (WAP) applications, for example. Because WAP protocol does not support cookies, the only way to identify a client is by transferring session information as part of the request URL. Note that WAP devices have a limit to the length of the URL they can transmit.

It is also applicable for multiframed pages, for example, for which different frames are related to accessing different sessions.

As mentioned, sessions can be implemented with two underlying mechanisms: cookies and URL rewriting. URL rewriting involves placing a session ID in the URL, as in http://www.ucny.com/shoppingcart/retrieve;jsessionid=863F3D316?Id=777.

According to the Open Web App Security Project and basic common sense, URL rewriting has obvious security risks. Because the session ID appears in the URL, it may be easily seen by third parties:

- End users often copy and paste such links without knowing the attached session ID compromises their security.
- Server log files usually record the "Referer" header, which will record session IDs in the log.

Third-party access to session IDs simply means that private user information is wide open to attack. Thus, many argue that URL rewriting is a dangerous practice and should be avoided. If cookies are used instead, the session ID does not appear in the URL.

It's possible that some websites may use cookies to track user browsing patterns. As a result, some users turn off cookies in an attempt to protect their privacy. However, given the seriousness of the preceding security issue, many would argue that turning off cookies is actually much worse for user privacy. That is, the risk of compromising personal data through session hijacking seems to far outweigh concerns about tracking personal browsing patterns. Options for managing URL rewriting include the following:

- Disabling them at the server level
- Disabling them at the application level

An attractive option is a servlet filter. The filter wraps the response object with an alternate version, which changes response.encodeURL(String) and related methods into no-operations. In the case of public websites, you will need to decide if requiring browsers to keep cookies enabled is acceptable in each case.

Maintaining State Using JEE Session Beans

If appropriate, you can also hold state with stateful session beans or entity classes. Entity classes allow state to be persisted to the database.

JPA Entities

The Java Persistence API (JPA) coordinates the management of relational data in JEE and Java Standard Edition applications. JPA's inclusion in EJB 3, coupled with its popularity, flow from the fact that entity beans, in previous EJB specifications, involved complicated code and a heavy resource footprint. Moreover, they could be used only in Java EE application servers. That said, you might reasonably use JPA entities to hold client session state if you intend to have long-lived state. For example, if you want to provide a shopping cart (for example, the Amazon model) that remembers all the items the customer has considered buying and then display those items when the customer returns to your site three weeks later, then an entity class might be appropriate. In this case, the real issue is whether you feel that this data belongs in a database.

Stateful Session Beans

Stateful session beans are designed to handle client session state. They do this efficiently via the container's ability to swap out a bean if memory becomes short. If your application needs to maintain conversational state, then this state must be stored somewhere and must be communicated from that storage location to the appropriate part of the system when needed. Instead of using a stateful session bean, as mentioned, one could store all state on the client as cookies. This approach scales well from a memory point of view because each client has new storage for its own state. However, from a network bandwidth perspective, each time that the client makes a request, the client has to use additional bandwidth to send any state that the server might require. Increased bandwidth could be problematic if the clients have slow connections. In addition, there is a cost in processing time to convert client data into application-usable state objects. You could also store all state in the web tier. This approach is a reasonable alternative if the web tier is the main user of the state. If, however, the business tier is the main user of the state, you can consider using session beans local to the web tier. Additionally, you can store all state in the database. This approach adds additional load on the database. Moreover, this approach creates additional network traffic between the database and whatever tier is using the state information. If the state must be long-term persistent for other reasons, this approach becomes a reasonable option.

EXERCISE 6-1

Session State

Question: If the web server or container is spending more of its time managing state than servicing clients, then should you reconsider the use of servlets to track and manage client session state?
Answer: In this case, it is usually preferred to store only enough data for session tracking (for example, small identifiers such as "cart id #") and to store the larger portion of session data in a stateful session bean.

Servlets

As previously mentioned, servlets can function to track and manage client session state. This is valid where presentation data is client specific. If the data is client specific, there is a degree of control on when the data needs to be passed to and from the web tier.

Business process and workflow make up the functional aspects of the business model. They capture the use-case activities and map them onto the significant data-oriented tasks. You assign these functional aspects to components of the business model. Presentation technologies (such as JSF/JSP technology components) and persistence technologies (such as JPA entities) are not well suited to defining and managing business processes directly.

CERTIFICATION OBJECTIVE 6.02

Identify Appropriate Uses for JSP and Servlet Technology, and JavaServer Faces in a Given Java EE Application

The web tier is responsible for bridging the gap between the user interface and the domain model of the business tier. Its goal is to provide the server-side programmatic support for the client tier, as dictated by the information architecture, without actually implementing any business logic. From an architectural standpoint, it is far from trivial. An improperly architected web tier can have profound effects on the systemic qualities of the overall enterprise application. Some of the core responsibilities of the web tier include:

- Delegating service requests to the business tier
- Dispatching presentation to the client interface
- Managing access to content
- Managing resource security concerns

Servlets

A servlet is a Java program that runs on a Java EE server and produces dynamic HTML pages, typically in response to client requests. The pages are then sent back to the client's web browser. The life cycle of a servlet (shown in Figure 6-1) is controlled by the container in which the servlet has been deployed. When a request is mapped to a servlet, the container performs the following steps. If an instance of the servlet does not exist, the web container loads the servlet class. It then creates an instance of the servlet class. It initializes the servlet instance by calling the init method. From then on, based on user requests, it invokes the service method passing request and response objects. When the container needs to remove the servlet, it finalizes the servlet by calling the servlet's destroy method.

FIGURE 6-1 The servlet life cycle

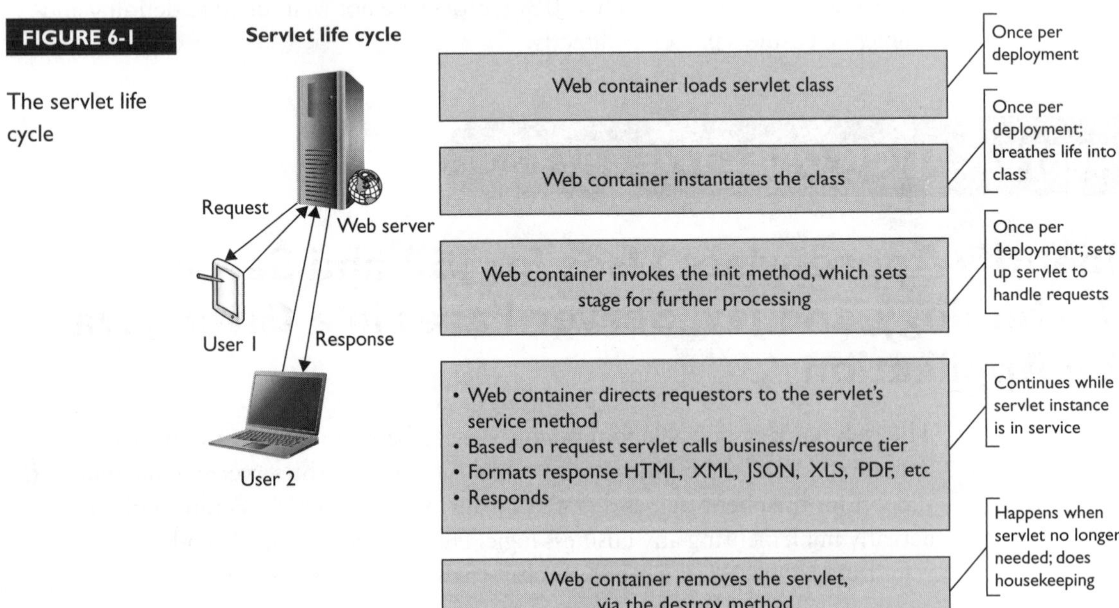

The output format for servlets typically is HTML, but the servlet can MIME many output formats: XML, XLS, PDF, and so on.

Before returning HTML pages, a servlet can perform any operation that a Java application can perform. For example, in a business environment, servlets access the business objects so that you can send custom HTML pages and forms with embedded data to your end users. Because servlets contain Java code, they are best suited for programs that perform processing over presentation.

JavaServer Page

A JSP is a text-based document that includes HTML, JSP tags, and Java code (including calls to JavaBeans and servlets). It cleanly separates content creation from presentation logic.

A JSP page services requests as a servlet. Thus, the life cycle (shown in Figure 6-2) and many of the capabilities of JSP pages are determined by Java servlet technology. When a request is mapped to a JSP page, the web container first checks whether the JSP page's servlet is older than the JSP page. If the servlet is older, the web container translates the JSP page into a servlet class and compiles the class. During development, one of the advantages of JSP pages over servlets is that the build process is performed automatically.

It focuses on rapid development and easy modification of the user interface. It focuses on presentation. JSPs are servlets that are written differently. The JSP technology separates the user interface from dynamic content generation so that designers can change the overall page layout without altering the dynamic content. The JSP technology supports a reusable component-based design. A key feature of the JSP technology is page generation, HTML-like tags, and scriptlets written in the Java programming language that encapsulate the logic that generates the content for the page. By separating the presentation design from the application logic that generates the data, the JSP-enabled pages make it easier for organizations to reuse and share application logic through custom tags and JavaBeans-based components. This also separates the job responsibilities of the web designer and the Java programmer. For example, custom tags and beans can be developed by the Java programmer and implemented by the web designer.

JavaServer Faces

A JSF is a server-side component framework for web applications. It implements the Model-View-Controller (MVC) framework as well as provides separation of navigational and data flow.

FIGURE 6-2

The JSP life cycle

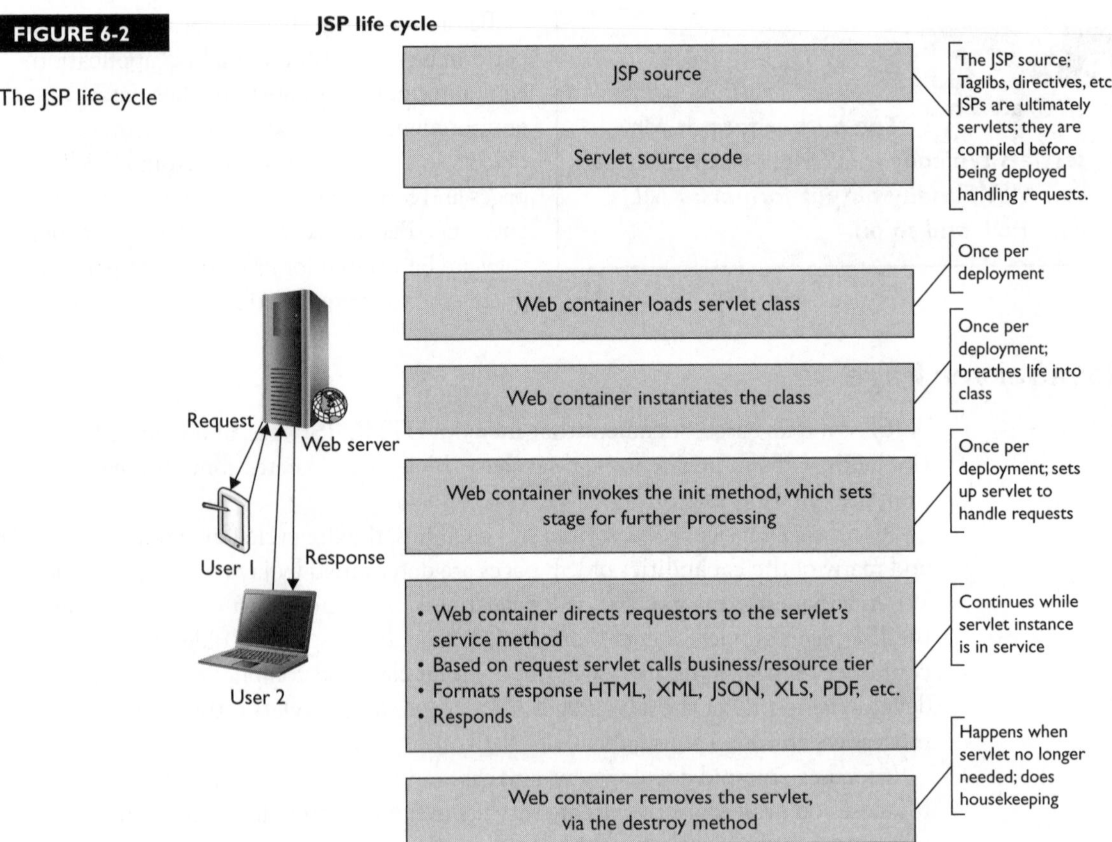

The life cycle of a JavaServer Faces page (shown in Figure 6-3) is somewhat similar to that of a JSP page: the client makes an HTTP request for the page, and the server responds with the page translated to HTML. However, the JavaServer Faces life cycle differs from the JSP life cycle in that it is split up into multiple phases in order to support the sophisticated UI component model. This model requires that component data be converted and validated, component events be handled, and component data be propagated to beans in an orderly fashion. A JavaServer Faces page is also different from a JSP page in that it is represented by a tree of UI components, called a "view." During the life cycle, the JavaServer Faces implementation must build the view while considering the state saved from a previous submission of the page. When the client submits a page, the JavaServer

FIGURE 6-3

The JSF life cycle

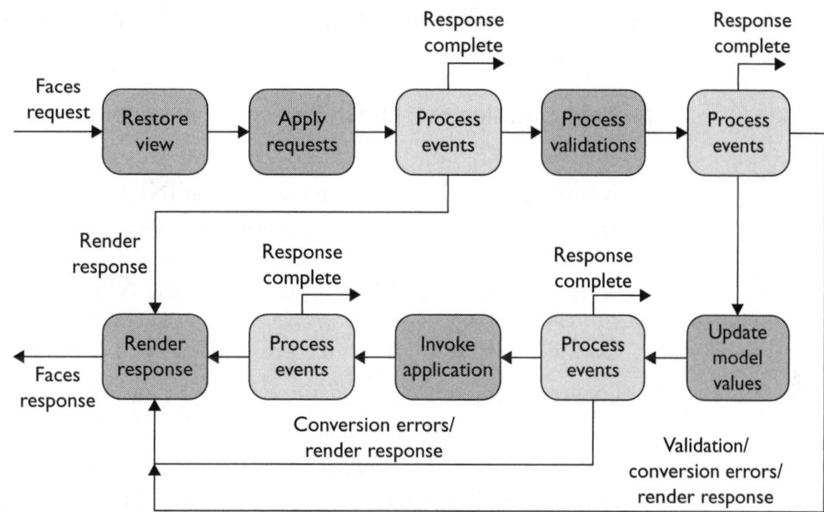

Faces implementation performs several tasks, such as validating the data input of components in the view and converting input data to types specified on the server side. The JavaServer Faces implementation performs all these tasks as a series of steps in the JavaServer Faces request-response life cycle.

Watch ***In Java EE 6, JSF 2 has deprecated JSP as its view layer, replacing it with the more JSF-centric Facelets.***

JSF is a component-based framework for developing web-based applications. JSF provides a framework for using robust UI components in a consistent manner. JSF provides a RAD environment for building web applications. JSF is developer tool centric so that developers can use visual editors to create applications. JSF also combines the functionality of a JSP with a built-in controller. These parts make JSF a true MVC framework.

As mentioned, Facelets replaces JSPs as the view layer in Java EE 6/JSF 2. Facelets support templating via composite components. Facelets allows the developer to create reusable composition components. For example, you can take an existing JSP page and turn it into a reusable component. Facelets help to resolve the mismatch between JSP's dynamic content and JSF's component-based model. Facelets were designed with the JSF life cycle in mind. Using Facelets, you create templates that build a component tree, not a servlet. This supports greater reuse at the component level. Facelets also eliminate the need to write custom tags to use JSF components, because Facelets use JSF custom components natively. Java

EE applications use the following parts of the JNDI specifications to find other distributed objects:

- An application-level interface used by client programs to access a naming and directory service
- A service-provider interface used by the JNDI API to communicate with a provider of a naming and directory service, in a vendor-independent manner

Client applications use JNDI properties and the API to:

- Connect with a JNDI service provider by establishing an initial context
- Locate an object by its registered name by calling a lookup operation from the initial context. The server implements the JNDI Service Provider Interface (SPI) library, which generalizes access to different types of JNDI provider implementations, such as Remote Method Invocation (RMI) Registry, Common Object Services Naming, Lightweight Directory Access Protocol (LDAP), and others. This enables different types of directory-service and naming-service implementations to be transparently used by the Java EE container.

Scripting Languages

Interpreted scripting languages, such as Perl, PHP, and possibly Python (an interpreted language that uses an intermediate representation), have been popular for some time—the "P" in the LAMP acronym. They provide the ability to preview the application in that there is no compilation step before deployment, and provide immediate viewing of dynamic behavior through a web server that supports the script handler. Scripting languages have always been popular for smaller projects, due to the rapidity of development. That rapidity, however, is often accomplished through a sacrifice of separation of concerns (SoC), even though frameworks exist for most scripting languages to support SoC. The use of scripting languages for the web tier of enterprise applications has found mainstream acceptance, especially with the new media companies that handle e-mail and SMS marketing. Most scripting languages have a bridge technology that allows communication with enterprise Java technology components. There are, however, scripting languages that run inside the JRE with greater degrees of integration with Java enterprise applications.

Web Tier Input Data Validation

Whether using JSPs, JSFs, or any scripting language, a validation framework should provide a common set of validators, validation via configuration, and the ability to customize validators. Also, where necessary, it provides local, remote, and web service–based service providers and run-time JavaScript validator generation for the client tier. Note that Java EE 6 introduces Bean Validation. Moreover, JSF includes built-in and custom validators. Client-side validation should be performed on the server as well. Regardless of the extent of data validation taking place in the client tier, data validation must also take place on the server side. Ideally, a ubiquitous data validation mechanism cuts across the web, business, and integration tiers as an application service. Some client tier validators found in RIA Ajax frameworks can make XMLHttpRequest callbacks to the server at run time for validation within the server. Bean Validation affords a standard framework for validation, in which the same set of validations can be shared by all the layers of an application. Bean Validation offers a framework for validating Java classes written according to JavaBeans conventions. You use annotations to specify constraints on a JavaBean—you can annotate a JavaBean class, field, or property. You can also extend or override these constraints through XML descriptors. A validator class then validates each constraint. You specify which validator class to use for a given type of constraint. Some client tier validators found in RIA Ajax frameworks can make XMLHttpRequest callbacks to the server at run time for validation within the server. A great user interaction pattern that fits this feature quite nicely is the attempt to select a user handle in a website registration form. The framework could validate the user's selected handle by invoking an XMLHttpRequest callback to the server-side validator that checks to make sure that the handle the user wants is not already selected. The end user could be told to select another handle before they actually submitted the form. JSF has a number of built-in validations and also comes with a powerful validation framework for plugging in custom validators.

Control and Logic Concerns

So how do we handle the management of view components, data entities, web framework–related logic, and the delegation of requests for business logic to the business tier? Within the MVC architecture, all data and business logic are encapsulated inside the model. The original MVC had an event-based mechanism for the model to communicate state changes to the view. Because HTTP is a request/response-oriented communication, the view has to explicitly make a request of model state if it is not returned with the result condition. The controller has two responsibilities:

- Dispatching of service requests to the model
- Dispatching of views to the end user

The components within the model might be somewhat coupled to the MVC framework. Because it is considered good practice to keep your business data and logic completely decoupled, what goes on in this model needs to be scrutinized.

Model-View-Controller: Model/Controller

One thing that has evolved in web tier development is the true meaning of a model. The Service to Worker pattern subrogates the idea of a model to the concerns of the business tier. Figure 6-4 illustrates the MVC/Service to Worker overlap. Specifically, the Service to Worker pattern just applies to the state machine relationship between a service dispatcher and business delegates. A front controller is the front door to the web application. It is implemented as a servlet or filter that all requests must come through. It may invoke business delegates directly for domain model operations that provide support for the web framework itself, or pass business logic requests to the

FIGURE 6-4

The MVC/Service to Worker

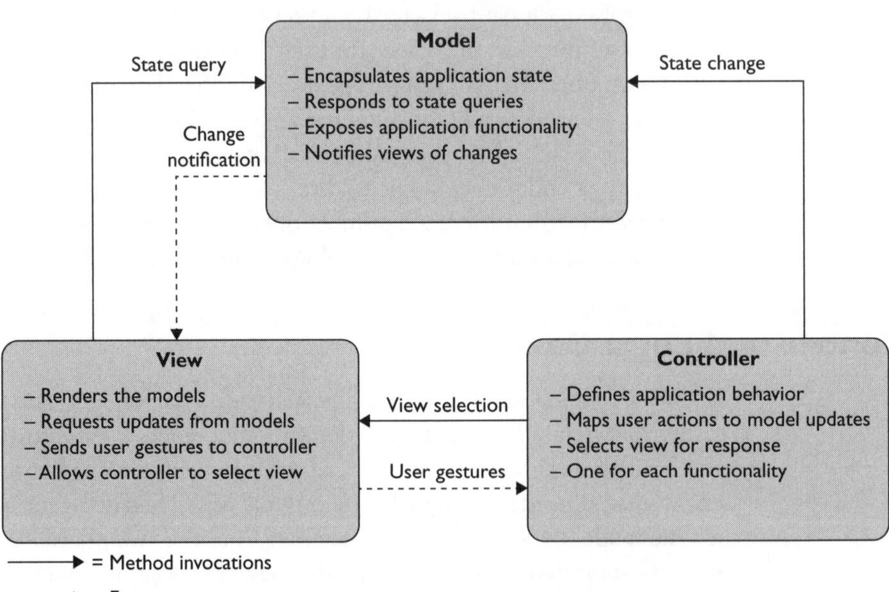

service dispatcher for dispatching to the appropriate domain model components through business delegates.

Service to Worker Pattern

The service dispatcher routes business logic requests to the appropriate business delegate. The business delegate calls the appropriate domain model component in the business tier. The business delegate then persists the value object returned from the business delegate to the appropriate scope (page, request, session, or application) and returns a result condition to the service dispatcher. If there are no further business logic operations to perform on the request, the final result condition is passed to the view dispatcher. The view dispatcher decides what view component to dispatch to the end user based on the result condition for the user's request. The view then accesses the value object in the appropriate scope and renders the final view for the user. Views can also use view helpers to help render pages and get access to business logic through business delegates for situations where service dispatching is not needed. This can be a useful architectural mechanism to easily add behavioral concerns to a running process prior to, or immediately after, its invocation.

Web Flow

Web flow is the term used to describe a process flow of user interactions through a series of web pages in a wizard-style fashion. Frameworks that provide for web flow management build on top of the Service to Worker request dispatching pattern as robust state management mechanisms. They provide a managed context for piecing together the user interactions into a workflow. Some frameworks even offer GUIs to assist in the web flow definition process. There is a classic balance between security and functionality that an architect must find. Typically the organization/enterprise will have a single sign-on for authentication/authorization. Once a user has been reasonably authenticated, the user must be authorized before accessing resources. The process of determining the appropriateness of the user to access a resource is referred to as "authorization," which can be based on the user, a group to which the user belongs, or a role to which the user is assigned. For Java enterprise applications, there are two layers of authorization: one within the web tier and another within the business tier. Web tier resource authorization can be achieved by defining the access control within the Web.xml deployment descriptor. It is applied to resources based on URL matching patterns. Assuming you are using Enterprise JavaBeans (EJB) within the business tier, the access to specific methods within EJBs can also be controlled using a deployment descriptor.

CERTIFICATION OBJECTIVE 6.03

Identify the Benefits of Using an EJB Container with a Web Container Instead of a Web Container Alone

An enterprise bean is a server-side component that encapsulates the business logic of an application. The business logic is the code that fulfills the purpose of the application. In an equity-trading application, for example, the enterprise beans might implement the business logic in methods called checkProductPrice and orderProduct. By invoking these methods, clients can access the equity services for a securities product (for example, an equity) provided by the application.

Benefits of Enterprise Beans

Enterprise beans may facilitate the development of large, distributed applications. The first benefit derives from the fact that the EJB container provides system-level services to enterprise beans; therefore, the bean developer can concentrate on solving business problems. The EJB container, rather than the bean developer, is responsible for nonfunctional services, such as transaction management and security authorization. Second, because the beans rather than the clients contain the application's business logic, the client developer can focus on the presentation of the client. An absolute benefit is that the client developer does not have to code the routines that implement business rules or access databases. As a result, the clients are thinner—a benefit that is particularly important for clients that run on small devices. Third, because enterprise beans are loosely coupled and portable components, the application assembler can build new applications from existing beans. Provided that they use the standard APIs, these applications can run on any compliant Java EE server.

Accessing Enterprise Beans

Clients access enterprise beans either through a no-interface view or through a business interface. The business interface or no-interface view defines the client's view of an enterprise bean. Well-designed interfaces and no-interface views simplify the development and maintenance of Java EE applications. Clients obtain references to EJBs though dependency injection or JNDI.

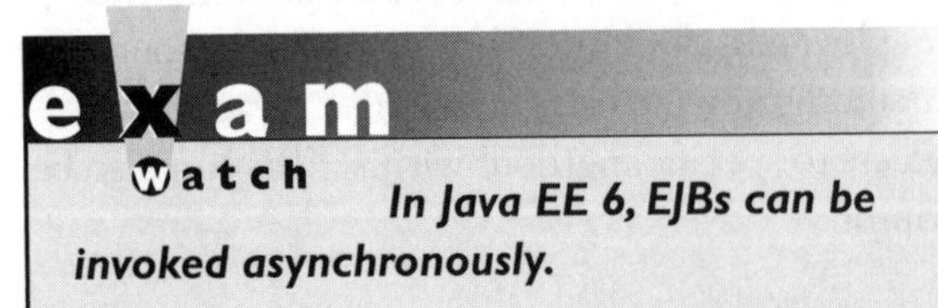

In Java EE 6, EJBs can be invoked asynchronously.

A no-interface view of an enterprise bean exposes the public methods of the enterprise bean implementation class to clients. Clients using the no-interface view of an enterprise bean may invoke any public methods provided by the enterprise bean implementation class or any superclasses of the implementation class.

A business interface is a standard Java programming language interface that contains the business methods of the enterprise bean. A client can access a session bean only through the methods defined in the bean's business interface or through the public methods of an enterprise bean that has a no-interface view. All other aspects of the enterprise bean (method implementations and deployment settings) are hidden from the client.

Not only do clean interfaces and no-interface views shield the clients from any complexities in the EJB tier, but they also allow the enterprise beans to change internally without affecting the clients. For example, if you change the implementation of a session bean business method, you won't have to alter the client code. But if you were to change the method definitions in the interfaces, you might have to modify the client code as well. Therefore, it is important that you design the interfaces and no-interface views carefully to isolate your clients from possible changes in the enterprise beans. Session beans can have more than one business interface. Session beans should, but are not required to, implement their business interface(s).

The client of an enterprise bean obtains a reference to an instance of an enterprise bean through either dependency injection (using Java programming language annotations) or JNDI lookup (using the Java Naming and Directory Interface syntax) to find the enterprise bean instance. Dependency injection is commonly used in obtaining an enterprise bean reference. Clients that run within a Java EE server-managed environment, JavaServer Faces web applications, JAX-RS web services, other enterprise beans, or Java EE application clients support dependency injection using the javax.ejb.EJB annotation. Applications that run outside a Java EE server-managed environment, such as Java SE applications, must perform an explicit lookup. JNDI supports a global syntax for identifying Java EE components to simplify this explicit lookup.

Accessing an Asynchronous Session Bean

One of the powerful features introduced in EJB 3.1 is the ability to invoke session bean methods asynchronously. For an asynchronous invocation, control returns to the client before the container dispatches the invocation to an instance of the bean. This allows the client to continue processing in parallel while the session bean method performs its operations.

What Type of Access Is Appropriate

When you design a Java EE application, one of the first decisions you make is the type of client access allowed by the enterprise beans: remote, local, or web service. Whether to allow local or remote access depends on the following factors:

- *Is there a tight or loose coupling of related beans?* Tightly coupled beans depend on one another. For example, if a session bean that processes equity orders calls a session bean that e-mails a confirmation message to the customer, these beans are tightly coupled. Tightly coupled beans are good candidates for local access. Because they fit together as a logical unit, they typically call each other often and would benefit from the increased performance that is possible with local access.
- *What type of client is in use?* If an enterprise bean is accessed by application clients, it should allow remote access. In a production environment, these clients almost always run on machines other than those on which the application server is running. If an enterprise bean's clients are web components or other enterprise beans, the type of access depends on how you want to distribute your components.
- *Are the components distributed?* Java EE applications are scalable because their server-side components can be distributed across multiple machines. In a distributed application, for example, the server that the web components run on may not be the one on which the enterprise beans they access are deployed. In this distributed scenario, the enterprise beans should allow remote access.
- *What are the performance requirements?* Owing to such factors as network latency, remote calls may be slower than local calls. On the other hand, if you distribute components among different servers, you may improve the application's overall performance. Both of these statements are generalizations; performance can vary in different operational environments. Nevertheless, you should keep in mind how your application design might affect performance. If you aren't sure which type of access an enterprise bean should have, choose remote access. This decision gives you more flexibility. In the future, you can distribute your components to accommodate the growing demands on your application. Although it is uncommon, it is possible for an enterprise bean to allow both remote and local access.

Handling Local Clients

A local client has these characteristics:

- It must run in the same application as the enterprise bean it accesses.
- It can be a web component or another enterprise bean.
- To the local client, the location of the enterprise bean it accesses is not transparent.

The no-interface view of an enterprise bean is a local view. The public methods of the enterprise bean implementation class are exposed to local clients that access the no-interface view of the enterprise bean. Enterprise beans that use the no-interface view do not implement a business interface. The local business interface defines the bean's business and life cycle methods. Client access to an enterprise bean that exposes a local, no-interface view or business interface is accomplished through either dependency injection or JNDI lookup.

Handling Remote Clients

A remote client of an enterprise bean has the following traits:

- It can run on a different machine and a different JVM from the enterprise bean it accesses. (It is not required to run on a different JVM.)
- It can be a web component, an application client, or another enterprise bean.
- To a remote client, the location of the enterprise bean is transparent.
- The enterprise bean must implement a business interface. That is, remote clients may not access an enterprise bean through a no-interface view.

Handling Web Service Clients

A web service client can access a Java EE application in multiple ways. The client can access a web service created with JAX-WS. Also, a web service client can invoke the business methods of a stateless session bean. Message beans cannot be accessed by web service clients. Provided that it uses the correct protocols (SOAP, HTTP, WSDL), any web service client can access a stateless session bean, whether or not the client is written in the Java programming language. The client doesn't need to know what technology implements the service: stateless session bean, JAX-WS, or some other technology. In addition, enterprise beans and web components can be clients of web services. This flexibility enables you to integrate Java EE applications with web services. A web service client accesses a stateless session bean through the bean's web service endpoint implementation class. By default, all public methods in the bean class are accessible to web service clients.

Session Beans

A session bean encapsulates business and processing logic invoked programmatically by a client over local, remote, or web service client views. A session bean accesses an application that is deployed on the server, and the client invokes the session bean's methods. The session bean performs work for its client, executing business tasks inside the server. Clients can access an enterprise bean via CDI or JNDI. Session beans are not persistent.

There are three types of session beans:

- **Stateless session bean (SLSB)** The interaction is contained in a single method call and the process does not maintain client state.
- **Stateful session bean (SFSB)** The interaction may invoke many methods, and processes can span multiple method requests, thus necessitating the maintaining of a client state.
- **Singleton session bean** Instantiated once per application and exists for the life cycle of the application. It is designed as you would expect for applications in which a single enterprise bean instance is shared concurrently accessed by multiple clients.

As mentioned, a stateless session bean does not maintain a conversational state with the client. When a client invokes the methods of a stateless bean, the bean's instance variables may contain a state specific to that client, but only for the duration of the invocation. When the method is finished, the client-specific state should not be retained. Except during method invocation, all instances of a stateless bean are equivalent, allowing the EJB container to assign an instance to any client. That is, the state of a stateless session bean should apply across all clients. A stateless session bean can implement a web service, but a stateful session bean cannot.

The state of an object is portrayed by the values of its instance variables. In a stateful session bean, the instance variables represent the state of a unique client/bean session. Because the client interacts/talks with its bean, this state is known as the "conversational" state. As its name suggests, a stateful session bean is similar to an interactive session. What puts the "state" in a stateful session bean is that it is not shared; it contains specific data for only one client. The state is retained for the duration of the client/bean session. If the client removes the bean, the session ends and the state disappears. Note that because the client/conversational state has to be maintained for a stateful bean, the stateful session bean can have at most one client at all times. A stateless session bean, as we know, need not maintain the client state, thus allowing the EJB container to assign an instance to any client. Because stateless beans do not care about the client state, they can effectively service a large number of client (scalable). A stateless session bean can be used to implement a web service, although it is not possible when it comes to a stateful singleton.

exam watch

In Java EE 6, EJBs can be co-located in the same WAR file as other components such as web components. Also, using CDI, EJBs can be injected into other components, enabling direct calls to the EJBs from components in other tiers without requiring intervening or helper objects.

Singleton session beans are new in Java EE 6. They are instantiated once per application and exist only for that application life cycle (no pool of beans). They are designed to be shared across concurrent access by clients to maintain stateful values between client invocations. Applications that use a singleton session bean may specify that the singleton should be instantiated upon application startup, which allows the singleton to perform initialization tasks for the application. The singleton may perform cleanup tasks on application shutdown as well, because the singleton will operate throughout the life cycle of the application.

Stateful session beans are appropriate in certain situations—for example, if the bean's state represents the interaction between the bean and a specific client (for example, a shopping cart) or the bean needs to hold information about the client across method invocations. Additionally, if the bean mediates between the client and the other components of the application, presenting a simplified view to the client, or if behind the scenes the bean manages the work flow of several enterprise beans, then stateful session beans may be the appropriate vehicle. Alternatively, to improve performance, you might choose a stateless session bean if, for example, the bean's state has no data for a specific client or if the bean implements a web service. Singleton session beans are appropriate when state needs to be shared across the application and a single enterprise bean needs to be accessed by multiple threads concurrently.

Message-Driven Bean (MDB)

An MDB is a stateless EJB that asynchronously consumes JMS messages and, as such, is never called directly by a client. This type of bean normally acts as a JMS message listener, which is similar to an event listener, but it receives JMS messages instead of events. The messages can be sent by any Java EE component (an ESB, an application client, another enterprise bean, or a web component) or by a JMS application or system that does not use Java EE technology. Message-driven beans can process JMS messages or other kinds of messages.

CERTIFICATION OBJECTIVE 6.04

Identify the Differences Between Client Pull and Server Push Architectures

Browsers have always been driven by user input. You click a link, an icon, or an image and some data comes to you. As soon as people saw that, they wanted servers to be able to push new data to the browser. An obvious example is a businessman who wants to see new stock quotes every two minutes. Until recently, that has not been easily done. Browsers recently added two complementary methods for generating dynamic documents: server push and client pull.

With the server push idea, the server sends data. The browser displays the data and leaves the connection open. The server sends more data whenever it is configured to do so, and the browser displays it, leaving the connection open based on configuration.

As for the client pull idea, the server sends data, including a command that may set a timer, at which time it will execute a call to the server for fresh data. So after the specified time has elapsed, the client either gets the new data or reloads the current data if nothing is new.

In server push, an HTTP connection is held open for an indefinite period of time (until the server sends a terminator, or until the client interrupts the connection). In client pull, an HTTP connection is never held open. Instead, the client is told when to open a new connection and what data to get.

A simple use of client pull is to periodically reload a document:

```
HTML><HEAD>
<META HTTP-EQUIV="Refresh" CONTENT=60>
<title>StockQuote1</title>
</HEAD><BODY>
<h1>Twitter price is 2000 yen</h1>
</BODY></HTML>
```

Note the document reloads itself once a minute. If we wanted to wait two minutes, we use this HTML command:

```
<META HTTP-EQUIV="Refresh" CONTENT=120>
```

Make sure the META tag is inside the HEAD of your HTML document, before any displayed text or images. You can interrupt the infinite reloading by pressing the Back button. You can also cause another document to be reloaded in place of the current document.

The META tag would be this:

```
<META HTTP-EQUIV="Refresh" CONTENT="12;
URL=http://ucny.com/stockfeed/twitter.txt">
```

Be sure to use the full pathname in the URL (for example, http://whatever/whatever). Do *not* use a relative URL. The following example shows two HTML documents, doc2.html and doc3.html, each of which causes the other to load (so if you load one, your browser will flip back and forth between them forever).

Here is StockQuote2.html:

```
<HTML><HEAD>
<META HTTP-EQUIV=REFRESH CONTENT="1;
      URL= http://ucny.com/stockfeed/ StockQuote3.html">
<title> StockQuote2</title>
</HEAD><BODY>
<h1>Bill is greater!</h1>
</BODY></HTML>
```

Here is doc3.html:

```
<HTML><HEAD>
<META HTTP-EQUIV=REFRESH CONTENT="1;
      URL= http://ucny.com/stockfeed/ StockQuote2.html ">
<title> StockQuote3</title></HEAD><BODY>
<h1>Sell Everything</h1></BODY></HTML>
```

When you load one of the documents, the browser will load the other in one second, then the first in another second, then the second again in another second, and so on indefinitely. How do you stop it? The easiest way is either to close the window or quickly change the URL address. Note that the reload interval can be zero seconds. This will cause the browser to load the new data as soon as it possibly can (after the current data is fully displayed). The HTML data can be of any type: a table, an image, an audio clip, whatever.

Server push is the other dynamic document method, complementing client pull. Unlike client pull, server push uses a connection that is held open over multiple responses, so the server can send more data any time it wants. The major advantage is that the server has total control over when and how often new data is sent. Also, this method can be more efficient because new HTTP connections do not have to be opened all the time. Also, server push is easily interruptible (you can just hit Stop and interrupt the connection).

CERTIFICATION OBJECTIVE 6.05

Identify the Benefits and Drawbacks of Using a Browser to Access Asynchronous, Lightweight Processes on the Server

One of the most important aspects about building smooth and responsive HTML5 applications is the synchronization between all the different parts of the application, such as data fetching, processing, animations, and user interface elements.

The main difference with a desktop or a native environment is that browsers do not give access to the threading model and provide a single thread for everything accessing the user interface (that is, the DOM). This means that all the application logic accessing and modifying the user interface elements is always in the same thread, hence the importance of keeping all the application work units as small and efficient as possible and taking advantage of any asynchronous capabilities the browser offers as much as possible.

Browser Asynchronous APIs

Fortunately, browsers provide a number of asynchronous APIs such as the commonly used XHR (XMLHttpRequest or "Ajax") APIs as well as the IndexedDB, SQLite, HTML5 Web workers, and HTML5 Geolocation APIs, to name a few. Even some DOM-related actions are exposed asynchronously, such CSS3 animation via the transitionEnd events.

The way browsers expose asynchronous programming to the application logic is via events or callbacks. In event-based asynchronous APIs, developers register an event handler for a given object (for example, an HTML element or another DOM object) and then call the action. The browser will perform the action, usually in a different thread, and trigger the event in the main thread when appropriate. For example, code using the XHR API, an event-based asynchronous API, would look like this:

```
// Create the XHR object to do GET to /data resource
var xhr = new XMLHttpRequest();
xhr.open("GET","data",true);


// register the event handler
xhr.addEventListener('load',function(){
  if(xhr.status === 200){
      alert("We got data: " + xhr.response);
  }
},false)

// perform the work
xhr.send();
```

The CSS3 transitionEnd event is another example of an event-based asynchronous API:

```
// get the html element with id 'findSellStock'
var findSellStockElem = document.getElementById("findSellStock");

// register an event handler
// ('transitionEnd' for FireFox, 'webkitTransitionEnd' for webkit)
findSellStockElem.addEventListener("transitionEnd",function(){
  // will be called when the transition has finished.
```

```
    alert("The Stock has been found");
  });

  // add the CSS3 class that will trigger the animation
  // Note: some browsers delegate some transitions
  //       developer does not and should not have to care about it.
  findSellStockElemen.classList.add('sellStock')
```

Other browser APIs such as SQLite and HTML5 Geolocation are callback based, meaning that the developer passes a function as an argument that will get called back by the underlying implementation with the corresponding resolution.

For example, for HTML5 Geolocation, the code looks like this:

```
// call and pass the function to callback when done.
navigator.geolocation.getCurrentPosition(function(position){
            alert('Lat: ' + position.coords.latitude + ' ' +
                  'Lon: ' + position.coords.longitude);
});
```

In this case, we just call a method and pass a function that will get called back with the requested result. This allows the browser to implement this functionality synchronously or asynchronously and give a single API to the developer regardless of the implementation details.

Making Applications "Asynchronous Ready"

Beyond the browser's built-in asynchronous APIs, well-architected applications should expose their low-level APIs in an asynchronous fashion as well, especially when they do any sort of I/O or computational-heavy processing. For example, APIs to get data should be asynchronous and should *not* look like this:

```
// WRONG: this will make the UI freeze when getting the data
var data = getData();
alert("We got data: " + data);
```

This API design requires the getData() to be blocking, which will freeze the user interface until the data is fetched. If the data is local in the JavaScript context, this might not be an issue; however, if the data needs to be fetched from the network or even locally in a SQLite or index store, this could have dramatic impact on the user experience.

The right design is to proactively make asynchronous all application APIs that could take some time to process, from the beginning, because retrofitting synchronous application code to be asynchronous can be a daunting task.

For example, the simplistic getData() API would become something like this:

```
getData(function(data){
   alert("We got data: " + data);
});
```

The nice thing about this approach is that it forces the application UI code to be asynchronous centric from the beginning and allows the underlying APIs to decide whether or not they need to be asynchronous in a later stage. Note that not all the application APIs need or should be asynchronous. The rule of thumb is that any API that does any type of I/O or heavy processing should be exposed asynchronously from the start, even if the first implementation is synchronous.

Handling Failures from Asynchronous Processes

One catch of asynchronous programing is that the traditional try/catch way to handle failures does not really work anymore because errors usually happen in another thread. Consequently, the callee needs to have a structured way to notify the caller when something goes wrong during the processing. In an event-based asynchronous API, this is often accomplished by the application code querying the event or object when receiving the event. For callback-based asynchronous APIs, the best practice is to have a second argument that takes a function that would be called in case of a failure with the appropriate error information as an argument.

Our getData call would look like this:

```
// getData(successFunc,failFunc);
getData(function(data){
  alert("We got data: " + data);
}, function(ex){
  alert("oops, some problem occurred: " + ex);
});
```

Using $.Deferred

One limitation of the preceding callback approach is that it can become really cumbersome to write even moderately advanced synchronization logic. For example, if you need to wait for two asynchronous API calls to be done before making a third one, code complexity can rise quickly:

```
// first do the get data.
getData(function(data){
  // then get the location
  getLocation(function(location){
```

```
    alert("we got data: " + data + " and location: " + location);
  },function(ex){
    alert("getLocation failed: "  + ex);
  });
},function(ex){
  alert("getData failed: " + ex);
});
```

Things can even get more complex when the application needs to make the same call from multiple parts of the application, because every call will have to perform these multistep calls. A pattern called Promises and an implementation in jQuery core called $.Deferred provide a solution to asynchronous programming.

The trending Promises pattern defines that the asynchronous API returns a Promise object, which is kind of a "promise that the result will be resolved with the corresponding data." To get the resolution, the caller gets the Promise object and calls a callback function (e.g., `done(successFunc(data))`, which will tell the Promise object to call this `successFunc` function when the "data" is resolved.

So, the getData call example becomes this:

```
// get the promise object for this API
var dataPromise = getData();
// register a function to get called when the data is resolved
dataPromise.done(function(data){
  alert("We got data: " + data);
});
// register the failure function
dataPromise.fail(function(ex){
  alert("component failure occurred: " + ex);
});
// Note: we can have as many dataPromise.done(...) as we want.

dataPromise.done(function(data){

  alert("We asked it twice, we get it twice: " + data);

});
```

Here, we get the dataPromise object first and then call the .done method to register a function we want to get called back when the data gets resolved. We can also call the .fail method to handle the eventual failure. Note that we can have as many .done or .fail calls as we need because the underlying Promise implementation (jQuery code) will handle the registration and callbacks. With this pattern, it is relatively easy to implement more advanced synchronization code, and jQuery already provides the most common, such as the javascript $.when.

For example, the nested `getData/getLocation` callback would become something like this:

```
// assuming both getData and getLocation return their respective Promise
var combinedPromise = $.when(getData(), getLocation())

// function will be called when both getData and getLocation resolve
combinePromise.done(function(data,location){
  alert("We got data: " + dataResult + " and location: " + location);
});
```

Note: jQuery. `Deferred` facilitates the asynchronous function. For example, the function `getData` could look something like this:

```
function getData(){
  // 1) create the jQuery Deferred object that will be used
  var deferred = $.Deferred();

  // ---- AJAX Call ---- //
  XMLHttpRequest xhr = new XMLHttpRequest();
  xhr.open("GET","data",true);

  // register the event handler
  xhr.addEventListener('load',function(){
    if(xhr.status === 200){
      // 3.1) RESOLVE the DEFERRED (this will trigger all the done()...)
      deferred.resolve(xhr.response);
    }else{
      // 3.2) REJECT the DEFERRED (this will trigger all the fail()...)
      deferred.reject("HTTP error: " + xhr.status);
    }
  },false)

  // perform the work
  xhr.send();
  // Note: could and should have used jQuery.ajax.
  // Note: jQuery.ajax return Promise, but it is always a good idea to wrap it
  //       with application semantic in another Deferred/Promise
  // ---- /AJAX Call ---- //

  // 2) return the promise of this deferred
  return deferred.promise();
}
```

When getData() is called, it first creates a new jQuery.`Deferred` object (1) and then returns its Promise (2) so that the caller can register its done and fail functions. Then, when the XHR call returns, it either resolves the `Deferred` object or rejects it. Calling `deferred.resolve` will trigger all the `done(...)` functions and other Promise functions (for example, then and pipe), and calling `deferred.reject` will call all the fail() functions. Here are some good use cases where `Deferred` can be very useful:

- **Data access** Exposing data access APIs as $.Deferred is often the right design. This is obvious for remote data, because synchronous remote calls would completely ruin the user experience. However, it is also true for local data because often the lower-level APIs (for example, SQLite and IndexedDB) are asynchronous themselves. The Deferred API's $.when and .pipe are extremely powerful to synchronize and chain asynchronous subqueries.
- **UI component display** Advanced HTML Component frameworks should use `Deferred` as well. Without going too much into the detail, when an application needs to display different parts of the user interface, having the life cycle of those components encapsulated in Deferred allows greater control of the timing.
- **Any browser asynchronous API** For normalization purpose, it is often a good idea to wrap the browser API calls as Deferred. This takes literally four to five lines of code each, but will greatly simplify any application code. As shown in the preceding getData/getLocation pseudo-code, this allows the applications code to have one asynchronous model across all types of API (browsers, application specific, and compound).
- **Caching** This is kind of a side benefit, but can be very useful on some occasions. Because the Promise APIs—for example, .done(..) and .fail(..)—can be called before or after the asynchronous call is performed, the Deferred object can be used as a caching handle for an asynchronous call. For example, a CacheManager could just keep track of Deferred for given requests and then return the Promise of the matching Deferred if it has not be invalidated. The beauty is that the caller does not have to know if the call has already been resolved or is in the process of being resolved; its callback function will get called exactly the same way.

Although the $.Deferred concept is simple, it can take time to get a good handle on it. However, given the nature of the browser environment, mastering asynchronous programing in JavaScript is a must for any serious HTML5 application developer. The Promise pattern and the jQuery implementation are tremendous tools to make asynchronous programming reliable and powerful.

CERTIFICATION SUMMARY

This chapter has identified the benefits and drawbacks of web tier techniques such as URL Rewriting and cookies to manage the HTTP session state. We also identified when to use JSP, Servlets, and JavaServer Faces. With respect to browsers, we reviewed client pull and server as well as the benefits of using Browser and Ajax to access asynchronous server processes. The web tier is certainly a dynamic development environment. A good architect needs to stay current and open to the new HTML5/CSS development techniques as well as "disconnected" applications using WebSQL and IndexedDB client data resources.

TWO-MINUTE DRILL

Identify the Benefits and Drawbacks of Using URL Rewriting and Cookies to Manage HTTP Session State

- The client tier can store state with cookies or URL rewriting.
- URL rewriting can store only enough state to tie a browser to a particular client session.
- Cookies can hold up to 4,096 bytes each.
- State stored in cookies must pass from the client to the presentation tier before it can be used.
- You can hold state on the presentation tier with the HTTPSession object, which is a collection that can hold any nonprimitive type.
- The web container ties the HTTPSession object to the client either with the use of cookies or URL rewriting, so no programming effort is required to perform this function.

Identify Appropriate Uses for JSP and Servlet Technology, and JavaServer Faces in a Given Java EE Application

- A JSP is a text-based document that includes HTML, JSP tags, and Java code (including calls to JavaBeans and servlets).
  - It cleanly separates content creation from presentation logic.
  - It focuses on rapid development and easy modification of the user interface as well as focuses on presentation.
- A JSF is a server-side component framework for web applications.
  - It implements the Model-View-Controller (MVC) framework.
  - It provides separation of navigational and data flow.
  - In Java EE 6, JSF 2 has deprecated JSP as its view layer, replacing it with the more JSF-centric Facelets.

Identify the Benefits of Using an EJB Container with a Web Container Instead of a Web Container Alone

- The benefits of an EJB container:
  - The EJB container provides system-level services to enterprise beans, so the bean developer can concentrate on solving business problems. The EJB container, rather than the bean developer, is responsible for nonfunctional services, such as transaction management and security authorization.
  - The beans rather than the clients contain the application's business logic, so the client developer can focus on the presentation of the client. An absolute benefit is that the client developer does not have to code the routines that implement business rules or access databases.
  - Enterprise beans are loosely coupled and portable components; the application assembler can build new applications from existing beans.

Identify the Differences Between Client Pull and Server Push Architectures

- The differences between client pull and server push:
  - With the server push idea, the server sends data. The browser displays the data and leaves the connection open. The server sends more data whenever it is configured to do so, and the browser displays it, leaving the connection open based on configuration.
  - With the client pull idea, the server sends data, including a command that may set a timer, at which time it will execute a call to the server for fresh data. So after the specified time has elapsed, the client either gets the new data or reloads the current data if nothing is new.
  - In server push, an HTTP connection is held open for an indefinite period of time (until the server sends a terminator, or until the client interrupts the connection).
  - In client pull, an HTTP connection is never held open. Instead, the client is told when to open a new connection and what data to get.

Identify the Benefits and Drawbacks of Using a Browser to Access Asynchronous, Lightweight Processes on the Server

- ❑ The benefits and drawbacks of using a browser to access server processes:
  - ❑ Browsers provide a number of asynchronous APIs, such as the commonly used XHR (XMLHttpRequest or "Ajax") APIs, as well as IndexedDB and SQLite. The way browsers expose asynchronous programming to the application logic is via events or callbacks.
  - ❑ In event-based asynchronous APIs, developers register an event handler for a given object (for example, HTML elements or other DOM objects) and then call the action.
  - ❑ The browser will perform the action usually in a different thread and will trigger the event in the main thread when appropriate.

SELF TEST

The following questions will help you measure your understanding of the material presented in this chapter. Read all the choices carefully because there may be more than one correct answer. Choose all correct answers for each question.

Identify the Benefits and Drawbacks of Using URL Rewriting and Cookies to Manage HTTP Session State

1. Which of the following is true about the client tier?

A. The client tier can store state with cookies.

B. The client tier can maintain state via URL rewriting.

C. The client tier cannot store state using JPA or a database.

D. Security constraints make it impossible to store state.

2. Which of the following statements are true?

A. URL rewriting can store only enough state to tie a browser to a particular client session.

B. Cookies can hold up to 1,024 bytes each.

C. You can hold state on the presentation tier with the HTTPSession object.

D. Use of cookies places a limit on the number of concurrent clients.

3. How can the application become aware that an HttpSession object has been added to or removed from a session?

A. Through the javax.servlet.http.HttpSessionBindingListener interface

B. Through the javax.servlet.http.HttpSessionActivationListener interface

C. Through the javax.servlet.http.HttpSessionRemovalListener interface

D. Through the javax.servlet.http.HttpSessionAdditionListener interface

4. If the client turns off cookies and your application uses session objects, which of the following must be done to ensure that session tracking can be handled properly?

A. Calling the response's encodeURL(URL) method on all URLs returned by a servlet

B. Including the session ID in the URL

C. Invoking the isRequestedSessionFromCookie() method of HttpServletRequest

D. Invoking the isRequestedCookieFromSession() method of HttpServletRequest

5. Which of the following are potential security risks created by URL rewriting?
   A. Users can copy and paste the attached session ID.
   B. Server log files may record the "Referer" header, which will record session IDs in the log.
   C. The session ID appears in the URL.
   D. The cookie can be hijacked and the client's machine can be corrupted.
6. You can hold state with stateful session beans or entity classes.
   A. True
   B. False

Identify Appropriate Uses for JSP and Servlet Technology, and JavaServer Faces in a Given Java EE Application

7. Which of the following are *not* core responsibilities of the web tier?
   A. Delegating service requests to the business tier
   B. Dispatching presentation to the client interface
   C. Managing access to content
   D. Handling database updates
8. Which of the following are *not* attributes of a servlet?
   A. It can be written using JavaScript.
   B. It's a Java program that runs on a Java EE or server.
   C. The output format for servlets is exclusively HTML.
   D. It can access a relational database.
9. Which of the following are *not* attributes of a JSP?
   A. It can be written using JavaScript.
   B. It compiles to Java program that runs on a Java EE or server.
   C. The output format for servlets is exclusively HTML.
   D. It can access a relational database.
10. Which of the following are *not* attributes of a JSF?
   A. JSF combines the functionality of a JSP with a built-in controller.
   B. JSF implements the Model-View-Controller (MVC) framework.
   C. JSPs are the JSF view layer in Java EE 6.
   D. A JSF can access a relational database.

11. Which of the following are responsibilities of the MVC Controller?
    A. Dispatching of service requests to the model
    B. Accessing the database
    C. Dispatching of views to the end user
    D. Performing business logic

12. Which of the following are responsibilities of the Controller/ServiceDispatcher?
    A. The service dispatcher routes business logic requests to the appropriate business delegate model.
    B. It calls the appropriate domain model component in the business tier.
    C. The dispatching of views to the end user.
    D. It persists the value object returned from the business delegate to the appropriate scope.

13. Which of the following are responsibilities of the Controller/ViewDispatcher?
    A. The view dispatcher decides what view component to dispatch to the end user based on the result condition for the user's request
    B. It accesses the value object in the appropriate scope and renders the final view for the user.
    C. The dispatching of views to the end user.
    D. It persists the value object returned from the business delegate to the appropriate scope.

Identify the Benefits of Using an EJB Container with a Web Container Instead of a Web Container Alone

14. Which of the following are benefits derived from the EJB container?
    A. The EJB container provides nonfunctional services such as transaction management to enterprise beans.
    B. Because the beans rather than the clients contain the application's business logic, the client developer can focus on the presentation of the client.
    C. It facilitates dispatching of views to the end user.
    D. Because enterprise beans are loosely coupled and portable components, the application assembler can build new applications from existing beans.

15. In Java EE 6, EJBs can be invoked asynchronously.
    A. True
    B. False

16. How do you obtain a reference to an enterprise bean reference?
    A. JDBC lookup
    B. JNDI lookup
    C. Dependency injection
    D. LDAP lookup
17. When accessing an enterprise bean, a local client must have which of the following characteristics?
    A. It must run in the same application as the enterprise bean it accesses.
    B. For the local client, the location of the enterprise bean it accesses is not transparent.
    C. It cannot be a web service.
    D. It can be a web component or another enterprise bean.
18. When accessing an enterprise bean, a remote client must have which of the following characteristics?
    A. It can run on a different machine and a different JVM from the enterprise bean it accesses.
    B. It can be a web component, an application client, or another enterprise bean.
    C. The enterprise bean must implement a business interface. That is, remote clients may not access an enterprise bean through a no-interface view.
    D. It cannot be a web component or another enterprise bean.
19. When a web service client accesses a Java EE application, which of the following statements are true?
    A. The client can access a web service created with JAX-WS.
    B. A web service client can invoke the business methods of a stateless session bean.
    C. The enterprise bean must implement a business interface. That is, remote clients may not access an enterprise bean through a no-interface view.
    D. Message beans cannot be accessed by web service clients.
20. With respect to a Java EE session bean, what statements are true?
    A. For a stateless session bean (SLSB), the interaction is contained in a single method call and the process does not maintain client state.
    B. For a stateful session bean (SFSB), the interaction may invoke many methods, and processes can span multiple method requests, thus necessitating the maintaining of a client state.
    C. A singleton session bean is instantiated once per application and exists for the life cycle of the application.
    D. Message session beans cannot be accessed by web service clients.

21. With respect to Java EE singleton session beans, which of the following statements are true?

A. A singleton session is instantiated once per application.

B. A singleton session bean exists in a pool of beans.

C. A singleton session bean exists for the life cycle of the application.

D. A singleton session bean must be instantiated upon application startup.

22. With respect to Java EE stateful session beans, which of the following statements are true?

A. Stateful session beans are appropriate if a bean's state represents the interaction between the bean and a specific client.

B. Stateful session beans improve performance.

C. Stateful session beans exists for the life cycle of the application.

D. Stateful session beans manages the work flow of several enterprise beans for the client.

23. With respect to message-driven beans (MDBs), which of the following statements are true?

A. MDBs are stateless EJBs that asynchronously consumes JMS messages.

B. MDBs are called directly by the client.

C. MDBs exist for the life cycle of the application.

D. MDBs asynchronously consume JMS messages.

Identify the Differences Between Client Pull and Server Push Architectures

24. With respect to server push and client pull, which of the following statements are true?

A. In client pull, an HTTP connection is held open.

B. In client pull, the mechanism may include a command that can set a timer, at which time it will execute a call to the server for fresh data.

C. With server push, the browser displays the data and leaves the connection open.

D. With server push, the server asynchronously sends new data.

Identify the Benefits and Drawbacks of Using a Browser to Access Asynchronous, Lightweight Processes on the Server

25. With respect to browser access to server-based asynchronous processes, what statements are true?

A. The way browsers expose asynchronous programming to the application logic is via events or callbacks.

B. Browsers provide a number of asynchronous APIs such as the commonly used XHR (XMLHttpRequest or "Ajax") APIs, as well as IndexedDB, SQLite, HTML5, to name a few.

C. With the server push idea, the browser displays the data and leaves the connection open.

D. With the server push idea, the server synchronously sends new data.

SELF TEST ANSWERS

Identify the Benefits and Drawbacks of Using URL Rewriting and Cookies to Manage HTTP Session State

1. ☑ **A** and **B**. The client tier can store state with cookies or URL rewriting.
   ☒ **C** and **D** are incorrect. You can utilize a JPA database/data store entity to separate the persistence logic from the other aspects of the application. Although URL rewriting is security problematic, you can maintain state.

2. ☑ **A, C,** and **D.** URL rewriting can store only enough state to tie a browser to a particular client session. Because state stored in cookies must pass from the client to the presentation tier before it can be used, this places a limit on the number of concurrent clients because of the network bandwidth used. You can hold state on the presentation tier with the HTTPSession object.
   ☒ **B** is incorrect. Cookies can hold up to 4,096 bytes each.

3. ☑ **A.** When the object is added to or removed from a session in order to receive this notification, your object must implement the javax.servlet.http.HttpSessionBindingListener interface.
   ☒ **B, C,** and **D** are incorrect. These are not proper interfaces.

4. ☑ **A, B,** and **C.** To perform URL rewriting, use the encodeURL() method of the HttpServletResponse object. You can perform a check whether a session has been retrieved from a cookie using the isRequestedSessionFromCookie() method of HttpServletRequest object.
   ☒ **D** is incorrect. Because isRequestedCookieFromSession() is not a real method, you cannot invoke it.

5. ☑ **A, B,** and **C.** URL rewriting has obvious security risks. Because the session ID appears in the URL, it may be easily seen by third parties. End users often copy and paste such links without knowing the attached session ID compromises their security. Server log files usually record the "Referer" header, which will record session IDs in the log. Third-party access to session IDs simply means that private user information is wide open to attack.
   ☒ **D** is incorrect. No cookie to be hijacked.

6. ☑ **A.** If appropriate, you can also hold state with stateful session beans or entity classes. Entity classes allow state to be persisted to the database.
   ☒ **B** is incorrect. You can hold state with stateful session beans or entity classes.

Identify Appropriate Uses for JSP and Servlet Technology, and JavaServer Faces in a Given Java EE Application

7. ☑ **D.** Handling database updates is *not* a core responsibility of the web tier.
☒ **A, B,** and **C** are incorrect. The core responsibilities of the web tier include delegating service requests to the business tier, dispatching presentation to the client interface, and managing access to content.

8. ☑ **A** and **C.** These are *not* attributes of a servlet. Servlets cannot be written using JavaScript. The output format for servlets includes HTML, XML, and other MIME formats.
☒ **B** and **D** are incorrect. These are attributes of a servlet. Servlets are Java programs that run on a Java EE and can access relational databases.

9. ☑ **C.** This is *not* an attribute of a JSP. The output format for servlets includes HTML, XML, and other MIME formats.
☒ **A, B,** and **D** are incorrect. Attributes of JSPs are as follows: they are compiled to servlets, which are Java programs that run on a Java EE, they can include HTML and JavaScript, and they can access relational databases.

10. ☑ **C.** This is *not* an attribute of JSF. Facelets replace JSPs as the view layer in Java EE 6/JSF 2.
☒ **A, B,** and **D** are incorrect. JSF implements the Model-View-Controller (MVC) framework. It provides separation of navigational and data flow. JSF is a component-based framework for developing web-based applications. JSF also combines the functionality of a JSP with a built-in controller. These parts make JSF a true MVC framework.

11. ☑ **A** and **C.** The controller has two responsibilities: dispatching of service requests to the model and dispatching of views to the end user.
☒ **B** and **D** are incorrect. These are responsibilities of the MVC Model or Service to Worker.

12. ☑ **A, B,** and **D.** The MVC Model or Service to Worker subrogates the idea of a model to the concerns of the business tier. It may invoke business delegates directly for domain model operations that provide support for the web framework itself, or pass business logic requests to the service dispatcher for dispatching to the appropriate domain model components through business delegates. The service dispatcher routes business logic requests to the appropriate business delegate. The business delegate calls the appropriate domain model component in the business tier.
☒ **C** is incorrect. This is the responsibility of the MVC Controller.

13. ☑ **A, B,** and **C.** The view dispatcher decides what view component to dispatch to the end user based on the result condition for the user's request. The view then accesses the value object in the appropriate scope and renders the final view for the user.
☒ **D** is incorrect. This is the responsibility of the MVC Model or Service to Worker.

Identify the Benefits of Using an EJB Container with a Web Container Instead of a Web Container Alone

14. ☑ **A, B,** and **D.** The first benefit derives from the fact that the EJB container provides system-level services to enterprise beans, so the bean developer can concentrate on solving business problems. The EJB container, rather than the bean developer, is responsible for nonfunctional services, such as transaction management and security authorization. Also, because the beans rather than the clients contain the application's business logic, the client developer can focus on the presentation of the client. Finally, because enterprise beans are loosely coupled and portable components, the application assembler can build new applications from existing beans. Provided that they use the standard APIs, these applications can run on any compliant Java EE server.
☒ C is incorrect. This is the responsibility of the MVC View dispatcher.

15. ☑ **A.** True, in Java EE 6, EJBs can be invoked asynchronously.
☒ B is incorrect. In Java EE 6, EJBs can be invoked asynchronously.

16. ☑ **B** and **C.** Dependency injection is one way of obtaining an enterprise bean reference. Clients that run within a Java EE server-managed environment, JavaServer Faces web applications, JAX-RS web services, other enterprise beans, and Java EE application clients support dependency injection using the javax.ejb.EJB annotation. Applications that run outside a Java EE server-managed environment, such as Java SE applications, must perform an explicit lookup. JNDI supports a global syntax for identifying Java EE components to simplify this explicit lookup.
☒ A and D are incorrect. These are not used to obtain a reference to an enterprise bean reference.

17. ☑ **A, B,** and **D.** A local client can run on a different machine and a different JVM from the enterprise bean it accesses. It can be a web component, an application client, or another enterprise bean. To a remote client, the location of the enterprise bean is transparent. The enterprise bean must implement a business interface.
☒ C is incorrect. It can be a web service.

18. ☑ **A, B,** and **C.** The client can access a web service created with JAX-WS. Also, a web service client can invoke the business methods of a stateless session bean. Message beans cannot be accessed by web service clients. Provided that it uses the correct protocols (SOAP, HTTP, WSDL), any web service client can access a stateless session bean, whether or not the client is written in the Java programming language. In addition, enterprise beans and web components can be clients of web services.
☒ D is incorrect. It can be a web component or another enterprise bean.

19. ☑ **A, B,** and **C.** The client can access a web service created with JAX-WS. A web service client can invoke the business methods of a stateless session bean. The enterprise bean must implement a business interface. That is, remote clients may not access an enterprise bean through a no-interface view.
☒ D is incorrect. Message beans can be accessed by web service clients.

20. ☑ **A, B,** and **C.** In a stateless session bean (SLSB), the interaction is contained in a single method call and the process does not maintain client state. In a stateful session bean (SFSB), the interaction may invoke many methods, and processes can span multiple method requests, thus necessitating the maintaining of a client state. A singleton session bean is instantiated once per application and exists for the life cycle of the application.
☒ D is incorrect. There are no message session beans.

21. ☑ **A, B,** and **C.** Applications that use a singleton session bean may specify that the singleton should be instantiated upon application startup, which allows the singleton to perform initialization tasks for the application. The singleton may perform cleanup tasks on application shutdown as well, because the singleton will operate throughout the lifecycle of the application. A singleton session bean is instantiated once per application and exists for the life cycle of the application.
☒ D is incorrect. A singleton session bean *may* be instantiated upon application startup.

22. ☑ **A** and **D.** Stateful session beans are appropriate in certain situations—for example, if the bean's state represents the interaction between the bean and a specific client (for example, shopping cart) or the bean needs to hold information about the client across method invocations. Additionally, if the bean manages the work flow of several enterprise beans, then stateful session beans may be the appropriate vehicle.
☒ B and C are incorrect. To improve performance, you might choose a stateless session bean if, for example, the bean's state has no data for a specific client or if the bean implements a web service. Singleton session beans exists for the life cycle of the application.

23. ☑ **A** and **D.** An MDB is a stateless EJB that asynchronously consumes JMS messages.
☒ B and C are incorrect. An MDB is never called directly by a client and does not exist for the life cycle of the application.

Identify the Differences Between Client Pull and Server Push Architectures

24. ☑ **B, C,** and **D.** With the server push, the server sends data. The browser displays the data and leaves the connection open. The server sends more data whenever it is configured to do so and the browser displays it, leaving the connection open based on configuration. As for client pull, the server sends data, including a command that may set a timer, at which time it will execute a call to the server for fresh data. So after the specified time has elapsed, the client either gets the new data or reloads the current data if nothing is new. In server push, an HTTP connection is held open for an indefinite period of time (until the server sends a terminator, or until the client interrupts the connection).

☒ A is incorrect. In client pull, an HTTP connection is never held open. Instead, the client is told when to open a new connection and what data to get.

Identify the Benefits and Drawbacks of Using a Browser to Access Asynchronous, Lightweight Processes on the Server

25. ☑ **A, B and C.** Browsers expose asynchronous programming to the application logic via events or callbacks; they also provide a number of asynchronous APIs such as the commonly used XHR (XMLHttpRequest or "Ajax") APIs, as well as IndexedDB, SQLite. Server push uses a connection that is held open over multiple responses

☒ D is incorrect. Server push is asynchronous.

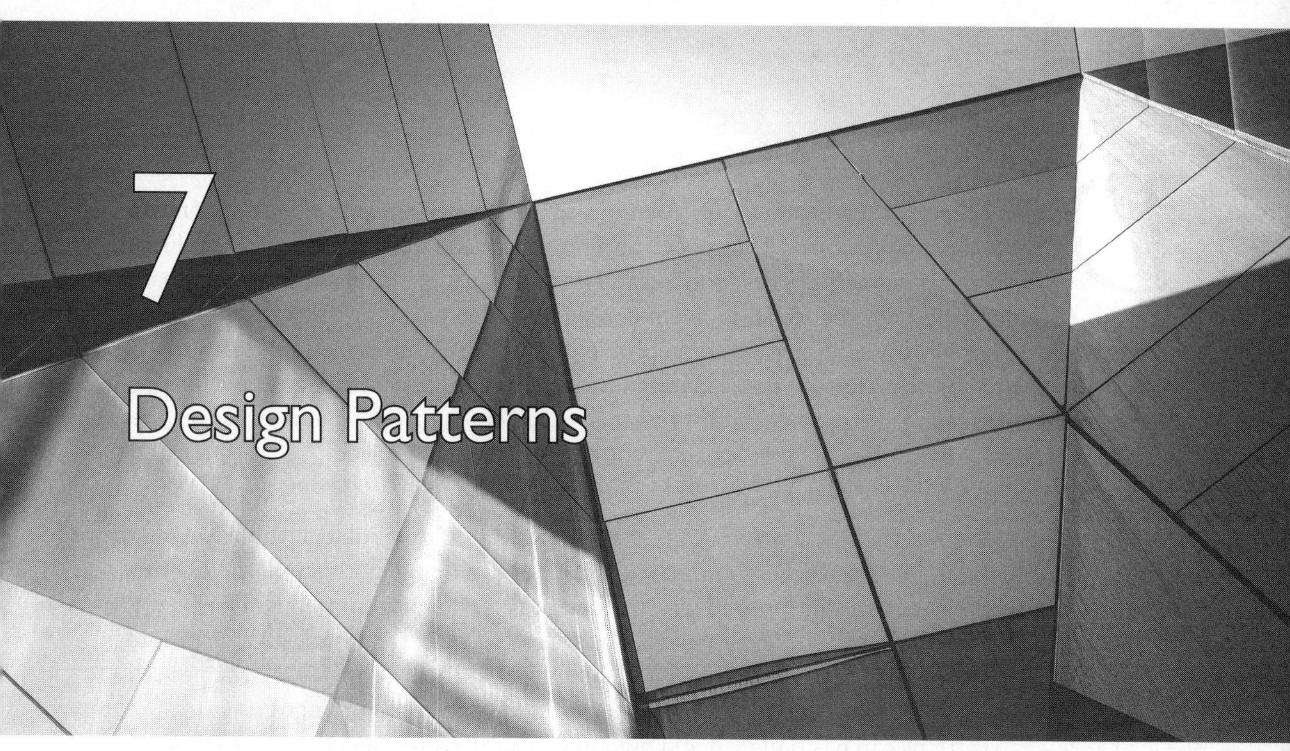

7 Design Patterns

CERTIFICATION OBJECTIVES

- 7.01 Select an Appropriate Gang of Four (GoF) Pattern for a Given Application Challenge
- 7.02 Identify a Gang of Four (GoF) Design Pattern, Using a Description of Its Features
- 7.03 Demonstrate Knowledge of Java EE Design Patterns
- 7.04 Identify the Use of the Law of Leaky Abstractions or a Specific Anti-Pattern in a Given Scenario
- ✓ Two-Minute Drill
- Q&A Self Test

Design *patterns* (or just *patterns*) are solutions to recurring problems in a given context amid competing concerns. They try to bring together and document the core solution to a given problem. They are identified and documented in a form that's easy to share, discuss, and understand. They are useful problem-solving documentation for software designers and are used repeatedly to help solve common problems that arise in the course of software engineering. Documentation for the design pattern should provide a discussion on the difficulties and interests surrounding the problem and arguments as to why the given solution balances these competing interests or constraints that are inherent in the issue being solved.

The value of the pattern is not just the solution to the problem; value can also be found in the documentation that explains the underlying motivation, the essential workings of the solution, and why the design pattern is advantageous. The pattern student will be able to experience all or at least some of the insight that went into providing the solution. This will undoubtedly help the designer to use the pattern and possibly adapt it or adjust it further to address needs accordingly.

Patterns can be combined and used in concert to solve larger problems that cannot be solved with just one pattern. Once the pattern student has become more familiar with these patterns, their combined applicability to a new set of problems will become much easier to identify. Design patterns address concerns in the following ways:

- They identify and name essential characteristics for addressing common software tasks.
- They provide details by specifying standard criteria that may include:
  - A problem statement
  - A list of forces that constrain the solution
  - A solution that defines class roles and participants
  - A list of strategies for well-known variations
  - The consequences or trade-offs that the solution imposes
  - A list of similar or related patterns

In order to make design patterns part of your development methodology, you must adopt and frequently use the vocabulary, recall the participants in the solution, and map roles to coding tasks.

Benefits of Using Design Patterns

Design patterns are beneficial because they describe a problem that occurs repeatedly, and then they explain the solution to the problem in a way that can be used many times over. Design patterns are helpful for the following reasons:

- They help designers quickly focus on solutions if the designers can recognize patterns that have been successful in the past.
- The study of patterns can inspire designers to come up with new and unique ideas.
- They provide a common language for design discussions.
- They provide solutions to real-world problems.
- Their format captures knowledge and documents best practices for a domain.
- They document decisions and the rationale that lead to the solution.
- They reuse the experience of predecessors.
- They communicate the insight gained previously.
- They describe the circumstances (when and where), the influences (who and what), and the resolution (how and why it balances the influences) of a solution.

Nevertheless, patterns are not the be-all and end-all, they are by no means a "silver bullet" or panacea, and they cannot be universally applied to all situations. You can't always find the solution to every problem by consulting the pattern playbook.

Design Patterns by Gamma et al., AKA the "Gang of Four" (GoF)

The Gang of Four—Erich Gamma, Richard Helm, Ralph Johnson, and John Vlissides, authors of the classic reference *Design Patterns: Elements of Reusable Object-Oriented Software* (Addison-Wesley, 2005)—described a pattern as "a solution to a problem in a context." These three elements—problem, solution, and context—are the essence of a pattern. As with all pattern creators, the GoF used a template to document patterns. Before we review the 23 patterns documented by the GoF, let's take a look at the format for these patterns.

Format for the GoF Design Patterns

The following table shows the elements and sections for the GoF Design Patterns format.

Element/Section	Description
Name	Used to help convey the essence of the pattern.
Classification	Categories are: ■ **Creational** Patterns concerned with creation ■ **Structural** Patterns concerned with composition ■ **Behavioral** Patterns concerned with interaction and responsibility
Intent	What problem does the pattern address? What does it do?
Also Known As	Other common names for the pattern.
Motivation	Scenario that illustrates the problem.
Applicability	Situations in which the pattern can be used.
Structure	Diagram representing the structure of classes and objects in the pattern. The GoF uses Object Modeling Technique (OMT) or Booch notation. Today, Unified Modeling Language (UML), which is a unification of OMT, Booch, and others, is commonly used.
Participants	Classes and/or objects participating in the design pattern along with their responsibilities.
Collaborations	How the participants work together to carry out their responsibilities.
Consequences	What objectives does the pattern achieve? What are the trade-offs and results?
Implementation	Implementation details (pitfalls, hints, or techniques) to consider. Are there language-specific issues?
Sample Code	Sample code.
Known Uses	Examples from the real world.
Related Patterns	Comparison and discussion of related patterns; scenarios where this pattern can be used in conjunction with another.

Benefits of a Specified GoF Design Pattern

This next table shows the benefits for each of the GoF design patterns:

GoF Design Pattern	Benefits
Abstract Factory	Isolates client from concrete (implementation) classes. Makes the exchanging of object families easier. Promotes consistency among objects.
Builder	Permits you to vary an object's internal representation. Isolates the code for construction and representation. Provides finer control over the construction process.
Factory Method	Removes the need to bind application-specific classes into the code. The code interacts solely with the resultant interface and therefore will work with any classes that implement that interface. Because creating objects inside a class is more flexible than creating an object directly, it enables the subclass to provide an extended version of an object.
Prototype	Allows adding or removing objects at run time. Specifies new objects by varying their values or structure. Reduces the need for subclassing. Allows dynamic configuring of an application with classes.
Singleton	Controls access to a single instance of the class. Reduces namespace usage. Permits refinement of operations and representation. Permits a variable number of instances. Is more flexible than class methods (operations).
Adapter	Allows two or more previously incompatible objects to interact. Allows reusability of existing functionality.
Bridge	Enables the separation of implementation from the interface. Improves extensibility. Allows the hiding of implementation details from the client.
Composite	Defines class hierarchies consisting of primitive and complex objects. Makes it easier to add new kinds of components. Provides the flexibility of structure with a manageable interface.
Decorator	Provides greater flexibility than static inheritance. Avoids the need to place feature-laden classes higher-up the hierarchy. Simplifies coding by allowing you to develop a series of functionality-targeted classes, instead of coding all of the behavior into the object. Enhances the extensibility of the object, because changes are made by coding new classes.

GoF Design Pattern	Benefits
Facade	Provides a simpler interface to a complex subsystem without reducing the options provided by the subsystem. Shields clients from the complexity of the subsystem components. Promotes looser coupling between the subsystem and its clients. Reduces the coupling between subsystems, provided that every subsystem uses its own Facade pattern and other parts of the system use the Facade pattern to communicate with the subsystem.
Flyweight	Reduces the number of objects to deal with. Reduces memory and storage devices if the objects are persisted.
Proxy	Remote proxy shields the fact that the implementation resides in another address space. Virtual proxy performs optimizations—for example, by creating objects on demand.
Chain of Responsibility	Reduces coupling. Adds flexibility when assigning responsibilities to objects. Allows a set of classes to act as one; events produced in one class can be sent to other handler classes within the composition.
Command	Separates the object that invokes the operation from the object that performs the operation. Simplifies adding new commands, because existing classes remain unchanged.
Interpreter	Makes it easier to change and extend the grammar. Makes implementing the grammar straightforward.
Iterator	Supports variations in the traversal of a collection. Simplifies the interface to the collection.
Mediator	Decouples colleagues. Simplifies object protocols. Centralizes control. Individual components become simpler and much easier to deal with because they do not need to pass messages to one another. Components do not need to contain logic to deal with their intercommunication and are therefore more generic.
Memento	Preserves encapsulation boundaries. Simplifies the originator.
Observer	Abstracts the coupling between the subject and the observer. Provides support for broadcast-type communication.
State	Keeps state-specific behavior local and partitions behavior for different states. Makes any state transitions explicit.
Strategy	Provides a substitute to subclassing. Defines each behavior within its own class, eliminating the need for conditional statements. Makes it easier to extend and incorporate new behavior without changing the application.
Template Method	For code reuse.

If you are new to design patterns, you may find the following table useful. It provides a suggestion for the sequence in which you can more easily study the GoF design patterns.

Sequence	Design Pattern	Classification	Comment
1	Factory Method	Creational	Frequently used and also well utilized by other patterns.
2	Strategy	Behavioral	Frequently used, so early familiarity helps.
3	Decorator	Structural	Considered the "skin" to the "guts" of Strategy.
4	Composite	Structural	Often used along with Chain of Responsibility, Interpreter, Iterator, and Visitor.
5	Iterator	Behavioral	Looping through anything is widespread in computing, so why not through objects, too?
6	Template Method	Behavioral	Helps to reinforce your understanding of Strategy and Factory Method.
7	Abstract Factory	Creational	Used to create more than one type of a group of objects.
8	Builder	Creational	Another way to create, similar to Factory Method and Abstract Factory.
9	Singleton	Creational	You want only one copy of something.
10	Proxy	Structural	Controlled access to a service is needed.
11	Adapter	Structural	Used to gain access to a service with an incompatible interface.
12	Bridge	Structural	Decouples the function from the implementation.
13	Mediator	Behavioral	Yet another middleman.
14	Façade	Structural	Single interface simplifying multiple interfaces in a subsystem.
15	Observer	Behavioral	A form of the publish/subscribe model.
16	Chain of Responsibility	Behavioral	Passes the message along until it's dealt with.
17	Memento	Behavioral	Backs up and restores an object's state.
18	Command	Behavioral	Separates invoker from performer.
19	Prototype	Creational	Similar to cloning.
20	State	Behavioral	Object appears to change class and alter its behavior.
21	Visitor	Behavioral	Object that represents an operation that operates on elements of an object structure.
22	Flyweight	Structural	Allows you to utilize sharing to support large numbers of objects efficiently.
23	Interpreter	Behavioral	Defines a grammar and an interpreter that uses the grammar to interpret sentences.

CERTIFICATION OBJECTIVE 7.01

Select an Appropriate Gang of Four (GoF) Pattern for a Given Application Challenge

We will now review each of the Gamma et al. design patterns, starting first with those that are used to create objects (Creational), and then moving on to those that are concerned with composition of classes and objects (Structural), and finally covering those that are concerned with the interaction and responsibility of objects (Behavioral).

GoF Creational Design Patterns

Creational design patterns are concerned with the way objects are created. These patterns are used when a decision must be made at the time a class is instantiated. Typically, the details of the concrete class that is to be instantiated are hidden from (and unknown to) the calling class by an abstract class that knows only about the abstract class or the interface it implements. The following creational patterns are described by the GoF:

- Abstract Factory
- Builder
- Factory Method
- Prototype
- Singleton

Abstract Factory

The Abstract Factory pattern's intent is to provide an interface to use for creating families of related (or dependent) objects without actually specifying their concrete classes. For a given set of related abstract classes, this pattern supplies a technique for creating instances of those abstract classes from an equivalent set of concrete subclasses. On some occasions, you may need to create an object without having to know which concrete subclass of object to create.

The Abstract Factory pattern is also known as Kit. The UML representation is shown in Figure 7-1.

FIGURE 7-1

UML for the Abstract Factory pattern

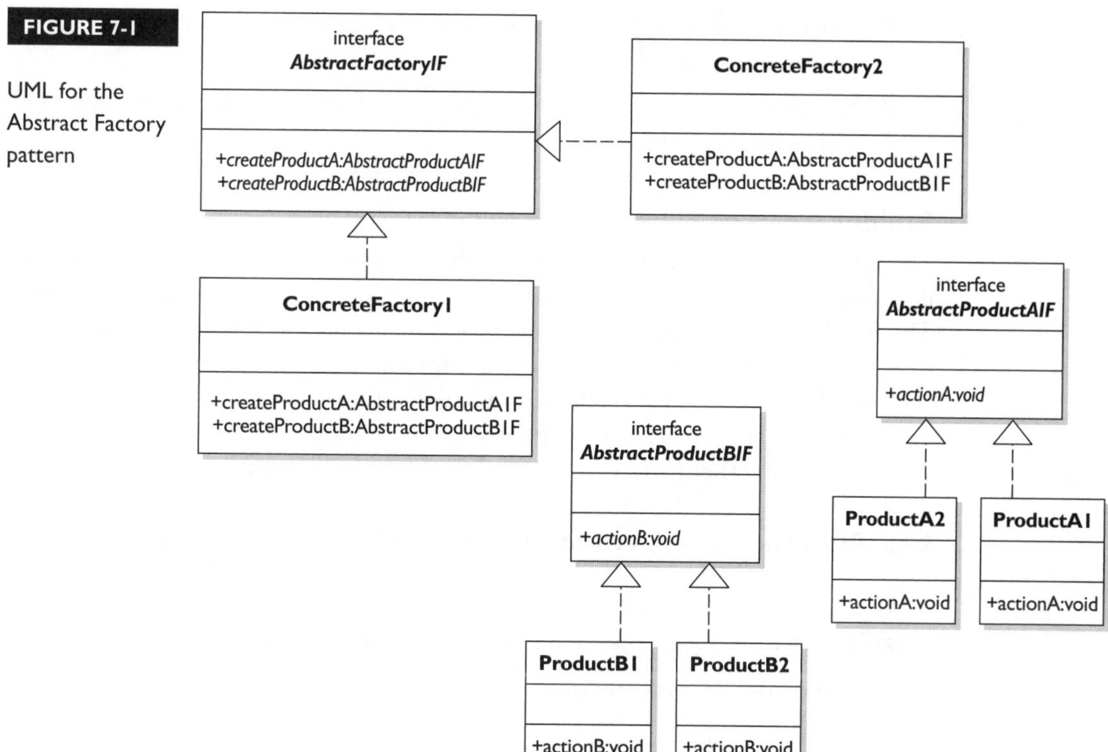

Benefits Following is a list of benefits of using the Abstract Factory pattern:

- It isolates the client from concrete (implementation) classes.
- It eases the exchanging of object families.
- It promotes consistency among objects.

Applicable Scenarios The following scenarios are most appropriate for the Abstract Factory pattern:

- The system needs to be independent of how its objects are created, composed, and represented.
- The system needs to be configured with one of multiple families of objects.

- The family of related objects is intended to be used together, and this constraint needs to be enforced.
- You want to provide a library of objects that does not show implementations and only reveals interfaces.

Builder

The Builder pattern's intent is to separate the construction of a complex object from its representation so that the same construction process can create different objects. The Builder pattern is useful when several kinds of complex objects with similar rules for assembly need to be joined at run time but result in different object types. It achieves this by separating the process of building the object from the object itself.

The Builder pattern creates complex objects in multiple steps instead of in a single step, as in other patterns. The UML is shown in Figure 7-2.

Benefits The following benefits are achieved when using the Builder pattern:

- It permits you to vary an object's internal representation.
- It isolates the code for construction and representation.
- It provides finer control over the construction process.

FIGURE 7-2 UML for the Builder pattern

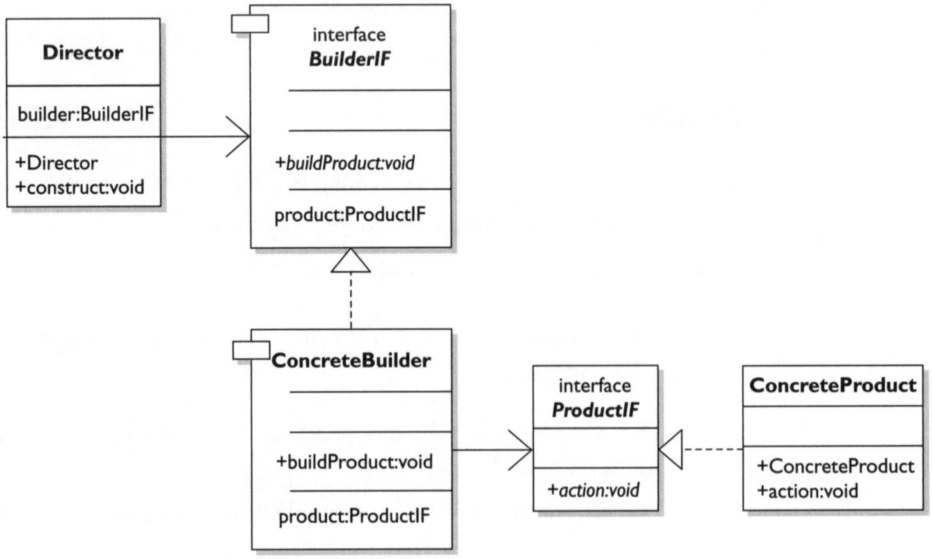

Applicable Scenarios The following scenarios are most appropriate for the Builder pattern:

- The algorithm for creating a complex object needs to be independent of the components that compose the object and how they are assembled.
- The construction process is to allow different representations of the constructed object.

Factory Method

The Factory Method pattern's intent is to define an interface for creating an object but letting the subclass decide which class to instantiate. In other words, the class defers instantiation to subclasses. The client of the Factory Method never needs to know the concrete class that has been instantiated and returned. Its client needs to know only about the published abstract interface.

The Factory Method pattern is also known as Virtual Constructor. Figure 7-3 shows the UML.

Benefits Following is a list of benefits of using the Factory Method pattern:

- It removes the need to bind application-specific classes into the code. The code interacts solely with the resultant interface, so it will work with any classes that implement that interface.

FIGURE 7-3

UML for the Factory Method pattern

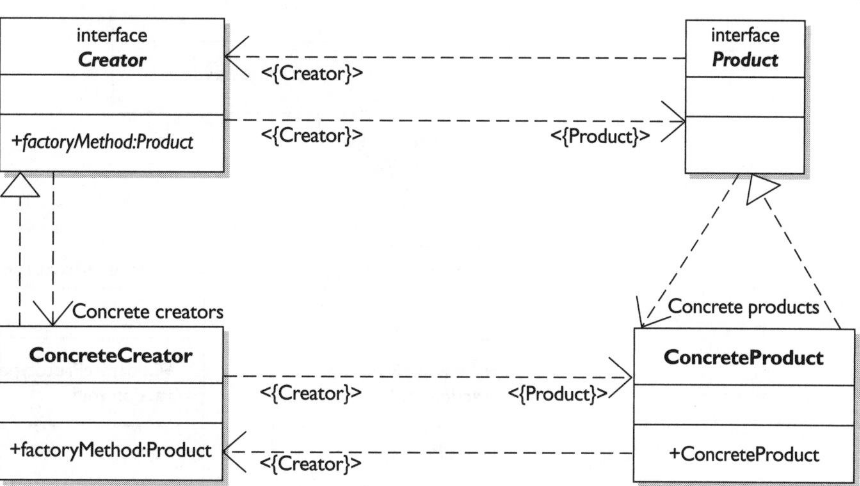

- Because creating objects inside a class is more flexible than creating an object directly, it enables the subclass to provide an extended version of an object.

Applicable Scenarios The following scenarios are most appropriate for the Factory Method pattern:

- A class is not able to anticipate the class of objects it needs to create.
- A class wants its subclasses to specify the objects it instantiates.
- Classes assign responsibility to one of several helper subclasses, and you want to localize the knowledge of which helper subclass is the delegate.

Prototype

The Prototype pattern's intent is to specify the kinds of objects that need to be created using a prototypical instance, and to then be able to create new objects by copying this prototype. The copying of objects in Java is typically done by the `clone()` method of `java.lang.Object`. The UML is shown in Figure 7-4.

FIGURE 7-4

UML for the Prototype pattern

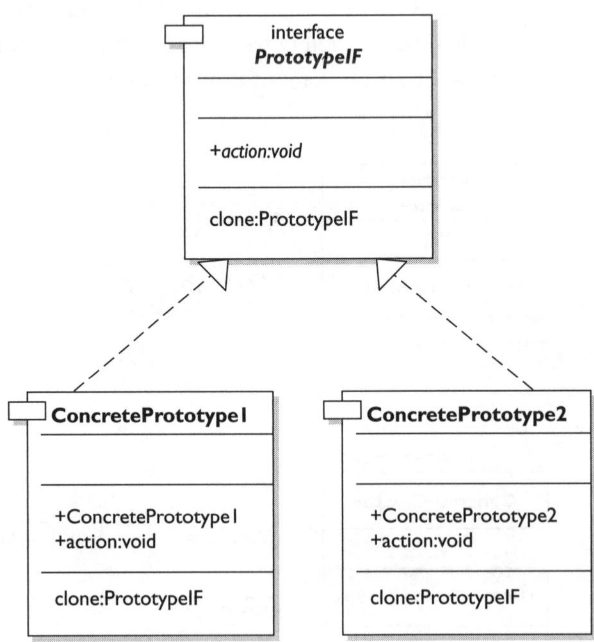

Benefits Following are the benefits of using the Prototype pattern:

- It lets you add or remove objects at run time.
- It lets you specify new objects by varying its values or structure.
- It reduces the need for subclassing.
- It lets you dynamically configure an application with classes.

Applicable Scenarios The following scenarios are most appropriate for the Prototype pattern:

- The classes to instantiate are specified at run time.
- You need to avoid building a class hierarchy of factories that parallels the hierarchy of objects.
- Instances of the class have one of only a few different combinations of state.

Singleton

The Singleton pattern's intent is to ensure that a class has only one instance and provides a global point of access to it. It ensures that all objects that use an instance of this class are using the same instance. Figure 7-5 shows the UML.

Benefits Following are the benefits of using the Singleton pattern:

- It controls access to a single instance of the class.
- It reduces namespace usage.
- It permits refinement of operations and representation.
- It can also permit a variable number of instances.
- It is more flexible than class methods (operations).

FIGURE 7-5

UML for the Singleton pattern

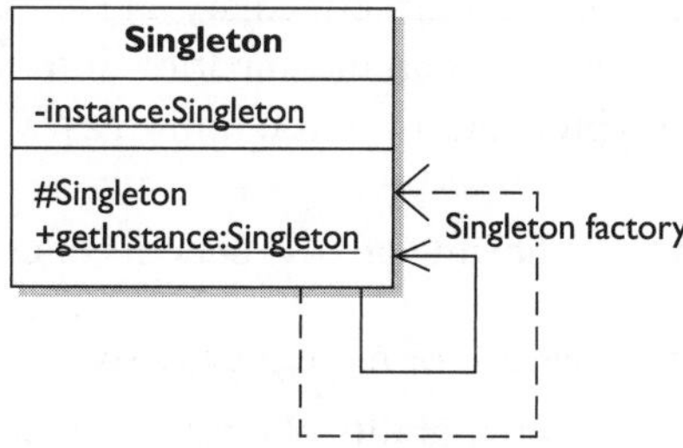

Applicable Scenario The scenario most appropriate for the Singleton pattern is when a single instance of a class is needed and must be accessible to clients from a well-known access point.

GoF Structural Design Patterns

Structural patterns are concerned with composition or the organization of classes and objects, how classes inherit from each other, and how they are composed from other classes.

Common structural patterns include the Adapter, Proxy, and Decorator patterns. These patterns are similar in that they introduce a level of indirection between a client class and a class it wants to use. Their intents are different, however. Adapter uses indirection to modify the interface of a class to make it easier for a client class to use it. Decorator uses indirection to add behavior to a class, without unduly affecting the client class. Proxy uses indirection transparently to provide a stand-in for another class.

The following structural patterns are described by GoF:

- Adapter
- Bridge
- Composite
- Decorator
- Facade
- Flyweight
- Proxy

Adapter

The Adapter pattern converts the interface of a class into an interface that a client requires. It acts as an intermediary and lets classes work together that couldn't otherwise because of an incompatible interface.

The Adapter pattern is also known as Wrapper. The UML is shown in Figure 7-6.

Benefits Following are the benefits of using the Adapter pattern:

- It allows two or more previously incompatible objects to interact.
- It allows reusability of existing functionality.

FIGURE 7-6

UML for the Adapter pattern

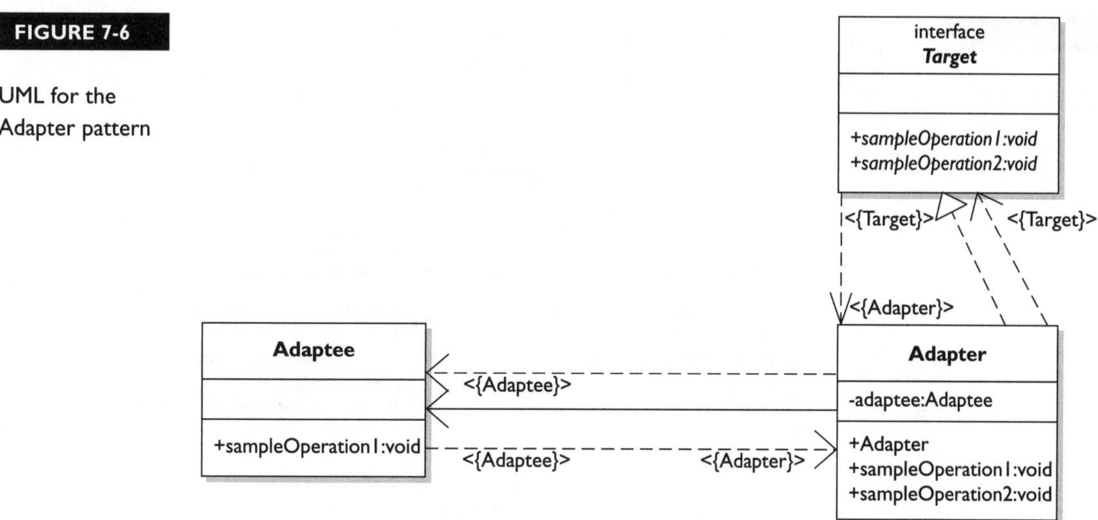

Applicable Scenarios The following scenarios are most appropriate for the Adapter pattern:

- An object needs to utilize an existing class with an incompatible interface.
- You want to create a reusable class that cooperates with classes that don't necessarily have compatible interfaces.
- You need to use several existing subclasses but do not want to adapt their interfaces by subclassing each one.

Bridge

The Bridge pattern's intent is to decouple the functional abstraction from the implementation so that the two can be changed and can vary independently.

The Bridge pattern is also known as Handle/Body. The UML is shown in Figure 7-7.

Benefits Following is a list of benefits of using the Bridge pattern:

- It enables the separation of implementation from the interface.
- It improves extensibility.
- It allows the hiding of implementation details from the client.

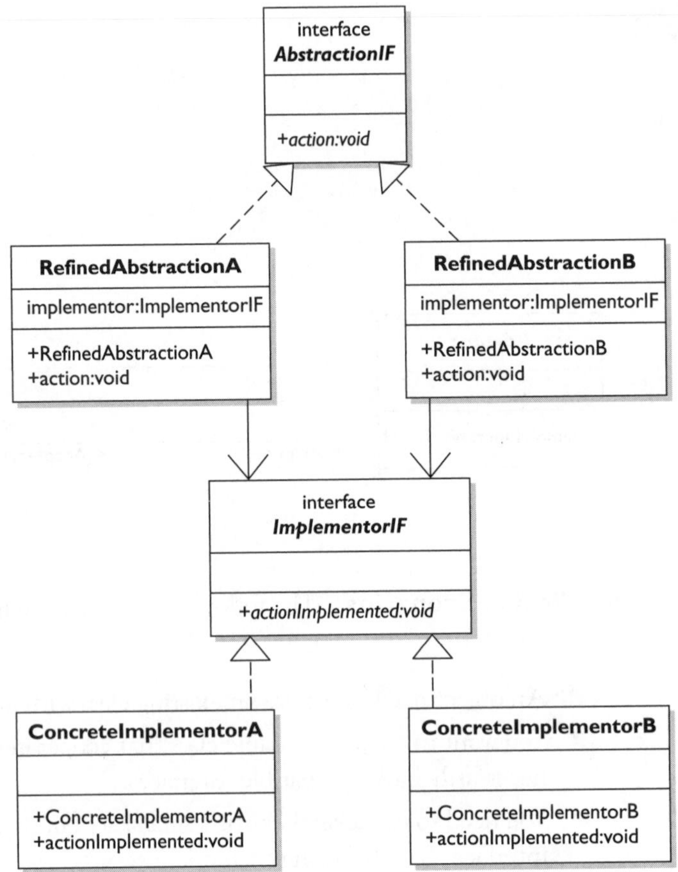

FIGURE 7-7

UML for the Bridge pattern

Applicable Scenarios The following scenarios are most appropriate for the Bridge pattern:

- You want to avoid a permanent binding between the functional abstraction and its implementation.
- Both the functional abstraction and its implementation need to be extended using subclasses.
- Changes to the implementation should not impact the client (not even a recompile).

Composite

The Composite pattern's intent is to allow clients to operate in a generic manner on objects that may or may not represent a hierarchy of objects.

The UML is shown in Figure 7-8.

Benefits

Following are benefits of using the Composite pattern:

- It defines class hierarchies consisting of primitive and complex objects.
- It makes it easier for you to add new kinds of components.
- It provides flexibility of structure with a manageable interface.

Applicable Scenarios The following scenarios are most appropriate for the Composite pattern:

- You want to represent a full or partial hierarchy of objects.
- You want clients to be able to ignore the differences between the varying objects in the hierarchy.

FIGURE 7-8

UML for the Composite pattern

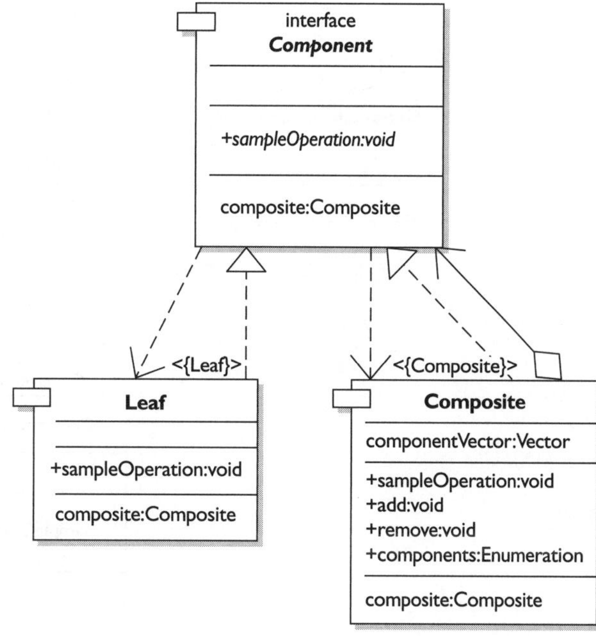

- The structure is dynamic and can have any level of complexity—for example, using the Composite View from the Java EE Patterns Catalog, which is useful for portal applications.

Decorator

An alternative to subclassing to extend functionality, the Decorator pattern's intent is to attach flexible additional responsibilities to an object dynamically. The Decorator pattern uses composition instead of inheritance to extend the functionality of an object at run time.

The Decorator pattern is also known as Wrapper. The UML is shown in Figure 7-9.

FIGURE 7-9

UML for the Decorator pattern

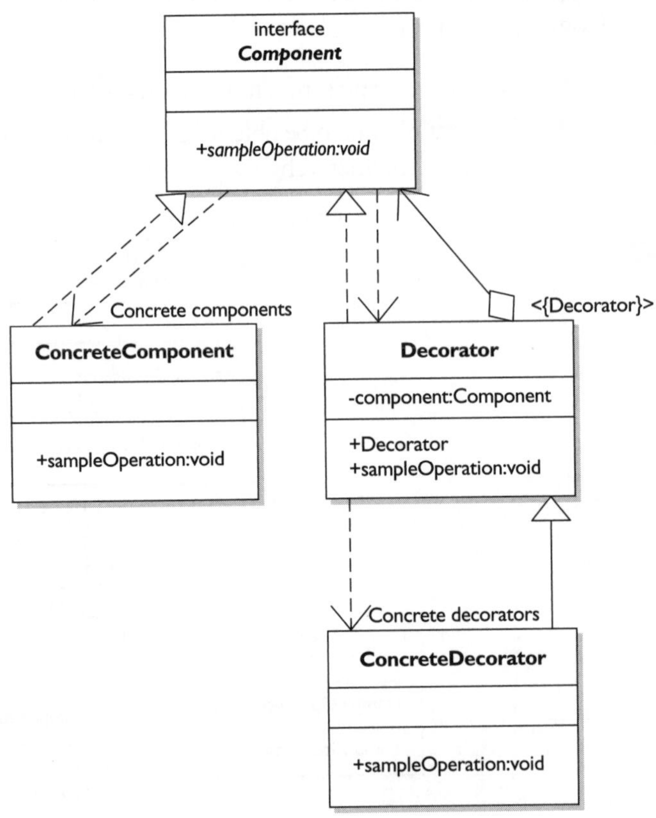

Benefits Following is a list of benefits of using the Decorator pattern:

- It provides greater flexibility than static inheritance.
- It avoids the need to place feature-laden classes higher up the hierarchy.
- It simplifies coding by allowing you to develop a series of functionality-targeted classes, instead of coding all of the behavior into the object.
- It enhances the extensibility of the object, because changes are made by coding new classes.

Applicable Scenarios The following scenarios are most appropriate for the Decorator pattern:

- You want to transparently and dynamically add responsibilities to objects without affecting other objects.
- You want to add responsibilities to an object that you may want to change in the future.
- Extending functionality by subclassing is no longer practical.

Facade

The Facade pattern's intent is to provide a unified and simplified interface to a set of interfaces in a subsystem. The Facade pattern describes a higher-level interface that makes the subsystem(s) easier to use. Practically every Abstract Factory is a type of Facade. Figure 7-10 shows the UML.

FIGURE 7-10

UML for the Facade pattern

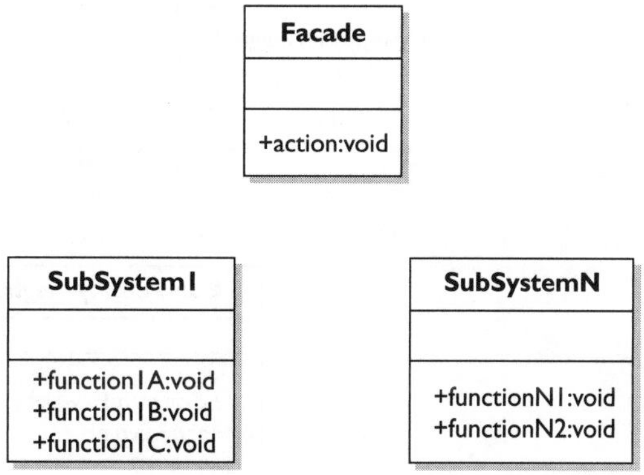

Benefits Following is a list of benefits of using the Facade pattern:

- It provides a simpler interface to a complex subsystem without reducing the options provided by the subsystem.
- It shields clients from the complexity of the subsystem components.
- It promotes looser coupling between the subsystem and its clients.
- It reduces the coupling between subsystems provided that every subsystem uses its own Facade pattern and other parts of the system use the Facade pattern to communicate with the subsystem.

Applicable Scenarios The following scenarios are most appropriate for the Facade pattern:

- You need to provide a simple interface to a complex subsystem.
- Several dependencies exist between clients and the implementation classes of an abstraction.
- Layering the subsystems is necessary or desired.

Flyweight

The Flyweight pattern's intent is to utilize sharing to support large numbers of fine-grained objects in an efficient manner. Figure 7-11 shows the UML.

FIGURE 7-11

UML for the Flyweight pattern

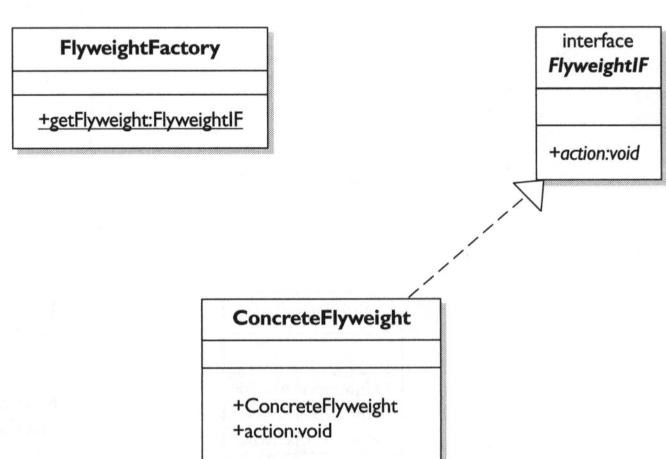

Benefits Following are benefits of using the Flyweight pattern:

- It reduces the number of objects to deal with.
- It reduces the amount of memory and storage devices required if the objects are persisted.

Applicable Scenarios The following scenarios are most appropriate for the Flyweight pattern:

- An application uses a considerable number of objects.
- The storage costs are high because of the quantity of objects.
- The application does not depend on object identity.

Proxy

The Proxy pattern's intent is to provide a surrogate or placeholder for another object to control access to it. The most common implementations are remote and virtual proxy.

The Proxy pattern is also known as Surrogate. Figure 7-12 shows the UML.

Benefits Following is a list of benefits of using the Proxy pattern:

- The remote proxy can shield the fact that the implementation resides in another address space.
- The virtual proxy can perform optimizations—for example, by creating objects on demand.

FIGURE 7-12

UML for the Proxy pattern

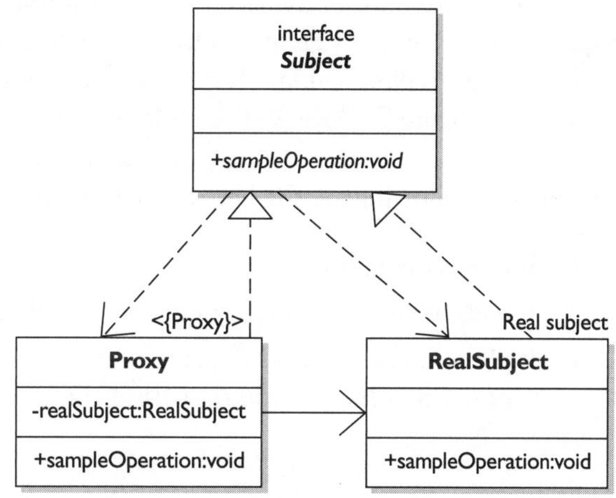

Applicable Scenario The Proxy pattern is appropriate when a more versatile or sophisticated reference to an object, rather than a simple pointer, is needed.

GoF Behavioral Design Patterns

Behavioral patterns are concerned with the interaction and responsibility of objects. They help make complex behavior manageable by specifying the responsibilities of objects and the ways they communicate with each other.

The following behavioral patterns are described by GoF:

- Chain of Responsibility
- Command
- Interpreter
- Iterator
- Mediator
- Memento
- Observer
- State
- Strategy
- Template Method
- Visitor

Chain of Responsibility

The Chain of Responsibility pattern's intent is to avoid coupling the sender of a request to its receiver by giving multiple objects a chance to handle the request.

The request is passed along the chain of receiving objects until an object processes it. Figure 7-13 shows the UML.

Benefits Following are the benefits of using the Chain of Responsibility pattern:

- It reduces coupling.
- It adds flexibility when assigning responsibilities to objects.
- It allows a set of classes to act as one; events produced in one class can be sent to other handler classes within the composition.

FIGURE 7-13

UML for the Chain of Responsibility pattern

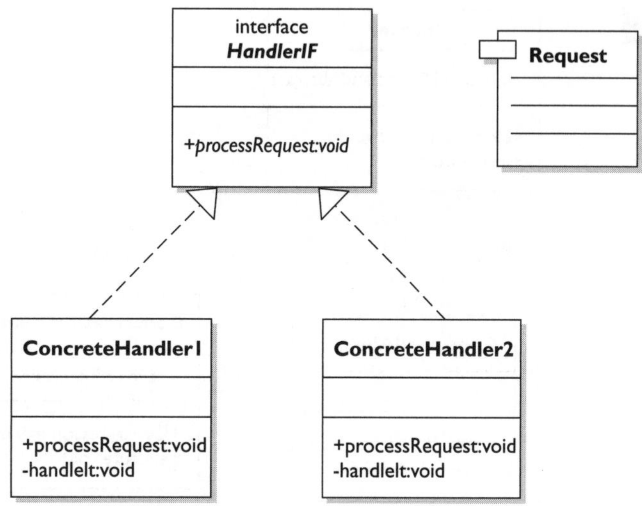

Applicable Scenarios The following scenarios are most appropriate for the Chain of Responsibility pattern:

- More than one object can handle a request, and the handler is unknown.
- A request is to be issued to one of several objects, and the receiver is not specified explicitly.
- The set of objects able to handle the request is to be specified dynamically.

Command

The Command pattern's intent is to encapsulate a request as an object, thereby letting you parameterize clients with different requests, queue or log requests, and support rollback types of operations.

The Command pattern is also known as Action or Transaction. The UML is shown in Figure 7-14.

Benefits Following is a list of benefits of using the Command pattern:

- It separates the object that invokes the operation from the object that actually performs the operation.
- It simplifies adding new commands, because existing classes remain unchanged.

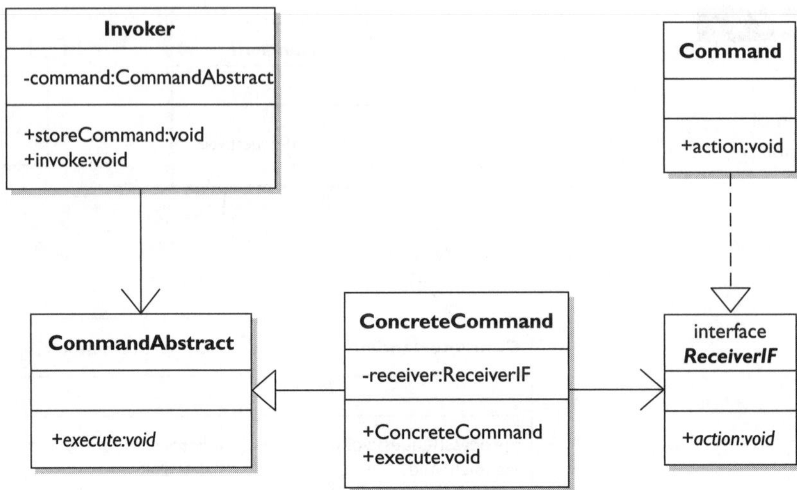

FIGURE 7-14

UML for the Command pattern

Applicable Scenarios The following scenarios are most appropriate for the Command pattern:

- You need to parameterize objects according to an action to perform.
- You create, queue, and execute requests at different times.
- You need to support rollback, logging, or transaction functionality.

Interpreter

The Interpreter pattern's intent is to define a representation of the grammar of a given language, along with an interpreter that uses this representation to interpret sentences in the language. The UML is shown in Figure 7-15.

Benefits Following is a list of benefits of using the Interpreter pattern:

- It is easier to change and extend the grammar.
- Implementing the grammar is straightforward.

Applicable Scenarios The following scenarios are most appropriate for the Interpreter pattern:

- The grammar of the language is not complicated.
- Efficiency is not a priority.

FIGURE 7-15

UML for the Interpreter pattern

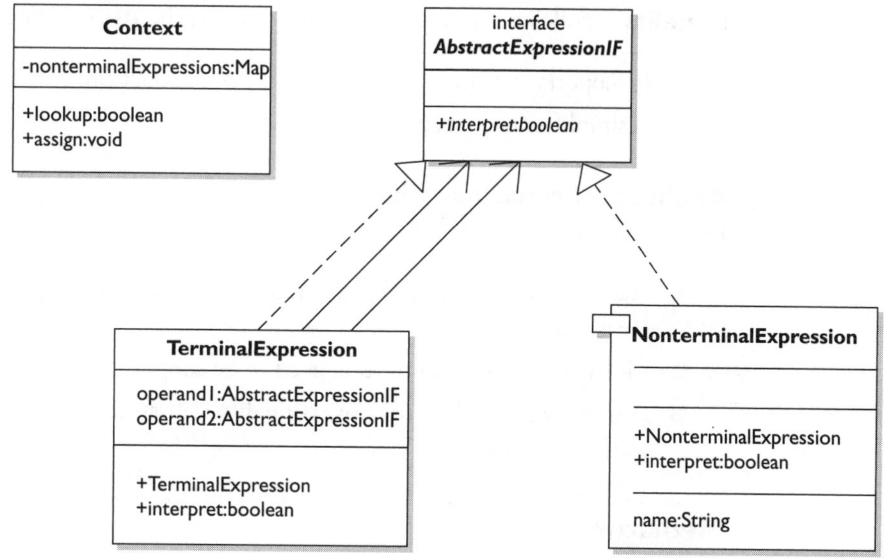

Iterator

The Iterator pattern's intent is to provide a way to access the elements of an aggregate object sequentially without exposing its underlying implementation. `java.util.Enumeration` and `java.util.Iterator` are examples of the Iterator pattern.

The Iterator pattern is also known as Cursor. The UML is shown in Figure 7-16.

FIGURE 7-16

UML for the Iterator pattern

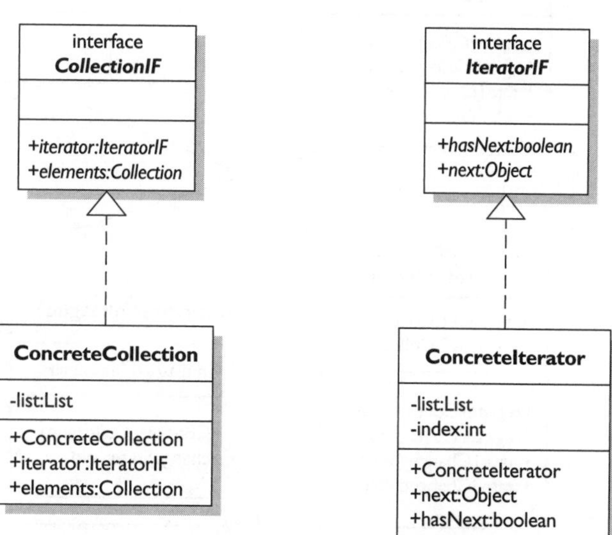

Benefits Following is a list of benefits of using the Iterator pattern:

- It supports variations in the traversal of a collection.
- It simplifies the interface to the collection.

Applicable Scenarios The following scenarios are most appropriate for the Iterator pattern:

- Access to a collection object is required without having to expose its internal representation.
- Multiple traversals of objects need to be supported in the collection.
- A universal interface for traversing different structures needs to be provided in the collection.

Mediator

The Mediator pattern's intent is to define an object that encapsulates how a set of objects interacts. It helps to promote a looser coupling by keeping objects from referring to each other explicitly, therefore allowing any interaction to vary independently. The UML is shown in Figure 7-17.

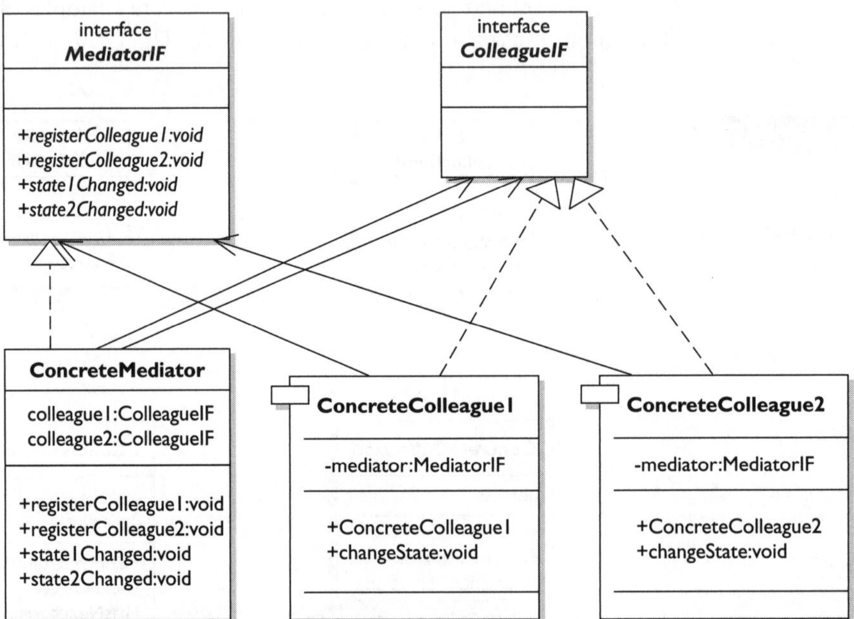

FIGURE 7-17

UML for the Mediator pattern

Benefits Following is a list of benefits of using the Mediator pattern:

- It decouples colleagues.
- It simplifies object protocols.
- It centralizes control.
- The individual components become simpler and much easier to deal with because they do not need to pass messages to one another.
- The components do not need to contain logic to deal with their intercommunication and are therefore more generic.

Applicable Scenarios The following scenarios are most appropriate for the Mediator pattern:

- A set of objects communicates in complex but well-defined ways.
- Custom behavior distributed between several objects is required without subclassing. It is commonly used structurally in message-based systems. The messages themselves are the means by which related objects are decoupled.

Memento

The Memento pattern's intent is to capture and internalize an object's internal state so that objects can be restored to this state later. It must do this without violating encapsulation.

The Memento pattern is also known as Token. The UML is shown in Figure 7-18.

Benefits Following is a list of benefits of using the Memento pattern:

- It preserves encapsulation boundaries.
- It simplifies the originator.

FIGURE 7-18

UML for the Memento pattern

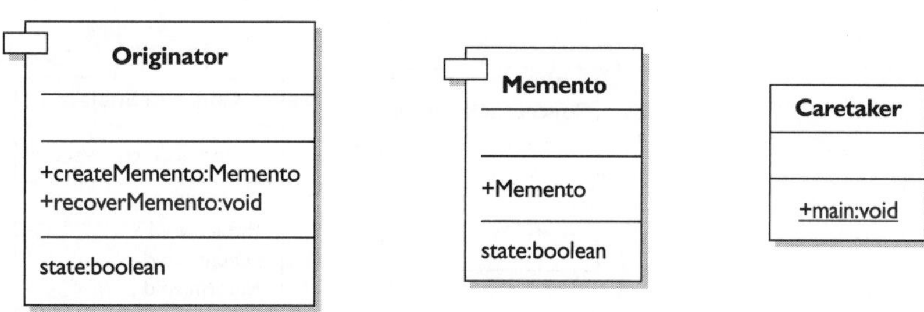

Applicable Scenarios The following scenarios are most appropriate for the Memento pattern:

- A snapshot containing enough information regarding the state of an object can be saved so that it can be restored to the complete state using the snapshot information later.
- Using a direct interface to obtain the state would impose implementation details that would break the rules of encapsulation for the object.

Observer

The Observer pattern's intent is to define a one-to-many dependency so that when one object changes state, all its dependents are notified and updated automatically. Java provides support for implementing the Observer pattern via the `java.util.Observer` interface and the `java.util.Observable` class.

The Observer pattern is also known as Dependents or Publish-Subscribe. The UML is shown in Figure 7-19.

Benefits Following is a list of benefits of using the Observer pattern:

- It abstracts the coupling between the subject and the observer.
- It provides support for broadcast-type communication.

FIGURE 7-19

UML for the Observer pattern

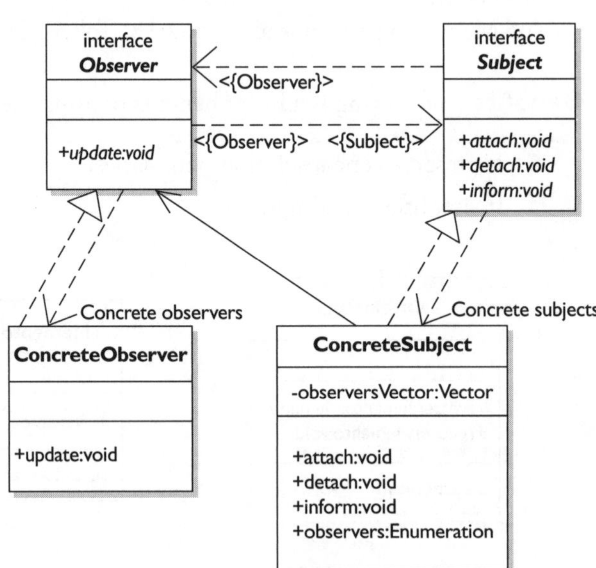

Applicable Scenarios The following scenarios are most appropriate for the Observer pattern:

- A change to an object requires changing other objects, and the number of objects that need to be changed is unknown.
- An object needs to notify other objects without making any assumptions about the identity of those objects.

State

The State pattern's intent is to allow an object to alter its behavior when its internal state changes, appearing as though the object itself has changed its class. Another view of the intent of the State pattern is to encapsulate the states of an object as discrete objects, with each object belonging to a separate subclass of an abstract state class.

The State pattern is also known as Objects for States and acts in a similar way to the Receiver in the Command pattern. The UML is shown in Figure 7-20.

Benefits Following is a list of benefits of using the State pattern:

- It keeps state-specific behavior local and partitions behavior for different states.
- It makes any state transitions explicit.

FIGURE 7-20

UML for the State pattern

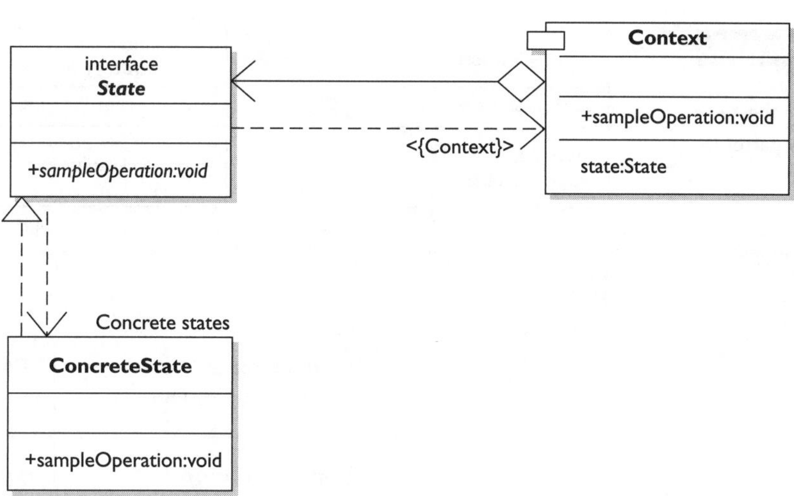

Applicable Scenarios The following scenarios are most appropriate for the State pattern:

- The behavior of an object depends on its state, and it must be able to change its behavior at run time according to the new state.
- Operations have large, multipart conditional statements that depend on the state of the object.

Strategy

The Strategy pattern's intent is to define a family of functionality, encapsulate each one, and make them interchangeable. The Strategy pattern lets the functionality vary independently from the clients that use it.

The Strategy pattern is also known as Policy. The UML is shown in Figure 7-21.

Benefits Following is a list of benefits of using the Strategy pattern:

- It provides a substitute to subclassing.
- It defines each behavior within its own class, eliminating the need for conditional statements.
- It makes it easier to extend and incorporate new behavior without changing the application.

FIGURE 7-21

UML for the Strategy pattern

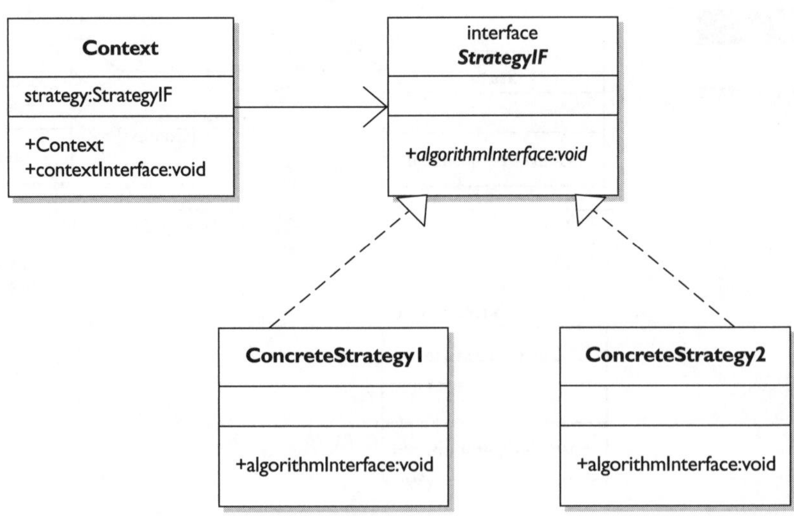

Applicable Scenarios The following scenarios are most appropriate for the Strategy pattern:

- Multiple classes differ only in their behaviors. The servlet API is a classic example of this.
- You need different variations of an algorithm.
- An algorithm uses data that is unknown to the client.

Template Method

The Template Method pattern's intent is to define the skeleton of a function in an operation, deferring some steps to its subclasses. The Template Method lets subclasses redefine certain steps of a function without changing the structure of the function. The HttpServlet does this in the servlet API. The UML is shown in Figure 7-22.

Benefit The Template Method pattern is a very common technique for reusing code.

Applicable Scenarios The following scenarios are most appropriate for the Template Method pattern:

- You want to implement the nonvarying parts of an algorithm in a single class and the varying parts of the algorithm in subclasses.
- Common behavior among subclasses should be moved to a single common class, avoiding duplication.

FIGURE 7-22

UML for the Template Method pattern

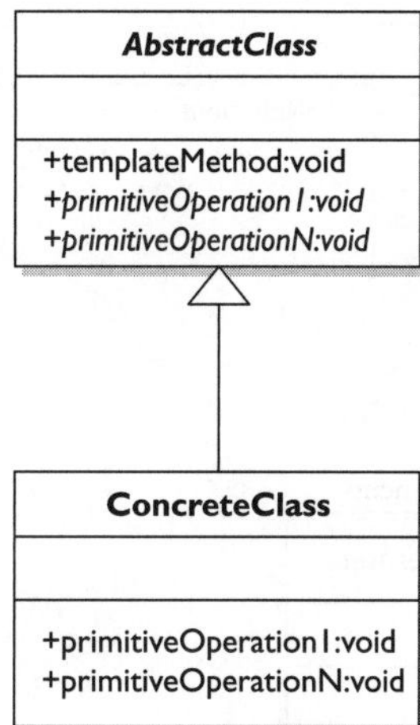

Visitor

The Visitor pattern's intent is to represent an operation to be performed on elements of an object structure. The Visitor pattern allows for the addition of a new operation without changing the classes of the elements on which it is to operate. Figure 7-23 shows the UML.

Benefits Following are the benefits of using the Visitor pattern:

- It simplifies the addition of new operations.
- It gathers related operations while separating unrelated ones.

Applicable Scenarios The following scenarios are most appropriate for the Visitor pattern:

- An object structure contains many objects with differing interfaces and there is a need to perform operations on these objects in a way that depends on their concrete classes.
- Many distinct and unrelated operations need to be performed on objects in a structure and there is a need to avoid cluttering the classes with these operations.
- The classes defining the object structure rarely change but you frequently need to define new operations that perform over the structure.

Now that we've covered each of the Gang of Four (GoF) Design Patterns, let's review scenarios and also identify the design pattern that is most appropriate as a solution.

FIGURE 7-23 UML for the Visitor pattern

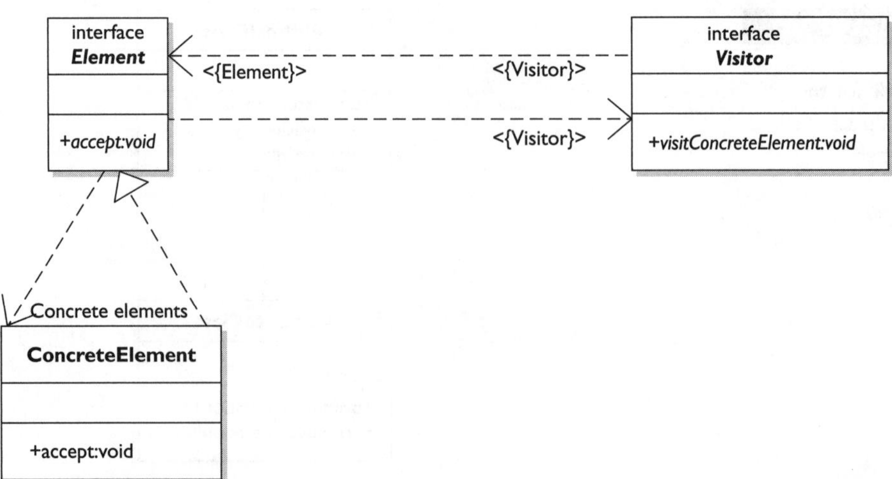

SCENARIO & SOLUTION

Given Scenarios	Appropriate Design Pattern
The system needs to be independent of how its objects are created, composed, and represented. The system needs to be configured with one of multiple families of objects. The family of related objects is intended to be used together, and this constraint needs to be enforced. You want to provide a library of objects that does not show implementations but only reveals interfaces.	Abstract Factory
The algorithm for creating a complex object needs to be independent of the components that compose the object and how they are assembled. The construction process is to allow different representations of the constructed object.	Builder
A class is not able to anticipate the class of objects it needs to create. A class wants its subclasses to specify the objects it instantiates. Classes delegate responsibility to one of several helper subclasses, and you want to localize the knowledge of which helper subclass is the delegate.	Factory Method
The classes to instantiate are specified at run time. You want to avoid building a class hierarchy of factories that parallels the hierarchy of objects. Instances of the class have one of only a few different combinations of state.	Prototype
A single instance of a class is needed, and it must be accessible to clients from a well-known access point.	Singleton
You want to utilize an existing class with an incompatible interface. You want to create a reusable class that cooperates with classes that don't necessarily have compatible interfaces. You need to use several existing subclasses but do not want to adapt their interfaces by subclassing each one.	Adapter
You want to avoid a permanent binding between the functional abstraction and its implementation. Both the functional abstraction and its implementation need to be extended using subclasses. Changes to the implementation should not impact the client (not even a recompile).	Bridge

SCENARIO & SOLUTION

Given Scenarios	Appropriate Design Pattern
You want to represent a full or partial hierarchy of objects. You want clients to be able to ignore the differences between the varying objects in the hierarchy. The structure is dynamic and can have any level of complexity.	Composite
You want to transparently and dynamically add responsibilities to objects without affecting other objects. You want to add responsibilities to an object that you may want to change in the future. Extending functionality by subclassing is no longer practical.	Decorator
You want to provide a simpler interface to a more complex subsystem. Several dependencies exist between clients and the implementation classes of an abstraction. You want to layer the subsystems.	Facade
The application uses a considerable number of objects. The storage costs are high because of the quantity of objects. The application does not depend on object identity.	Flyweight
You need a more versatile or sophisticated reference to an object, rather than a simple pointer.	Proxy
More than one object can handle a request and the handler is unknown. A request is to be issued to one of several objects and the receiver is not specified explicitly. The set of objects able to handle the request is to be specified dynamically.	Chain of Responsibility
You need to parameterize objects by an action to perform. You specify, queue, and execute requests at different times. You need to support rollback, logging, or transaction functionality.	Command
The grammar of the language is not complicated and efficiency is not a priority.	Interpreter
Access to a collection object is required without having to expose its internal representation. You need to support multiple traversals of objects in the collection. You need to provide a universal interface for traversing different structures in the collection.	Iterator

SCENARIO & SOLUTION

Given Scenarios	Appropriate Design Pattern
A set of objects communicates in complex but well-defined ways. Custom behavior distributed between several objects is required without subclassing.	Mediator
A snapshot containing enough information regarding the state of an object can be saved so that it can be restored to the complete state using the snapshot information later. Using a direct interface to obtain the state would impose implementation details that would break the rules of encapsulation for the object.	Memento
A change to an object requires changing other objects, and the number of objects that need to be changed is unknown. An object needs to notify other objects without making any assumptions about the identity of those objects.	Observer
The behavior of an object depends on its state, and it must be able to change its behavior at run time according on the new state. Operations have large multipart conditional statements that depend on the state of the object.	State
Multiple classes differ only in their behavior. You need different variations of an algorithm. An algorithm uses data that is unknown to the client.	Strategy
You want to implement the nonvarying parts of an algorithm in a single class and the varying parts of the algorithm in subclasses. Common behavior among subclasses should be moved to a single common class, avoiding duplication.	Template Method
An object structure contains many objects with differing interfaces and you need to perform operations on these objects in a way that depends on their concrete classes. Many distinct and unrelated operations need to be performed on objects in a structure and you need to avoid cluttering the classes with these operations. The classes defining the object structure rarely change but you frequently need to define new operations that perform over the structure.	Visitor

CERTIFICATION OBJECTIVE 7.02

Identify a Gang of Four (GoF) Design Pattern, Using a Description of Its Features

Study each GoF design pattern diagram shown earlier. The following table has a brief description of the features and the design pattern associated with each diagram.

Pattern's Functionality	Pattern Name
Provides an interface for creating families of related or dependent objects without specifying the concrete classes.	Abstract Factory
Separates construction of a complex object from its representation so that the construction process can create different representations.	Builder
Defines an interface for creating an object, letting subclasses decide which class to instantiate. Allows a class to defer the actual instantiation to subclasses.	Factory Method
Specifies the kinds of objects to create using a prototypical instance, and creates new objects by copying this prototype.	Prototype
Ensures a class has only one instance, and provides a global point of access to it.	Singleton
Converts the class's interface into another interface that the client expects. Lets classes work together that couldn't otherwise do so because of incompatible interfaces.	Adapter
Decouples abstraction from its implementation so that the two can vary independently.	Bridge
Composes objects into tree structures to represent part-whole hierarchies. Lets clients treat individual objects and compositions of objects in a uniform manner.	Composite
Attaches added responsibilities to an object dynamically. Provides a flexible alternative to subclassing to extend functionality.	Decorator
Provides a unified interface to a set of interfaces in one or more subsystems. Defines a higher-level interface that makes the subsystems easier to use.	Facade
Uses sharing to support large numbers of fine-grained objects in an efficient manner.	Flyweight
Provides a placeholder or surrogate for another object to control access to it.	Proxy

Pattern's Functionality	Pattern Name
Avoids coupling the sender of a request to its receiver by giving more than one object a chance to handle the request. The receiving objects are chained together and pass the request along the chain until it is handled.	Chain of Responsibility
Encapsulates a request as an object, allowing the client to be parameterized with different requests, to queue or log requests, and to be able to support undo operations.	Command
Given a language, defines a representation for its grammar along with an interpreter of the grammar that uses the representation to interpret sentences in the language.	Interpreter
Provides a way to access the elements of a collection (aggregate) object sequentially without having to expose the underlying representation.	Iterator
Defines an object that encapsulates how a set of objects interacts. Promotes loose coupling by keeping objects from referring to each other directly and varying their interaction independently.	Mediator
Without violating encapsulation, captures and externalizes an object's internal state so that the object's essential state can be restored later.	Memento
Defines a one-to-many dependency among objects so that when one object changes state, all its dependents (subscribers) are notified and updated automatically.	Observer
Allows an object to alter its behavior when its internal state changes; the object will appear to change its class.	State
Defines a family of algorithms, encapsulating each one, and makes them interchangeable. Lets the algorithm vary independently from the clients that use it.	Strategy
Defines the skeleton of an algorithm (function) in an operation, deferring some steps to subclasses. Lets subclasses redefine certain steps of an algorithm without changing the algorithm's structure.	Template Method
Represents an operation to be performed on the elements of an object structure. Lets you define a new operation without changing the classes of the elements on which it operates.	Visitor

The following table shows the alternate names for certain GoF design patterns.

Pattern Name	Also Known As
Abstract Factory	Kit
Factory Method	Virtual Constructor
Adapter	Wrapper
Bridge	Handle/Body
Decorator	Wrapper
Proxy	Surrogate
Command	Action or Transaction
Iterator	Cursor
Memento	Token
Observer	Dependents or Publish-Subscribe
State	Objects for States
Strategy	Policy

Java EE Patterns

Java EE patterns have been revamped and are now also included in all parts of the examination. The presentation tier is no longer covered, but there are patterns for the business tier and integration tier as well as patterns for infrastructure.

You will find it essential to study Java EE patterns for all parts of the exam and to include them as part of your solution.

CERTIFICATION OBJECTIVE 7.03

Demonstrate Knowledge of Java EE Design Patterns

Similar to the GoF design patterns (covered earlier in this chapter), the Java EE patterns are broken down into the various sections that address the tiers or areas that make up a large part of an application. The Java EE patterns break down into the following tiers or areas:

- Business component patterns
- Integration patterns
- Infrastructural patterns

Where applicable, each Java EE pattern will be broken down and described in the following sub-sections: "Problem," "Forces," "Solution," "Conventions," "Strategies," and "Consequences."

Business Component Patterns

The business component provides the services required by application clients and contains the business logic. All business processing for the application is gathered and placed in this component. Using Enterprise JavaBean (EJB) components is one of the ways to implement business processing in this tier.

Here are the Java EE patterns available for business components:

- Fluid Logic
- Gateway
- Persistent Domain Object
- Service
- Service Facade

We will now cover each of these business component patterns.

Fluid Logic

The primary function of the Fluid Logic pattern is to incorporate scripted business logic into a service.

Problem When business rules change rapidly, Java's strong typing and the Java EE deployment model may hinder adaptation to the changes that do not affect the type or class structure.

Forces

- Building a domain-specific language (DSL) is impractical.
- The type and structure of your services will not be affected by the change in logic.
- You can afford not to depend on static type-checking.
- You want to change some elements of the business logic on demand.
- You want to script business logic.

Solution

- Java SE 6 supports JSR-223 or "Scripting for the Java Platform."
- Use `javax.script.ScriptEngine` as an alternative strategy to the Service pattern.
- Redeployment is not required.

Consequences

- Redeployment is not required.
  - Poor performing script will still cause issues.
- Executes in the context of the EJB.
  - Attached entities can be passed to the script.
  - Script security context is the JVM SecurityManager.
  - Transaction service is available.
  - Other container services are available.
- There is no type-safety checking.
  - Use thorough testing to compensate.

Gateway

The primary function of the Gateway pattern is to directly expose Persistent Domain Objects (PDOs) to the presentation tier or client. This pattern is also known as an anti-Service Facade.

Problem

- PDOs are passive artifacts—all Java Persistence API (JPA) entities (PDOs) detach after a transaction and client loses state.
- Client-side changes have to be merged with the persistence layer—a whole graph of objects transported back to the server.
- Clients cannot access an EntityManager.
- Code for merging small updates from the client gets more clumsy.
    - Monolithic Service Facades probably evolve from these requirements.

Forces

- The application may add columns to the data.
- PDOs are locally accessible by reference and encapsulate logic.
- Application access to the persistence layer is not restricted.
    - Data change is user driven.
    - Data validation is nontrivial.

Solution

- Expose a PDO directly to the presentation layer with a Gateway.
- Inject an entity manager and declare the persistence context type with

```
@PersistenceContext(type=PersistenceContextType.EXTENDED)
EntityManager em;
```

- Annotate the `save()` method (or other methods as needed) with

```
@TransactionAttribute(TransactionAttributeType.REQUIRES_NEW)
```

    - By design, a flush to the persistence layer is always triggered.
- Inject the Gateway into a stateful web component.

Conventions

- Name a Gateway after the cached root entity that it supports (it doesn't need to contain word "Gateway").
- Create a Gateway in the same package as a Service Facade.

Strategies

- **Server-Side Gateway** Dependency injection means a Server-Side Gateway does not require a business interface. It can serve container-managed callers in either the web or business container.
- **Rich Internet Application (RIA) Gateway** Requires a way to inject an EntityManager outside the container. This is not a standardized solution, but the RIA platform typically provides a supporting mechanism.
- **Hybrid Gateway** A proxy that acts on the client's behalf within the business container. The most flexible approach that can be considered is part-Gateway, part-Facade.

Consequences

- Gateways are stateful with a 1:1 relationship with the client.
- Entity state is managed by transaction.
  - Bridges concerns such as lazy loading and complex object management.
- Inverse of a Service Facade.
- When a PDO is reused, you may get the benefit of caching.
  - Exposes PDOs directly to the presentation tier.

Persistent Domain Object

The primary function of the Persistent Domain Object pattern is to encapsulate logic with the data on which it operates.

Problem Distributed applications are frequently architected in a procedural way. Business logic is decomposed into tasks and resources, which are mapped into rules and services and anemic, persistent entities.

- Shallow relationship with the data.
- Decomposed into rules or services.
- Anemic domain model (see "Anti-Patterns" later in this chapter).
- Requires type-checking, which can dominate business logic.

Forces

- Business logic becomes complex and variance driven.
- Database design is JPA compatible (reasonably named tables and columns, tables are not overly normalized).
- Validation rules are sophisticated and focus on domain objects (persisted in database).
- You want an object-oriented model.

Solution

- Conduct object-oriented type-checking.
  - Leverage polymorphic behavior with generics.
- Model the application with objects.
- Move type-checking from the service to the domain object.
- Separate the design of the persistence layer.
- Use method-chaining supported by a Builder in order to construct complex object graphs.

Conventions

- The name of the PDO is derived from the target domain.
- Put PDOs in a subpackage called "domain" (or "entity"). Name the containing package after the business domain.
- Getters and setters are not obligatory—they should be justified by a demonstrated need.
- PDO is a JPA entity that contains domain logic and not the technology. Technical details of the data are less important.
- PDO business logic should always execute in an attached state.
  - Remote access requires a fat client or Rich Internet Application (RIA) platform.

Strategies

- **DSL/test/domain-driven** Test-driven strategy favors developing in an incremental, unit-testable manner.

- **Data Bound PDO** Inverse of DSL/test/domain-driven. Applies JavaBean property naming convention to expose data; changes can be observed in an event-driven way.
- **Fat PDO** Direct access to the database and very similar to a Data Access Object (DAO) approach. Useful for workarounds (for example, when the database design is not compatible with JPA).

Consequences

- Domain expertise closer to where data is captured.
- Easier to maintain complex logic.
  - Promotes a fluent interface.
- Object-oriented techniques replace branching type-checks.
- PDO is an annotated Plain Old Java Object (POJO).
  - Simplifies unit testing.
- PDOs should not operate in a detached state:
  - Logic can change the object without syncing.
  - Not suitable to pass between layers.

Service Facade

The primary function of the Service Facade pattern is to expose a coarse-grained business service interface.

Problem

- Business logic is spread out over fine-grained components and services—network latency becomes is an issue.
- Requirements dictate the need for domain-oriented service.
- Services have their own access views.
- Services have their own transaction boundaries.

Forces

- Business methods must have a stable interface with a flexible implementation.
- Component state should be consistent after each invocation.
- The API may be defined as part of a separate effort.

- The API must be available to a remote client.
- Implementation should be encapsulated.

Solution

- Create a stateless session bean (and in exceptional cases, a stateful session bean) with a local business interface.
- Only create a remote interface for RIA or non-Java clients.
- Servlets, web components, or backing beans use the local business interface.

Conventions

- Deploy with REQUIRES_NEW transaction attribute, because it cannot participate in an existing transaction.
- Put Service Facade code in a domain subpackage with a name suffix of "facade" or "boundary."
- Used with domain-oriented components.

Strategies

- **CRUD** Behaves like a Data Access Object (DAO) implemented with a no-interface view. Recommended when a requirement exists for a facade that simply delegates calls to a database.
- **Dual-View** Separates calls made available locally but not remotely (make the local interface a "versioned interface" of the remote one to achieve this).
- **Multichannel** Details the steps needed to expose a facade to a RESTful client and/or other clients not tightly integrated into Java.
- **IIOP** A specific multichannel strategy that offers a way to incorporate Common Object Request Broker Architecture (CORBA) clients into the EJB 3 model.

Consequences

- Decouple clients from business components.
- Define a clear point of entry.
- Encourage intuitive, domain-oriented method naming.
- Establish a contract among business and presentation objects.
- Provide transactional consistency by design.

Service

The primary function of the Service pattern is to decompose business requirements into technical implementations with a restricted view. A Service is a procedural activity. It realizes activities or subprocesses containing cross-cutting, domain object–independent logic.

Problem The Service Facade pattern exposes a coarse-grained, service-oriented interface (methods) to a client and as such:

- Direct implementation of these methods may overlap.
- Service-oriented methods do not map well to the implementation and data because they are usually written in a procedural way (for example, step 1, step 2, step 3, … , final step).
- Each step adds a round trip to the server (when exposed to the client).
- Client interfaces should express the result, not all of the intermediate steps to obtain it.

Forces

- Should be available to a Service Facade only.
- Implementation may not be business oriented.
- Methods should be idempotent or able to participate in a transaction.
- Should be an independent, fine-grained component.
- Confine visibility to the business tier.

Solution

- Use Service to decompose coarse-grained methods.
- Give it well-defined, reusable responsibility.
- Enforce local-only visibility.
- Use a Facade or other boundary component to initiate a transaction or support remoting.

Conventions

- Create a subpackage in the domain that Service supports.
- Do not use the word "Service" in the name.

- Deploy with a MANDATORY transaction attribute.
- The preference is to use a local, stateless session bean.

Strategies

- **Stateless session bean** Provides stateless session and container-provided transaction management (preferred to the POJO approach).
- **POJO** Use when a stateless session bean isn't viable or if it has already become part of the existing framework and therefore becomes the strategy of choice.
- **DAO hybrid** Adapts to already-existing complex queries that should be maintained separately from the services they support. An example is a Service that extends a DAO containing complex data access logic.

Consequences

- Replacement for J2EE Session Facade pattern.
- Promotes reuse of fine-grained logic.
- Adds complexity:
  - Decomposed from business requirement.
  - Tempting to future-proof for future requirements.
- Favors service-oriented applications.

The following table is a list of scenarios addressed by the business tier Java EE patterns.

SCENARIO & SOLUTION

Given Scenarios	Appropriate Business Tier Java EE Pattern
Incorporate "change on demand" scripted business logic into a service.	Fluid Logic
Directly expose Persistent Domain Objects (PDOs) to the presentation tier or client.	Gateway
Maintain OO principles by encapsulating logic with the data on which it operates.	Persistent Domain Object
Expose a coarse-grained (higher-level) business service interface.	Service Facade
Decompose business requirements into technical implementations with a restricted view.	Service

Integration Patterns

The integration tier is responsible for accessing external resources and systems, such as relational and nonrelational data stores and any legacy applications. A business tier object uses the integration tier when it requires data or services that reside at the resource level. The components in this tier can use JDBC, Java EE connector technology, or some other proprietary software to access data at the resource level.

Here are the Java EE patterns available for the integration tier:

- Asynchronous Resource Integrator
- Data Access Object
- Data Transfer Object
- Web Service Broker

We will now cover in detail each of these integration patterns.

Asynchronous Resource Integrator

The Asynchronous Resource Integrator integrates asynchronous messages with transaction services within the business container. It provides a standardized approach to integrating message-driven beans (MDB) with other managed beans in the business container.

Problem

More services are leveraging the asynchronous benefits of messaging. Transactions require a consistent (synchronous) scope.

Forces

- Need to incorporate asynchronous messages into a business transaction.
- When a rollback situation occurs, the code should not acknowledge message receipt, then the messaging server can redeliver the message.

Solution

- Provide a JMS destination.
- Provide a message-driven bean to extract the message payload.

- Handle broken or incorrectly typed messages.
    - Convert validated payloads into parameters.
    - Delegate parameters to the EJB.
- Enable transactions with the service using the transaction attribute type MANDATORY and do not acknowledge the message after a rollback.

Strategies For integration in the front end:

- Messages that originated from the presentation or client tier are accepted.
- Parameters should be coarse grained.
- User-oriented data formats (JSON and XML) are included.

For integration in the back end:

- Legacy naming conventions for destinations are followed.
- Messages from a legacy system are accepted.
- The message type may be proprietary or inflexible.
- The payload may require a complex extraction into parameters.

Conventions

- When possible, you should name destinations by their domain.
- Use a service-oriented name and suffix (for example, MDB, Listener).
- Package front-end strategy implementations with the services or facades they support.
- Package back-end implementations with other integration-oriented packages.

Consequences

- Fire-and-forget message handling is straightforward, whereas two-way messaging isn't.
- Increased scalability compared to synchronous-only strategies.
- Integration testing is difficult.
- It does not help with proprietary message types.
- Some products supply a bridge for REST operations (for example, ActiveMQ and OpenMQ).
- Strict message type-checking leads to tighter coupling.

Data Access Object

The Data Access Object (DAO) encapsulates data access logic and decouples access to disparate data sources. The pattern is based on the rate-of-change principle. DAOs isolate logic for accessing data in a similar way to the Collecting Parameter implementation pattern (not a Java EE pattern).

Problem The DAO pattern is a prominent concept in many data-driven application frameworks.

- The premise is to bundle data to expose it to clients.
- It promotes separation of concerns, which helps because business logic and data access logic frequently change at different rates.
- Previously used to address the limits of some container-managed persistence (CMP) vendors.

Forces The revised DAO pattern addresses these conditions:

- JPA EntityManager resolves many of the issues that J2EE DAOs were built to overcome.
- Some data sources are not compatible with JPA.
- Need a simple way to test data access.
- Need to decouple proprietary data sources from business logic.
- Want clear demarcation between service-oriented applications and the data they use.
- Want to separate code (complex query versus simple CRUD).

Solution

- The client is a session bean that accesses the DAO.
- The DAO is a local stateless session bean that can:
  - Encapsulate the data-access API.
  - Separate domain logic from proprietary access logic.
- The EntityManager is itself is an implementation of a generic DAO.

Strategies

- Abstract DAO strategy uses an abstract class. If many business methods simply wrap the data access calls, extending the abstract class that captures them avoids redundancy.
- **Attached-result DAO** Identifies the preferred state for an entity when a query returns. Subsequent logic is simpler if the transaction scope is still in effect.
- **Detached-result DAO** Identifies a data source that does not support JPA. In this case, the data must be retrieved with a `@NamedQuery` that is mapped to a Data Transfer Object (DTO).
- **Back-end integration DAO** Refers to a data source whose access is proprietary. This requires a Java Connector Architecture (JCA) connector to access the source.
- **Domain-specific DAO** Uses compile-time knowledge of the returned object type. A domain-specific layer, added to the DAO, can perform the casting work.
- **Generic DAO** Wraps EntityManager methods to return generic types. The client needs to correctly cast the returned objects, unless the query parameters infer the return type.

Consequences

- Adds an interface and its implementation to the code.
  - These have to be updated with entity logic changes.
  - Has inherently leaky abstractions (see "Anti-Patterns," later in this chapter).
- Centralized reusable data access logic; however, coding reuse may be unrealistic or unlikely.
- Potentially overlapping code with JPA's facilities.
- Probably the least awkward approach for proprietary data APIs.

exam watch

The DAO pattern favors a stateless session bean for its implementation. The considerable benefits are as follows:

- ***A 1:1 thread relationship between the caller and the bean method, which means that the method is guaranteed to execute within a single thread.***
- ***The transaction is invoked by default.***
- ***Entities included in the transaction become attached, and they can be managed by the bean.***

Data Transfer Object

The Data Transfer Object (DTO or TO) makes data available across a service boundary. The DTO pattern is a copy of some underlying data. DTO patterns weigh the inherent problems of duplicating data against the expediency of delivering it where it is needed.

Problem Data Transfer Objects expose back-end data to a client or presentation tier.

- This is problematic in J2EE (prior to JEE 5) for the following reasons:
  - Entity beans supported a remote capability.
  - The container supported two persistence management schemes.
  - The CMP 2.x standard did not support serialization.
- Java EE addresses some issues, however:
  - JPA does not expose data.
  - Entities have attached and detached states.
  - Service-oriented applications should not see raw data.

Forces

- Need a common data interface for several client types.
- Entity data is connected to a complex schema, but has to be exposed in a simple way.
- Need multiple views of the same data in one domain.
- Need to supply object-oriented data in a transferable form.
- Metadata support needed to support UI development.

Solution

- TransferObject is a simple POJO that can be Serializable or Externalizable (which is overkill in a single JVM deployment).
- Getters can be used for each data column.
- The component must create, populate, and return the DTO to the caller.

Strategies

- **Builder-style DTO** Each method that contributes to the object under construction returns a reference to the object. Using several methods all of which return a reference to the current object, it is possible to express a complex construction as a chain of methods in one statement. This technique helps to form what is known as a "fluent interface."

- **Builder-style immutable DTO** Declares required fields as final, which forces those values to be set in the constructor. This approach precludes the use of setter methods for those fields. Optional elements can then be added through builder methods.
- **Client-specific DTO strategy** Uses annotations to supply metadata with the payload data. If one goal of the DTO is to support presentation of data, this strategy can help clients to convert data into parameters.

Note that the Builder design pattern is a GoF structural pattern.

Consequences

- Transfer objects replicate data.
- Transfer objects are per-value objects, whereas EntityManager objects are per-reference objects.
- Consider using read-only entities.

Web Service Broker

Web Service Broker makes business services available as web services. The Web Service Broker pattern is carried over from previous versions of Java EE. Although in Java EE 6 it may be viewed as unnecessary, the pattern highlights a method for decorating an existing service so that it can be made available as a web service. The Web Service Broker is a like a protocol-compliant facade (see the GoF Adapter pattern).

Problem and Forces Exposing business services directly as web services may create the following conditions/issues:

- Exposes methods that are not service oriented
- Exposes methods that are too fine grained
- Requires additional monitoring, logging, or security code
- Requires reworking of several methods

Solution

- The WebServiceBroker component can handle a web service request and invoke the Service component.
- EndPointProcessor may receive the request and invoke the WebServiceBroker.
- The WebServiceBroker component can be a stateless session bean or a POJO.

Strategies

- For custom XML messaging, write a custom EndPointProcessor component.
- For Java API for XML Web Services, implement an EndPointProcessor via JAX-WS.
- Use the Java API for RESTful Web Services (JAX-RS).
- For Client-Broker, EJB 3.1 brokers can be injected into a servlet.

Consequences The advantage is:

- The client and service protocols are separated.

The disadvantages are:

- Adds a layer of indirection.
- Relies on a local interface. Business components with a remote interface may produce different side effects from thrown exceptions.
- Web service protocols may increase network overhead.

The following table is a list of scenarios addressed by an integration tier Java EE pattern.

SCENARIO & SOLUTION

Given Scenarios	Appropriate Integration Tier Java EE Pattern
Integrate asynchronous messages with transaction services within the business container.	Asynchronous Resource Integrator
Reduce the amount of coupling and complexity between business and resource tiers, while still centralizing the access to the resource tier.	Data Access Object
Make data available across a service boundary.	Data Transfer Object
Make business services available as web Services.	Web Service Broker

Infrastructure Patterns

Infrastructure patterns provide a model approach to handling common requirements. They stress portability among Java EE servers and use dependency injection and annotations to reduce code plumbing. They are also useful for encapsulating artifacts of old APIs.

Here are the Java EE patterns available for the infrastructure:

- Bean Locator
- Resource Binder
- Service Starter
- Singleton

We will now cover each of these infrastructure patterns.

Bean Locator

The Bean Locator pattern encapsulates JNDI services and provides them for non–Java EE clients.

Problem

- Java Naming and Directory Interface (JNDI) API predates Java EE and Java SE 5.
- A checked exception is used: `NamingException`.
- An object is returned.
- EJB 3.1 supports a global naming convention:

  ```
  java:global[/<app-name>]/<module-name>/<bean-name>#[<FQ-interface-name>]
  ```

- Neither form is convenient for clients.
- Standalone clients and POJOs cannot use dependency injection (DI) as a workaround.

Forces

- JNDI details should always be hidden from users because:
  - Building global names is subject to typos.
  - JNDI method plumbing is awkward.

- You want a lookup service that can execute either inside or outside the container.
- You want a service that is client neutral.

Solution

- Encapsulate the JNDI lookup code in a utility class.
- Add a Builder-style `GlobalJNDIName` as a static inner class.

Consequences

- Construction of `GlobalJNDI` is tied to the Properties object.
  - File I/O may become a hotspot.
- If testing reveals a hotspot, consider optimizations such as caching.
- Solution is portable across Java EE–compliant environments.
- Performance hits occur at bean creation time.
  - May not be noticeable by remote clients due to network latency.
- The `computeBeanName()` method is slow on the first call.

Resource Binder

The Resource Binder pattern allows you to register custom resources with the application server.

Problem Each application server vendor provides the ability to register custom resources with the server. Although the Java EE specification does not offer a standardized approach, this feature is commonly available in the following ways:

- Web-based administration utility with a drill-down or wizard-based process
- Command-line interface with vendor-specific syntax

Forces

- You want a convenient way to register custom resources, as simple as the way Bean Locator works for lookup services.
- The process should avoid proprietary application server bindings.
- You want to inject custom resources into managed beans.
- Resources are stateless and do not require life cycle management.

Solution

- Implement a `CustomResource` as a POJO.
- Inject the `CustomResource` into a `CustomResourceClient`.
- Use a `ResourceBinder` to add the `CustomResource`.
- Use annotations to assert the necessary order.

Consequences

- Injectability of custom resources reduces code plumbing.
- This can increase server startup time.
  - Depends on resource startup requirements.
  - Should complete before business methods are called.
- The SPI for resource binding is server specific.
  - Resource Binder relies on JNDI but should be tested with each server product.

Service Starter

The Service Starter pattern ensures that a session bean starts at deployment time.

Problem

- Infrastructural beans frequently need to be initialized before a client calls business logic.
- Prior to EJB 3.1, there was no standard way to initialize a bean upon deployment.

Forces

- Need a general approach to start services eagerly.
- The approach must address stateless session beans, which are normally invoked on demand.

Solutions and Strategies

- For EJB 3.0:
  - Inject a bean into a servlet.
  - Call a bean starter method from the servlet's `init()` method.

- For EJB 3.1 and later:
- Use a singleton bean with an `@PostConstruct` method.
- If you want to load a bean before the Service Starter, use the `@DependsOn` annotation.

Consequences

- There are various ways to implement:
  - Servlet 2.5
  - Servlet 3.0
  - Java EE 6 Singleton
- Inconsistent schemes can cause startup code to execute multiple times.

Singleton

The Singleton implements a single instance of a resource, per JVM—and you almost always run more than one JVM in an enterprise application!

Problem Implementing a portable, homegrown Singleton pattern in an EJB container is not possible, because:

- Thread control is out of the developer's hands.
- Thread pooling (size and behavior) is not defined by the specification.

Therefore, it isn't possible to build an efficient read-only cache under these circumstances.

Forces

- Build a Singleton that is portable across implementations.
- The Singleton must be read-only or must provide synchronization control during updates.

Solution

- EJB 3.1 standardizes a Singleton as a per-JVM instance.
- A Singleton provides:
  - Shared state
  - Concurrency (managed by container)

- A Singleton does not provide startup services.
- For the most part, Singleton and Service Starter have the same underpinnings.

Strategies

- Gatekeeper
  - Enables legacy-resource throttling.
  - Suitable for single-node environments.
  - Useful if a JCA-based throttle is too heavy.
- Caching Singleton
  - Can wrap an existing solution (for example, Ehcache, Memcached, or Hazelcast).
  - Can build your own.

Consequences

- Hard-wired solution for EJB 3.1 and beyond.
- Can create a bottleneck with locking type:
  - `@ConcurrencyManagement(ConcurrencyManagementType.CONTAINER)`.
  - `@Lock(LockType.WRITE)`.
  - For read-only cache use `@Lock(LockType.READ)`.
- Can improve performance as part of a cache implementation, but this can also exhaust memory (work out limits with load/stress testing).
- Does not satisfy high-availability requirements.

The following table is a list of scenarios addressed by infrastructure Java EE patterns.

SCENARIO & SOLUTION

Given Scenarios	Appropriate Infrastructure Java EE Pattern
Encapsulate JNDI services and also provide them for non–Java EE clients.	Bean Locator
Register custom resources with the application server.	Resource Binder
Ensure that a session bean starts at deployment time.	Service Starter
Implement a single instance of a resource per JVM.	Singleton

Interceptor Patterns

Interceptor patterns provide an aspect-oriented programming (AOP) approach to the Java EE platform. They are supported by session and message-driven beans and can be contained within the beans or as separate classes. They can be applied with annotations and configured with deployment descriptors. Intercepted classes or methods use annotations such as `@Interceptors(...)`. Interceptor methods use `@AroundInvoke`, and interceptor timeouts use `@AroundTimeout`.

Here are the Java EE Interceptor patterns:

- Context Holder
- Dependency Injection Extender
- Payload Extractor
- Thread Tracker

We will now cover each of these infrastructure patterns.

Context Holder

The Context Holder shares data among participants in a transaction.

Problem

- In Java EE, there is no standard way to pass context-oriented information among participants in a transaction.

Forces

- Need to add data to a thread within the programming restrictions enforced by the container.
- The target environment may use multiple thread pools, and `ThreadLocal` might not suffice.
- A solution should not require changes to the parameter list of a bean.
- A portable solution is ideal.

Solution

- Java EE supports object type `TransactionSynchronizationRegistry` for each transaction.
- In single-pool targets, `ThreadLocal<T>` is suitable.

- The `@Resource` annotation is used for injection. The Service Facade is a good candidate.
- All beans participating in the transaction will have access to the registry.

Strategies

- Use `TransactionSynchronizationRegistry`:
  - Most portable, but predates Java generics.
  - Requires transaction context.
  - Supports managed classes.
- Use `ThreadLocal`:
  - Effective but less portable.
  - Requires 1:1 association between thread and method.
  - No support for dependency injection, but as such supports all participants.
- Either strategy requires casting of fetched objects.

Consequences

- Context Holder is a cross-cutting approach that removes complexity from business services.
- The `TransactionSynchronizationRegistry` strategy's performance depends on the container implementation.
- Performance of the `ThreadLocal` approach depends on the Java SE implementation.
- `ThreadLocal` may break with complex pool implementations.

Dependency Injection Extender

The Dependency Injection Extender provides bootstrap capability for clients of other frameworks.

Problem Google's Guice and SpringSource's Spring components have different forms of injection control that are incompatible with Java EE's dependency injection. They cannot be deployed directly as EJBs.

Forces

- You do not want to modify these components to integrate them into the Java EE framework.
- EJBs should not be aware of any difference in these components.
- You want these components to participate in an EJB's transaction and security context.
- You want to integrate legacy components (from other frameworks) into an EJB application.

Solution

- Interceptors provide a reusable, cross-cutting service.
- Use an interceptor to provide bootstrap support and injection services for legacy components.
- The Injector instantiates its legacy component and uses `@PostConstruct` to bootstrap creation.
- The Injector injects the instance on a method using `@AroundInvoke` and for the class using `@PostConstruct`.
- EJB declares the Injector as an interceptor.

Strategies

- **Stateful session bean** Does not require a per-method approach to injection. Because of the one-to-one relationship between client and stateful session, simply include the injection of the legacy component and the bootstrap logic together in a method that is annotated with `@PostConstruct`.
- **Stateless session bean** Typically has a many-to-one relationship with clients, so a method interceptor is required (unless all the methods are themselves idempotent).
- **Transactional integration** The transaction context is already started by the container.

Consequences

- Implementation is portable across Java EE servers.
- Interceptors and dependency injection use reflection, but database access latency can cancel out the hit to performance.

- Testing the interceptor implementation in an EJB 3.0 container is very difficult; however, the embeddable EJB 3.1 container is useful for unit testing.

Payload Extractor

The Payload Extractor performs message typecasting and payload validation in a common class or utility.

Problem

- The message type received by an MDB's `onMessage()` method requires casting and testing checks that may fail or throw an exception.
- There's no way to tell message producers that they are sending messages of the wrong type or payload (that is, poison messages).
- Rolling messages back may create a Hot Potato situation.
- Dropped messages get lost in a fire-and-forget scenario.

Forces

- You want to redirect poison (wrong type or payload) messages to an appropriate "invalid message" destination.
- You want to validate inbound message types before they reach the `onMessage()` method.
- You want to validate the payload before it reaches the business logic.
- You prefer a transaction-based solution.

Solution

- Use interceptor to:
  - Validate the message type.
  - Extract the payload.
  - Delegate the payload to a business method.
  - Delegate invalid messages to a handler bean.
- The handler bean sends invalid messages (type or payload), consumed from the destination, to a dead-letter queue or "invalid message" destination.

Strategies

- Handling errors:
  - Returning a consumed and unprocessed message has to be a reliable process.
  - The return mechanism (dead-letter queue and so on) should follow site practice.

Consequences

- Extractor logic is separated into its own class, providing reusable cross-cutting logic.
- Easy to add or remove interceptors.
- Unit-testing on the consumer method is much simpler.
- Reflection is relatively expensive.

Thread Tracker

The Thread Tracker names threads, making them easier to identify during monitoring.

Problem

- Session bean methods run in a single service thread.
- Service threads are generic and are typically named by function and instance (for example, httpSSLWorkerThread-8080-3).
- Correlating deadlocks or latency to a business method requires a clearer identification and association.

Forces A thread-tracker needs to be:

- Applicable to any session bean
- Straightforward to disable and undeploy
- Portable across Java EE implementations

Solution

- Intercept the business methods with a Tracker class.
- Save the original thread name and rename it after a business purpose in a `try` block.
- Restore the original thread name in a `finally` block.
- Annotate interceptors for production use (or use deployment descriptors).

Consequences

- Solution may not be permitted by the target environment.
  - It is not supported by EJB spec.
  - The target could throw `AccessControlException` and/or `SecurityException`.
  - Glassfish v3 allows it.
- Performance bottlenecks may occur on frequently called methods.
  - `InvocationContext` may be reflection based (which is slow).
  - Load testing is essential.
  - MDBs may be a better use case.
- Monitoring solutions may not refresh thread names, but logging will be reliable.

The following table is a list of challenges and scenarios addressed by the Interceptor Java EE patterns.

SCENARIO & SOLUTION

Given Scenarios	Appropriate Interceptor Java EE Pattern
Share data among participants in a transaction in a portable way.	Context Holder
Provide bootstrap capability for clients of other frameworks (for example, Guice or Spring).	Dependency Injection Extender
Provide a common class for message typecasting and payload validation.	Payload Extractor
Make it easier to identify thread names for monitoring and logging.	Thread Tracker

Unlike earlier versions of the exam, knowledge of Java EE patterns is now required for Part I, and you will also find it necessary to use them in Parts II and III.

CERTIFICATION OBJECTIVE 7.04

Identify the Use of the Law of Leaky Abstractions or a Specific Anti-Pattern in a Given Scenario

In this section we cover both the Law of Leaky Abstractions and the anti-patterns that will be tested in the exam.

Law of Leaky Abstractions

The Law of Leaky Abstractions is not an actual anti-pattern, but it is a common underlying cause of negative impacts on a system. It speaks to the fact that the larger and more complex abstractions become, the more likely they are to become leaky or error prone. A short quote from Joel Spolsky is often cited to sum this up: "All non-trivial abstractions, to some degree, are leaky."

Again, in summary:

- The Law of Leaky Abstractions is not an actual anti-pattern but a common underlying cause.
- Layered software forces one to rely on "high-level" abstractions.
- Shielding or hiding complexity means some crucial details go unmentioned.
- Lack of awareness of latent details leads to errors in practice.

In Part I of the exam, you are guaranteed to see a question on the Law of Leaky Abstractions!

Anti-Patterns

Anti-patterns identify and document habits and practices that have a negative impact on system. The goal is that by studying anti-patterns, an architect can learn to avoid them and use preferred alternates. Many Java EE patterns are designed to avoid these habits and practices by documenting proven techniques. For the purposes of the examination and for an architect, anti-patterns are grouped into three types:

- Integration tier anti-patterns
- Business tier anti-patterns
- Presentation tier anti-patterns

Integration Tier Anti-Patterns

Here is the list of integration tier anti-patterns:

- Anemic Domain Model
- Fat Message
- Hot Potato
- Monolithic Consumer
- Not Pooling Connections

We will now cover each of these integration tier anti-patterns.

Anemic Domain Model

The Anemic Domain Model is the anti-pattern that describes a model containing little (or no) business logic.

Problem

- Business logic is implemented separately from the domain objects (or data) on which it operates.

Symptoms and Consequences

- Violates the principle of encapsulation
- Forces public access to data, which tightens coupling
- Requires an extra layer (DTOs) to negotiate multiple data consumers

Solution

- Apply the PDO pattern to put data with its logic.
- So many J2EE-based applications are bound to this model by the platform. Possibly a good reason to upgrade to a newer release of Java EE.

Fat Message

The Fat Message is the anti-pattern that describes a message containing a large amount of data in the payload.

Problem

- The payload of an asynchronous message may be fat.

Symptoms and Consequences

- High network latency.
- Degradation of messaging server scalability.
- Unmarshaling message payload is compute-intensive.

Solutions

- Review the Enterprise Integration Patterns (EIP) Splitter pattern.
- Refactor the payload to include only data that is relevant to the business service.
- Pass an ID or other reference instead of the large payload and let the recipient look up the data.

Hot Potato

The Hot Potato is the anti-pattern that describes when a messaging server continues to send a message that cannot be acknowledged by a consumer because the transaction keeps failing.

Problem

- Messaging servers redeliver messages until they receive an acknowledgement from a consumer.
- A transaction that rolls back on each attempt may not acknowledge the message, causing a continuous resend (loop).

Symptoms and Consequences

- This is an infinite loop.
- The system shows high utilization but low throughput.

Solution

- If a transaction rolls back, acknowledge the message and forward it through another means (e-mail or to an error destination) for problem resolution.
- Implement a resend threshold on the messaging server. When the threshold is reached, reassign the message to a dead-letter queue.

Monolithic Consumer

The Monolithic Consumer is the anti-pattern that describes when any business logic is placed in the consuming MDB instead of placing it in another class (e.g., another EJB or POJO).

Problem

- Business logic is put in the `onMessage()` method of an MDB.
- Logic is invoked only after a JMS message is received.

Symptoms and Consequences

- Clients cannot access business logic directly with a business method.
- Unit testing the business logic is very difficult.

Solution

- Confine the message-driven bean to:
  - Validating and processing the payload.
  - Calling the right business method.
- Synchronous clients can also invoke the service (and unit tests too).
- The Asynchronous Resource Integrator pattern embraces this approach.

Not Pooling Connections

The Not Pooling Connections anti-pattern describes when instead of utilizing a connection pool, a database connection is created and destroyed for each request.

Problem

- Creating and destroying a database connection for each query is expensive (and slow).

Symptoms and Consequences

- Slow response times.
- Poor scalability.
- Driver initialization and lookup code is duplicated across the system.

Solution

- Use a connection pool.
- Use the DataSource interface.

Business Tier Anti-Patterns

Here is the list of business tier anti-patterns:

- Cacheless Cow
- Conversational Baggage
- Golden Hammers of Session State
- Local and Remote Interfaces Simultaneously
- Sledgehammer for a Fly

We will now cover each of these business tier anti-patterns.

Cacheless Cow

The Cacheless Cow is the anti-pattern that describes when frequently retrieved, but seldom changed, resources are not placed in a cache.

Problem

- When fairly static resources are repeatedly used without a caching strategy in place, then server and network resources are over-utilized (wasted).

Symptoms and Consequences

- Scalability is constrained by the per-request round trips between the container and the external resource.

Forces

- A stored result may suffice for as many or more requests than when new data is needed.
- A reasonable size for a cache can be determined from normal application use.
- There is enough memory to cache enough results to achieve a useful hit rate.
- Fast concurrent reads can be satisfied while also protecting data as it is being modified.

Solution

- Java EE `EntityManager` provides built-in caching.
- Consider a cache for other service boundaries where objects get reused:
  - On a client-facing web server
  - Between clients and web tier components
  - Between web and business tier components
- Consider vendor-provided caching solutions.
- Consider cache-oriented patterns such as Command (GoF).

Conversational Baggage

The Conversational Baggage anti-pattern describes a scenario when a stateful session bean is utilized though a stateless session bean is sufficient.

Problem

- By default, many tasks in enterprise applications use a stateful session.

Symptoms and Consequences

- Application scalability is reduced by increased container service demand.
- Stateful services that do the same work in a stateless form appear more resource intensive.

Solution

- Use a stateless session as the default model.
- Justify a stateful session bean by listing the benefits that can be proven.

Golden Hammers of Session State

The Golden Hammers of Session State is the anti-pattern that describes when a single location approach is chosen to persist session state.

Problem There are well-known common places to store session state:

- In the client tier with cookies
- In the presentation tier with an `HttpSession` class
- In the business tier with a stateful session bean

Symptoms and Consequences

- Committing to one location often requires workarounds.
- The benefit of a central site for session data is arguable.
- Performance varies for each application when using the site.

Solution When making a session state tool choice, consider the following:

- Implications of losing the data. (Is it okay for this scenario?)
- Location of the data to be used.
- Size and type of the data.
- Types of clients supported.

Local and Remote Interfaces Simultaneously

The Local and Remote Interfaces Simultaneously anti-pattern that describes when a local and remote interfaces are provided to both fine and course grained services.

Problem

- Local interface methods may throw `RemoteException`.
- Remote interfaces should only be coarse grained.

Symptoms and Consequences

- Different side effects between local and remote clients.
- Poor performance if service is fine grained.

Solution

- Separate coarse-grained from fine-grained services.
- Allow remote access only to coarse-grained services.
- Consider a Service Facade boundary for remote clients.
- Allow local or no-view access only to fine-grained services.

Sledgehammer for a Fly

The Sledgehammer for a Fly anti-pattern describes when EJB, a technology that comes with extra overhead, is chosen over a simple POJO where only lightweight processing is the requirement.

Problem

- EJB components are container managed, which implies some extra overhead.
- For lightweight objects, this cost may outweigh its benefits.

Symptoms and Consequences

- Additional complexity; no apparent benefit
- More code and objects than are needed
- Possible impact on scaling and performance

Solution

- If your code does not use the following container services, use a POJO:
  - Concurrency
  - Entity interaction
  - Interceptors
  - Life cycle management
  - Timers
  - Transaction management

Presentation Tier Anti-Patterns

This is the list of presentation tier anti-patterns:

- Ad Lib TagLibs
- Embedded Navigational Information
- Including Common Functionality in Every Servlet

We will now cover each of these presentation tier anti-patterns.

Ad Lib TagLibs

The Ad Lib TagLibs anti-pattern describes when logic is placed in a JSP custom tag library instead of within a POJO.

Problem

- A model or controller's logic may be moved from a JSP page into a custom tag.

Symptoms and consequences:

- Custom tags are difficult for rich clients to use.
- Custom tags with model/controller logic may need many attributes.
- Custom tags are an extra layer of development and maintenance compared to a POJO.

Solution

- When creating custom tags, ask where the underlying logic will be easiest to maintain.

Embedded Navigational Information

The Embedded Navigational Information anti-pattern describes when resource locations are embedded into a JSP.

Problem

- JSP pages often include URL and file references on the page.
- JSP pages must be updated every time a filename or URL changes.

Symptoms and Consequences

- Users receive (404) Page Not Found errors until the JSP code is corrected.
- The application flow is obscured.

Solution

- Use the Front Controller pattern (a J2EE Pattern) and logical resource mapping; URLs are unlikely to change frequently.
- Use custom tags to include fragments instead of the `jsp:include` action or the `<%@include>` directive. An include custom tag maps a generic attribute value, such as banner, to a specific resource.

Including Common Functionality in Every Servlet

The Including Common Functionality in Every Servlet anti-pattern describes when code is placed in the service methods of every servlet instead of in a single separate class.

Problem

- Every servlet invokes the same pre- and post-processing tasks in its service methods.

Symptoms and Consequences

- Tasks must be programmatically added and removed from multiple servlets.
- The servlets have poor organization and structure.

Solution

- Place these tasks in filters.
- Filters can be used with JSP pages and servlets.
- Intercepting Filter pattern (a J2EE pattern) is a solution for this anti-pattern.

The following table is a list of scenarios that signifies an anti-pattern.

SCENARIO & ANTI-PATTERN

Given Scenarios	Anti-Pattern
Business logic is implemented separately from the domain objects (or data) on which it operates.	Anemic Domain Model
Payload of an asynchronous message may be fat (very large size), causing network latency and compute-intensive payload marshaling/unmarshaling.	Fat Message
Messaging system is showing high utilization with very little throughput.	Hot Potato
Unable to easily test (or independently call) business logic placed in an MDB.	Monolithic Consumer
Slow throughput of application that is creating and destroying a database connection for each query.	Not Pooling Connections
Static-like resources are repeatedly used and the server and network resources are shown as being over-utilized.	Cacheless Cow
Stateful session beans are being used by default and are showing more resource-intensive usage.	Conversational Baggage
By edict, all applications for a particular company use the same approach for storing session state, and performance is adversely affected or session state is occasionally lost.	Golden Hammers of Session State
Experiencing different side effects between local and remote clients (for example, poor performance for fine-grained services).	Local and Remote Interfaces Simultaneously
The application uses EJBs instead of POJOs for all business components.	Sledgehammer for a Fly
A model or controller's logic has been moved from a JSP page into a custom tag, making it difficult to call from a rich client.	Ad Lib TagLibs
JSP pages must be updated every time a filename or URL changes.	Embedded Navigational Information
Every servlet is poorly structured, and each invokes the same processing tasks in its service methods.	Including Common Functionality in Every Servlet

CERTIFICATION SUMMARY

By studying this chapter, you now have an understanding of the Gang of Four's design patterns and some introductory material on Java EE patterns. You should also understand which are the most appropriate patterns to use for given scenarios.

Here are some of the key points from each certification objective in this chapter.

Select an Appropriate GoF Pattern for a Given Application Challenge

- The Abstract Factory is most appropriate when the system needs to be independent of how its objects are created, composed, and represented.
- The Adapter is most appropriate when you want to utilize an existing class with an incompatible interface.
- The Bridge is most appropriate when you want to avoid a permanent binding between the functional abstraction and its implementation.
- The Builder is most appropriate when the algorithm for creating a complex object needs to be independent of the components that compose the object and how they are assembled.
- The Chain of Responsibility is most appropriate when more than one object can handle a request and the handler is unknown.
- The Command is most appropriate when you need to parameterize objects by an action to perform.
- The Composite is most appropriate when you want to represent a full or partial hierarchy of objects.
- The Decorator is most appropriate when you want to transparently and dynamically add responsibilities to objects without affecting other objects.
- The Facade is most appropriate when you want to provide a simpler interface to a more complex subsystem.
- The Factory Method is most appropriate when a class is not able to anticipate the class of objects it needs to create.
- The Flyweight is most appropriate when the application uses a considerable number of objects.
- The Interpreter is most appropriate when the grammar of the language is not complicated and efficiency is not a priority.
- The Iterator is most appropriate when access to a collection object is required without having to expose its internal representation.

- The Mediator is most appropriate when a set of objects communicates in complex but well-defined ways.
- The Memento is most appropriate when a snapshot containing enough information regarding the state of an object can be saved so that it can be restored to the complete state using the snapshot information later.
- The Observer is most appropriate when a change to an object requires changing other objects, and the number of objects that need to be changed is unknown.
- The Prototype is most appropriate when the classes to instantiate are to be specified at run time.
- The Proxy is most appropriate when you need a more versatile or sophisticated reference to an object, rather than a simple pointer.
- The Singleton is most appropriate when a single instance of a class is needed, and it must be accessible to clients from a well-known access point.
- The State is most appropriate when the behavior of an object depends on its state and it must be able to change its behavior at run time according to the new state.
- The Strategy is most appropriate when multiple classes differ only in their behavior.
- The Template Method is most appropriate when you want to implement the nonvarying parts of an algorithm in a single class and the varying parts of the algorithm in subclasses.
- The Visitor is most appropriate when an object structure contains many objects with differing interfaces and you need to perform operations on these objects in a way that depends on their concrete classes.

Identify a Gang of Four (GoF) Design Pattern, Using a Description of Its Features

Review the Gang of Four (Gamma et al.) diagrams and associated descriptions that appear earlier in the chapter.

Demonstrate Knowledge of Java EE Design Patterns

- The Fluid Logic is most appropriate when you want to incorporate "change on demand" scripted business logic into a service.

- The Gateway is most appropriate when you want to directly expose Persistent Domain Objects (PDOs) to the presentation tier or client.
- The Persistent Domain Object is most appropriate when you want to maintain OO principles by encapsulating logic with the data on which it operates.
- The Service Facade is most appropriate when you want to expose a coarse-grained (higher-level) business service interface.
- The Service is most appropriate when you want to decompose business requirements into technical implementations with a restricted view.
- The Asynchronous Resource Integrator is most appropriate when you want to integrate asynchronous messages with transaction services within the business container.
- The Data Access Object is most appropriate when you want to reduce the amount of coupling and complexity between business and resource tiers, while still centralizing the access to resource tier.
- The Data Transfer Object is most appropriate when you want to make data available across a service boundary.
- The Web Service Broker is most appropriate when you want to make business services available as web services.
- The Bean Locator is most appropriate when you want to encapsulate JNDI services and to also provide them for non–Java EE clients.
- The Resource Binder is most appropriate when you want to register custom resources with the application server.
- The Service Starter is most appropriate when you want to ensure that a session bean starts at deployment time.
- The Singleton is most appropriate when you want to implement a single instance of a resource per JVM.
- The Context Holder is most appropriate when you want to share data among participants in a transaction in a portable way.
- The Dependency Injection Extender is most appropriate when you want to provide bootstrap capability for clients of other frameworks (for example, Guice or Spring).
- The Payload Extractor is most appropriate when you want to provide a common class for message typecasting and payload validation.
- The Thread Tracker is most appropriate when you want to make it easier to identify thread names for monitoring and logging.

Identify the Use of the Law of Leaky Abstractions or a Specific Anti-Pattern in a Given Scenario

Review the Law of Leaky Abstractions and anti-pattern descriptions that appear earlier in the chapter.

- ❑ The Law of Leaky Abstractions is a common underlying cause of negative impacts on a system. Larger and more complex abstractions become increasingly more likely to become leaky or error prone. In short, all non-trivial abstractions are leaky.
- ❑ Integration tier anti-patterns:
  - ❑ The Anemic Domain Model anti-pattern is when business logic is implemented separately from the domain objects (or data) on which it operates.
  - ❑ The Fat Message anti-pattern is when the payload of an asynchronous message may be fat.
  - ❑ The Hot Potato anti-pattern is when messaging servers redeliver messages until they receive an acknowledgement from a consumer. A transaction that rolls back on each attempt may not acknowledge the message, causing a continuous resend (loop).
  - ❑ The Monolithic Consumer anti-pattern involves putting business logic in the `onMessage()` method of an MDB and logic is invoked only after a JMS message is received.
  - ❑ The Not Pooling Connections anti-pattern is when a database connection is created and destroyed for each query (expensive and slow).
- ❑ Business tier anti-patterns:
  - ❑ The Cacheless Cow anti-pattern is when fairly static resources are repeatedly used without a caching strategy in place and the server and network resources are over-utilized (wasted).
  - ❑ The Conversational Baggage anti-pattern is when, by default, many tasks in enterprise applications use a stateful session.
  - ❑ The Golden Hammers of Session State anti-pattern is when session state is stored in the wrong tier for the required functionality.
  - ❑ The Local and Remote Interfaces Simultaneously anti-pattern is when the local interface methods throw `RemoteException`, and remote interfaces should only be coarse grained.

- ❑ The Sledgehammer for a Fly anti-pattern is when EJB components are used instead of POJOs for lightweight processing. EJB components are container-managed, implying extra overhead. The extra overhead is not needed for lightweight processing objects.

❑ Presentation tier anti-patterns:

- ❑ The Ad Lib TagLibs anti-pattern is when a model or controller's logic contained in a JSP page should be moved into a custom tag.
- ❑ The Embedded Navigational Information anti-pattern is when JSP pages include URL and file references and therefore must be updated every time a filename or URL changes.
- ❑ The Including Common Functionality in Every Servlet anti-pattern is when every servlet invokes the same pre- and post-processing tasks in its service methods.

SELF TEST

The following questions will help you measure your understanding of the material presented in this chapter. Read all the choices carefully and choose the correct answers for each question.

Select an Appropriate Gang of Four (GoF) Pattern for a Given Application Challenge

1. The Factory Method design pattern is useful when a client must create objects having different ____________.

A. subclasses

B. ancestors

C. sizes

D. similarities

2. What design pattern limits the number of instances a class can create?

A. Command

B. Limiter

C. Strategy

D. Singleton

3. Iterators are useful when dealing with which of the following types of classes?

A. Dynamic

B. Collection

C. Singleton

D. Small

4. What pattern isolates client from concrete (implementation) classes?

A. Isolator

B. State

C. Prototype

D. Abstract Factory

5. What pattern makes it easier for you to add new kinds of components?

A. Proxy

B. Visitor

C. Composite

D. Flyweight

6. What pattern provides a simple interface to a complex subsystem?
   A. Facade
   B. Bridge
   C. State
   D. Proxy
7. What pattern allows you different variations of an algorithm?
   A. Memento
   B. Strategy
   C. Variation
   D. Flyweight
8. What pattern can be used so that an object is notified when another object changes?
   A. Subscriber
   B. Publisher
   C. Observer
   D. Memento

Identify a Gang of Four (GoF) Design Pattern, Using a Description of Its Features

9. What is the Abstract Factory pattern also known as?
   A. Kit
   B. Wrapper
   C. Cursor
   D. Virtual Constructor
10. Which pattern can be used when a class is not able to anticipate the class of objects it needs to create?
    A. Abstract Factory
    B. Factory Method
    C. Command
    D. Chain of Responsibility
11. What pattern is also known as Virtual Constructor?
    A. Abstract Factory
    B. Memento
    C. Wrapper
    D. Factory Method

12. Which pattern decouples the function from the implementation?
    A. Proxy
    B. Decorator
    C. Bridge
    D. Observer
13. What is the Adapter pattern also known as?
    A. Surrogate
    B. Wrapper
    C. Token
    D. Proxy
14. Which pattern provides a single interface to simplify many subsystem interfaces?
    A. Proxy
    B. Facade
    C. Adapter
    D. Bridge
15. What pattern is also known as Handle/Body?
    A. Proxy
    B. Adapter
    C. Abstract Factory
    D. Bridge
16. Which pattern reduces coupling and allows a set of classes to act as one?
    A. Chain of Responsibility
    B. Command
    C. Memento
    D. Factory Method
17. What is the Decorator pattern also known as?
    A. Wrapper
    B. Adapter
    C. Composite
    D. Strategy
18. Which pattern is a very common technique for reusing code?
    A. Template Method
    B. Command
    C. Singleton
    D. State

19. What pattern is also known as Surrogate?

A. Observer
B. Bridge
C. Proxy
D. Decorator

20. What is the Command pattern also known as?

A. Action
B. Transaction
C. Wrapper
D. Surrogate

21. The Command design pattern ____________ a request in an object.

A. separates
B. encapsulates
C. processes
D. decouples

22. Which of the following elements are part of the Gang of Four (GoF) Design Pattern format?

A. Problem
B. Solution
C. Consequences
D. Intent

Demonstrate Knowledge of Java EE Design Patterns

23. Which of the following aspects may prevent the Thread Tracker pattern from working?

A. Java specification
B. Target environment
C. Logging tool in use
D. Interceptor annotation

24. Which of the following requirements are suitable for the Singleton pattern?

A. Establishing a load order for servlets
B. Implementing a per-JVM instance
C. Implementing a per-server instance
D. A and B
E. B and C

25. To create a proper Payload Extractor, you must guarantee that:
    A. Transactions cannot roll back.
    B. The message type is valid.
    C. Consumed messages will be forwarded.
    D. The payload isn't large.
26. Which annotation describes a prerequisite class to the class being annotated?
    A. `@Attach`
    B. `@DependsOn`
    C. `@Inject`
    D. `@Depends`
27. The Service and Gateway patterns are ____________.
    A. interchangeable
    B. least popular
    C. fungible
    D. direct opposites
28. Which pattern ensures that a session bean executes at deployment time?
    A. Context Holder
    B. Service Starter
    C. Resource Binder
    D. Singleton
29. Which of the following can encapsulate JNDI services and provide them for non–Java EE clients?
    A. Resource Binder
    B. Singleton
    C. Bean Locator
    D. Persistent Domain Object
30. Which pattern can be used to register custom resources with the application server?
    A. Resource Binder
    B. Bean Locator
    C. Persistent Domain Object
    D. Singleton

31. To allow Spring components to participate in an EJB's transaction and security context, which pattern would you choose?

A. Context Holder

B. Dependency Injection Extender

C. Thread Tracker

D. Gateway

32. Which pattern is used to validate an asynchronous message payload to avoid a Hot Potato anti-pattern?

A. Context Holder

B. Resource Binder

C. Payload Extractor

D. Asynchronous Resource Integrator

33. Which pattern is used to portably share data among participants in a transaction?

A. Persistent Domain Object

B. Data Transfer Object

C. Context Holder

D. Gateway

34. Which one of the following is the pattern that makes it easier to identify functions and instances for a service thread in a log file?

A. Thread Tracker

B. Log4j

C. Context Holder

D. Resource Binder

Identify the Use of the Law of Leaky Abstractions or a Specific Anti-Pattern in a Given Scenario

35. Which of the following best summarizes the Law of Leaky Abstractions?

A. Code that relies entirely on complex abstract interfaces could be an anti-pattern.

B. It is the only cause of anti-patterns.

C. All abstractions are anemic and leak.

D. Software fails in the long run.

36. What makes a Hot Potato anti-pattern difficult to identify?

A. The server is located outside an air-conditioned environment.

B. Queues deliver a single message at a time.

C. Message-driven beans cannot easily be debugged.

D. The message server is remote.

37. Which anti-pattern describes the scenario where business logic is implemented separately from the domain objects (or data) on which it operates?

A. Fat Object

B. Monolithic Consumer

C. Hot Potato

D. Anemic Domain Model

38. Which of the following is the anti-pattern that describes the scenario where performance is observed to be slow for a method in a component that connects to a database, performs a query, and then disconnects from the database?

A. Anemic Query Model

B. Not Pooling Connections

C. Inadequate Covering Key

D. Missing Index

39. What anti-pattern may exist in the situation where you have fairly static resources that are being repeatedly called and used?

A. Cacheless Cow

B. Time to Live

C. Sledgehammer for a Fly

D. Bazooka for a Fly

40. Which anti-pattern is potentially incurred if, instead of POJO, an EJB component is used for all business logic regardless of complexity?

A. Conversational Baggage

B. Bazooka for a Fly

C. Sledgehammer for a Fly

D. Monolithic Consumer

41. What anti-pattern exists when all JSP pages have URL and file references?

A. Embedded Navigational Information

B. Ad Lib TagLibs

C. Including Common Functionality

D. Conversational Baggage

SELF TEST ANSWERS

Identify the Most Appropriate Design Pattern for a Given Scenario

1. ☑ **A**. The Factory Method design pattern is useful when a client must create objects having different subclasses.
☒ **B, C,** and **D** are incorrect. The Factory Method design pattern is not useful in these situations.

2. ☑ **D**. The Singleton pattern limits the number of instances a class can create.
☒ **A, B,** and **C** are incorrect. These do not limit the number of instances a class can create.

3. ☑ **B**. Iterators are useful when dealing with Collection classes.
☒ **A, C,** and **D** are incorrect. These are not appropriate for the Iterator pattern.

4. ☑ **D**. Abstract Factory isolates client from concrete (implementation) classes.
☒ **A, B,** and **C** are incorrect. These patterns do not isolate the client from concrete classes.

5. ☑ **C**. Composite makes it easier for you to add new kinds of components.
☒ **A, B,** and **D** are incorrect. These patterns do note make it easier to add new kinds of components.

6. ☑ **A**. Facade provides a simple interface to a complex subsystem.
☒ **B, C,** and **D** are incorrect. These patterns do not provide a simple interface to a complex subsystem.

7. ☑ **B**. Strategy allows you different variations of an algorithm.
☒ **A, C,** and **D** are incorrect. These patterns do not allow different variations of an algorithm.

8. ☑ **C**. Observer can be notified when another object changes.
☒ **A, B,** and **D** are incorrect. These patterns do not notify an object when another object is changed.

Identify a GoF Design Pattern, Using a Description of Its Features

9. ☑ **A**. The Abstract Factory pattern is also known as Kit.
☒ **B, C,** and **D** are incorrect. These are not valid aliases for Abstract Factory.

10. ☑ **B**. The Factory Method pattern can be used when a class is not able to anticipate the class of objects it needs to create.
☒ **A, C,** and **D** are incorrect. These can't be used to address the feature required.

11. ☑ **D**. The Factory Method pattern is also known as the Virtual Constructor.
☒ **A, B,** and **C** are incorrect. These are not valid aliases for Virtual Constructor.

12. ☑ C. The Bridge pattern decouples the function from the implementation.
☒ A, B, and D are incorrect. These can't be used to address the feature required.

13. ☑ B. The Adapter pattern is also known as the Wrapper.
☒ A, C, and D are incorrect. These are not valid aliases for Adapter.

14. ☑ B. The Facade pattern provides a single interface for simplifying multiple interfaces in a subsystem.
☒ A, C, and D are incorrect. These can't be used to address the feature required.

15. ☑ D. The Bridge pattern is also known as Handle/Body.
☒ A, B, and C are incorrect. These are not valid aliases for Handle/Body.

16. ☑ A. The Chain of Responsibility pattern reduces coupling and allows a set of classes to act as one.
☒ B, C, and D are incorrect. These can't be used to address the feature required.

17. ☑ A. The Decorator pattern is also known as the Wrapper.
☒ B, C, and D are incorrect. These are not valid aliases for Decorator.

18. ☑ A. The Template Method pattern is a very common technique for reusing code.
☒ B, C, and D are incorrect. These can't be used to address the feature required.

19. ☑ C. The Proxy pattern is also known as Surrogate.
☒ A, B, and D are incorrect. These are not valid aliases for Surrogate.

20. ☑ A and B. The Command pattern is also known as Action or Transaction.
☒ C and D are incorrect. These are not valid aliases for Command.

21. ☑ B. The Command design pattern encapsulates a request in an object.
☒ A, C, and D are incorrect. These are not valid descriptions of the Command pattern.

22. ☑ C and D. Consequences and Intent are valid elements in the (GoF) Design Pattern format.
☒ A and B are incorrect. These are not valid elements in the (GoF) Design Pattern format.

Demonstrate Knowledge of Java EE Design Patterns

23. ☑ B. The target environment may prevent the Thread Tracker pattern from working.
☒ A, C, and D are incorrect. These will not prevent the Thread Tracker pattern from working.

24. ☑ B. Implementing a per-JVM instance is the correct requirement for the Singleton pattern.
☒ A, C, D, and E are incorrect. These are not the correct requirements for the Singleton pattern.

25. ☑ C. To create a proper Payload Extractor, you must guarantee that consumed messages will be forwarded.
☒ A, B, and D are incorrect. These are not the correct guarantees for a Payload Extractor.

26. ☑ **B.** `@DependsOn` is the correct annotation for a prerequisite class to be called from the class being annotated.
☒ **A, C,** and **D** are incorrect. These are not the correct annotations for a prerequisite class to be called from the class being annotated.

27. ☑ **D.** Service and Gateway patterns are direct opposites.
☒ **A, B,** and **C** are incorrect. These can't be used to describe the Service and Gateway patterns.

28. ☑ **B.** The Service Starter pattern ensures that a session bean executes at deployment time.
☒ **A, C,** and **D** are incorrect. These patterns do not ensure that a session bean executes at deployment time.

29. ☑ **C.** The Bean Locator pattern encapsulates JNDI services and also provides them for non–Java EE clients.
☒ **A, B,** and **D** are incorrect. These patterns do not encapsulate JNDI services and provide them for non–Java EE clients.

30. ☑ **A.** The Resource Binder pattern can be used to register custom resources with the application server.
☒ **B, C,** and **D** are incorrect. These patterns do not register custom resources with the application server.

31. ☑ **B.** The Dependency Injection Extender pattern allows Spring components to participate in an EJB's transaction and security context.
☒ **A, C,** and **D** are incorrect. These patterns do not allow Spring components to participate in an EJB's transaction and security context.

32. ☑ **C.** The Payload Extractor pattern is used to validate an asynchronous message payload to avoid a Hot Potato anti-pattern.
☒ **A, B,** and **D** are incorrect. These patterns do not validate an asynchronous message payload to avoid a Hot Potato anti-pattern.

33. ☑ **C.** The Context Holder pattern is used to portably share data among participants in a transaction.
☒ **A, B,** and **D** are incorrect. These patterns do not share data among participants in a transaction in a portable way.

34. ☑ **A.** The Thread Tracker pattern makes it easier to identify service thread functions and instances in a log.
☒ **B, C,** and **D** are incorrect. These patterns do not make it easier to identify service thread functions and instances in a log.

Identify the Use of the Law of Leaky Abstractions or a Specific Anti-Pattern in a Given Scenario

35. ☑ A. The Law of Leaky Abstractions, in summary, states that code that relies entirely on an abstract interface could be an anti-pattern.

☒ **B, C,** and **D** are incorrect. None of these choices are not the best summarization of the Law of Leaky Abstractions.

36. ☑ B. Queues delivering a single message at a time make a Hot Potato anti-pattern difficult to identify.

☒ **A, C,** and **D** are incorrect. These choices do not make the Hot Potato anti-pattern difficult to identify or even apply to the Hot Potato anti-pattern.

37. ☑ D. The Anemic Domain Model anti-pattern describes the scenario where business logic is implemented separately from the domain objects (or data) on which it operates.

☒ **A, B,** and **C** are incorrect. These are not the accepted anti-patterns that fit the given scenario.

38. ☑ B. The Not Pooling Connections anti-pattern describes the scenario where performance is observed to be slow for a method in a component that connects to a database, performs a query, and then disconnects from the database.

☒ **A, C,** and **D** are incorrect. These are not the accepted anti-patterns that fit the given scenario.

39. ☑ A. The Cacheless Cow anti-pattern may exist in the situation where you have fairly static resources being repeatedly called and used.

☒ **B, C,** and **D** are incorrect. These are not the accepted anti-patterns that fit the given situation.

40. ☑ C. The Sledgehammer for a Fly anti-pattern is potentially incurred if, instead of POJO, an EJB component is used for all business logic regardless of complexity.

☒ **A, B,** and **D** are incorrect. These are not the accepted anti-patterns potentially incurred in the given situation.

41. ☑ A. The Embedded Navigational Information anti-pattern exists when all JSP pages have URL and file references.

☒ **B, C,** and **D** are incorrect. These are not the accepted anti-patterns that exist in the given situation.

8 Security

CERTIFICATION OBJECTIVES

- 8.01 Identify Elements of the Security Model in the Java SE Environment for Remote Clients, Including Web Start, Applets, and the Role of the SecurityManager Class
- 8.02 Select Appropriate Locations to Implement Java EE Security Technologies or Features in a UML Component and Deployment Diagram
- 8.03 Classify Security Threats to an Enterprise Application and Select the Measures an Architect Can Propose to Mitigate Them
- 8.04 Identify Techniques Associated with Declarative and Programmatic Security, Including the Use of Annotations, Deployment Descriptors, and JAAS Technology
- 8.05 Identify the Security Technologies That Apply to an Application's Code, Messaging, and Transport Layers
- ✓ Two-Minute Drill
- Q&A Self Test

In an enterprise computing environment, the failure, compromise, or lack of availability of computing resources can jeopardize the life of the enterprise. To survive, an enterprise must identify, minimize, and, where possible, eliminate threats to the security of enterprise computing system resources. The term *resources,* for our purposes, refers to goods and services. A *good* is a tangible property—that is, the physical server. A *service* is an intangible property such as software or data. A *threat* against a resource is basically an unauthorized use of a good or a service.

The Java EE security environment enables security constraints to be defined at deployment time as opposed to requiring that platform-specific security measures be embedded within an application. Java EE application developers are shielded from the complexity of implementing security features, which makes applications portable to a wide variety of security environments.

The Java EE platform allows a developer and then a deployer to define access control rules (declaratively) that are interpreted when the application is deployed to a server. Developers do not need to implement login mechanisms within code for each application they create; they can rely on the Java EE container to provide standard login methods. These features allow an application to work across a variety of security implementations without code change.

CERTIFICATION OBJECTIVE 8.01

Identify Elements of the Security Model in the Java SE Environments for Remote Clients, Including Web Start, Applets, and the Role of the SecurityManager Class

The following is a list of the Java Standard Edition (SE) security elements you will need to know about for the exam:

- Java Web Start
- Java Applet
- Java SecurityManager

- Java Authentication and Authorization Service (JAAS)
- Java Cryptography Extension (JCE)
- Java Generic Security Services (GSS)
- Java Secure Sockets Extension (JSSE)
- Simple Authentication and Security Layer (SASL)
- Java SE security utilities

Java Web Start

The Java Web Start software allows a user to download and run Java applications, in the form of Java archives (JARs) from the Web. It provides the user with a single-click method to launch the application. During launch, it checks the application's website and automatically downloads a new version, if available, prior to starting.

The JAR files that are downloaded are unsigned, and when launched by Web Start they execute in an restricted environment, more commonly known as a *sandbox*. Within this environment the following restrictions exist for the application:

- No access to the local disk.
- JAR files can only be downloaded from the same domain (host).
- Network connections can only be to the same domain (host).
- No SecurityManager can be installed.
- No native libraries.
- Limited access to system properties. The application has read/write access to properties that are defined in the Java Network Launch Protocol (JNLP) file. The application has read access to same properties that a Java applet running in a browser has (see the following section).

Java Applet

A Java applet is a program that a browser (with Java technology installed) can download from the Web and run in the context of the browser. Applets are either unsigned or can be signed by a certificate from a recognized certificate authority. Unsigned applets, when accepted to run by the user, will run in a restricted environment (a.k.a. sandbox) that only allows safe operations. Signed applets, when user accepts the certificate, can run outside the sandbox and potentially have access to additional capabilities on the local environment.

Note that applets that are loaded from the local file system (from a directory in the user's `CLASSPATH`) have none of the restrictions that applets loaded over the network do.

The following operations are permitted for unsigned (and implicitly signed) applets:

- Create a thread.
- Display HTML documents.
- Invoke public methods of other applets on the same page.
- Make network connections to the domain (host) from which they were downloaded.
- Read secure system properties.

When launched via JNLP, applets can also perform the following operations:

- Access the shared system-wide clipboard.
- Access printing functions.
- Open, read, and save files on the client.
- Store data on the client, decide how applets should be downloaded and cached, and more. (See the JNLP API documentation for more information.)

The following operations are *not* permitted for unsigned applets:

- Access the local file system, executable files, system clipboard, and printers.
- Connect to domains other than the host from which they were downloaded.
- Load native libraries.
- Change the existing or install a new SecurityManager.
- Create a ClassLoader.
- Read certain system properties.

The Security Manager

The base Java security model is composed of three parts:

- **Verifier** Helps ensure type safety.
- **Class Loader** Loads/unloads classes dynamically from the Java run time.
- **Security Manager** Gatekeeper guarding potentially dangerous operations.

The objective focuses on the role of the `SecurityManager` class, so let's look at that part in more detail.

Role of the `SecurityManager` Class

The role of the `SecurityManager` class is to keep track of who is allowed to perform risky operations—for example, access to files, network sockets, and printers. The default `SecurityManager` prevents almost all operations when requested by *untrusted* code, but allows *trusted* code to pretty much do whatever it wants. Java uses the `SecurityManager` as follows:

- Java class calls a potentially dangerous Java API operation (for example, open a file).
- Java API calls `SecurityManager` to check if the operation is permitted:
  - If the operation is permitted, `SecurityManager` returns without throwing an exception and the Java API operation executes, returning the operation response (if any) to the calling Java class.
  - If the operation is not permitted, `SecurityManager` throws `SecurityException`. Java API catches and throws this exception to the calling Java class.

Untrusted Code and SecurityManager For untrusted code, the `SecurityManager` is set up to perform the following:

- Prevent installation of new class loaders.
- Protect threads and thread groups from each other.
- Control the execution of other application programs.
- Control access to other application processes.
- Control access to system resources such as print queues, clipboards, event queues, system properties, and windows.
- Control the ability to shut down the VM.
- Control file system operations such as read, write, and delete. Access to local files is strictly controlled.
- Control network socket operations such as connect and accept.
- Control access to Java packages (or groups of classes), including access to security enforcement classes.

Using encryption-based authentication methods, the `SecurityManager` in concert with other mechanisms can set up much more sophisticated rules for trusted, partially trusted, and untrusted applets.

More Java SE Security Features/Mechanisms

The following are additional security features/mechanisms supported by the Java SE (Standard Edition) environment:

- **Java Authentication and Authorization Service (JAAS)** JAAS is a set of APIs that enable services to authenticate and enforce access controls upon users. It provides a pluggable and extensible framework for programmatic user authentication and authorization.
- **Java Cryptography Extension (JCE)** JCE provides a framework and implementations for encryption, key generation and key agreement, and Message Authentication Code (MAC) algorithms. Support for encryption includes symmetric, asymmetric, block, and stream ciphers.
- **Java Generic Security Services (GSS)** GSS is a token-based API used to securely exchange messages between applications. It offers application programmers uniform access to security services.
- **Java Secure Sockets Extension (JSSE)** JSSE provides a framework and an implementation for Secure Sockets Layer (SSL) and Transport Layer Security (TLS) protocols. JSSE includes functionality for data encryption, server authentication, message integrity, and client authentication to enable secure communications.
- **Simple Authentication and Security Layer (SASL)** SASL is a standard that specifies a protocol for authentication and possible establishment of a security layer between client and server applications.

Java SE also provides utilities for managing keystores, security certificates, and policy files; generating and verifying JAR signatures; and obtaining, listing, and managing Kerberos tickets.

CERTIFICATION OBJECTIVE 8.02

Select Appropriate Locations to Implement Java EE Security Technologies or Features in a UML Component and Deployment Diagram

This section identifies the locations where Java EE security technology can be implemented. We use a UML component diagram and a UML deployment diagram to illustrate the locations.

Java EE Security Depicted within UML Component Diagram

A UML component diagram represents how components are wired together to form a larger, more complex component or a software system. An architect can use a UML component diagram to show the internal structure of a component, as well as the provided and required interfaces.

Figure 8-1 depicts a UML component diagram that identifies the locations, or security ports, where Java EE security technology can be implemented. The UML diagram depicts authentication and authorization via a security component.

Java EE Security Depicted within UML Deployment Diagram

A UML deployment diagram represents the network of processing resource elements and the configuration of software components on each physical element. An architect can use a UML deployment diagram to show how the logical tiers of an application architecture are configured into a physical network. A UML deployment diagram is composed of hardware nodes, software components, software dependencies, and communication relationships.

FIGURE 8-1 UML component diagram with Java EE security

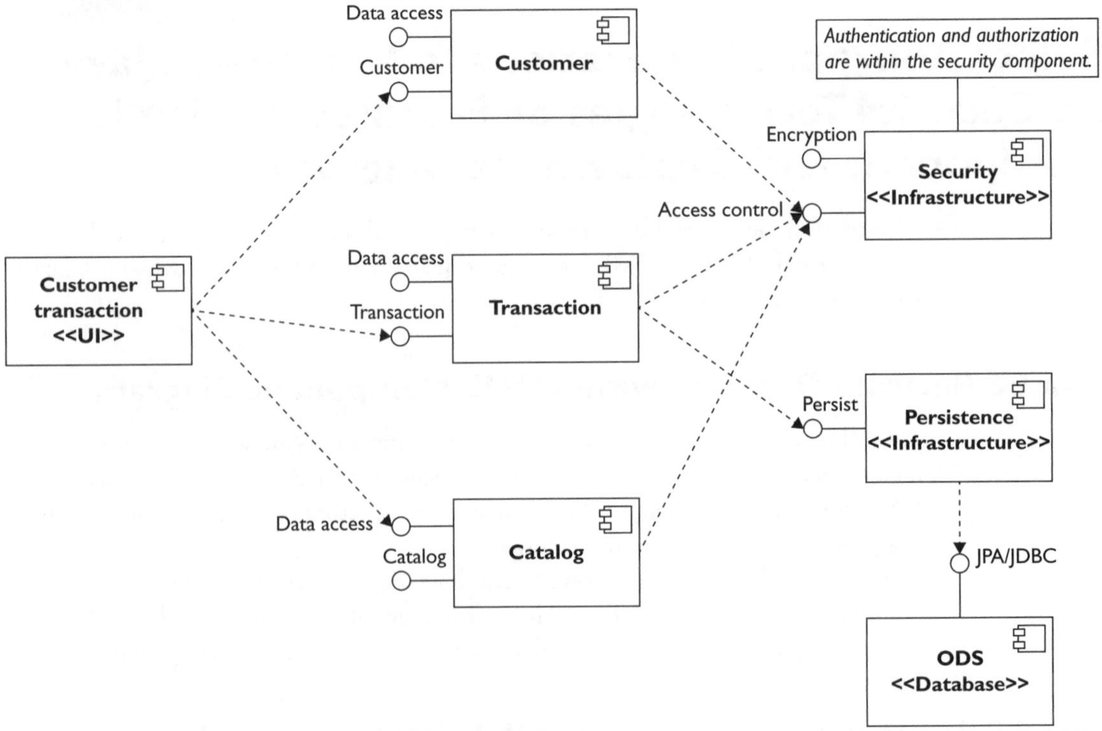

Although UML diagrams do not appear in Part I of the exam, you must include and refer to them in Parts 2 and 3.

Figure 8-2 depicts a UML deployment diagram that identifies the locations (for example, firewalls and DMZs) where Java EE security technology can be implemented.

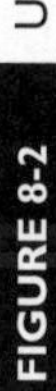

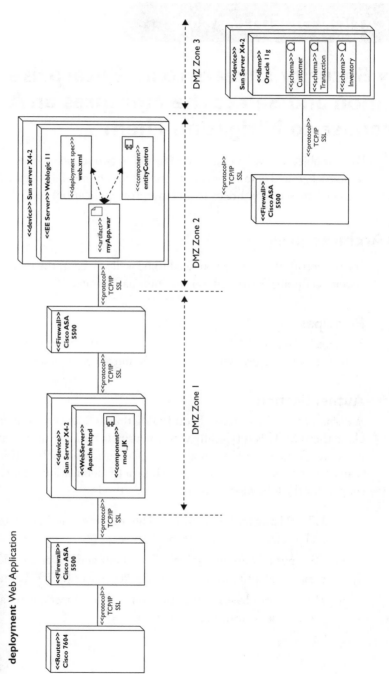

FIGURE 8-2 UML component diagram with Java EE security

deployment Web Application

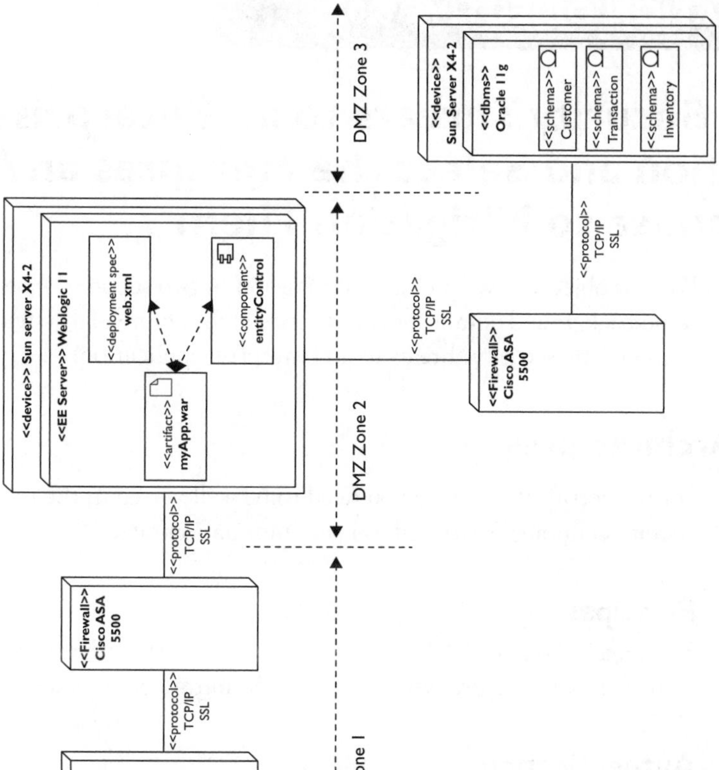

CERTIFICATION OBJECTIVE 8.03

Classify Security Threats to an Enterprise Application and Select the Measures an Architect Can Propose to Mitigation Them

For this objective, we provide information in two sections. The first section provides some background details for the security architecture of a system. The second section classifies the security threats to an enterprise application.

Security Architectures

For the certification exam you need to be well versed in the following security system technologies utilized to keep information safe.

Principal

The *principal* is a uniquely identified person or system that can be authenticated by a security module before system access is permitted or denied.

Authentication

Authentication is the process of confirming that an identified principal is who they claim they are. This is typically with the principal supplying a username/ID and a password. Authentication can also take place using biometrics (for example, retina scan or more commonly a fingerprint). Java EE application servers come with support for the following authentication methods:

- **HTTP basic authentication** The web server authenticates the username and password entered within a browser.
- **SSL mutual authentication** The client and server use x509 certificates to establish identity over a Secure Sockets Layer (SSL) channel.
- **HTML form-based authentication** A developer creates an HTML form to capture identification information.

Authorization

Authorization is the process where an authenticated principal (user or system) is permitted or prevented access to a resource based on the permissions set up directly or indirectly through membership to a group or associated role. The Java EE platform uses a role-based access control mechanism. A principal can be associated with one or more roles (for example, guest user, regular user, administrator), and these roles can have zero or more permissions assigned to them.

Protecting Messages

Messages can be transmitted either in encrypted form or in clear form with a message signature attached (an enciphered digest of the message contents, which is costly in terms of CPU cycles).

Auditing/Logging

Auditing/logging are required to help document when a system is under attack. When steps are taken to prevent it, subsequent logging can demonstrate if the issue has been remediated.

Cryptography

Cryptography is the name given to the techniques that allow information to be temporarily transformed as it passes through public view, making it unreadable. There are two forms of cryptography: symmetric and asymmetric.

Symmetric Cryptography

The key used to transform a message between its original and encrypted form is shared by the sender and recipient. The major consequences being:

- Key must be securely shared between sender and recipient.
- Algorithm that uses the key to transform data is not considered a part of the security system and may be made public. There is a demand on system resources to encrypt and decrypt information.

Asymmetric Cryptography Asymmetric cryptography is also commonly known as public key cryptography. Unlike the single key used in symmetric cryptography, this form uses two mathematically related keys: one known (public) and one secret (private). The known (public) key is used to encrypt plain text or to verify a digital signature. The secret (private) key is used to decrypt cipher text or to create a digital signature.

Security Threats

This section classifies the security threats to an enterprise application and then details the measures that an enterprise architect can take to mitigate those threats. Security threats potentially allow hackers to compromise a network, access and destroy data, and take control of machines. Here is the list of security threats:

- Code injection
- Denial of service
- Man-in-the-middle
- Impersonation
- Eavesdropping
- Packet sniffing
- Password cracking
- Phishing
- Replay
- Repudiation
- Social engineering

We will now look in more detail at each of these threats.

Code Injection

Code injection can be used to introduce code—most commonly either SQL or HTML/Script (cross-site scripting)—into a computer program (for example, a browser) to change the course of execution. The following are mitigation strategies for code injection attacks:

- Validate all input (for example, accept known and valid values, and only proceed when all are valid).
- Use input and output encoding (for example, escaping dangerous characters).
- Use coding practices such as parameterized SQL queries (a.k.a. prepared SQL statements).

Denial of Service

A denial of service (DoS) attack—more commonly carried out as a distributed denial of service (DDoS) attack, one that uses a large number of geographically distributed computers—is an attempt to initiate a large number of requests for a computer resource so that it becomes unavailable for its intended audience. Strategies to address this type of attack typically involve some kind of filtering of the incoming traffic:

- Rules can be set up in firewalls to allow or deny certain protocols, ports, or IP addresses.
- Switches can be used that have comprehensive rate-limiting and Access Control List (ACL) capabilities.
- Routers can be used with (simplistic) rate-limiting and ACL capabilities.
- Application front-end hardware can be used that analyzes data packets as they enter the system and then prioritizes them accordingly (for example, high priority for administrator requests, normal priority for intended use requests, and low priority for the malicious requests).

Man-in-the-Middle

A man-in-the-middle attack is a form of active eavesdropping in which the attacker makes independent connections with the victims and relays messages between them, making them believe that they are talking directly to each other over a private connection when in fact the entire conversation is controlled by the attacker. The following are mitigation strategies using authentication techniques that defend against man-in-the-middle attacks:

- Use public key infrastructures (PKIs) to mutually authenticate messages between two entities.
- Use stronger mutual authentication, including biometrics (fingerprint, retina scan) or secret keys and passwords, in addition to a secure channel (for example, SSL).

Impersonation

Impersonation attacks involve compromising the authentication scheme used between two parties, in order to allow the attacker to impersonate the first party, as far as an interaction with the second party is concerned. The same techniques used to address man-in-the-middle (MITM) attacks are relevant to stop impersonation attacks.

Eavesdropping

Man-in-the-middle (MITM) attacks assume that the attacker wishes to affect the interaction between the two victim parties in the channel. However, the attacker may simply wish to "eavesdrop" on the channel, so as to "copy" (and presumably take advantage of) the information carried over the channel. The mitigation strategy to defend against eavesdropping attacks is to implement encryption at the transport and message layer levels.

Packet Sniffing

A malicious intruder can capture and analyze network traffic using a packet sniffer. Any username and password combinations transmitted in clear text can be captured and the associated account compromised. The mitigation strategy to defend against packet-sniffing attacks is to avoid clear-text username and password and use SSL.

Password Cracking

Password-cracking (or brute force) attacks are used to repeatedly attempt to log in as a known principal by guessing the password. In this scenario an application is used to try passwords made up of all possible combinations of legal characters in sequence. The mitigation strategy to defend against brute force password-cracking attacks is to introduce rules for passwords:

- Use a sufficient number of characters (for example, at least eight) that contain a mix of at least one upper- and lowercase letter, numbers, and special characters.
- Lock the user out of the system if more than a specified number of login attempts fail (for example, more than three).

Phishing

A phishing attack is one where a user is misdirected to a fake version of the system and then tricked into releasing sensitive information (for example, the security questions for a forgotten password). This information is then used by the attack source to gain access to the system. The following are mitigation strategies that defend against phishing attacks:

- **Education** Teach customers to recognize legitimate e-mails. For example, use a customer-selected image that must appear in every e-mail.
- **Personalization** Stay clear of using generically addressed e-mail such as "Dear Customer." Instead, use "Dear <*InsertFirstName*>," which is much harder for a attacker to re-create in a bulk e-mail. You can go even further by consistently including more personalization items in every e-mail

communication with a user. For example, full name, partial account number, partial address, and postal code are simple for a legitimate company to include in the e-mail body, but impossible for a malicious attacker.

- Use digital e-mail signatures to further authenticate the e-mail and minimize the risk of it being dumped into a spam folder. Some digital signature technologies are:
  - Domain Keys Identified Mail (DKIM)
  - Domain-based Message Authentication, Reporting & Conformance (DMARC)
  - Sender Policy Framework (SPF)

Replay

A replay attack is a form of network attack, similar to the man-in-the-middle attack, in which a valid data transmission is maliciously or fraudulently repeated later on. This is carried out either by the originator or by an adversary who intercepts the data and retransmits it. The following are mitigation strategies for replay attacks:

- Use session token(s) in each message. A session token is a one-time use identifier.
- Use nonce(s) in each message. A nonce is a random (or pseudo-random) number that is used only once.
- Use timestamp(s) in each message.

All of these are variations on the theme of tagging data with a unique data point that allows the receiver to recognize a duplicate (already processed) message and take the appropriate action (typically to ignore it, but still log it and possibly notify a security administrator).

Repudiation

Repudiation consists of claiming that either the content of a request was corrupted or the authentication of the sender was compromised and therefore the request should be invalidated. The following are mitigation strategies for repudiation attacks:

- Use digital signatures. A digital signature consists of text that is encrypted using the private key of an entity (sender). The sender's public key is used to decrypt the signature to verify its authenticity.
- Use public/private cryptography with a trusted Certificate Authority (CA).

Social Engineering

Social engineering attacks exploit the very nature of human beings to achieve the threat objective. This attack typically comes in the form of interaction with an individual (for example, e-mail message, telephone call, or even in person). With the objective of gaining trust being paramount, the attack usually employs elements of empathy, urgency, and some degree of believability. The mitigation strategy for social engineering attacks is employee education.

CERTIFICATION OBJECTIVE 8.04

Identify Techniques Associated with Declarative and Programmatic Security, Including the Use of Annotations, Deployment Descriptors, and JAAS Technology

In this section, we examine the ways that Java EE applications can be set up to enforce a desired security policy. In Java EE applications there are three roles responsible for administering security:

- **Application component provider/application assembler** The application component provider/application assembler is responsible for creating a security view of the application. This is done by annotating (explicitly with Java annotations or within entries of the standard deployment descriptor) the classes and methods of the enterprise application in order to provide information to the application deployer about which methods need to have restricted access.
- **Application deployer** The application deployer takes the security view created by the application component provider/application assembler and configures the Java EE application for the operational environment. This includes mapping the logical security to the physical security of the application container.

- **System administrator** From a security perspective, the system administrator is responsible for setting up the list of users and assigning those users to a security group (or role). The system administrator is also responsible for setting up a default principal to role mapping, anonymous users, default users, and propagated identities.

Security Model

The separation of the business logic from security logic of application components is achieved by the container-based security model. There are two approaches to implementing and configuring how an application should perform security services: declarative and programmatic. We will now examine each of these in detail.

exam watch ***Although specific developer-level security coding knowledge is not required, you will find that a general understanding at the developer level will make it much easier to pass the exam.***

Declarative Security

In declarative security, the application's security structure is defined using rules and permissions contained within an XML file called the *standard deployment descriptor*. The standard deployment descriptor is a document packaged along with an application component. The application deployer is responsible for assigning the required rules and permissions granted to the application in the deployment descriptor. The deployment descriptor contains a logical security model for the application; it also contains the valid users and roles for the system and the specific resources and operations that those users and roles can access and execute. At deployment, the application deployer will also create and supply vendor-specific deployment descriptors. These map the logical model to the physical security services provided by the application server product.

The three types of Java EE components use different formats (schemas) for their deployment descriptors:

- Web components use a web application deployment descriptor named web.xml that is contained in the Web Archive (WAR) file.
- Web service components use a deployment descriptor named webservices.xml.
- Enterprise bean components use a deployment descriptor named META-INF/ejb-jar.xml that is contained within the EJB Java Archive (JAR) file.

Annotations

A Java annotation is a form of metadata that can be added to application source code. In Java EE 5, annotations were introduced to specify which users were authorized to access protected methods of enterprise applications. For enterprise beans there are some limitations to using this simplified approach, and continued use of the standard deployment descriptor to specify security information is preferred.

Declarative security is generally considered the preferred approach over programmatic security because changing and deploying one or two deployment descriptors compared to potentially many class files will have less of a production deployment impact. Annotations are considered declarative, but because they are contained within code, you may make the mistake of identifying them as programmatic. However, like declarations in deployment descriptors, they are to be resolved by an application deployer during deployment and then evaluated at run time.

Programmatic Security

In programmatic security, the application's security structure is embedded in application source code. Programmatic security is needed in the event that declarative security is not sufficient to express the security model of an application (for example, where the access control decisions need to use a degree of complexity, or dynamic rules or policies, that cannot be expressed declaratively). The Java API for programmatic security consists of methods on the EJBContext interface for enterprise bean components, HttpServletRequest interface for web components, and WebServiceContext interface for web service components. These methods allow components to make business logic decisions based on the security role of the identified caller.

Securing Web Components

In Java EE 6, web component developers are encouraged to define the security view for an application by using annotations or deployment descriptors. Figure 8-3 depicts a web application.

In the Java EE platform, web components can be implemented with Java servlets and JavaServer Pages (JSP). There are a few security elements that cannot be specified as annotations for all types of web applications, so these need to be defined

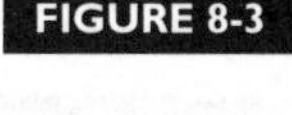
FIGURE 8-3

Web component application

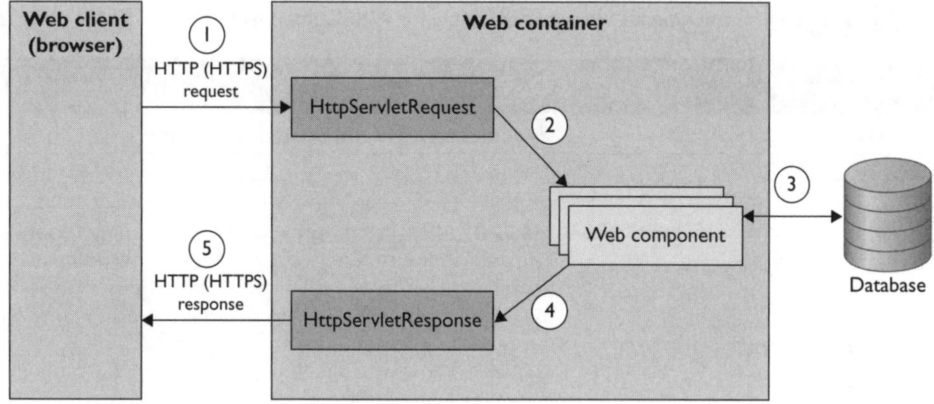

in the deployment descriptor. The next set of tables and a code listing excerpt show the specific elements, annotations, and methods that can be used for securing web component applications. Table 8-1 shows the top-level elements that can be defined in the deployment descriptor for a web component application.

TABLE 8-1 Deployment Descriptor Elements for Web Components: Declarative Security

Element	Description
`security-constraint`	Defines the access privileges to a collection of resources using URL mappings.
`web-resource-collection`	URL patterns (`url-pattern`) and HTTP methods (`http-method`) that describe a set of resources to be protected. Possible values for `http-method` are `POST`, `GET`, `PUT`, and `DELETE`.
`auth-constraint`	Specifies if authentication is to be used and the role names (`role-name`) authorized to perform the constrained requests.
`user-data-constraint`	Specifies how data is protected when transported between a client and a server (`transport-guarantee`). Possible values for `transport-guarantee` are: **`CONFIDENTIAL`** Requires that data be transmitted in a way to prevent other entities from observing the contents of the transmission. **`INTEGRAL`** Requires that the data be sent between client and server such that it cannot be changed in transit. **`NONE`** Container must accept the constrained requests on any connection, including an unprotected one. Java EE servers treat the `CONFIDENTIAL` and `INTEGRAL` values identically, usually requiring SSL.

TABLE 8-1 Deployment Descriptor Elements for Web Components: Declarative Security (*continued*)

Element	Description
`login-config`	Specifies an authentication mechanism.
`auth-method`	Defines the authentication mechanism. Possible values are: **`NONE`** There is no authentication method. **`BASIC`** Requires that the server request a username and password from the web client and verify that the username and password combination match a database of authorized users in the specified or default realm. **`DIGEST`** Like `BASIC`, but the client sends a one-way cryptographic hash of the password and additional data. **`FORM`** Allows the developer to present a custom login screen and error pages for a browser to present. **`CLIENT-CERT`** This method is typically used for identifying the user by their X.509 certificate. Also used to enable mutual authentication over SSL.
`realm-name`	The realm name for `BASIC` authentication.
`form-login-config`	The login and error pages for `FORM` authentication.

Here is a sample code snippet defining the security elements within a web application (web.xml) deployment descriptor:

```
<!-- Security constraint #1 -->
<security-constraint>
    <web-resource-collection>
        <web-resource-name>Protected Area</web-resource-name>
        <url-pattern>/security/protected/*</url-pattern>
        <http-method>PUT</http-method>
        <http-method>DELETE</http-method>
        <http-method>GET</http-method>
        <http-method>POST</http-method>
    </web-resource-collection>
    <auth-constraint>
        <role-name>standarduser</role-name>
    </auth-constraint>
</security-constraint>
<!-- Security constraint #2 -->
<security-constraint>
    <web-resource-collection>
        <web-resource-name>Protected Area 2</web-resource-name>
        <url-pattern>/security/protected2/*</url-pattern>
```

```
        </web-resource-collection>
        <auth-constraint>
            <role-name>poweruser</role-name>
        </auth-constraint>
    </security-constraint>
    <!-- Security roles -->
    <security-role>
        <role-name>standarduser</role-name>
    </security-role>
    <security-role>
        <role-name>poweruser</role-name>
    </security-role>
    <!-- Authentication method -->
    <login-config>
        <auth-method>FORM</auth-method>
        <realm-name>file</realm-name>
        <form-login-config>
            <form-login-page>/login.xhtml</form-login-page>
            <form-error-page>/error.xhtml</form-error-page>
        </form-login-config>
    </login-config>
```

Table 8-2 shows the metadata annotations that can be used in a web component application.

Table 8-3 shows the programmatically defined security that can be used in a web component application.

TABLE 8-2 Metadata Annotations for Web Components: Declarative Security

Annotation	Description
`@ServletSecurity`	Specify HTTP constraints in general (`HttpConstraint`) and for specific methods (`httpMethodConstraint`).
`@HttpMethodConstraint`	Specify constraints on HTTP methods via the subelements `EmptyRoleSemantic` (the default authorization semantic), `RolesAllowed` (for the names of the authorized roles), `TransportGuarantee` (for the data protection requirements). Valid constants are `CONFIDENTIAL` and `NONE`.
`@HttpConstraint`	Security constraints to be applied to all HTTP protocol methods for which a corresponding `HttpMethodConstraint` element does *not* occur within the `ServletSecurity` annotation.

TABLE 8-3 Security Methods for Web Components: Programmatic Security

Method on HttpServletRequest	Description
`authenticate`	Initiates authentication of the caller by the container from within an unconstrained request context. A login window displays and prompts for the username and password to be authenticated.
`getRemoteUser`	If the remote user is not authenticated, this method returns `null`. If the remote user is authenticated, this method returns the name of the remote user associated with the container with the request.
`getUserPrincipal`	If the remote user is not authenticated, this method returns `null`. If the remote user is authenticated, this method returns `java.security.Principal`, calling `getName()` on `Principal` for the name of remote user.
`isUserInRole`	If the remote user is not authenticated, this method returns `false`. If the remote user is authenticated, this method checks if the remote user is in a specific security role.
`login`	The application can determine username and password information and use this method to log in. This is a programmatic alternative to the declarative approach of using form-based authentication in the deployment descriptor.
`logout`	Allows an application to reset the caller identity of a request.

Securing Enterprise Bean Components

In Java EE 6, enterprise bean developers are encouraged to define the security view for an application by using annotations or deployment descriptors. Figure 8-4 depicts an enterprise bean component application.

The following set of tables show the specific elements, annotations, and methods that can be used for securing enterprise bean component applications. Table 8-4 shows the top-level elements that can be defined in the deployment descriptor for an enterprise bean component application. Table 8-5 shows the annotations that can be used in an enterprise bean component application. Table 8-6 shows the programmatic security methods that can be used in an enterprise bean component application.

FIGURE 8-4 Enterprise bean application

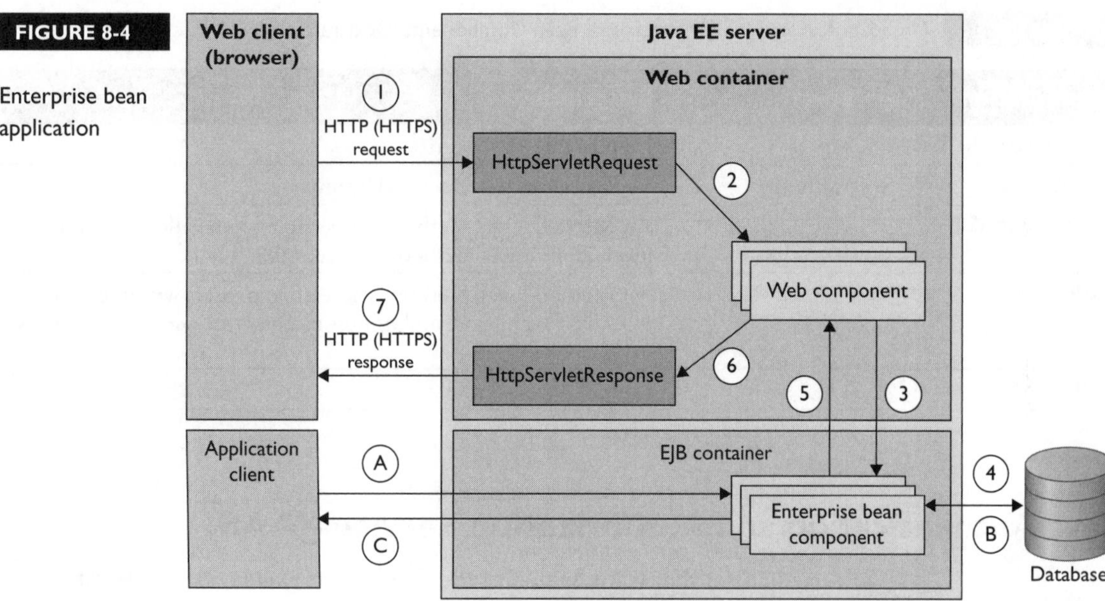

TABLE 8-4 Deployment Descriptor Elements for Enterprise Bean Components: Declarative Security

Element	Description
`security-identity`	Specifies (or overrides annotation for) security identity. Values are `use-caller-identity` and `run-as`.
`method-permission`	Specifies role names (`role-name`) authorized to perform the method.

TABLE 8-5 Metadata Annotations for Enterprise Bean Components: Declarative Security

Annotation	Level	Description
`@DeclareRoles`	Type	Defines roles for security.
`@DenyAll`	Method	Method cannot be accessed by anyone.
`@PermitAll`	Type or Method	For Method level, method is accessible to all callers. For Type level, all business methods are accessible to all callers.
`@RolesAllowed`	Type or Method	For Method level, method is accessible to users within given roles. For Type level, all business methods are accessible to users within given roles.
`@RunAs`	Type	Defines "run-as" role.

Java Authentication and Authorization Service (JAAS)

JAAS, a mechanism that is integrated in the JVM, allows Java code to identify users (authentication) and roles before allowing or denying access to resources or functionality controlled by the JVM (authorization). It supports pluggable authentication and authorization modules. This allows existing security services to be more easily integrated into a Java solution.

TABLE 8-6 Security Methods for Enterprise Bean Components: Programmatic Security

Method on EJBContext	Description
getCallerPrincipal	If the caller is not authenticated, this method returns `null`. If the caller is authenticated, this method returns `java.security.Principal`, calling `getName()` on `Principal` for the name of the caller.
isCallerInRole	If the caller is authenticated, this method checks whether the caller is in a specific security role. If the caller is not authenticated, this method returns `false`.

CERTIFICATION OBJECTIVE 8.05

Identify the Security Technologies That Apply to an Application's Code, Messaging, and Transport Layers

Security features for authenticating users and authorizing access to application functions and associated data are provided by the component container for Java EE. They can be implemented declaratively or programmatically, and they can be applied across the application, messaging, and transport layers. We will now cover the Java EE security features within each of these layers.

Application-Layer Security

In Java EE, component containers are responsible for providing application-layer security, which is tailored to the needs of the application. Within this layer, firewalls can be used to protect the communication stream and all associated application resources. Java EE security offers fine-grained access control to application functions using declarative and programmatic security approaches (see the other parts of this chapter for details). However, these security approaches apply only within an application and cannot transfer to applications executing in additional environments. This is less of an issue with individual enterprise-level applications, but in modern web- and service-based applications data is expected to pass across application boundaries, so one needs to use all the application-layer security in conjunction with message- and transport-layer security for a secure solution.

Table 8-7 shows the advantages and disadvantages of application-layer security.

TABLE 8-7 Application-Layer Security: Advantages and Disadvantages

Advantages	Disadvantages
Security completely tailored to the application's needs.	Security attributes are not transferable between applications.
Fine-grained application-specific security settings are available.	Multiple protocols support increases in vulnerability.
	Point of vulnerability is close to (or with) the data.

Message-Layer Security

In message-layer security, security information is contained within the SOAP message and/or SOAP message attachment, which allows security information to travel along with the message or attachment. For example, a portion of the message may be signed by a sender and encrypted for a particular receiver. When sent from the initial sender, the message may pass through intermediate nodes before reaching its intended receiver. In this scenario, the encrypted portions continue to be opaque to any intermediate nodes and can be decrypted only by the intended receiver. For this reason, message-layer security is also sometimes referred to as end-to-end security. For SOAP messages, the WS-Security specification focuses on the following:

- Authentication using security token validation. Assertions are validated by a message recipient, for an unsigned username/password style token, or by an authorized third party, such as a Certificate Authority (CA) for a signed token (x509 cert or Kerberos ticket).
- Message integrity using XML signatures (part of WS-Security).
- Message confidentiality using XML encryption (part of WS-Security).

Table 8-8 shows the advantages and disadvantages of message-layer security.

Transport-Layer Security

Transport-layer security is provided by the transport mechanisms used to transmit information over the wire between clients and providers; thus, transport-layer security relies on secure HTTP transport (HTTPS) using Secure Sockets Layer (SSL).

TABLE 8-8 Message-Layer Security: Advantages and Disadvantages

Advantages	Disadvantages
Maintained along with message over hops; can be used with intermediaries along the way, and after message arrives at destination.	Relatively complex.
Can be selectively applied to different portions of a message and, when using XML WS-Security, to message attachments.	Adds processing overhead.
Independent of application environment and transport protocol.	

TABLE 8-9 Transport-Layer Security: Advantages and Disadvantages

Advantages	Disadvantages
Relatively simple.	Tight coupling with transport protocol.
Applies to the message body and attachments.	All-or-nothing approach, so one cannot selectively apply security to portions of a message. Message is protected only while in transit. At the point of delivery, protection is removed automatically.
	Not an end-to-end solution, simply a point-to-point solution.

Transport security is a point-to-point security mechanism that can be used for authentication, message integrity, and confidentiality. When running over an SSL-protected session, the server and client can authenticate each other and negotiate an encryption algorithm and cryptographic keys before the application protocol transmits or receives its first byte of data. Security is active from the time the data leaves the client until it arrives at its destination, or vice versa, even across intermediaries. The problem is that the data is not protected once it gets to the destination. One solution is to encrypt the message before sending.

Table 8-9 shows the advantages and disadvantages of transport-layer security.

CERTIFICATION SUMMARY

By studying this chapter, you will have an understanding of the Java EE security technologies that will be tested on the examination. The high-level elements are the Java SE Security Model, the SecurityManager Class, locations to depict security features in UML diagrams, security threats and mitigation strategies, declarative and programmatic security, and the security technology that can be applied in code and within the messaging and transport layers.

TWO-MINUTE DRILL

Here are some of the key points from each certification objective in Chapter 8.

Identify Elements of the Security Model in the Java SE Environment for Remote Clients, Including Web Start, Applets, and the Role of the SecurityManager Class

- ❑ Java Web Start allows a user to download and run a Java application via a single click, and it automatically downloads a new version if available prior to starting.
- ❑ A Java applet is a program that a browser (with Java technology installed) can download from the Web and run in the context of the browser. There are unsigned and signed types.
- ❑ The role of the `SecurityManager` is to keep track of who is allowed to perform risky operations (for example, access to files, network sockets, and printers). The default `SecurityManager` prevents almost all operations when requested by untrusted code, but lets trusted code execute the same.

Select Appropriate Locations to Implement Java EE Security Technologies or Features in a UML Component and Deployment Diagram

- ❑ Review the diagrams for this objective. The diagrams are not tested in Part 1 of the examination, but should be considered for use in your solutions for Parts 2 and 3.

Classify Security Threats to an Enterprise Application and Select the Measures an Architect Can Propose to Mitigate Them

- ❑ Code injection, commonly SQL or HTML/Script (cross-site-scripting), introduces code to change the course of execution. Mitigation techniques include validating input, encoding input and output, and good coding practices (for example, prepared SQL statements).
- ❑ (Distributed) denial of service involves initiating a large number of requests for a computer resource so that it becomes generally unavailable. This attack can be mitigated mainly by filtering traffic in firewalls, routers, switches, or custom front-end hardware.

- Man-in-the-middle involves active eavesdropping, with the attacker connected between the victims and relaying messages between them. This attack can be mitigated with public key infrastructures and stronger mutual authentication (biometrics such as fingerprint and retina scans), secret keys, and passwords.
- Impersonation involves compromising the authentication between two parties. This attack can be mitigated using the same techniques used to address man-in-the-middle attacks.
- Eavesdropping is essentially a passive man-in-the-middle attack. This attack can be mitigated using encryption at the transport and message levels.
- Packet sniffing involves capturing packet data looking for information in clear text. This attack can be mitigated using encryption.
- Password cracking involves brute force attacks to guess passwords. This attack can be mitigated with a stronger password policy (eight characters, mixed-case letters, numbers, and special characters) and a lockout after several login attempt failures (for example, more than three).
- Phishing uses a fake version of the system to trick victim into releasing sensitive information. This attack can be mitigated with education, personalization, and digital e-mail signatures (DKIM, DMARC, and SPF).
- Replay is where valid data transmission is maliciously or fraudulently repeated. This attack can be mitigated by tagging data with a unique data point that allows the receiver to recognize a duplicate (already-processed) message.
- Repudiation involves claiming that either the content of a request was corrupted or the authentication of the sender was compromised and therefore the request should be invalidated. This attack can be mitigated with digital signatures and public/private cryptography with a trusted Certificate Authority (CA).
- Social engineering is an attack whose objective is to gain trust using elements of empathy, urgency, and some degree of believability. This attack can be mitigated via employee education.

Identify Techniques Associated with Declarative and Programmatic Security, Including the Use of Annotations, Deployment Descriptors, and JAAS Technology

- JAAS technology supports pluggable authentication and authorization modules.
- Security for web components:
  - The (declarative) security deployment descriptor elements are `security-constraint`, `web-resource-collection`, `auth-constraint`, `user-data-constraint`, `login-config`, `auth-method`, `realm-name`, and `form-login-config`. Refer to Table 8-1 for the full explanation and use of each element.
  - The (declarative) security metadata annotations are `@ServletSecurity`, `@HttpMethodConstraint`, and `@HttpConstraint`. Refer to Table 8-2 for the full explanation and use of each annotation.
  - The (programmatic) security methods are `authenticate`, `getRemoteUser`, `getUserPrincipal`, `isUserInRole`, `login`, and `logout`. Refer to Table 8-3 for the full explanation and use of each method.
- Security for enterprise bean components:
  - The (declarative) security deployment descriptor elements are `security-identity`, and `method-permission`. Refer to Table 8-4 for the full explanation and use of each element.
  - The (declarative) security metadata annotations are `@DeclareRoles`, `@DenyAll`, `@PermitAll`, `@RolesAllowed`, and `@RunAs`. Refer to Table 8-5 for the full explanation and use of each annotation.
  - The (programmatic) security methods are `getCallerPrincipal` and `isCallerInRole`. Refer to Table 8-6 for the full explanation and use of each method.

Identify the Security Technologies That Apply to an Application's Code, Messaging, and Transport Layers

- For the application layer, use the declarative (deployment descriptor and annotations) and programmatic security features of Java EE. Also utilize firewalls to protect access to application servers.
- For the message layer, use WS-Security (only for SOAP messages).
- For the transport layer, use the Secure Socket Layer (SSL) protocol.

SELF TEST

The following questions will help you measure your understanding of the material presented in this chapter. Read all the choices carefully because there may be more than one correct answer. Choose all correct answers for each question.

Identify Elements of the Security Model in the Java SE Environment for Remote Clients, Including Web Start, Applets, and the Role of the SecurityManager Class

1. Which of the following is not part of the security features or security model of the Java SE environment?
   A. JAAS
   B. Applet
   C. WS-Security
   D. Web Start

2. Which of the following is possible for a unsigned Java applet?
   A. Access local file system.
   B. Run an executable file.
   C. Access system clipboard.
   D. Print a document.
   E. None of the above.

3. Which of the following is the mechanism by which all applets that are loaded over a network are prevented from accessing security-sensitive resources, such as the local file system?
   A. IPSec
   B. Sandbox
   C. Java SDK
   D. JAAS

Select Appropriate Locations to Implement Java EE Security Technologies or Features in a UML Component and Deployment Diagram

4. Which of the following is not a valid location for Java EE security features on a UML diagram?
   A. DMZ
   B. SSL transport
   C. Firewall
   D. Load balancer

Classify Security Threats to an Enterprise Application and Select the Measures an Architect Can Propose to Mitigate Them

5. Which one of the following is a mitigation strategy for a distributed denial of service (DDoS) attack?

A. Switch filter

B. Encryption

C. Secret keys

D. Encoding input and output

6. The support help desk has reported a very high number of incidents with locked-out customers who need their password reset. What type of attack is the most likely?

A. Eavesdropping

B. Code injection

C. Phishing

D. Brute force

7. Which of the following is the recommended approach to prevent replay attacks?

A. Encrypt messages.

B. Use nonce in messages.

C. Digital signature.

D. Port filtering.

8. Which one of the following can result from a failure to validate input from an HTML form?

A. Code injection

B. Session hijacking

C. Phishing

D. Unsafe object

Identify Techniques Associated with Declarative and Programmatic Security, Including the Use of Annotations, Deployment Descriptors, and JAAS Technology

9. Which of the following is a valid security annotation for a Java EE web component?

A. `@Deny`

B. `@Permit`

C. `@ServletSecurity`

D. `@Login`

10. Which of the following is a valid security deployment descriptor element for a Java EE web component?

A. `<deny-role>`

B. `<auth-permit>`

C. `<login-schema>`

D. `<web-resource-collection>`

11. Which of the following is a valid security method for a Java EE web component?

A. `getCallerPrincipal`

B. `isUserInRole`

C. `isCallerInRole`

D. `getProtocol`

12. Which of the following is a valid security annotation for a Java EE enterprise bean component?

A. `@Deny`

B. `@Permit`

C. `@RunAs`

D. `@Roles`

13. Which of the following is a valid security deployment descriptor element for a Java EE enterprise bean component?

A. `<method-permission>`

B. `<ejb-security>`

C. `<ejb-home>`

D. `<identity>`

14. Which of the following is a valid security method for a Java EE enterprise bean component?

A. `getRemoteUser`

B. `getUserPrincipal`

C. `isCallerInRole`

D. `getRemotePrincipal`

Identify the Security Technologies That Apply to an Application's Code, Messaging, and Transport Layers

15. Which of the following security technologies can be applied to the application layer?

A. Declarative security

B. Programmatic security

C. Firewalls

D. All of the above

16. Which of the following security technologies can be applied to the message layer?

A. Firewalls

B. WS-Security

C. IPSec

D. All of the above

17. Which of the following security technologies can be applied to the transport layer?

A. Message digest

B. Intercepting filter

C. Secure Sockets Layer

D. Digital fingerprint

SELF TEST ANSWERS

Identify Elements of the Security Model in the Java SE Environment for Remote Clients, Including Web Start, Applets, and the Role of the SecurityManager Class

1. ☑ **C.** WS-Security is not part of the security features or security model of the Java SE environment.
   ☒ **A, B,** and **D** are incorrect. These are security features or parts of the security model of the Java SE environment.

2. ☑ **E.** None of these actions is permitted for an unsigned Java applet.
   ☒ **A, B, C,** and **D** are incorrect. These actions are not permitted for an unsigned Java applet.

3. ☑ **B.** A sandbox is responsible for controlling access to security-sensitive resources.
   ☒ **A, C,** and **D** are incorrect. These mechanisms do not prevent applets from accessing security-sensitive resources.

Select Appropriate Locations to Implement Java EE Security Technologies or Features in a UML Component and Deployment Diagram

4. ☑ **D.** A load balancer is not a valid location for Java EE security features on a UML diagram.
   ☒ **A, B,** and **C** are incorrect. These are all valid locations for Java EE security features on a UML diagram.

Classify Security Threats to an Enterprise Application and Select the Measures an Architect Can Propose to Mitigate Them

5. ☑ **A.** Using a switch filter is the mitigation strategy for a distributed denial of service attack.
   ☒ **B, C,** and **D** are incorrect. These do not apply to DDOS attacks.

6. ☑ **D.** Brute force (password-cracking) is the most likely attack for this scenario.
   ☒ **A, B,** and **C** are incorrect. None of these is the most likely attack for this scenario.

7. ☑ **B.** Using a nonce is a mitigation strategy for replay attacks.
   ☒ **A, C,** and **D** are incorrect. These are not mitigation strategies for replay attacks.

8. ☑ **A.** Code injection can result from a failure to validate input from an HTML form.
   ☒ **B, C,** and **D** are incorrect. These are not the result of a failure to validate input from an HTML form.

Identify Techniques Associated with Declarative and Programmatic Security, Including the Use of Annotations, Deployment Descriptors, and JAAS Technology

9. ☑ **C.** `@ServletSecurity` is a valid security annotation for a Java EE web component.
☒ **A, B,** and **D** are incorrect. These are not valid security annotations for a Java EE web component.

10. ☑ **D.** `<web-resource-collection>` is a valid security deployment descriptor element for a Java EE web component.
☒ **A, B,** and **C** are incorrect. These are not valid security deployment descriptor elements for a Java EE web component.

11. ☑ **C.** `isUserInRole` is a valid security method for a Java EE web component.
☒ **A, B,** and **D** are incorrect. These are not valid security methods for a Java EE web component.

12. ☑ **C.** `@RunAs` is a valid security annotation for a Java EE enterprise bean component.
☒ **A, B,** and **D** are incorrect. These are not valid security annotations for a Java EE enterprise bean component.

13. ☑ **A.** `<method-permission>` is a valid security deployment descriptor element for a Java EE enterprise bean component.
☒ **B, C,** and **D** are incorrect. These are not valid security deployment descriptor elements for a Java EE enterprise bean component.

14. ☑ **C.** `isCallerInRole` is a valid security method for a Java EE enterprise bean component.
☒ **A, B,** and **D** are incorrect. These are not valid security methods for a Java EE enterprise bean component.

Identify the Security Technologies That Apply to an Application's Code, Messaging, and Transport Layers

15. ☑ **D.** All of these security technologies (declarative security, programmatic security, and firewalls) can be applied to the application layer.
☒ **A, B,** and **C** are incorrect. Each answer given can be applied to the application layer, but all of them are applicable.

16. ☑ **B.** WS-Security can be applied to the message layer.
☒ **A, C,** and **D** are incorrect. Firewalls and IPSec do not apply to the message layer; therefore, "All of the above" is also incorrect.

17. ☑ **C.** Secure Sockets Layer (SSL) can be applied to the transport layer.
☒ **A, B,** and **D** are incorrect. Message digest, intercepting filter, and digital fingerprint do not relate to the transport layer.

A

Java (EE) Enterprise Architect Certified Master Assignment

This appendix presents a case study that will help you to prepare for and complete the assignment for the Oracle Certified Master, Java EE 6 Enterprise Architect (OCMJEA) certification, also referred to within this book as Part 2 architecture (or P2A). The assignment does not require any coding, because it is an architecture and design project. The assignment and essay parts of the exam are in place to test your fundamental architect skill in being able to identify and call out the most significant technical risks for the given scenario and to mitigate these risks in the documented solution. To keep the amount of work involved to a reasonable level, the programs you create will be restricted in capability and simpler than anything you would actually create for a real-world client. You will be graded on correctly solving the technical and performance requirements.

Your project will be evaluated on a large number of objective criteria that fall into the following categories:

- **Class Diagram** This category covers how well your class diagram(s) address the object model needed to satisfy the requirements.
- **Component Diagram** This category covers how well your component diagram(s) convey the structure of the architecture in satisfying the requirements.
- **Sequence Diagram** This category covers how well your sequence diagram(s) satisfy the requirements of the assignment.
- **Deployment Diagram** This category covers how well your deployment diagram(s) convey the architecture at deployment.

Additionally, each category is evaluated on UML compliance.

In this appendix, we present you with a securities trading application that includes use cases, a domain object model, and additional requirements. Most systems in the real world start off with requirements, and the exam assignment chooses to define the requirements in use cases and a domain model. As the architect for the application, you must develop the class diagram(s), component diagram(s), sequence diagram(s), and deployment diagram(s) to describe your architecture.

Scenario

You have been assigned the role of architect for Bank of New Amsterdam (BNA), a Wall Street securities clearing corporation that interacts with hundreds of correspondent trade brokers and their respective customers. The primary goal is to help the firm by facilitating the customers' ability to trade securities on the Web. To be successful, a trading firm (broker-dealers) must transition their firm to a customer-centric, web-based environment. The Internet is seen as the best way to maintain existing and grow new distribution channels, customers, and strategic partnerships. Basically, the challenge is to determine how this trading firm can develop a winning strategy to compete for customers and brokers who want the ease of trading securities via the Web.

The solution is the same for all businesses competing in the e-commerce world—a three-step approach to successful enterprise development:

1. Spend the time to understand what the client needs—in this case, web browser-based trading functionality.
2. Choose the right technology—in this case, Java and Java 6 Enterprise Edition (Java 6 EE).
3. Develop a team and teamwork atmosphere to implement the technology. Choose architects and developers skilled in trade processing and Java EE design and development.

Infrastructure

As with many large organizations, Bank of New Amsterdam (BNA) has several different operating systems running many kinds of software systems. The primary platform for the production business data is the IBM Mainframe S/390 (the mainframe). In addition, Microsoft Windows servers use Internet Information Services (IIS) and other Microsoft software to provide reporting capabilities, using a SQL Server shadow copy of the business data. BNA also has an investment in Oracle on the S/390. Several preexisting legacy applications provide trade-processing links to the major securities exchanges. These applications work well and have been developed and maintained for the past two decades, during which time a great deal of time and money has been spent. The applications do not need modification; instead, they need a new web front end to make them look good. The development environment is primarily Windows based.

The advantages of using the mainframe include its reliability, scalability, flexibility, and security. The mainframe has been running continuously for years in BNA without major problems. The mainframe can easily be amended to add hardware resources (such as CPU, memory, and disk) or networking hardware, to increase capacity without changing the operating system or application systems. In addition, the CPU, memory, and disk space can be redistributed as application requirements change.

Traditionally, the downside to the mainframe has been the user interface—the 3270 dumb terminal (the green screen), which is not user friendly. Prior to the commencement of BNA's Java project, another group spent a few months trying to develop Windows Active Server Pages (ASP) to talk to the mainframe. The only solution providing ASP reports, a portfolio management system, solved the interface problem, but it was difficult to connect to the mainframe using ASP for trading.

BNA has experienced difficulty getting the order messages to the mainframe. Along with performance problems, it seemed that every ASP order transaction required multiple dedicated connections to the SQL Server database. Fortunately, Java Database Connectivity (JDBC) connection pooling and Java's platform independence provided the performance and scalability that was needed. Moreover, it allowed BNA to take advantage of the mainframe for deployment and Windows for development. (Because budget is a limiting factor in an economic downturn, where every developer is competing for business, it is critical that you deliver a solution quickly that will integrate with an organization's existing infrastructure.)

The IBM HTTP server, WebSphere application server, and Oracle 11*g* relational database management system (RDBMS) all exist on the company's legacy IBM mainframe enterprise server.

Table A-1 describes the software components of the web front end.

Figure A-1 illustrates the enterprise architecture as a diagram, and Figure A-2 shows a Unified Modeling Language (UML) sequence diagram.

TABLE A-1 Web Front-End Software

Type of Component	Vendor/Component Name/Version	Description	Software/Hardware Required for Support
Application server	WebSphere Application Server 8.5	Serves up JSPs and servlets, runs EJBs, and provides JDBC connection pools to user data	IBM S/390, Windows 7 or 8
DBMS	Oracle 11g	Database required for application data (orderdb)	Oracle 11g
Browser	Microsoft Internet Explorer, Mozilla Firefox, or Google Chrome	Web browser required to support JavaScript	Compatible browser
XML tool	IBM/XML Parser for Java/XML4J	A library for parsing and generating XML documents	Windows 7 or 8

FIGURE A-1 Production architecture components

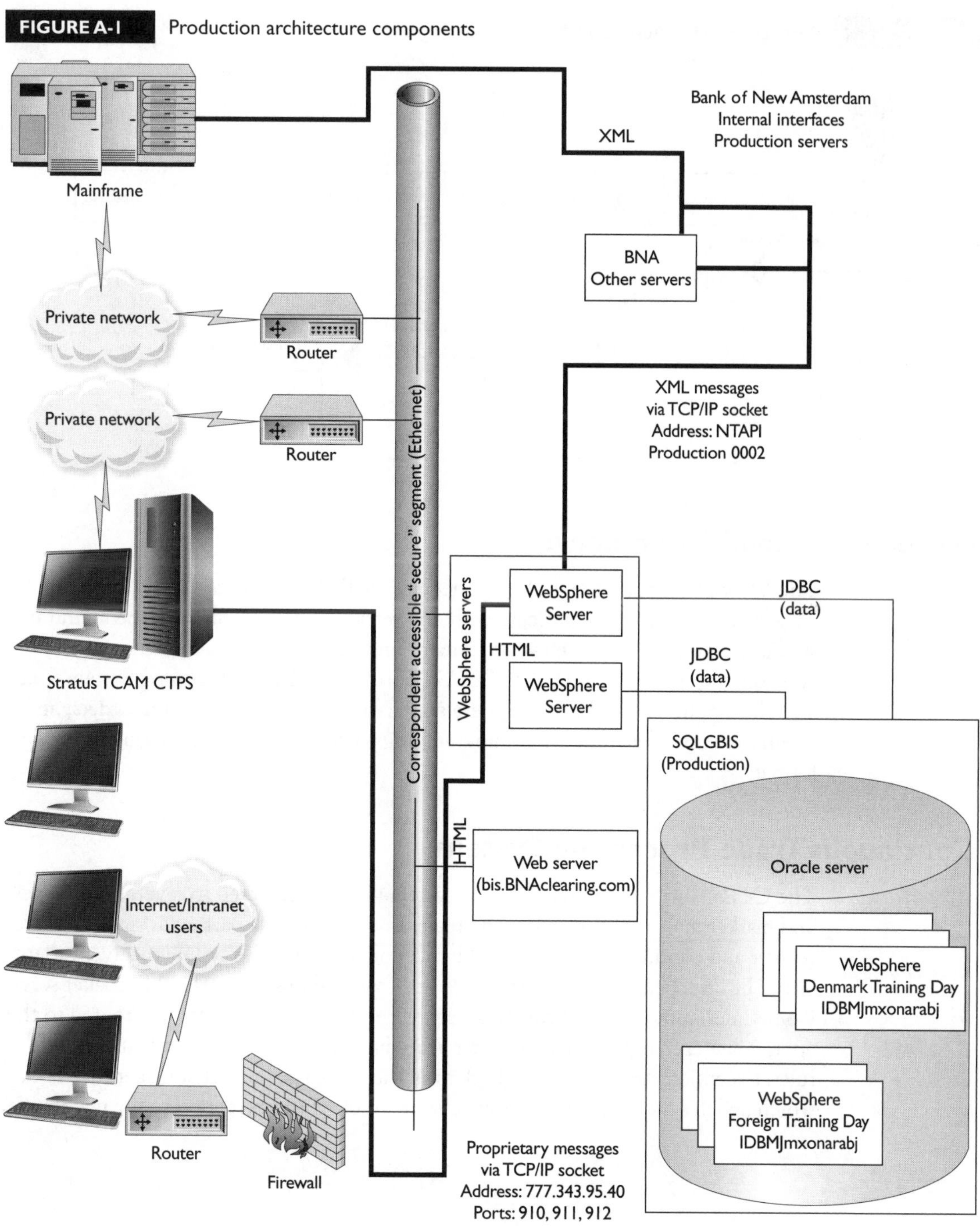

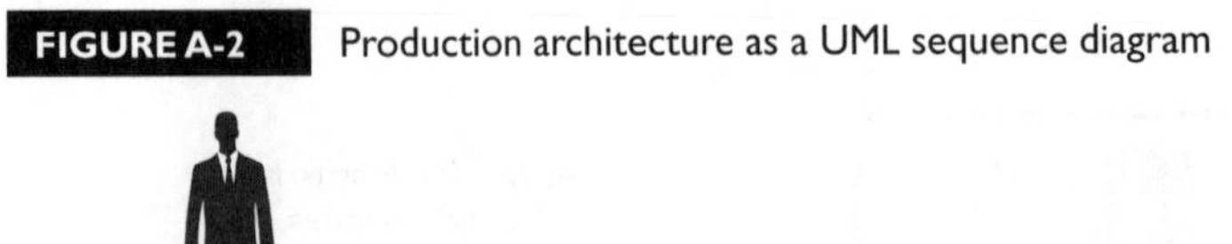

FIGURE A-2 Production architecture as a UML sequence diagram

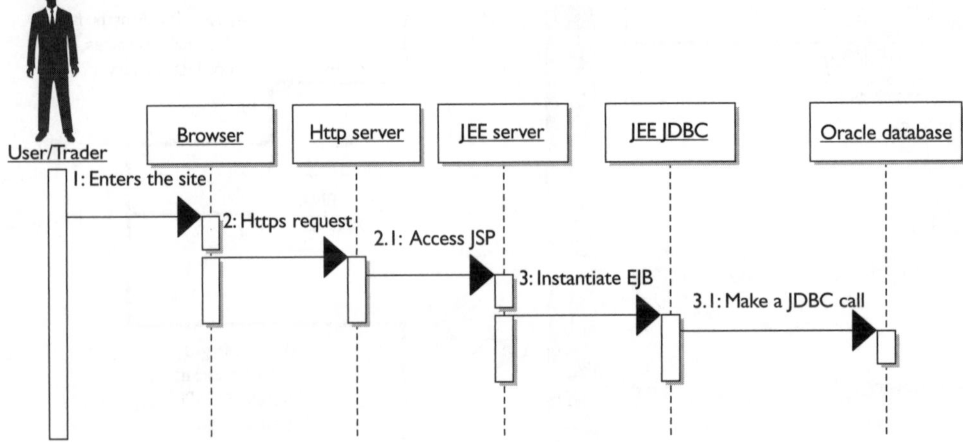

WebSphere Application Server

The WebSphere partition is also connected via TCP/IP sockets to the BNACS API. This API is used to communicate with and retrieve information from the mainframe system via an XML-based message format. Finally, the WebSphere partition is connected to the Stratus TCAM CTPS (Continuous Trade Processing System from TCAM) application. The WebSphere application sends and maintains orders, and it can look up order status by communicating with CTPS via a proprietary message format.

Continuous Trade Processing System

The CTPS system is an order-routing system that is connected to several exchanges and market makers (firms that stand ready to buy and sell a particular stock on a regular and continuous basis at a publicly quoted price). The system receives orders either by direct entry into its terminals or via an in-house-built TCP/IP socket server (sometimes known as the Stratus Gateway Interface). These orders are routed to the appropriate exchange or market maker according to a set of correspondent-defined rules. Executions are then passed back from the exchange or market maker to CTPS, which updates the order file and forwards the result of the execution to the mainframe.

SQLBIS Database Server

The SQLBIS database server was created to service BNA's trading website, Brokerage Information System (BIS). On the database server are several databases (or data *marts*) that are used by BIS and the BIS Trading Area to look up account and application access as well as cross-references and other information. The ORDERDB database was created exclusively to support the WebSphere applications. In development, the tables and views were created by developers and migrated to production by the database administration (DBA) group.

Model and Develop the Case Study

This section describes the case study trading application using text and diagrams (mostly UML diagrams). This task is not unlike what you as the assignment test taker must accomplish. UML diagrams and use cases can replace what was formerly called the "functional requirements" in an application development scenario. Moreover, UML is an adopted and widely accepted standard used to describe business processing. UML provides benefits to architects and enterprises by facilitating the construction of robust and maintainable business models, which can support the entire software development life cycle (SDLC).

The *use case model* describes the target functionality of a new application. A *use case* represents a unit of interaction between an actor and some function. A *use case diagram* describes an interaction between an actor and the system. It presents a collection of use cases and actors and typically specifies or characterizes the functionality and behavior of a enterprise application interacting with one or more external actors. The users and any system that may interact with the system are the *actors*. Actors help delimit the system and give a clearer picture of what it is supposed to do.

Use cases are developed on the basis of the actors' needs. This ensures that the system will turn out to be what the users expected. Use case diagrams contain stick figure icons that represent actors, association relationships, generalized relationships, packages, and use cases. A top-level use case diagram shows the context of a system and the boundaries of the system's behavior. One or more use case diagrams can be drawn to describe a part of an application system. Use cases can include other use cases as part of their behavior. A use case diagram shows the set of external actors and the system use cases in which the actors participate.

After the use case model is completed and signed off by the business managers, development begins in earnest. For the remainder of the appendix, we will mix some of the UML modeling techniques with the actual development product to illustrate the case study.

A use case model typically comprises the following interrelated components:

- Actor definition
- Business process model
- Sequence diagrams
- Class descriptions
- Class diagrams
- State transition (life cycle) diagrams

Actor Definition

The people involved in the business process are described as a series of actors, who may represent existing jobs or roles in the organization or may be completely new jobs or roles. Table A-2 shows the various actors involved in a business process and their roles.

Business Process Model

A number of *scenarios*—that is, specific examples of performing the task—are identified for each task that is carried out in the business process.

The *business process*, or task model, describes how the business processes will perform the necessary tasks with or without a computer application. It represents an important aspect of the business requirements because it describes from a user and business perspective what work is done. The model provides the basis for designing the functionality of the computer application.

TABLE A-2 Actors and Their Roles

Actor	Description
Customer	Trades with the application according to limits
Trader	Trades with the application without limits
Continuous trade processing system (CTPS)	Routes orders to the mainframe trading system
Mainframe trading system	Holds BNACS back office books and records
SQL (Oracle)	Contains the database reference data

A *business process model* is a model of one or more business processes. Each process has a process owner and process goals (such as encryption, authentication, authorization, cycle time, defect rate, and cost) and consists of a set of business activities (in sequence and/or parallel). Figure A-3 shows an example of a securities trade order and the processing steps it goes through from submission to completion.

Development Environment and Database Design

Before we begin the physical construction of the application components, we must make certain that prerequisite physical items such as infrastructure, development environment, and so on, are in place for use by the development team. In addition to an adequate workstation and the appropriate server(s), the Java EE project libraries and the development GUI presentation tool (such as JBuilder) are accessible to developers with the appropriate permissions in place. The RDBMS application database (in this case, Oracle), with current maintenance and whatever third-party or in-house Java EE development software, is ready for use from each workstation. Developers have been availed of the guidelines and naming standards that the project team agreed to use to develop both the database and the application.

Important for development is the preliminary physical database design used for the application. The database design at this point can differ from that of the final application database design, but it is eventually reconciled in terms of function back to the overall design.

This design of the trade system ORDERDB, shown in Figure A-4, meets the constraints of the DBMS, and because it is derived directly from a composite data model, it also satisfies the system requirements. The rules ensure that the physical design is valid and that it follows good practice. During development, no attempt is made to achieve good performance. Rather, the design provides a sound starting point for physical tuning when the design of both database and Java classes is adjusted to achieve performance objectives. The database characteristics can vary depending on the DBMS being used.

The key characteristics of many of the popular DBMS engines, such as Oracle, are built according to the following seven rules:

1. **Entities** Most entities on the composite data model become tables. The key-only entities may be paired with other key-only entities to form junction tables, which can speed up joins.
2. **Primary keys** The primary key of each entity becomes the primary key of the corresponding table. Specify a UNIQUE index for the entire primary key.

FIGURE A-3 A trade as a business process

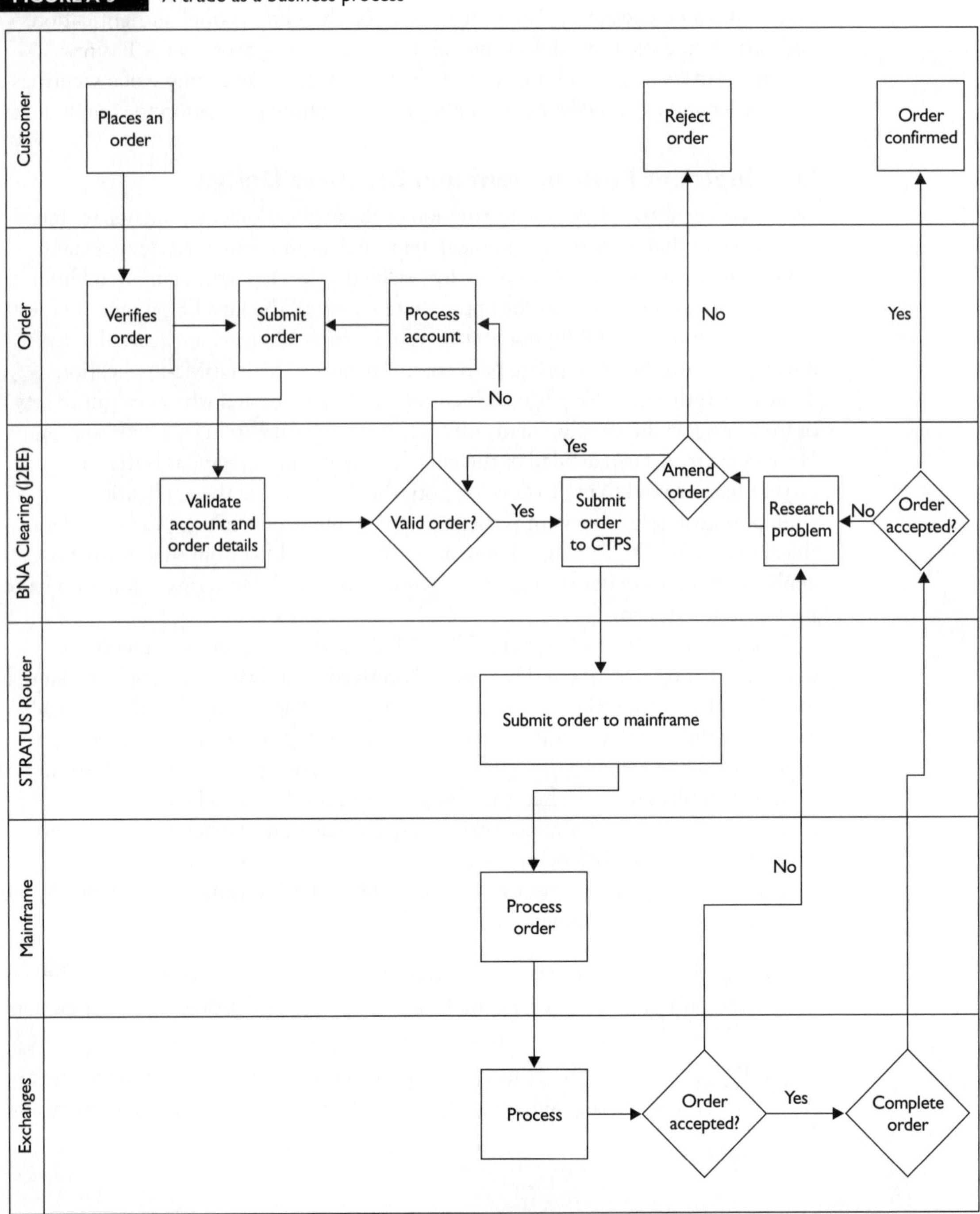

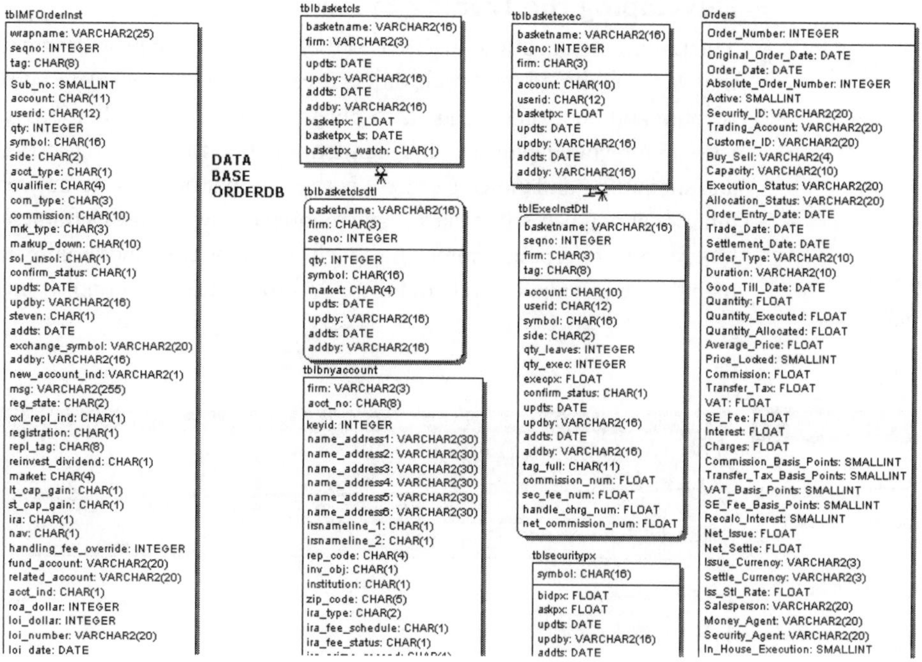

FIGURE A-4 The ORDERDB database

DATA BASE ORDERDB

tblMFOrderInst
wrapname: VARCHAR2(25)
seqno: INTEGER
tag: CHAR(8)
Sub_no: SMALLINT
account: CHAR(11)
userid: CHAR(12)
qty: INTEGER
symbol: CHAR(16)
side: CHAR(2)
acct_type: CHAR(1)
qualifier: CHAR(4)
com_type: CHAR(3)
commission: CHAR(10)
mrk_type: CHAR(3)
markup_down: CHAR(10)
sol_unsol: CHAR(1)
confirm_status: CHAR(1)
updts: DATE
updby: VARCHAR2(16)
steven: CHAR(1)
addts: DATE
exchange_symbol: VARCHAR2(20)
addby: VARCHAR2(16)
new_account_ind: VARCHAR2(1)
msg: VARCHAR2(255)
reg_state: CHAR(2)
cxl_repl_ind: CHAR(1)
registration: CHAR(1)
repl_tag: CHAR(8)
reinvest_dividend: CHAR(1)
market: CHAR(4)
lt_cap_gain: CHAR(1)
st_cap_gain: CHAR(1)
ira: CHAR(1)
nav: CHAR(1)
handling_fee_override: INTEGER
fund_account: VARCHAR2(20)
related_account: VARCHAR2(20)
acct_ind: CHAR(1)
roa_dollar: INTEGER
loi_dollar: INTEGER
loi_number: VARCHAR2(20)
loi_date: DATE

tblbasketols
basketname: VARCHAR2(16)
firm: VARCHAR2(3)
updts: DATE
updby: VARCHAR2(16)
addts: DATE
addby: VARCHAR2(16)
basketpx: FLOAT
basketpx_ts: DATE
basketpx_watch: CHAR(1)

tblbasketolsdtl
basketname: VARCHAR2(16)
firm: CHAR(3)
seqno: INTEGER
qty: INTEGER
symbol: CHAR(16)
market: CHAR(4)
updts: DATE
updby: VARCHAR2(16)
addts: DATE
addby: VARCHAR2(16)

tblbnyaccount
firm: VARCHAR2(3)
acct_no: CHAR(8)
keyid: INTEGER
name_address1: VARCHAR2(30)
name_address2: VARCHAR2(30)
name_address3: VARCHAR2(30)
name_address4: VARCHAR2(30)
name_address5: VARCHAR2(30)
name_address6: VARCHAR2(30)
irsnameline_1: CHAR(1)
irsnameline_2: CHAR(1)
rep_code: CHAR(4)
inv_obj: CHAR(1)
institution: CHAR(1)
zip_code: CHAR(5)
ira_type: CHAR(2)
ira_fee_schedule: CHAR(1)
ira_fee_status: CHAR(1)

tblbasketexec
basketname: VARCHAR2(16)
seqno: INTEGER
firm: CHAR(3)
account: CHAR(10)
userid: CHAR(12)
basketpx: FLOAT
updts: DATE
updby: VARCHAR2(16)
addts: DATE
addby: VARCHAR2(16)

tblExecInstDtl
basketname: VARCHAR2(16)
seqno: INTEGER
firm: CHAR(3)
tag: CHAR(8)
account: CHAR(10)
userid: CHAR(12)
symbol: CHAR(16)
side: CHAR(2)
qty_leaves: INTEGER
qty_exec: INTEGER
execpx: FLOAT
confirm_status: CHAR(1)
updts: DATE
updby: VARCHAR2(16)
addts: DATE
addby: VARCHAR2(16)
tag_full: CHAR(11)
commission_num: FLOAT
sec_fee_num: FLOAT
handle_chrg_num: FLOAT
net_commission_num: FLOAT

tblsecuritypx
symbol: CHAR(16)
bidpx: FLOAT
askpx: FLOAT
updts: DATE
updby: VARCHAR2(16)
addts: DATE

Orders
Order_Number: INTEGER
Original_Order_Date: DATE
Order_Date: DATE
Absolute_Order_Number: INTEGER
Active: SMALLINT
Security_ID: VARCHAR2(20)
Trading_Account: VARCHAR2(20)
Customer_ID: VARCHAR2(20)
Buy_Sell: VARCHAR2(4)
Capacity: VARCHAR2(10)
Execution_Status: VARCHAR2(20)
Allocation_Status: VARCHAR2(20)
Order_Entry_Date: DATE
Trade_Date: DATE
Settlement_Date: DATE
Order_Type: VARCHAR2(10)
Duration: VARCHAR2(10)
Good_Till_Date: DATE
Quantity: FLOAT
Quantity_Executed: FLOAT
Quantity_Allocated: FLOAT
Average_Price: FLOAT
Price_Locked: SMALLINT
Commission: FLOAT
Transfer_Tax: FLOAT
VAT: FLOAT
SE_Fee: FLOAT
Interest: FLOAT
Charges: FLOAT
Commission_Basis_Points: SMALLINT
Transfer_Tax_Basis_Points: SMALLINT
VAT_Basis_Points: SMALLINT
SE_Fee_Basis_Points: SMALLINT
Recalc_Interest: SMALLINT
Net_Issue: FLOAT
Net_Settle: FLOAT
Issue_Currency: VARCHAR2(3)
Settle_Currency: VARCHAR2(3)
Iss_Stl_Rate: FLOAT
Salesperson: VARCHAR2(20)
Money_Agent: VARCHAR2(20)
Security_Agent: VARCHAR2(20)
In_House_Execution: SMALLINT

3. **Alternate keys** Each alternate key becomes a UNIQUE secondary index.
4. **Foreign keys** Indexing each entity foreign key becomes a secondary NON-UNIQUE index.
5. **Referential integrity** Make each entity foreign key a FOREIGN KEY for the table, referencing the master of the supported relationship.
6. **Other non-unique keys** All other non-unique keys becomes a NON-UNIQUE index on the corresponding column(s).
7. **Exclusive relationships** If a detail entity has two or more mutually exclusive masters:
   - Provide foreign key indexes to support each relationship, as defined in Rule 4.
   - The foreign key columns for the relationships should all be defined as NULLS ALLOWED.
   - Maintenance of exclusivity must be handled by the program.

Developing the Trading System

The trading system is a browser-based user interface that provides trading functionality—that is, the ability to send trade orders (even baskets of stocks) and view customer account and trade order requests to BNA. Written in Java EE, it provides the customer with an integrated, platform-independent method for accessing account information and submitting and viewing orders via the Internet or a private network. All trading functionality is accessible via a single menu page, which uses a frameset with a header, footer, and a navigation frame on the left to expose the functionality in the right-side main frame (no pun intended). Figure A-5 shows the main trading frameset.

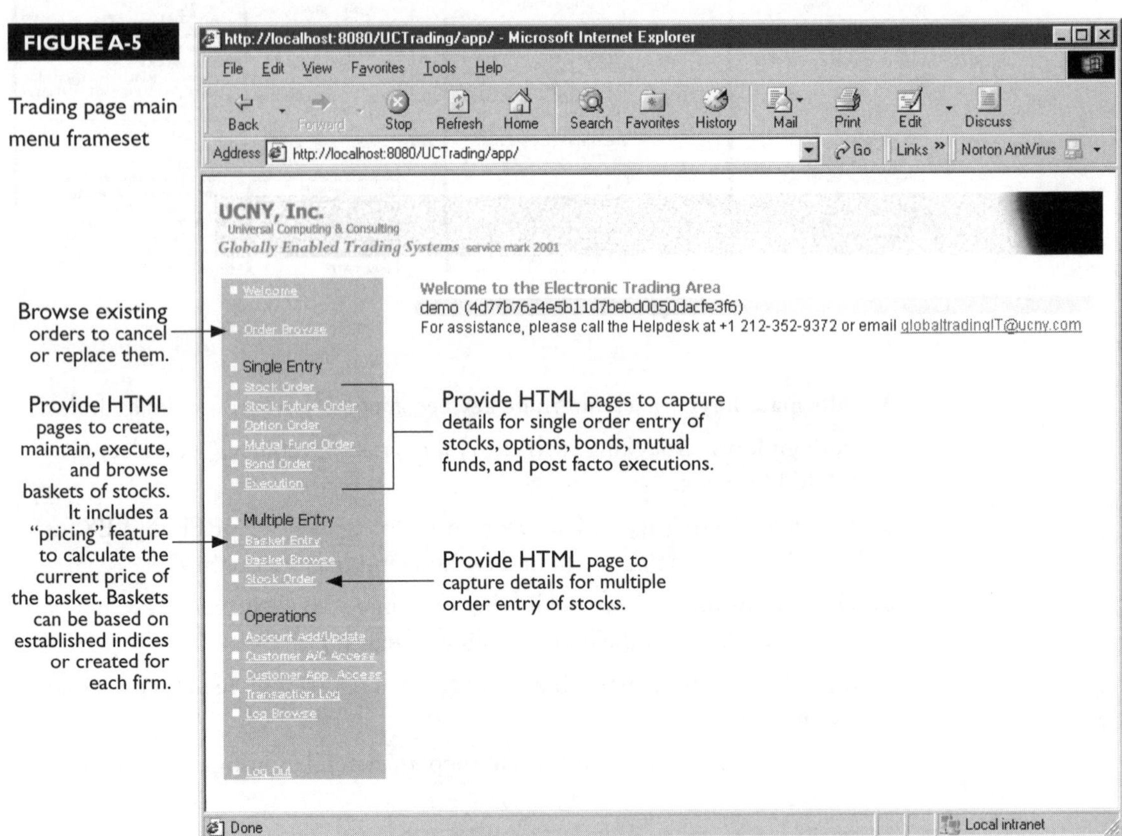

FIGURE A-5 Trading page main menu frameset

On the left side of the trading page is a frame that exposes the functionality that is currently available for trading—stocks, bonds, mutual funds, as well as baskets and multiple orders—along with some basic operational functionality used to maintain accounts and other external information. The main trading application page and operations page can be depicted as use case diagrams, as shown in Figures A-6 and A-7.

Table A-3 describes the use case task goals and scenarios.

Sequence Diagrams

Sequence diagrams are models of business processes that represent the different interactions between actors and objects in the system. Each process has a process owner and goals (such as cycle time, defect rate, and cost) and consists of a set

FIGURE A-6 Trading page functionality as a use case

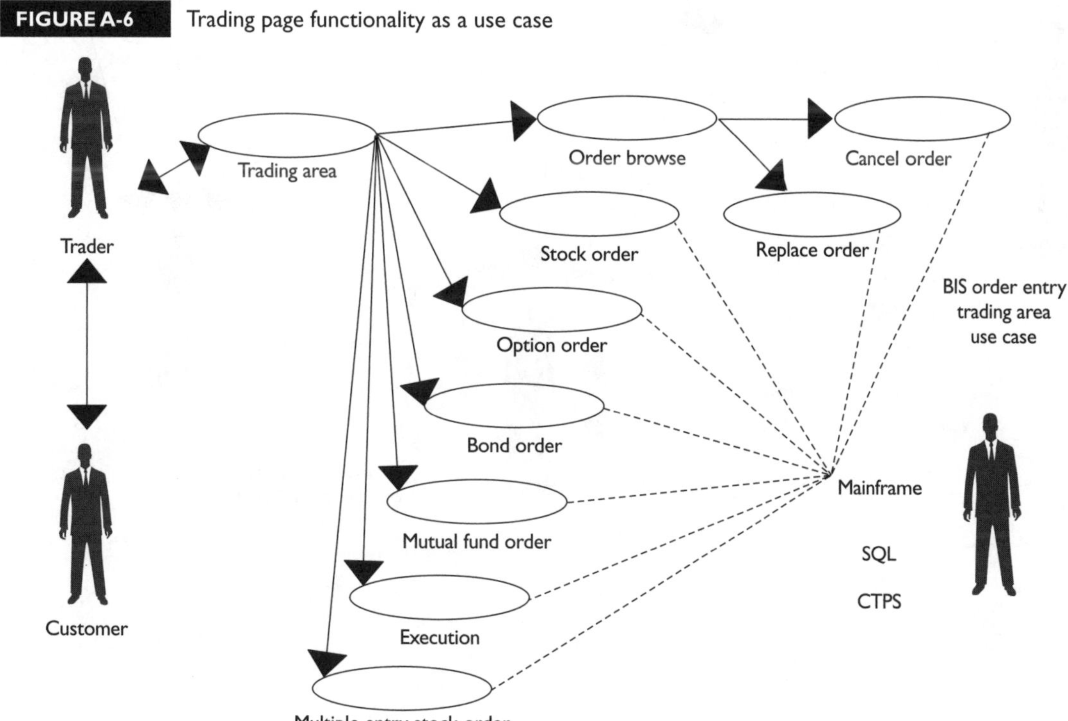

FIGURE A-7 Operations page functionality as a use case

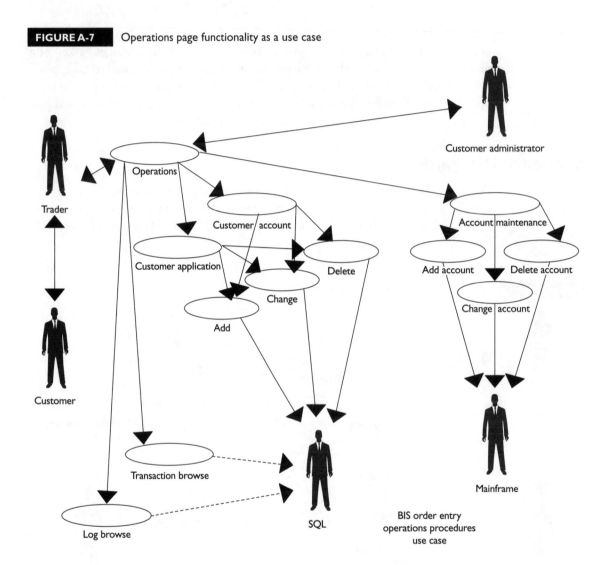

Customer administrator

Trader

Operations

Customer account

Account maintenance

Customer application

Delete

Add account

Delete account

Change

Change account

Add

Customer

Transaction browse

Mainframe

Log browse

SQL

BIS order entry
operations procedures
use case

TABLE A-3 Tasks and Scenarios

Task Name	Task Goal	Task Scenarios
All forms of order entry: equity, bonds, mutual funds, baskets	Send order to CTPS routed to the mainframe trading system.	Order information is keyed in, and information is edited and routed to CTPS and ultimately to the mainframe trading system for processing.
Order browse	Review/cancel/replace orders that have been previously sent to the CTPS-mainframe trading system.	Previously entered order information is edited and sometimes replaced; information is edited and routed to CTPS and ultimately to the mainframe trading system for processing.
Account maintenance	Add/update/delete retail customer accounts.	Account information is edited and sometimes replaced; information is edited and routed to the mainframe trading system for processing.
Customer application maintenance	Add/update/delete customer application entitlement.	Application information is edited and sometimes replaced; information is edited and routed to SQL for processing.
Customer account maintenance	Add/update/delete customer account/user entitlement.	Account/user information is edited and sometimes replaced; information is edited and routed to SQL for processing.

of business activities (in sequence and/or in parallel). Figure A-8 depicts the sequence of a trade order being placed by a customer as it moves through the Java EE application server for verification and onto the trade process router, to the mainframe, and then to the securities exchange, where the actual trade is executed. After a confirmed execution, each of the front-end processors is notified, and ultimately the customer is availed of the completed order and price.

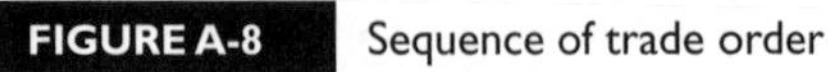

FIGURE A-8 Sequence of trade order

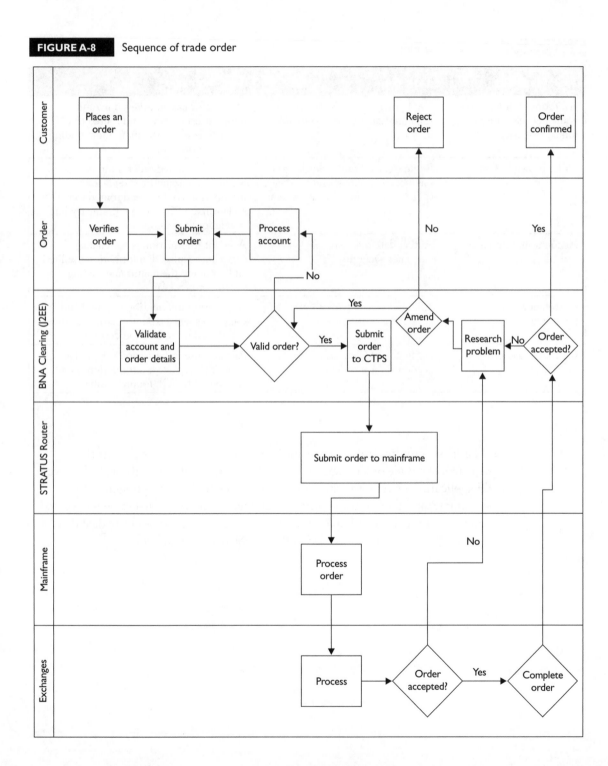

TABLE A-4 Business Classes and Descriptions

Class	Description
Customer	A person who orders securities
Potential Customer	A member of the general public who makes inquiries about the company's publications to potentially order publications from the company
Order	A request for a security
Order Inquiry	An inquiry from a customer concerning an order that has been placed
Delivery	When the security that is purchased is sent to the customer portfolio
Payment	The payment by a customer for securities ordered and/or received
Company	BNACS
Order Browse	A request to view all outstanding security orders
Order Cancel	A request to cancel all outstanding security orders
Order Replace	A request to replace all outstanding security orders

Class Descriptions

Table A-4 describes the business classes, some of which are included in the business process sequence diagram in Figure A-8.

Class Diagrams

Using the initial list of business classes, you develop class diagrams by identifying and defining the relationships among the classes. This is best done in an interactive development workshop with business partners. It is also useful to keep these diagrams on display on a whiteboard or other medium, and to develop it gradually as the project progresses. The diagrams can also be stored on a UML tool to provide access to all team members and other interested parties.

The class diagrams are also used to show relationships among classes. This aspect of the diagrams will tend to emerge later in the design process, as "lower-level" classes are identified. The class diagrams will improve the definition of the classes, which in turn may require changes to the sequence diagrams and, when developed, the state transition diagrams. These other diagrams will also have an impact on the class diagrams.

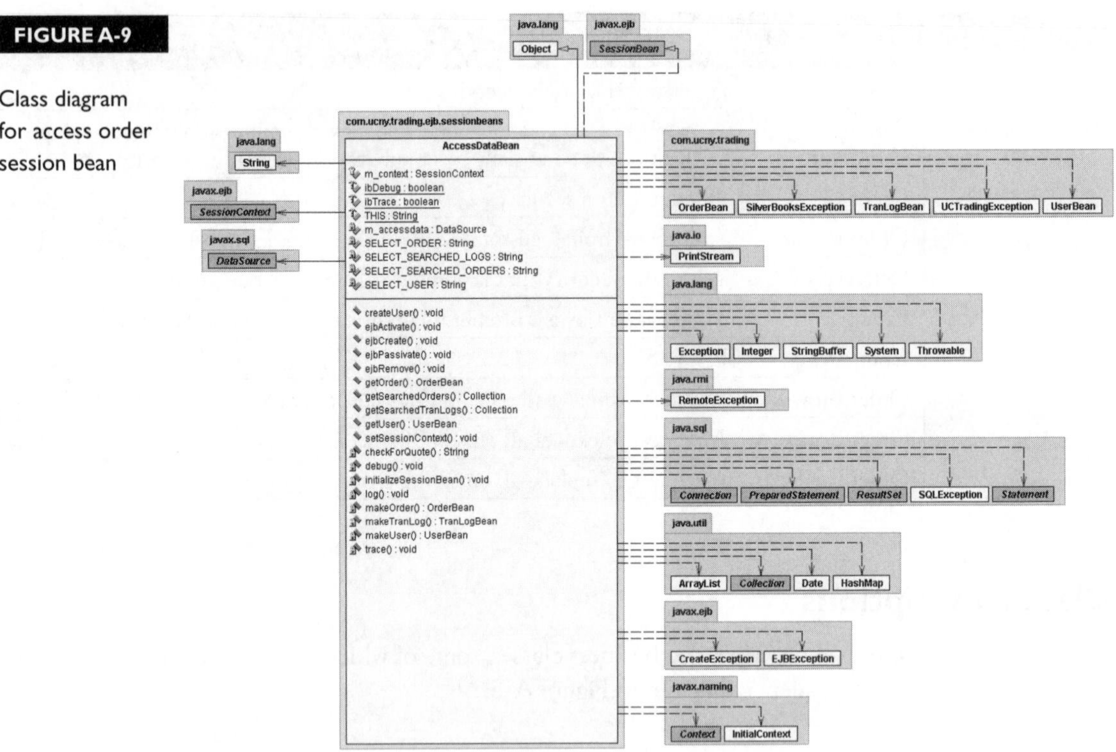

FIGURE A-9

Class diagram for access order session bean

Two important classes in terms of the back-end processing are the Enterprise JavaBeans (EJB) session beans that process orders: the `AccessOrderBean` will send and track orders, and the `AccessDataBean` will provide associated data pertaining to the customer and the associated order(s). Figures A-9 and A-10 are UML class diagrams illustrating the methods and associations for each of these classes.

State Transition (Life Cycle) Diagrams

It is useful to trace what happens to a class through the execution of a business process, or through the computer system that is developed to support the business process. The state transition diagrams show the various states in which a class can exist and the way in which the class changes from one state to another. Figure A-11 shows a state transition of trade order processing.

FIGURE A-10

Class diagram for access data session bean

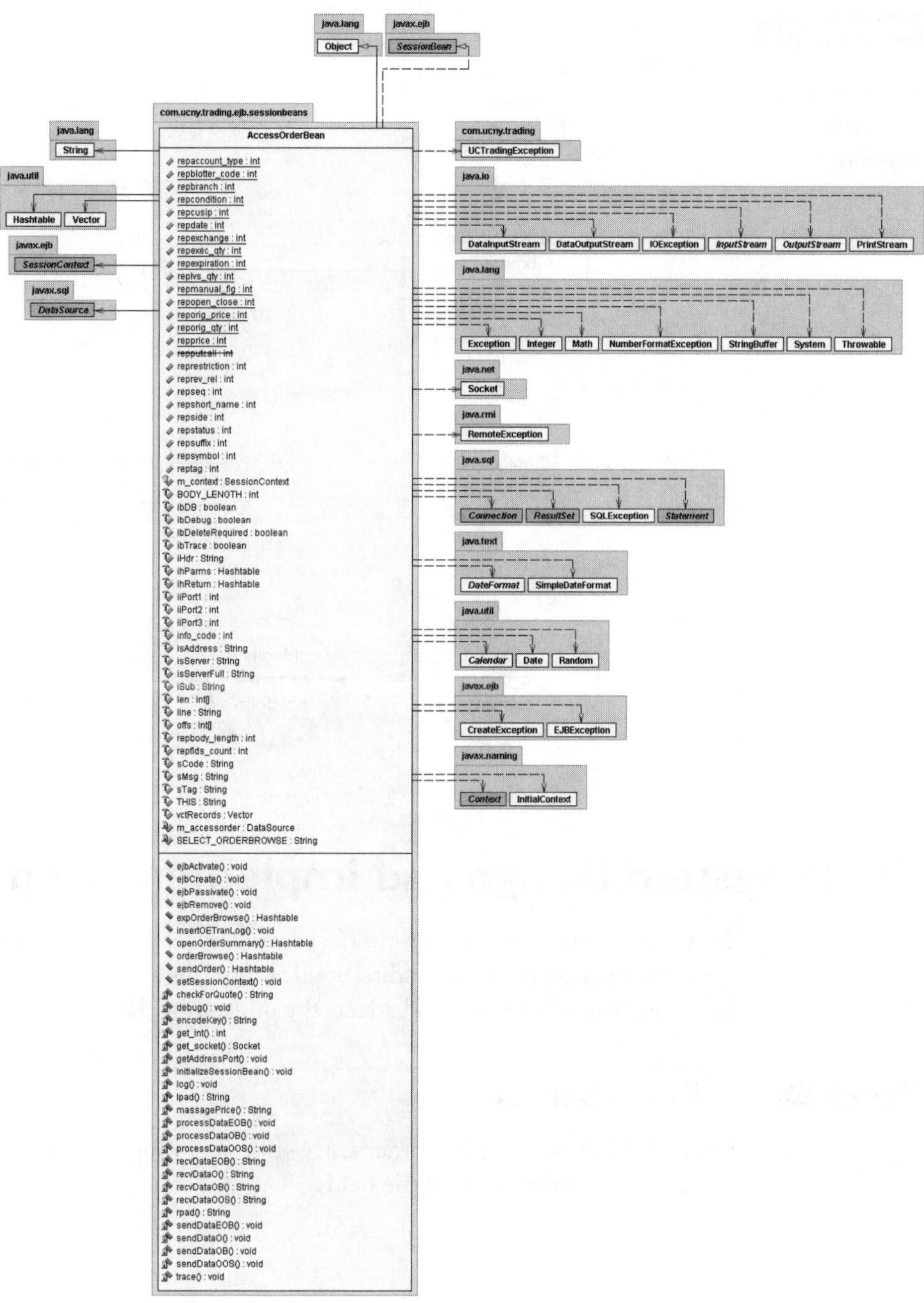

FIGURE A-11

State transition (life cycle) diagrams

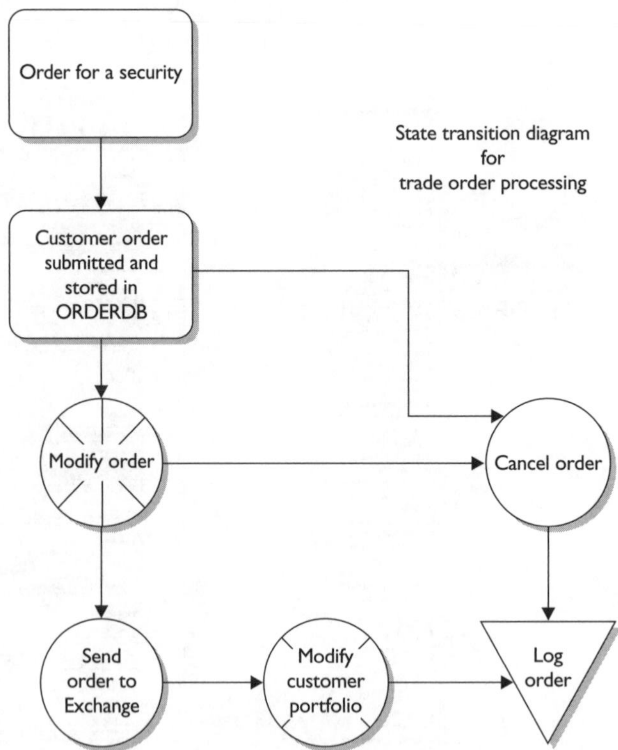

Trade System Design and Implementation

This section describes the user interface layout, class diagrams, controls, actions, and navigational aspects for the trading application. It is a comprehensive description of how the application works and affects the underlying data elements.

Stock Order Entry Screen

Figure A-12 shows the stock order entry screen, in which a buyer clicks Stock Order and enters information in all the fields.

FIGURE A-12

Equity trade order screen

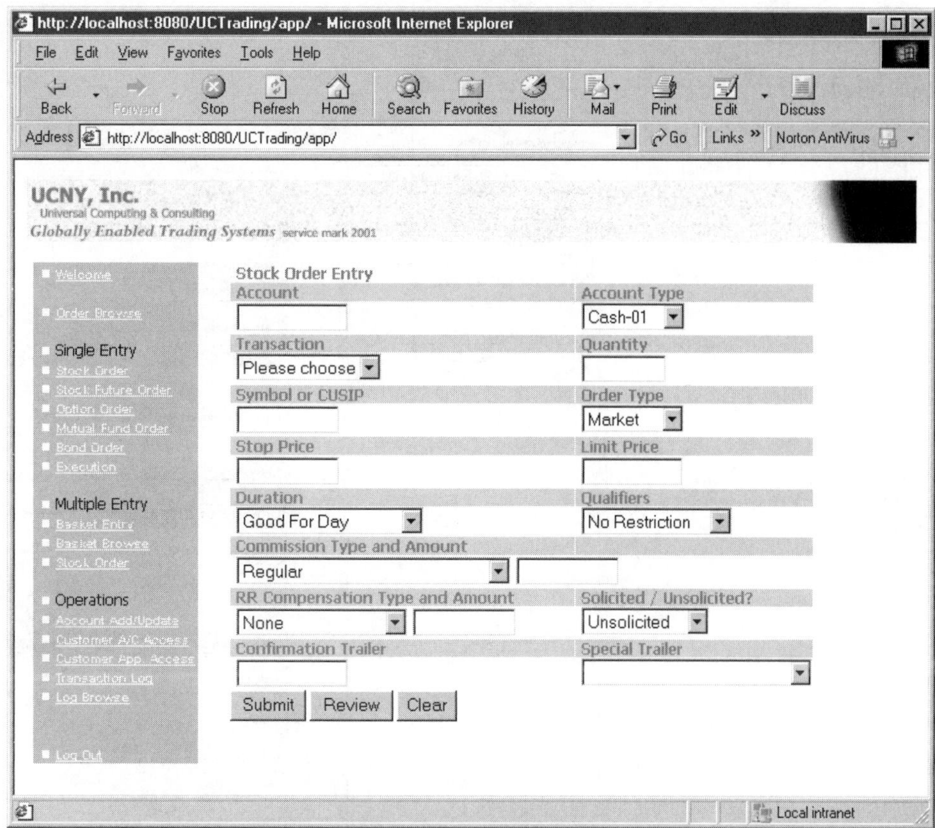

Figure A-13 shows a class diagram that identifies and defines the relationships between the classes.

In Figure A-14, you can see that a buy order has been placed for 100 shares of IBM at the market price for account 14112345678.

Table A-5 shows the controls and descriptions of the information entered as well as validity notes regarding what each control should contain.

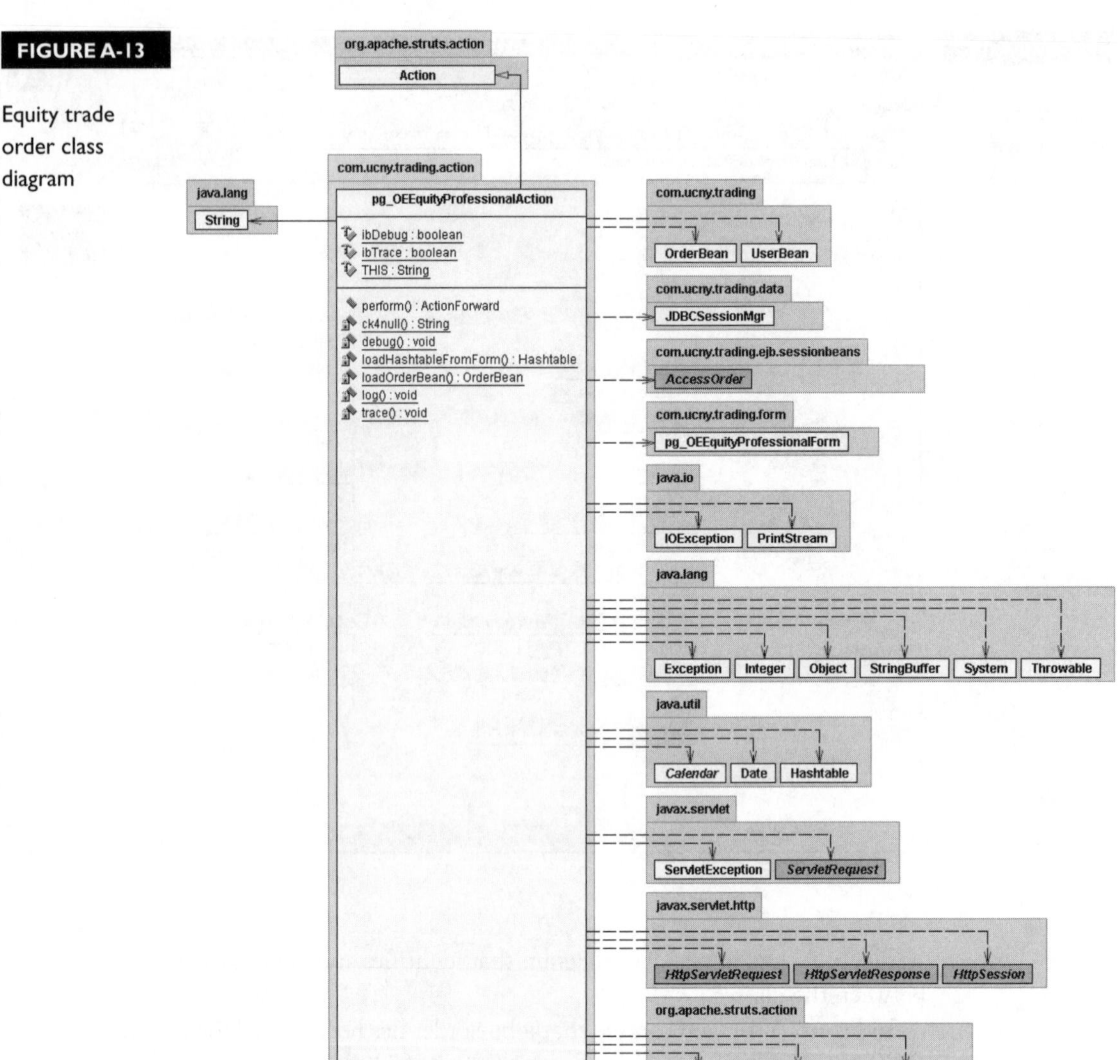

FIGURE A-13 Equity trade order class diagram

FIGURE A-14

Submission and execution of trade order

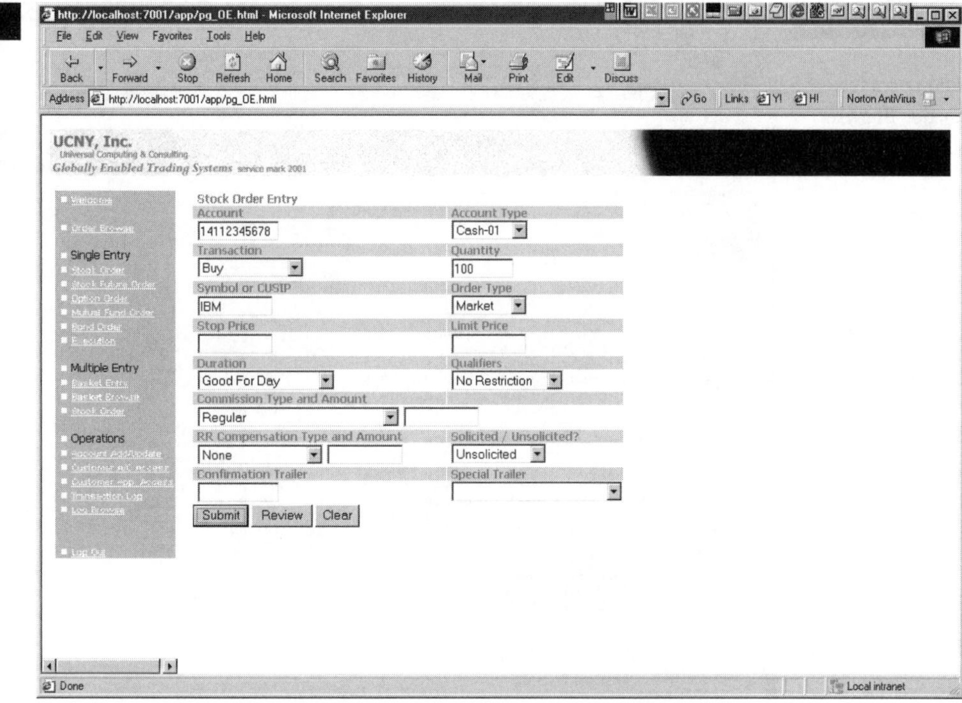

TABLE A-5 Controls on the Trading Page

Controls	Description
Account	The customer's account number. Valid values: This is from the Customer Information System CIS system.
Account Type	The valid values are Cash, Margin, and Short.
Transaction	Side of the transaction. Valid values are B, SL, SS, and Buy Cover.
Quantity	How many shares of the security. Valid values: Numeric/integer > 0.
Symbol or CUSIP	Security identifier/symbol or CUSIP. Valid values: Symbol checked against warehouse security table.
Messages	Green or red, depending on the result. Green is success; red is problematic. Note that in Figure A-14 this control is not visible prior to the order being submitted.
Submit button	Process the data and exit the form.
Review button	Review and exit the form.
Clear button	Cancel the data entered and exit the form.

FIGURE A-15

Equity trade Order Browse screen

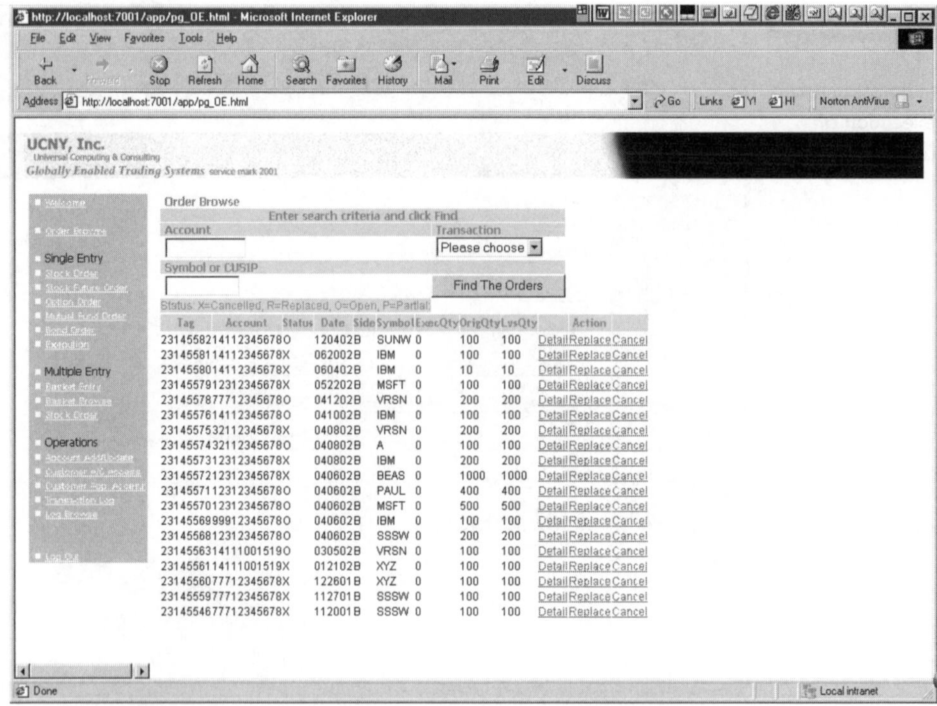

Figure A-15 shows the Order Browse screen, where you enter an account, a transaction side (that is, B for Buy or S for Sell), or a symbol and then click Find The Orders. All of the buy orders are shown here.

Figure A-16 shows a class diagram that identifies and defines the relationships among the classes.

Trade Application Packages

After all the application components are completed and the application is ready for deployment, a package diagram (or diagrams) can be used to describe associations among the component classes. Figures A-17, A-18, and A-19 show package diagrams for `com.ucny.trading`, `com.ucny.trading.ejb.sessionbeans`, `com.ucny.trading.data`, and `com.ucny.trading.action`, which tie together all the components (JSPs, EJBs, JavaBeans, and so on).

FIGURE A-16

Class diagram for equity trade Order Browse screen

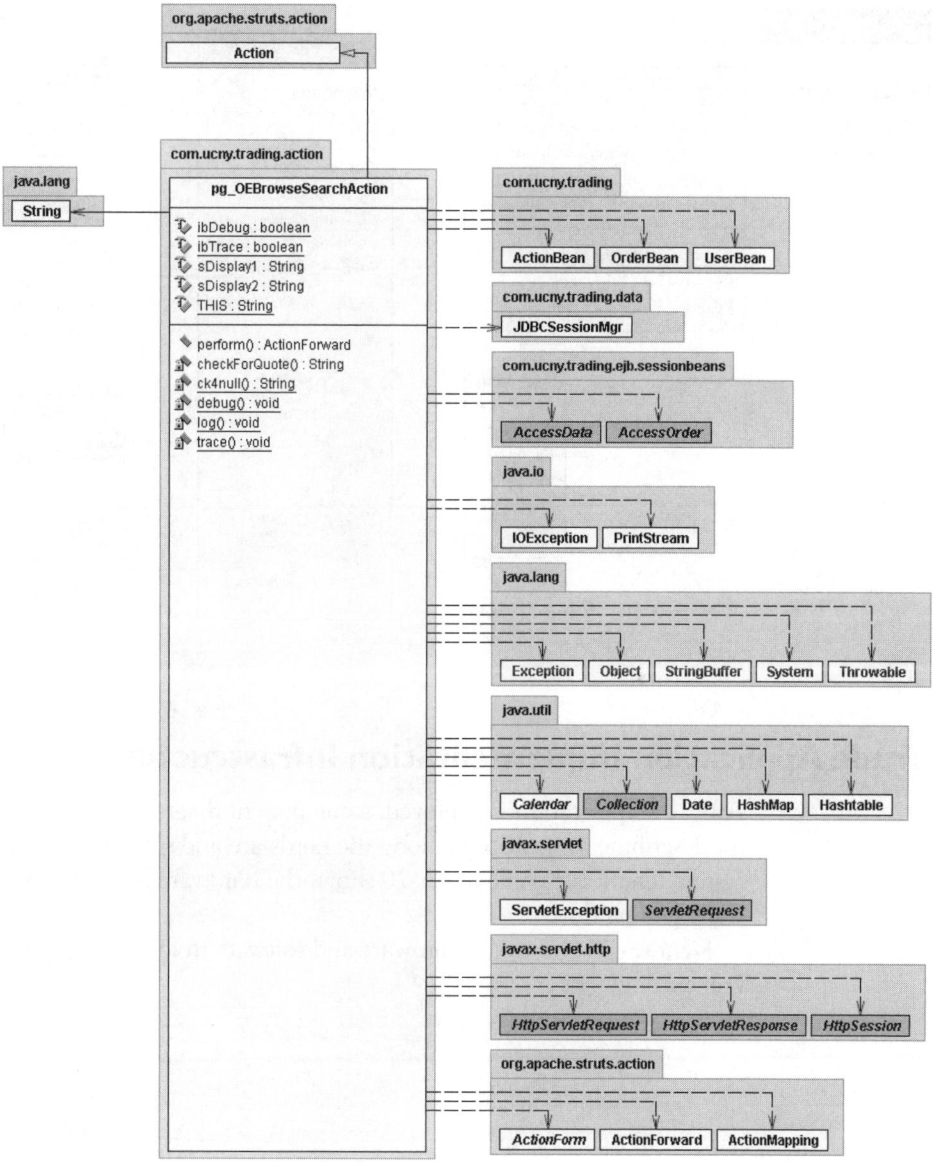

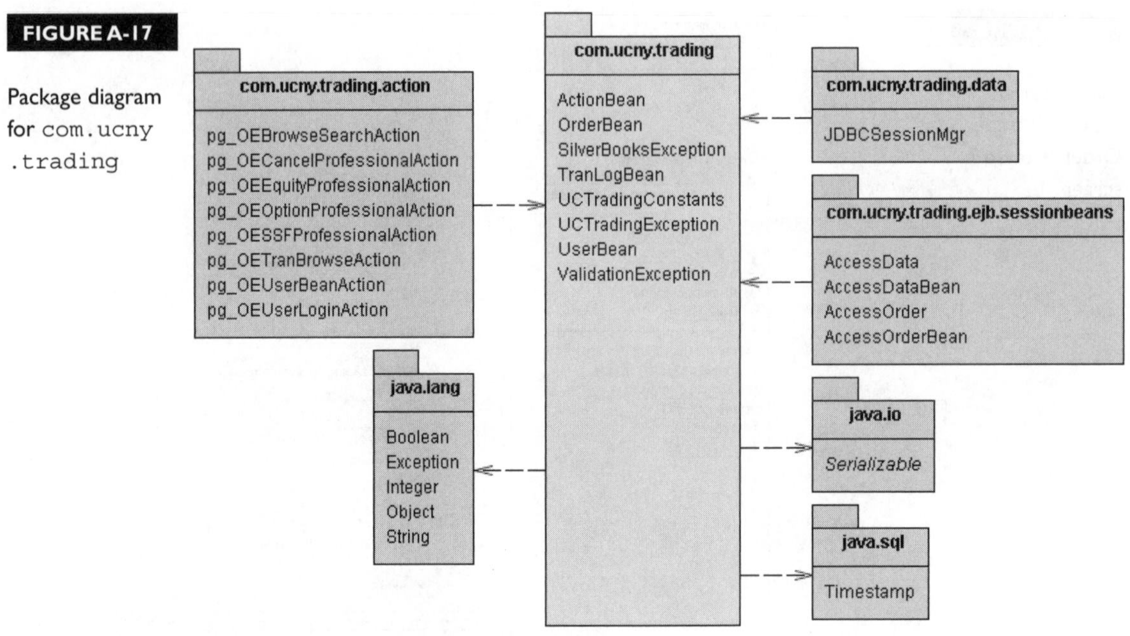

FIGURE A-17 Package diagram for `com.ucny.trading`

Trade Application Implementation Infrastructure

After the application is deployed, a component diagram (or diagrams) can be useful for describing associations among the hardware and software components and the system functionality. Figure A-20 shows the hardware and software involved in the trade process flow.

Figure A-21 shows the hardware and software involved in the security pricing process flow.

FIGURE A-18

Package diagram for `com.ucny.trading.ejb.sessionbeans`

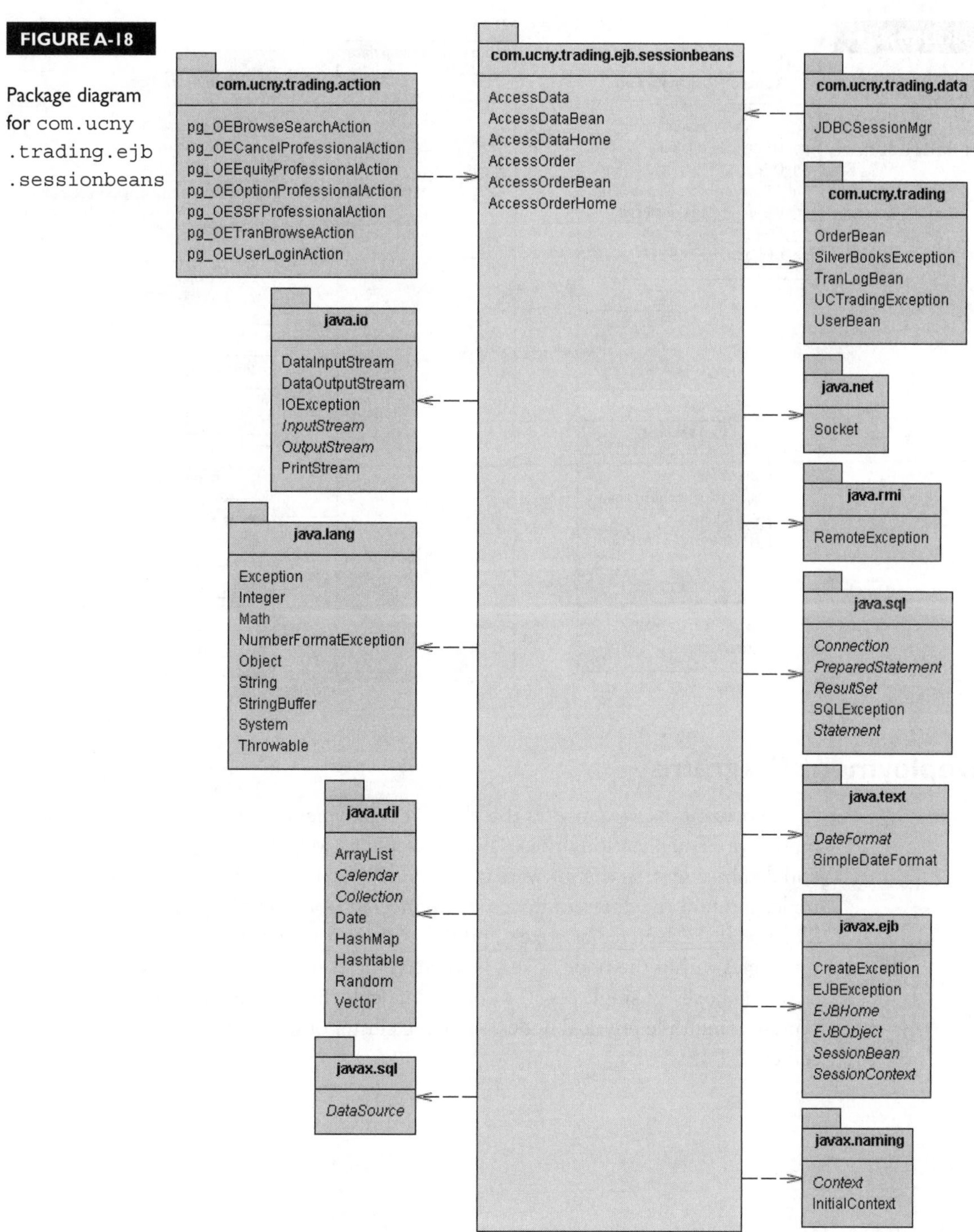

FIGURE A-19

Package diagram for `com.ucny.trading.data`

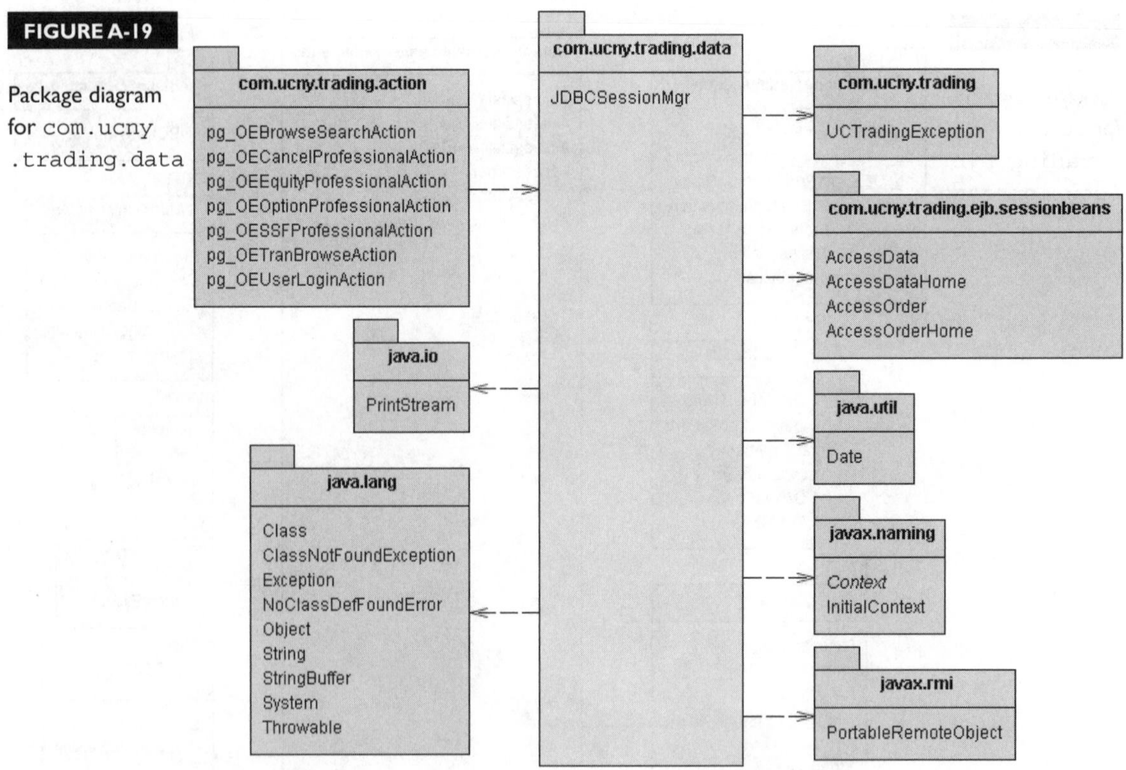

Deployment Diagrams

A deployment diagram models the physical deployment of artifacts on nodes. For most Java EE applications, these "nodes" would be web servers, application servers, and database servers, the software components ("artifacts") that run on each node, and how the different nodes are connected (for example, JDBC or REST). The nodes are depicted as boxes, and the artifacts for each node are depicted as rectangles within the node boxes. Nodes can have subnodes, which are depicted as nested boxes. A single box (or node) in a deployment diagram can conceptually represent multiple physical nodes, such as a cluster of web, application, or database servers.

FIGURE A-20 Hardware and software involved in the trade process flow

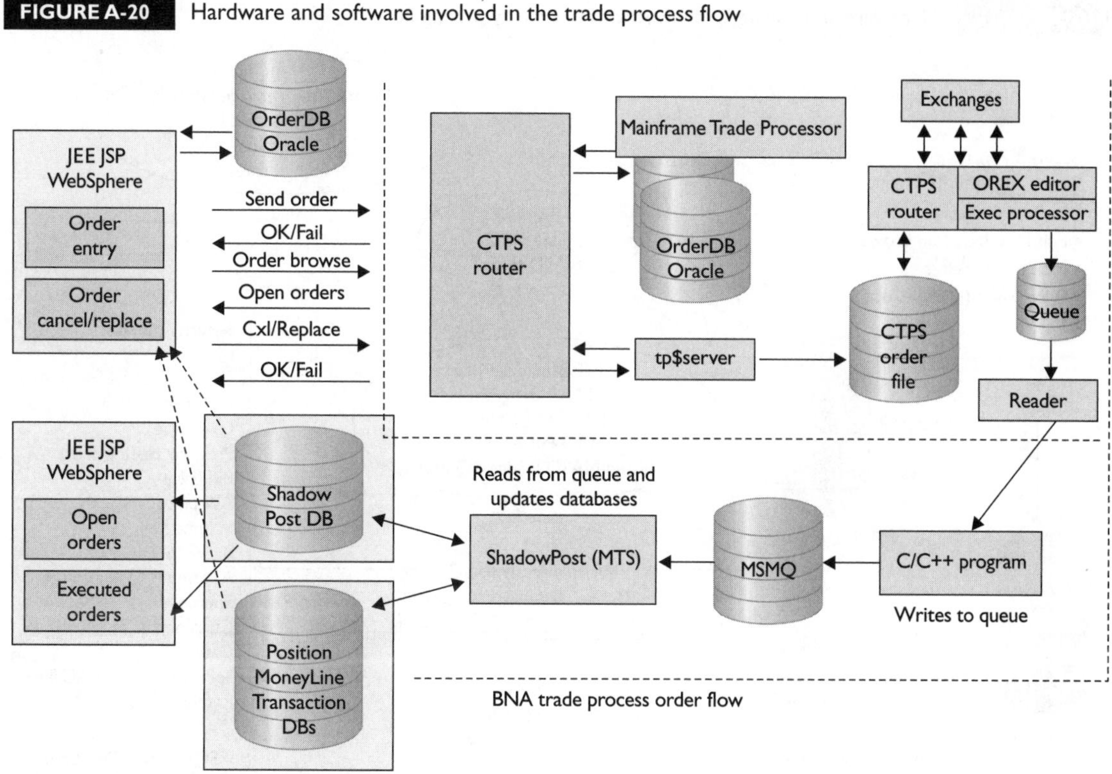

Deployment diagrams, as such, do not add significant marks to the overall submission, but they do convey that you, as an enterprise architect, have seriously considered the hardware and software needed in a production environment to make the solution a reality.

Figure A-22 shows the deployment diagram for the trading application.

FIGURE A-21 Hardware and software involved in the security pricing flow

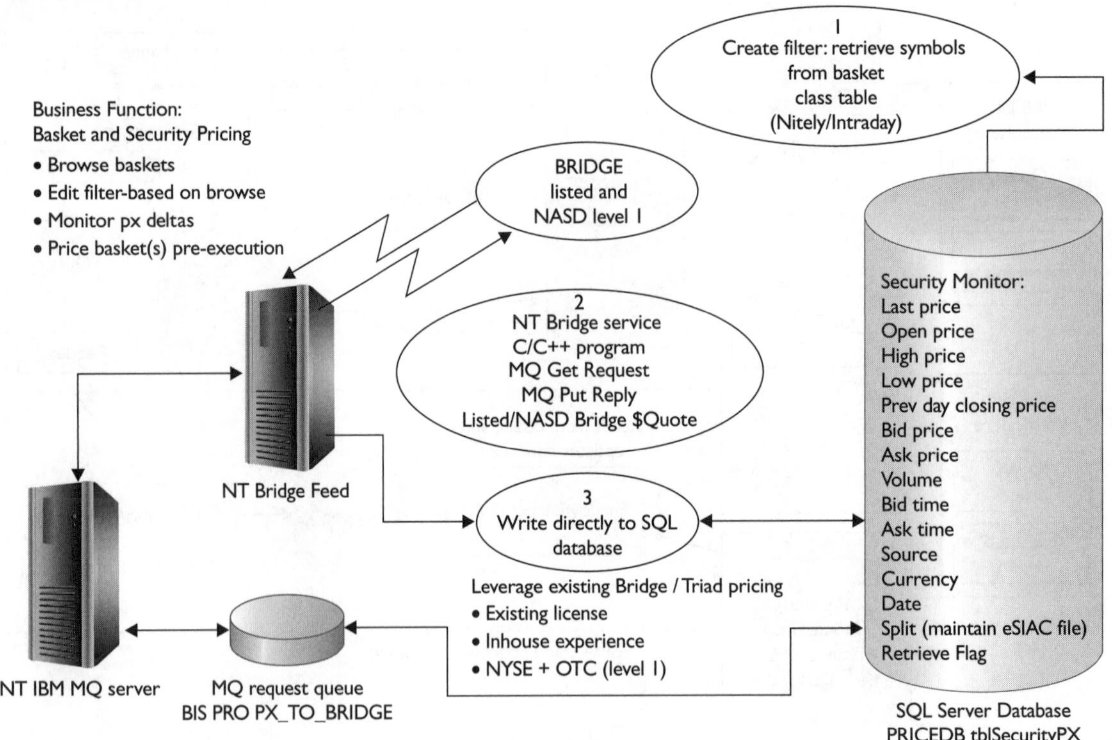

Security pricing

Assumptions:

- The NT Bridge machine will start a service at 4AM each business day
- It will establish a connection with Bridge and send a request for issues (currently approximately 4000)
- The service will issue MQ GET's to determine requests for symbols and their prices
- A special request message type will be set up to "throttle" the speed of the price feed delivery
- The service will issue MQ PUT's to reply with price information
- The queues are configured for destructive read

FIGURE A-22 Deployment diagram for the trading application

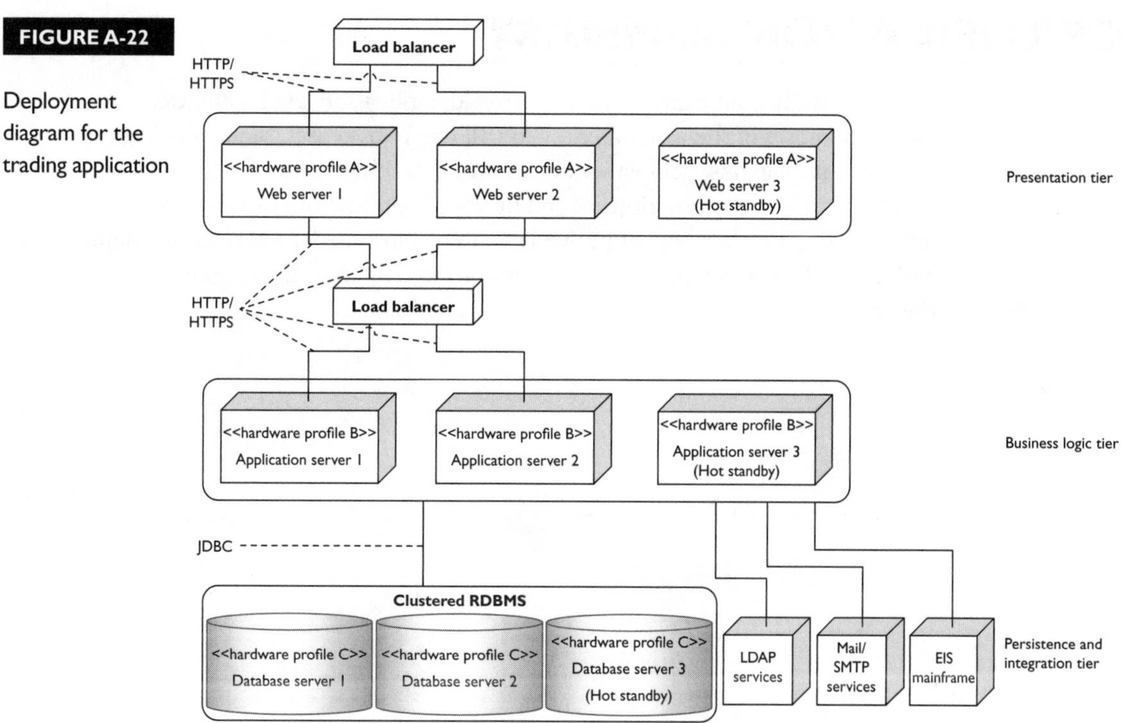

Final Tips

Apart from the obvious point of making it as easy as possible for the examiner to find the information necessary to grade and hopefully give a passing mark to your submission, here are some additional tips:

- Ensure your diagrams are clear and legible. Make sure that the tool you use to draw can output a diagram in an acceptable file and image format.
- Ensure that your assignment submission documents and focuses on the business solution.

CERTIFICATION SUMMARY

This case study is an example of a real-world application. As an architect, and for the purposes of the assignment, you will create use cases, sequence diagrams, component diagrams, deployment diagrams, and other types of diagrams to provide a clear picture of the functions of an enterprise application. Its infrastructure, functionality, and deployment particulars can be illustrated using UML in conjunction with other diagramming and text descriptions to help in evaluating and understanding the application.

B

Java (EE) Enterprise Architect Certified Master Essay Exam

The Part 2 architecture (P2A) is your proposed conceptual model of the objects, relationships, and processes that provide the solution. In Part 3, you are asked to review aspects of your P2A and explain and justify your design process. For example, you need to explain how your P2A identified and eliminated inefficiencies, such as superfluous steps in a process. During your P2A design, development, and representation of the architectural idea/solution, you hopefully will have developed documentation and an explanation of the relationship between the design process and the architectural outcome. This will enable you to successfully describe the orchestration of the various design instruments (for example, UML) and to communicate your architectural concept and its resolution during the allotted time. That said, this appendix presents some essay answer examples to general/typical questions posed in Part 3 and some tips on preparation.

You will be asked to appear at the testing center and in 120 minutes (two hours) provide your reasoning for all the choices made in Part 2. That said, you will have hopefully documented Part 2 architecture choices and their justification. In the real world of enterprise computing, decisions concerning architecture and infrastructure are formalized and include a compare/contrast survey of the alternatives. For the essay exam, you should take the time to formally answer the questions posed in this appendix. This will force you to review your application and to draft answers to typical questions included herein.

As mentioned, Part 3 is a set of essay questions related to your project. Exam Parts 2 and 3 should be done within six months after the assignment is downloaded. The essays we include in the chapters of this book should help you with this part. Eight essay questions appear in Part 3, and you get 120 minutes to complete them. As you saw in Appendix A, the Part 2 sample assignment requires that you architect a solution for a bank securities trading system. You will be graded on correctly solving the technical and performance requirements.

In Appendix A, we presented you with a securities trading solution. Most systems in the real world start off and perhaps end with architecture review and justification, which is what we will do in this appendix. You explain why your architecture is the best choice considering all the alternatives. The particular case study application in Appendix A was developed for a Wall Street clearing firm that interacted with hundreds of correspondent trade brokers and their customers. It was designed to help the firm by facilitating the customers' ability to trade securities on the Web. Typical Part 3 essay questions are:

- How does your design handle availability?
- How does your application interact and communicate with external systems and applications?

Because the questions are somewhat predictable, you should prepare and write some of them out as preparation. That said, let's begin.

The Case Study Infrastructure

Bank of New Amsterdam (BNA) has several different operating systems running many kinds of software systems. The primary platform for the production business data is the mainframe. In addition, peripheral Microsoft and Unix boxes provide Internet services and other software to provide reporting capabilities, using a SQL-based DBMS shadow copy of the business data. BNA also has an investment in SQL-based DBMS (for example, Oracle on the S/390). Several preexisting legacy applications provide trade-processing links to the major securities exchanges. These applications work well and have been developed and maintained for the past two decades, during which time a great deal of time and money has been spent to maintain them. The applications do not need modification; instead, they are constantly "facaded" using a browser/web front end to service the growing base of mobile devices.

The advantages of using the mainframe include its reliability, scalability, flexibility, and security. The mainframe has been running continuously for years in BNA without major problems. The mainframe can easily be amended to add hardware resources, such as CPU, memory, disk, and networking hardware, to increase capacity without changing the operating system or application systems. In addition, the CPU, memory, and disk space can be redistributed as application requirements change.

Java Database Connectivity (JDBC) connection pooling and Java's platform independence provide the performance and scalability needed. Because budget is a limiting factor in an economic downturn, where every developer is competing for business, it is critical that you deliver a solution quickly that will integrate with the organization's existing infrastructure. The clustered HTTP server, clustered application servers, and SQL-based enterprise relational database management system (RDBMS) are all in existence on the company's legacy IBM mainframe enterprise servers. The enterprise servers are clustered for failover and load balancing. They can handle JSF, JSPs, and servlets, they run SOAP and REST services as well as EJBs, and they provide JDBC connection pools and caching to access and update user data.

Application Servers

The application servers are also connected via TCP/IP sockets to the bank's mainframe set (BNACS API). This API is used to communicate with and retrieve information from the mainframe system via an XML/JSON-based message format. Finally, the JEE application server is connected to the bank's CTPS (the continuous trade-processing system) application. The JEE application server's application sends and maintains orders, and it can look up order status by communicating with CTPS via an XML/JSON message format.

Continuous Trade Processing

The CTPS system is an order-routing system that is connected to several exchanges and market makers (firms that stand ready to buy and sell a particular stock on a regular and continuous basis at a publicly quoted price). The system receives orders either by direct entry into its terminals or via an in-house-built interface. These orders are routed to the appropriate exchange or market maker according to a set of correspondent-defined rules. Executions are then passed back from the exchange or market maker to CTPS, which updates the order file and forwards the result of the execution to the mainframe.

SQLBIS Database Server

The SQLBIS database server was created to service BNA's trading website, Brokerage Information System (BIS). On the database server are several databases (or data *marts*) that are used by BIS and the BIS Trading Area to look up account and application access as well as cross-references and other information. The ORDERDB database was created exclusively to support the JEE application server's applications. In development, the tables and views were created by developers and migrated to production by the database administration (DBA) group.

Essay Questions and Sample Answers

As the exam site puts it, "This is another stimulating test to verify your architectural knowledge about design decisions." As you know by now, architectures can be implemented in many ways, with different design decisions. The questions on the exam will ask why you have chosen a certain way and why not another way. You need to answer such questions with a focused explanation. To that end, this section presents some typical questions and answers for Part 3.

How Does Your Design Handle Availability?

The availability of a system is the degree to which a system, subsystem, or equipment is operable and in a committable state. The conditions determining operability must be specified. Availability is the ratio of (a) the total time a functional unit is capable of being used during a given interval to (b) the length of the interval.

Because our trading application has users in every part of the globe, our required availability is virtually 168/168—that is, the application must be available for all 168 hours in a week, with the exception of holidays and some softer parts of the trading week (for example, weekends). Our availability objective, specified in decimal fractions, is 0.9998. To accomplish this, we employ the use of application server clustering for load balancing and failover. We keep our front-end UI components as stateless as possible by using granular services. Our enterprise mainframe is always online because it is the "books and records" of the firm, and today's risk compliance law mandates that it is constantly checking its pulse and responding to issues immediately. Additionally, we set up our trading application such that it always accepts orders, placing them in a message queue. We use our back-end application servers to handle the queued requests ("make a trade" and "get a price"), allowing us to spot and respond to spikes and add queue handlers as necessary—essentially providing redundancy and failover. Moreover, we review and audit all activity and monitor component thresholds to avoid failures.

How Does Your Design Handle Reliability?

Reliability is the ability of an item to perform a required function under stated conditions for a specified period of time. Reliability is also the probability that a functional unit will perform its required function for a specified interval under stated conditions. For example, in the trading application, the reliability of the "BUY" or "SELL" transaction is critical to the operation of the system. An outage transaction, for example, can effectively shut down the business. For users requesting a trade in markets that are not yet open, we can make the outage invisible to user: "I'll take your order and inform if there's a problem."

In the arena of Internet trading and ubiquitous computing, the consumer cannot be placed in the position of troubleshooting the computer system. Reliability is critical because, eventually, users expect the trading system to work just as well as any other appliance in their life—and even better. Our clustered solution provides load balancing and is capable of routing all traffic to a "round-robin" stack of servers; therefore, if any server is inoperable, it is removed from the stack.

The steps taken to promote availability also contribute to the reliability of the system. In a typical HA cluster, instances of an application run simultaneously on application servers in the cluster. Each has its own Java Virtual Machine. Because each server has its own JVM, if you update data in a local cache, the effects of the update will only be seen by that JVM. For that reason we employ a real-time distributed cache to keep data synchronized across the JVMs. To facilitate the stateless HTTP protocol, our application uses the HTTP session to store session information. In our clustered environment, we replicate session data in real time. This is done by saving the session data in a database and then enabling replication at the database level.

How Does Your Design Handle Scalability?

Scalability is the ability to support the required trading system availability and performance as the transactional load increases. In our trading system, we can respond and make transaction performance increases using "vertical scalability." For this we can add capacity (memory and CPUs) to existing servers. We can also respond and make transaction availability increases via "horizontal scalability" by adding servers. In terms of scalability, our trading system can scale to accommodate more users and higher transaction volumes in several different ways:

- We can upgrade the hardware platform. Our use of JEE servers is a solution that offers platform independence and enables rapid deployment and easier integration of new technology.
- We can improve the efficiency of communications. In a distributed environment, the communications overhead is often a performance bottleneck. We add session management to improve communication among clients and servers through session pooling.

- Our use of clustering provides transparent access to multiple servers to increase throughput during peak loads. The load balancing provided by clustering is necessary to support the unpredictable and uncontrollable demands of trading applications.
- We can improve communication between the application component server and various data sources through the use of connection pooling management.

Scalability is more a system problem than a CPU architecture problem. For this reason, we capture trading system metrics, for example, to measure the number of users in a 24-hour period, response time, as well as average and longest running transactions. These metrics provide answers so that we can include the following:

- Graceful degradation, all the way up to 100 percent system load
- The ability to add capacity incrementally (CPUs, memory, I/O, and/or disk storage) without disrupting system operation
- The ability to prioritize the workload so that unneeded work can be suspended at times of peak activity

We also employ techniques such as logical partitioning to shift system resources. Portions of the system resources can be assigned to the partitions, with the assignments enforced by the hardware. This allows resources to be shifted from development to production, or between different systems involved in production, by simply shifting the percentages assigned to the partitions. Capacity is affected by scalability—for example, one machine handles 500 transactions or five machines handle 100 transactions each.

How Does Your Design Handle Performance?

Performance is defined as the amount of work accomplished by an application as compared to the time and resources used. In the context of a web-based application, good performance involves short response time for a trading transaction, as well as high throughput and high availability of the application. Therefore, in a trading application, response time and response ratio are important to the success of the application. With Michael Lewis's "Flash Boys" as competition, large institutional users want "up to nanosecond" pricing information. When a trade is entered, the users want immediate execution and confirmation as well as the accurate price paid or received. The key in establishing good performance is to identify and control expensive transactions. The architect should state target performance criteria before implementing within a production environment. For example, the first visible response in an Internet securities trading application's browser view, when the application is under maximum specified load, must occur in less than three seconds, 95 percent of the time. Measurement is made at the enterprise's external firewall.

In the trading system, when measuring performance, the architect must consider and attempt to quantify the cost of an operation (data or computational), which can involve "round trips" across our application cluster of servers and across our network connections—before finally returning a response view to the user requestor. We include tables to capture system metrics, which are used to determine the real cost of each transaction. After analysis, we could improve performance by amending software to execute functions fast enough to meet goals. Response time (the time it takes to respond) and response ratio (the time it takes to perform the function) are important to a securities-trading application. Both figures should be as low as possible, but a ratio of 1 is the target. For example, suppose a user requests functionality requiring a great deal of processing or database searching, and it takes a minute to process. The user will not see a result for a minute—seemingly a long time to wait. However, if the result can be viewed in one minute plus 20 seconds (a response ratio of 1.3333), that is still good performance. Alternatively, suppose that the processing takes only 1 second, but the user does not see the result for 20 seconds (response ratio of 20); that is not good performance.

To start, we analyze the client environments and ensure that the proposed solutions will not only meet the business needs but ensure a reliable production IT environment. Before we went operational, we piloted the system to weed out performance problems that could disrupt our client business (securities trading) and result in loss of revenue. Our performance handling involved a number of accepted performance enhancement techniques. We set up a cluster of application servers (for example, WebSphere Process Server and Tomcat) that use a round-robin handling to ensure that we maintain our stated performance goals. We put in place metrics collection and analytics to measure response time. We responded by adding database performance enhancements such as indices and caching to speed up lookups and update processing. We used metrics to identify hot spots and used maintenance programs to clean and refresh components and their supporting data. See the answer for "How Does Your Design Handle Scalability," which allowed us to respond to performance issues quickly and without interruption to business.

How Does Your Design Handle Security?

Our goal for security is to protect resources and assets from loss. Resources include most importantly the integrity of the trade data, which directly affects the business, as well as other information, services, and equipment such as servers and networking components. Our security is controlled access to component services and protection such that data is appropriately managed. The security for the integrated network, Internet, server, and securities-trading application is controlled by one administrative tool, which is a manageable solution and what we aimed for. This approach provides Single Sign-On (SSO) to our rich infrastructure of network and system services. Obviously, firewalls and authentication mechanisms are also used to support Internet security. With enterprise-wide control, multiuser access is managed without requiring explicit securities-trading application code. We created software APIs to each environment's ACL to facilitate SSO and other security measures.

We not only have to ensure that trade data is accurate, but we have legal obligations with respect to Gramm–Leach–Bliley legislation covering financial data. Therefore, the security we put in place had to accomplish the following objectives:

- **Privacy** Preventing information disclosure to unauthorized persons
- **Integrity** Preventing corruption or modification of resources
- **Authenticity** Proof that a person has been correctly identified or that a message is received as transmitted
- **Availability** Assurance that information, services, and equipment are working and available for use

We broke out the risk based on a set of threats. These threats include accidental threats, intentional threats, passive threats (those that do not change the state of the system but may include loss of confidentiality but not of integrity or availability), and active threats (those that change the state of the system, including changes to data and to software).

We established a security policy (that is, a enterprise trading statement) defining the rules that regulate how we will provide security, handle intrusions, and recover from damage caused by security breaches. Based on our risk analysis and cost considerations, we engaged the users so they could understand these rules and agree to abide by them. Our objectives are facilitated in some ways by the enterprise, including firm-wide security services provided for implementing the security policy of an application (for example, the trading application). A standard set of such services includes the following:

- **Identification and authentication** Unique identification and verification of trading system users via certification servers and global authentication services (Single Sign-On services)
- **Access control and authorization** Rights and permissions that control what resources trading system users may access
- **Accountability and auditing** Services for logging activities on network systems and linking them to specific user accounts or sources of attacks
- **Data confidentiality** Services to prevent unauthorized data disclosure
- **Data integrity and recovery** Methods for protecting resources against corruption and unauthorized modification—for example, mechanisms using checksums and encryption technologies
- **Data exchange** Services that secure data transmissions over communication channels
- **Object reuse** Services that provide multiple users secure access to individual resources
- **Non-repudiation of origin and delivery** Services to protect against attempts by the sender to falsely deny sending the data, or subsequent attempts by the recipient to falsely deny receiving the data
- **Reliability** Methods for ensuring that systems and resources are available and protected against failure

Our enterprise infrastructure uses many diverse user authentication and authorization (Auth/Auth) credentials and access control lists. For the most part, Auth/Auth details and values are stored in the enterprise LDAP database. Spring's JAAS (Java Authentication and Authorization Service) is used to control the authentication and authorization in the application. Spring is configured to connect to the enterprise LDAP. Front-end access to each UI component (for example, Java Server Page) is controlled by a taglib (for example, Spring-Security). Once the user submits the form with a username/password, the application checks the details with LDAP. As mentioned previously, security is controlled by a firm-wide administration tool.

How Does Your Design Handle Extensibility?

Extensibility is the ability to extend a system vertically or horizontally with relative ease. This is achieved by loosely coupled interfaces and encapsulation. We use SOAP/REST services for most UI interfaces. The services communicate via extensible XML/JSON message formats. This ensures that functional requirements have limited impact on the application. It is critical in a trading system to be able to extend functionality. Extensibility requires careful modeling of the business domain to add new features based on a model. The securities-trading application is designed with separation of concerns: presentation tier, business tier, persistence tier, and integration tier. Each layer is loosely coupled with each other with good usage of design patterns, interfaces, and best practices of object-oriented design such as encapsulation and inheritance. Therefore, any change to subsystems will have less impact on systems that are using the subsystem as long the interfaces remain same. Even if there are changes, the impact will be minimal for adapting new changes. We have made use of granular services to handle the components of each transaction. The use of business domain controllers to assemble and invoke distinct services to create transactions makes our design extensible.

How Does Your Design Handle Maintainability?

Maintainability and adaptability of software are important to keep software running for a long time. Where possible, we have made use of object-oriented designs to be more flexible and adaptable than the older procedural designs, thus reducing maintenance costs. We make use of OO principles to reduce maintenance costs in the following way: we use object–oriented modeled business entities and processes to address the "separation of concerns." Thus, we are able to adapt to new functional requirements because the interface typically is not affected. Our object-oriented designs are easier to change in response to new trading business requirements. Our object-oriented design is focused on identifying stable business objects that can be made to interact in new ways (for example, "get a price" and "make a trade").

Because we are part of a large investment banking infrastructure, we make use of the established layers. We monitor the communication between two layers to determine how the securities-trading application can be partitioned at that point for physical distribution across tiers. In our case, layers represent component relationships in the service implementation. They are the application, virtual platform, securities-trading application infrastructure, enterprise services, and compute and storage layers, as detailed here:

- **Application** The securities-trading application layer is the user and business functionality of a system (for example, the .war or .ear files deployed on the application).
- **Virtual platform (component APIs)** The virtual platform layer contains interfaces to the securities trading application infrastructure component APIs (for example, REST Web Services and the servlets to "get a price" or "make a trade").
- **Application infrastructure (containers)** The application infrastructure layer contains products (for example, JBOSS and IBM's WebSphere) that provide for the operation and development of the application. The virtual platform components are housed in an application infrastructure container.
- **Enterprise services (OS and virtualization)** The enterprise services layer is composed of the operating system (for example, Linux) and software (for example, Oracle DBMS) that run on top of the compute and storage layer. This layer provides the interfaces to operating system and storage functions needed by the application infrastructure layer.
- **Compute and storage** The compute and storage layer consists of the physical hardware used in the enterprise architecture.

Due to the layered (loosely coupled) architecture, each layer addresses a particular need so that any enhancement to the trading application can be made easily. Also, each layer is loosely coupled with best design practices, which makes understanding, analyzing, and debugging the trading functionality as well as making changes easier.

How Does Your Design Handle Manageability?

With respect to the trading application, the ability to administer and manage the system resources to ensure the availability and performance of all system components is how we provide manageability of the trading application with respect to the other capabilities. Manageability refers to the set of services that ensures the continued integrity (or correctness) of the component application. It includes security, concurrency control, and server management. A metric example of manageability would be the number of staff hours per month required to perform normal upgrades. The trading application is one of many that is managed by BNA. That said, we have made use of their wide array of tools to ensure availability and performance of all system components and to alert all parties when system components are affected and unavailable for whatever reason.

How Does Your Design Handle Persistence?

Our trading application data is primarily stored on Unix-based Oracle servers. In front of the database are services that provide an API that insulates the developer from needing Hibernate/iBatis knowledge and avoids a tight coupling between frameworks and code. We have developed Spring-based services that manage sessions, access the data, and cache frequently used reference and other data to provide performance and integrity.

How Does Your Design Handle the Presentation Tier?

REST stateless services provide easy development for distributed applications. They also provide system-level services that free the developer to solve business problems. These services allow for scalability in distributed systems and facilitate transactions that ensure data integrity.

Because we use services to provide the majority of business rules, our front end can be varied. We use a combination of Java Server Faces (JSF), which provide rich JavaScript functionality but require skill to build efficient/performant UI pages. We also use Java Server Pages (JSP) with an MVC framework (for example, Spring MVC or Struts).

Before the Exam: Prepare and Practice

Writing a good essay requires synthesis of material that cannot be done in the minutes you have during the exam. In the days before the exam, you should:

- *Anticipate test questions*. Look at the questions from the online forums. Did you have to compare/contrast alternative approaches?
- *Practice writing*. You may decide to write a summary of each prototype question you have been discussing, or a short description of the application solution you've created for Part 2. Focus on clarity, conciseness, and understanding the differences between the nonfunctional requirements of an architecture.

- *Memorize key facts and names.* You will have to support your argument with evidence, and this may involve memorizing some key events, the names of theorists, and so on.
- *Organize your ideas.* Knowledge of the subject matter is only part of the preparation process. You need to spend some time thinking about how to organize your ideas. Let's say a question asks you to compare and contrast how you provide manageability for your application. The key components of an answer to this question must include the following:
  - A definition of the alternative approaches
  - A brief description of the issue
  - A comparison of the two alternative approaches
  - A clear and logical contrasting of the alternative approach (noting how and why they are different)

How to Proceed at the Exam

Many students start writing too soon after scanning the essay question. Do not do this! Instead, try the following:

- *Perform a "memory dump."* Write down all the information you had to memorize for the exam in note form.
- *Read the questions and instructions carefully.* Read over all the questions on the exam. If you simply answer each question as you encounter it, you may give certain information or evidence to one question that is more suitable for another. Be sure to identify all parts of the question.
- *Formulate a thesis that answers the question.* You can use the wording from the question. There is not time for an elaborate introduction, but be sure to introduce the topic, your argument, and how you will support your thesis (do this in your first paragraph).
- *Organize your supporting points.* Before you proceed with the body of the essay, write an outline that summarizes your main supporting points. Check to make sure you are answering all parts of the question. Coherent organization is one of the most important characteristics of a good essay.

- *Make a persuasive argument*. Most essays ask you to make some kind of argument. Although there are no right answers, there are more and less persuasive answers. What makes an argument persuasive?
  - A clear point that is being argued (a solid approach to the issue)
  - Sufficient evidence to support that approach
  - A logical progression of ideas throughout the essay
- *Review your essay*. Take a few minutes to reread your essay. Correct grammatical mistakes and check to see that you have answered all parts of each question.

Best of luck!

CERTIFICATION SUMMARY

This review of how to approach the essays after completion of the Part 2 case study provides some examples. As an architect, and for the purposes of the essay assignment, you should always document the reasoning behind the analysis and design decisions made during a development project. These documents will provide a clear picture of the enterprise application and the reasoning behind its infrastructure, functionality, and deployment particulars. It will also help in evaluating and extending and amending the application when the inevitable change occurs.

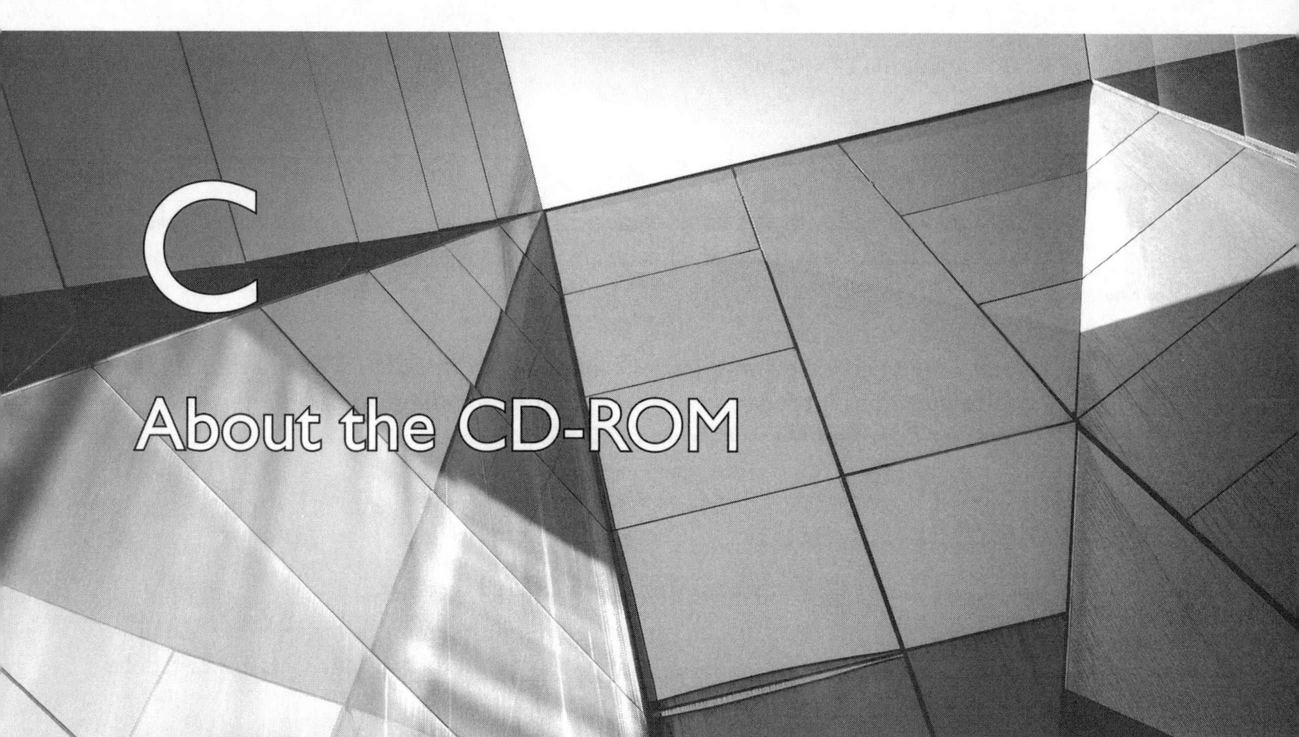

C

About the CD-ROM

The CD-ROM included with this book comes complete with Total Tester customizable practice exam software with 60 practice exam questions and a PDF copy of the book.

***Note** The practice exam questions included on the CD-ROM are multiple-choice questions intended to provide practice for the Java EE 6 Enterprise Architect Certified Master Exam (1Z0-807).*

System Requirements

The software requires Windows XP or higher and 30MB of hard disk space for full installation. To run the software, the screen resolution must be set to 1024×768 or higher. The PDF copy of the book requires Adobe Acrobat, Adobe Reader, or Adobe Digital Editions.

Total Tester Premium Practice Exam Software

Total Tester provides you with a simulation of the Java EE 6 Enterprise Architect Certified Master Exam (1Z0-807). You can also create custom exams from selected domains or chapters. You can further customize the number of questions and time allowed.

The exams can be taken in either Practice Mode or Exam Mode. Practice Mode provides an assistance window with hints, references to the book, explanations of the correct and incorrect answers, and the option to check your answer as you take the test. Exam Mode provides a simulation of the actual exam. The number of questions, the types of questions, and the time allowed are intended to be an accurate representation of the exam environment. Both Practice Mode and Exam Mode provide an overall grade and a grade broken down by domain.

To take a test, launch the program and select JEE6 Master Exam from the Installed Question Packs list. You can then select Practice Mode, Exam Mode, or Custom Mode.

Installing and Running Total Tester Premium Practice Exam Software

From the main screen you may install the Total Tester by clicking the Total Tester Practice Exams link. This will begin the installation process and place an icon on your desktop and in your Start menu. To run Total Tester, navigate to Start | (All) Programs | Total Seminars, or double-click the icon on your desktop.

To uninstall the Total Tester software, go to Start | Settings | Control Panel | Add/Remove Programs (XP) or Programs And Features (Vista/7/8), and then select the Total Tester program. Select Remove, and Windows will completely uninstall the software.

PDF Copy of the Book

The entire contents of the book are provided in PDF format on the CD-ROM. This file is viewable on your computer and many portable devices. Adobe Acrobat, Adobe Reader, or Adobe Digital Editions is required to view the file on your computer. A link to Adobe's website, where you can download and install Adobe Reader, has been included on the CD-ROM.

***Note** For more information on Adobe Reader and to check for the most recent version of the software, visit Adobe's website at www.adobe.com and search for the free Adobe Reader or look for Adobe Reader on the product page. Adobe Digital Editions can also be downloaded from the Adobe website.*

To view the PDF copy of the book on a portable device, copy the PDF file to your computer from the CD-ROM, and then copy the file to your portable device using a USB or other connection. Adobe offers a mobile version of Adobe Reader, the Adobe Reader mobile app, which currently supports iOS and Android. For customers using Adobe Digital Editions and an iPad, you may have to download and install a separate reader program on your device. The Adobe website has a list of recommended applications, and McGraw-Hill Education recommends the Bluefire Reader.

Technical Support

Technical Support information is provided in the following sections by feature.

Total Seminars Technical Support

For questions regarding the Total Tester software or operation of the CD-ROM, visit www.totalsem.com or e-mail support@totalsem.com.

McGraw-Hill Education Content Support

For questions regarding the PDF copy of the book, e-mail techsolutions@mhedu.com or visit http://mhp.softwareassist.com.

For questions regarding book content, e-mail customer.service@mheducation.com. For customers outside the United States, e-mail international_cs@mheducation.com.

access control The way by which interactions with resources are limited to collections of users or programs for the purpose of enforcing integrity, confidentiality, or availability constraints.

ACID The four properties that are guaranteed by a transaction: atomicity, consistency, isolation, and durability. Atomicity exists when either all of the changes are committed or, if for any reason the transaction cannot be completed, all of the changes are rolled back to their prior state. Consistency means that a transaction starts with data in a consistent state and ends with data in a consistent state. The data is said to be in a consistent state when it conforms to a set of invariants or rules, such as no duplicate keys or a column not allowing nulls. Isolation means that any given transaction must appear to be running all by itself on the database. The effects of any concurrent transaction are not visible to this transaction, and the effects of this transaction are not visible until the transaction is actually committed. Durability means that once a transaction is committed, its effects are guaranteed to continue even after the recovery of a subsequent system failure.

activation The process that transfers an EJB from secondary storage to memory. This is the complementary process to passivation.

Ajax (Asynchronous JavaScript and XML) Ajax is a group of related client-side web tools and techniques used to create asynchronous web applications. Web applications can send data to or receive data from a server asynchronously while the display and behavior of the existing page continues uninterrupted. Data can be retrieved using the XMLHttpRequest object. XML is not required, and JSON is often used instead. Ajax is not a single technology, but a group of technologies. HTML and CSS can be used in combination to mark up and style information.

applet A Java component that executes in an application or device—usually a web browser that supports the applet programming model.

applet container A container that supports the applet programming model.

application assembler Combines components into a deployable application unit.

application component provider Writes the business and application logic for the application by providing JavaServer Pages (JSP), JavaServer Faces (JSF), Java classes, and the required deployment descriptors.

authentication The process used by callers and service providers that proves they are to be "trusted." Authentication establishes the caller's identity and proves that they are an "authenticated" instance of an identity. The three types of authentication required on the Java EE platform are basic, form based, and mutual. The Java EE platform also supports digest authentication.

authorization The mechanism that controls caller access and interaction with application resources or components. The caller's credentials (identity), which can also be anonymous or arbitrarily set by the caller, can be determined via authentication contexts that are available to the called component. Access can then be determined by comparing the caller's credentials with the access control rules for the required component or resource.

basic authentication The web server authenticates a principal using the username and password obtained from the web client via its built-in authentication mechanism.

BMP (bean-managed persistence) The enterprise bean provider is responsible for creating the code for all the database access. Consequently, this technique provides much more control over how data is accessed.

BMT (bean-managed transaction) A transaction boundary defined and controlled by an enterprise bean.

business logic The code that implements the required functionality of an application.

caller principal The principal that identifies the caller of the enterprise bean method.

client certificate authentication A client authentication mechanism that uses an X.509 certificate to establish its identity.

CMP (container-managed persistence) The enterprise bean provider delegates the specifics of data access to the EJB container.

CMT (container-managed transaction) A transaction boundary defined and controlled by the EJB container.

component An application-level unit that is configurable at deployment time and supported by a container. The four types of components for the Java EE platform are enterprise beans, web components, applets, and application clients.

connector A standard extension mechanism that lets a container provide connectivity to enterprise information systems.

container An entity that provides life cycle management, security, deployment, run time, and component-specific services to components.

CORBA (Common Object Request Broker Architecture) The distributed object model defined by the Object Management Group (OMG).

credentials The security attributes of a principal.

deployer Installs modules and applications into the operational environment.

deployment The process of installing modules and applications into an operational environment.

deployment descriptor An XML file that accompanies each module or application. It describes specific configuration requirements that need to be resolved for the module or application to be installed successfully.

destination A JMS-administered object that is either a queue for a point-to-point messaging model or a topic for a publish/subscribe messaging model.

digest authentication An authentication mechanism in which a web client authenticates by sending the server a message digest as part of the HTTP request. This message digest is calculated by taking pieces of the message along with the client's password and passing them though a one-way hash algorithm.

durable subscription In a JMS publish/subscribe messaging system, known subscribers receive the messages when they are connected to the topic. If a known subscriber is not connected, JMS retains the messages until the subscriber reconnects or until the messages expire.

EAR (Enterprise Archive) file An archive that contains a Java EE enterprise application. An EAR file comprises WAR, EJB JAR, RAR, and JAR files.

EJB container A container within an EJB server or a Java EE application server that implements the run-time environment for enterprise beans, including security, concurrency, life cycle management, transaction, deployment, naming, and other services provided by the Java EE platform.

EJB container provider A vendor that supplies an EJB container.

EJB context Allows the enterprise bean (EJB) to use services provided by the EJB container and in doing so obtain information about the invoker of a client-invoked method.

EJB home object Provides the life cycle operations (create, find, and remove methods) for an enterprise bean. The EJB home object, which is generated by the container's deployment tools, implements the enterprise bean's home interface.

Any client wishing to use an enterprise bean will first locate its EJB home object via JNDI. Then it will call the life cycle operations (methods) provided by the EJB home object to reference the EJB object (remote reference to the enterprise bean).

EJB JAR (Java Archive) file An archive file that contains an EJB module.

EJB object An object that implements the remote interface of the enterprise bean. Clients of an EJB reference an EJB object and do not reference an enterprise bean instance directly.

EJB server A server that can host one or more EJB containers.

EJB server provider A vendor that supplies an EJB server.

enterprise bean A component that implements either a business function or a business entity. The component can be an entity, session, or message-driven bean.

enterprise bean provider The person or vendor that creates enterprise bean classes, remote and home interfaces, and deployment descriptor files, and then packages them into an EJB JAR file.

enterprise information system (EIS) The applications that maintain data for an enterprise. These applications offer a well-defined set of services that are exposed to callers as local and/or remote interfaces. Some examples of EIS are legacy mainframe transaction-processing and database systems.

Enterprise JavaBeans (EJB) Component architecture for the development and deployment of distributed, object-oriented, enterprise-level applications. EJBs are scalable, secure, and transactional.

entity bean An enterprise bean that represents data, uniquely identified by a primary key, which is persisted and maintained by a database. The entity bean is able to manage its own persistence (BMP), or it can leave this function to the EJB container.

form-based authentication An authentication mechanism that allows for the use of a custom HTML form as the user interface for capturing the authentication information.

handle An opaque, long-lived, and serializable reference to an enterprise bean instance.

home handle An object used to obtain a reference to the home interface.

home interface An object that provides the management or life cycle operations (create, remove, find) for an EJB. The home interface of a session bean has create and remove methods, and the home interface of an entity bean has create, find, and remove methods.

HTML (Hypertext Markup Language) A file format for creating hypertext documents on the Web.

HTTP (Hypertext Transfer Protocol) A web protocol based on TCP/IP that is used to fetch hypertext objects from remote hosts—for example, web pages, images, and binary files.

HTTPS The HTTP protocol layered over the Secure Sockets Layer (SSL) protocol. This provides a more secure transfer of data using encrypted data streams.

IIOP (Internet Inter-ORB Protocol) A protocol used for communication between CORBA object request brokers (ORBs).

Java API for Restful Web Service (JAX-RS) JAX-RS provides support for web services that conform to the Representational State Transfer (REST) architectural pattern. JAX-RS makes extensive use of annotations to simplify the development and deployment of web service clients and endpoints.

Java API For XML-based Web Services (JAX-WS) JAX-WS is a technology for building web services and clients that communicate using XML. For this, a web service operation invocation is represented by an XML-based protocol—for example, the Simple Object Access Protocol (SOAP). SOAP defines the envelope structure, encoding rules, and conventions for representing web service invocations and responses.

Java EE application server Provides EJB and/or web containers to support the run-time environment of a Java EE product.

Java EE product provider A vendor that supplies a Java EE product implemented as per the Java EE platform specification.

Java EE role The function performed by a party in the development and deployment phases of an application developed using Java EE technology. The roles are Application Component Provider, Application Assembler, Deployer, Java EE Product Provider, EJB Container Provider, EJB Server Provider, Web Container Provider, Web Server Provider, Tool Provider, and System Administrator.

JAR (Java Archive) file A file format that allows several files to be stored in a single file. JAR is compatible with ZIP archives.

Java EE Connector Architecture (JCA) JCA is a standardized access mechanism to and from enterprise information systems (EIS) from the Java EE platform. JCA is a generic architecture for connection to legacy systems.

JavaBeans component A portable, platform-independent, reusable component model that can be manipulated in a visual builder tool and coded into applications. To make this possible, JavaBeans must adhere to defined property and event interface conventions.

JavaMail Provides a standard and independent framework for Java client applications to use electronic mail. JavaMail provides the ability to do the following:

- Compose messages, including multipart messages with attachments.
- Send messages to particular servers.
- Retrieve and store messages in folders.

JCP Established in 1998 as the open, participative process to develop and revise the Java technology specifications, reference implementations, and test suites, the Java Community Process (JCP) program has fostered the evolution of the Java platform in cooperation with the international Java developer community.

JDBC Provides database-independent connectivity between Java and a wide range of data sources.

JMS (Java Message Service) Provides a common way for a Java application to create, send, receive, and read an enterprise messaging system's messages.

JMS provider An enterprise messaging system that implements the Java Message Service along with administrative and control functions.

JNDI (Java Naming and Directory Interface) An API that provides naming and directory functionality for Java classes.

JPA (Java Persistence API) The Java Persistence API is an application programming interface for the management of relational data in applications using Java Platform, Standard Edition and Java Platform, Enterprise Edition. Before EJB 3.0 and the JPA specification, developers used lightweight persistent objects and provided persistence frameworks such as Hibernate—this owing to the fact that entity beans, in previous EJB specifications, called for complicated code, a large footprint, and the need for Java EE application servers. Many features in third-party persistence frameworks were incorporated into the JPA.

JPQL (Java Persistence Query Language) JPQL is part of JPA, and it allows a developer to define queries for entities and their persistent state. JPQL uses a SQL-like syntax to select objects based on entity abstract schema types and the relationships that exist among them. JPQL is an object-oriented version of SQL.

JSF (JavaServer Faces) JavaServer Faces (JSF) is a Java specification for building component-based user interfaces for web applications. JSF 2 uses Facelets as its default templating system. Based on a component-driven UI design model, JavaServer Faces uses XML files called view templates or Facelets views. The FacesServlet processes requests, loads the view template, builds a component tree, processes events, and renders the response (for example, HTML language) to the client. The state of UI components is saved at the end of each request in a process and restored upon the next creation of that view. JSF can be used with Ajax to create rich user interfaces. The JSF 2.0 specification provides built-in support for Ajax by standardizing the Ajax request life cycle and providing simple development interfaces to Ajax events, allowing any event triggered by the client to go through proper validation, conversion, and finally method invocation, before returning the result to the browser.

JSON (JavaScript Object Notation) JSON is based on a subset of the JavaScript programming language. It is a lightweight data-interchange format that uses text, which humans can read and write and machines can parse and generate, to transmit data objects consisting of attribute/value pairs. It is now primarily used to transmit data between a server and web application, including those executing within a web browser or iOS/Android mobile application.

JSP (JavaServer Pages) JavaServer Pages use template data, custom elements, scripting languages, and server-side Java objects to return dynamic content to a client typically within a web browser. A JSP is a combination of HTML syntax and Java syntax that is executed at run time to create content for web-based clients dynamically. More advanced JSPs can use templates and custom tag libraries to further enhance their functionality and reusability.

JSR A Java Specification Request (JSR) is the document submitted to the Process Management Office (PMO) by one or more JCP members to propose the development of a new specification or significant revision to an existing specification for Java.

JTA (Java Transaction API) An API that allows applications and Java EE servers to use transactions.

JTS (Java Transaction Service) Defines the implementation of a transaction manager, which supports the Java Transaction API (JTA) and implements the Java mapping of the Object Management Group (OMG) Object Transaction Service (OTS) specification.

MDB (message-driven bean) An enterprise bean that consumes messages asynchronously. A client invokes an MDB by sending messages to the destination to which the MDB is listening.

ORB (Object Request Broker) Enables CORBA objects to locate and then communicate with one another.

OS principal A principal that exists for the operating system on which the Java EE platform is executing.

OTS (Object Transaction Service) Defines the interfaces that permit CORBA objects to participate in transactions.

passivation The process that transfers an enterprise bean from memory to secondary storage. This is the complementary process to activation.

persistence Protocol for moving the state of an entity bean between its instance variables and a persistent store (a database).

point-to-point messaging model A messaging model that uses queues. In JMS, clients can write messages to a queue and can read messages from a queue.

POJO (Plain Old Java Object) A POJO is a Java object not bound by any restriction other than those forced by the Java Language Specification.

primary key An object within a home that uniquely identifies an entity bean.

principal The identity assigned to a user that has been authenticated.

privilege A non-unique security attribute that can be shared by many principals, such as a group.

publish/subscribe messaging model A messaging model that uses topics. In JMS, clients can publish messages to a topic and multiple clients can subscribe and receive messages from a topic.

queue A destination used in the point-to-point messaging model.

realm A string passed on an HTTP request during basic authentication. It specifies the protection domain to be used for authentication.

remote interface An enterprise bean interface that defines the business methods a client can invoke.

resource adapter System-level software used by an EJB container or a client to connect to an EIS.

resource manager Provides shared access to a set of resources. It participates in transactions that are externally controlled and coordinated by a transaction manager.

RMI (Remote Method Invocation) A distributed object model that allows an object running in one Java virtual machine (JVM) to invoke methods on an object running in a different JVM.

RMI-IIOP An RMI implementation that uses CORBA's IIOP protocol. RMI-IIOP allows developers to code using the RMI APIs while the interprocess communication actually involves the IIOP protocol instead of the JRMP protocol with which RMI is usually associated.

role mapping Associating groups and/or principals known to the container to security roles specified within the deployment descriptor. Before the component is installed on the server, these security roles need to be mapped (associated) by the deployer.

security attributes A set of properties associated with a principal via an authentication protocol and/or a Java EE product provider.

security constraint The declarative way of protecting web resource collections. A security constraint consists of these parts: a web resource collection, an authorization constraint, and a user data constraint.

security context An object that encapsulates the shared security state between two entities.

security permission A mechanism used by the Java EE platform to convey the programming restrictions imposed upon application component providers.

security role An abstract logical grouping of users defined by an application assembler. When an application is deployed, roles are associated to security identities that actually exist in the deployment environment, such as principals or groups.

security view A set of security roles created by the application assembler.

server principal The operating system principal that the server is executing as.

service-oriented architecture (SOA) A strategy, or system integration process, for developing and integrating systems through interoperable standards-based services that are comprised of discrete pieces of software providing application functionality.

servlet A Java program that generates dynamic content and interacts with web clients using a request-response model.

servlet container Also called a web container. Provides services that facilitate the request-response model. It also decodes requests and formats responses. All servlet containers support HTTP and can optionally support other request-response protocols such as HTTPS.

servlet context An object that contains information about the web application that the servlet is executing as a part of. Through this object, a servlet can log events, obtain URL references to resources, and set and store context attributes for other servlets within the same context.

session An object used by servlets to track user interaction with a web application across multiple HTTP requests.

session bean An enterprise bean that performs operations for a client. A session bean is created by a client and typically exists only for the duration of a single client/server session. A session bean can be either stateful, in which it maintains conversational state across methods and transactions, or stateless.

SQL (Structured Query Language) The standardized relational database language for defining and maintaining database objects and manipulating the data within them.

SQL/J Standards that include specifications for embedding SQL statements within the Java programming language and for calling Java static methods as SQL stored procedures and user-defined functions.

SSL (Secure Socket Layer) A protocol that provides communication between a client and server to be encrypted for privacy. Servers must be authenticated, and clients are optionally authenticated.

stateful session bean A session bean that maintains a conversational state.

stateless session bean A session bean that does not maintain conversational state. All instances of the same stateless session bean are identical. (Singleton session beans offer similar functionality to stateless session beans but differ from them in that there is only one singleton session bean per application, as opposed to a pool of stateless session beans, any of which may respond to a client request.)

system administrator The individual responsible for configuring, administering, and maintaining computers, networks, and software systems.

topic A destination used in the publish-subscribe messaging model.

transaction An atomic unit of work that changes data from one state to another. A transaction can comprise one or more changes, all of which will either complete or roll back. Transactions allow several users to access the same data at the same time (concurrently).

transaction attribute A value defined in the deployment descriptor of an enterprise bean module. It tells the EJB container how to control the transaction scope when the enterprise bean's methods are invoked. The following are the possible values for a transaction attribute: Required, RequiresNew, Supports, NotSupported, Mandatory, and Never.

transaction isolation level The degree to which the intermediate state of the data being modified by a transaction can be seen by other concurrent transactions; also the degree to which the data being modified by other transactions can be seen by it.

transaction manager Provides the management functions and services required to support synchronization, transaction demarcation, transaction context propagation, and transactional resource management.

URI (Uniform Resource Identifier) A compact string of characters that identifies either an abstract or physical resource. A URI is an abstract superclass of the URL and URN concrete subclasses.

URL (Uniform Resource Locator) A standard way for referring to an arbitrary piece of data on the Web. Each URL is in the form *protocol://host/localinfo*, where *protocol* specifies the protocol to use (such as HTTP or FTP), *host* specifies the remote host where the resource exists, and *localinfo*, which is often a file name, is passed to the protocol handler on the remote host to actually find the resource.

URL path A URL passed in an HTTP request to invoke a servlet. It consists of a Context Path, a Servlet Path, and PathInfo. Context Path is the path prefix associated with the servlet context. Servlet Path, which starts with a slash (/) character, is the path section that corresponds to the servlet container mapping that activated the request. PathInfo is the part of the request path that is neither part of the Context Path nor the Servlet Path.

URN (Uniform Resource Name) A unique identifier for an entity that does not specify where the entity is actually located. A URN may be used to attempt to find an entity locally before looking it up on the Web. The URN allows the web location to change while still allowing the entity to be found.

WAR (Web Archive) file A JAR archive that contains a web application.

web application An Internet application, including applications that use Java technologies such as JavaServer Pages and servlets, as well as those that use non-Java technologies such as CGI and Perl.

web component A component that can be either a servlet or a JavaServer Page, and that provides service by responding to requests.

web container A container provided by a Java EE or web server that implements the Java EE web component contract. This defines the run-time environment and services for web components, including concurrency, deployment, life cycle management, security, transaction, and other services.

web module A unit that consists of one or more web components along with a web deployment descriptor.

web resource collection A list of URL patterns and HTTP methods that describe a set of resources to be protected via a security constraint.

web server Software that provides services to access the network (the Internet, an intranet, or an extranet). The web server hosts websites, supports HTTP (and possibly other protocols), and executes server-side programs such as servlets. On a Java EE platform, a web server provides services to one or more web containers.

web service Web services provide a standard means of interoperating, via Hypertext Transfer Protocol (HTTP), between software applications. Web services can be combined in a loosely coupled way to achieve complex operations.

XML (eXtensible Markup Language) A markup language that evolved from Standard Generalized Markup Language (SGML). It allows for the definition of tags (markup) needed to identify the content, data, and text in XML documents.

INDEX

A

F

G

H

I

J

K

L

M

N

O

P

S

T